Foreign Direct Investments (FDIs) and Opportunities for Developing Economies in the World Market

Venkataramanaiah Malepati
University of Gondar, Ethiopia

C. Mangala Gowri
University of Gondar, Ethiopia

A volume in the Advances in Finance, Accounting, and Economics (AFAE) Book Series

IGI Global
DISSEMINATOR OF KNOWLEDGE

Published in the United States of America by
IGI Global
Business Science Reference (an imprint of IGI Global)
701 E. Chocolate Avenue
Hershey PA, USA 17033
Tel: 717-533-8845
Fax: 717-533-8661
E-mail: cust@igi-global.com
Web site: http://www.igi-global.com

Library of Congress Cataloging-in-Publication Data

Names: Malepati, Venkataramanaiah, 1980- editor. | Gowri, C. Mangala, 1980- editor.
Title: Foreign direct investments (FDIs) and opportunities for developing economies in the world market / Venkataramanaiah Malepati and C. Mangala Gowri, editors.
Description: Hershey, PA : Business Science Reference, [2018]
Identifiers: LCCN 2017012417| ISBN 9781522530268 (hardcover) | ISBN 9781522530275 (ebook)
Subjects: LCSH: Investments, Foreign--Developing countries.
Classification: LCC HG5993 .F6568 2018 | DDC 332.67/3091724--dc23 LC record available at https://lccn.loc.gov/2017012417

This book is published in the IGI Global book series Advances in Finance, Accounting, and Economics (AFAE) (ISSN: 2327-5677; eISSN: 2327-5685)

British Cataloguing in Publication Data
A Cataloguing in Publication record for this book is available from the British Library.

Advances in Finance, Accounting, and Economics (AFAE) Book Series

ISSN:2327-5677
EISSN:2327-5685

Editor-in-Chief: Ahmed Driouchi, Al Akhawayn University, Morocco

MISSION

In our changing economic and business environment, it is important to consider the financial changes occurring internationally as well as within individual organizations and business environments. Understanding these changes as well as the factors that influence them is crucial in preparing for our financial future and ensuring economic sustainability and growth.

The **Advances in Finance, Accounting, and Economics (AFAE)** book series aims to publish comprehensive and informative titles in all areas of economics and economic theory, finance, and accounting to assist in advancing the available knowledge and providing for further research development in these dynamic fields.

COVERAGE

- Bankruptcy
- Behavioral Economics
- Economics of Risks, Uncertainty, Ambiguity, and Insurance
- Stock Market
- Entrepreneurship in Accounting and Finance
- Banking
- E-Accounting
- Economics of Innovation and Knowledge
- Microeconomics
- Field Research

IGI Global is currently accepting manuscripts for publication within this series. To submit a proposal for a volume in this series, please contact our Acquisition Editors at Acquisitions@igi-global.com or visit: http://www.igi-global.com/publish/.

The Advances in Finance, Accounting, and Economics (AFAE) Book Series (ISSN 2327-5677) is published by IGI Global, 701 E. Chocolate Avenue, Hershey, PA 17033-1240, USA, www.igi-global.com. This series is composed of titles available for purchase individually; each title is edited to be contextually exclusive from any other title within the series. For pricing and ordering information please visit http://www.igi-global.com/book-series/advances-finance-accounting-economics/73685. Postmaster: Send all address changes to above address.

Titles in this Series

For a list of additional titles in this series, please visit:
https://www.igi-global.com/book-series/advances-finance-accounting-economics/73685

Accountancy and the Changing Landscape of Integrated Reporting
Ioana Dragu (Babes-Bolyai University, Romania)
Business Science Reference • ©2018 • 303pp • H/C (ISBN: 9781522536222) • US $195.00

Economic Growth in Latin America and the Impact of the Global Financial Crisis
Mauricio Garita (Universidad del Valle de Guatemala, Guatemala) and Celso Fernando Cerezo Bregni (Universidad del Valle de Guatemala, Guatemala)
Business Science Reference • ©2018 • 193pp • H/C (ISBN: 9781522549819) • US $180.00

Uncertainties and Risk Assessment in Trade Relations
Marianne Ojo (George Mason University, USA)
Business Science Reference • ©2018 • 385pp • H/C (ISBN: 9781522541318) • US $225.00

Economic Reforms for Global Competitiveness
Denis Ushakov (International College Suan Sunandha Rajabhat University, Thailand & Russian Academy of National Economy and Public Administration–South, Russia)
Business Science Reference • ©2018 • 363pp • H/C (ISBN: 9781522538561) • US $235.00

Alternative Decision-Making Models for Financial Portfolio Management ...
Narela Spaseski (International University of Sarajevo, Bosnia and Herzegovina)
Business Science Reference • ©2018 • 333pp • H/C (ISBN: 9781522532590) • US $175.00

Ranking Economic Performance and Efficiency in the Global Market Emerging Research ...
Benjamen Franklen Gussen (University of Southern Queensland, Australia & Australian Law and Economics Association, Australia)
Business Science Reference • ©2018 • 372pp • H/C (ISBN: 9781522527565) • US $195.00

Financial Entrepreneurship for Economic Growth in Emerging Nations
Atsede Woldie (University of South Wales, UK) and Brychan Thomas (University of South Wales, UK)
Business Science Reference • ©2018 • 304pp • H/C (ISBN: 9781522527008) • US $225.00

For an entire list of titles in this series, please visit:
https://www.igi-global.com/book-series/advances-finance-accounting-economics/73685

IGI Global
DISSEMINATOR OF KNOWLEDGE

701 East Chocolate Avenue, Hershey, PA 17033, USA
Tel: 717-533-8845 x100 • Fax: 717-533-8661
E-Mail: cust@igi-global.com • www.igi-global.com

Editorial Advisory Board

Table of Contents

Detailed Table of Contents

credit to private sector, and regulatory quality have a significant effect on FDI. Policy makers in African countries need to adopt institutional reforms that could contribute to improving their state of governance, promote their investment climate, and help in attracting more FDI.

In the process of globalization of the world economy, foreign direct investment has a significant impact on economic growth and development of the national economy. To adequately facilitate the development of competitiveness, these countries usually intervene through measures and instruments of tax policy. One of the main tasks of developing countries is to create a favorable environment for investors, considering that this is one of the methods to ensure greater capital inflows. The main objective of this chapter is to assess the role of tax policy in achieving the competitiveness of developing countries. For the creators of tax policy, it is very important to constantly review the tax rules to ensure that the country is attractive for foreign investments. The results that were obtained indicate that tax incentives significantly influence the improvement of competitiveness and the attraction of multinational companies as a key holder of foreign direct investment.

This chapter investigates the relative strength of the contributions of trade openness and FDI inflows towards economic growth of Thailand, taking account of the importance of human capital and other conditioning factors as a source of technology transfer in facilitating growth. Using Granger causality tests conducted within a vector-error-correction framework, the authors find significant evidence of the complementarities between domestic investment and trade openness, providing support for import-led growth. In contrast, direct support for FDI-led growth is relatively weak, which implies that trade openness has played a more significant role than FDI in influencing Thai economic growth. However, the results reveal a subtle role for technology transfer through the complementary effect of trade on FDI, and FDI on government expenditure, which henceforth influences human capital development with spillovers into domestic investment and growth. This leads

The chapter has raised two critically important questions. First, is the M&A boom a one-time effect of privatization, or is it likely to be followed by a rise in Greenfield investment? Second, do these two types of FDI mode have different macroeconomic consequences in terms of aggregate investment and growth? The main purpose of this chapter is to analyze the two entry modes, mergers and acquisitions and Greenfield investment, specifically, and to present a comparative view of the same and how it leads to the economic growth of a nation. It is concluded that one should choose the right mode according to the different situation about the firms in the international market. The present chapter also concludes that Greenfields and M&As do have a positive homogenous effect on growth. Additionally, the enhancement of human capital is an important condition for the host countries to derive the maximum benefits from Greenfields and M&As. Also, there is empirical evidence of a two-way linkage between FDI and growth. However, the bidirectional relationship exists only for the M&A's growth nexus.

Although MNEs are important players in the present global world, there has been a debate regarding, on one hand, how MNEs contribute to the development of indigenous firms in host countries, and on the other hand, how indigenous suppliers are able to cope with their international technology demanding clients. This chapter analyzes the patterns of technology acquisition of 40 firms that supply eight multinational firms that belong to four different industries. It is possible to conclude that there are certain differences among foreign and indigenous suppliers as well across the industries they belong to. These differences are the result of a cumulative process over time, which reflect the different performances of the companies and their relationships with the environment.

The effect of governance on FDI inflows is firstly through the effect of institutions on investment environment of a country and secondly through the decreasing transaction costs, production costs, and uncertainty. The countries are divided into

Foreword

One of the most attractive buzz words in the literature of economics in the recent period is Foreign Direct Investment (FDI). Traditionally, FDI is considered as an effective instrument for economic growth of countries, particularly developing and less developing nations. It is believed that the FDI acts as panacea for cracking out of the vicious cycle of low-savings, low- income and for other socio-economic problems. The literature in the field advocates that FDI facilitates import of capital goods and advanced technical know-how. It is evident that the growth rate in FDI is so fast during the last two decades particularly in developing and less developing nations. The backdrop of liberalized economy pushed the most economies to frame appropriate policies to attract FDI from international frontiers. As the FDI is gaining much importance in the recent years with the back drop of globalised economy and liberalized policies, most of the developing and less developing countries ought to be significantly affected in a positive manner. The overwhelming enthusiasm among developing and less developing countries to attract FDI coupled with the actual results is sometimes contradictory.

In this book, authors have been made an attempt to recap various issues those may fit into the concept ‘the Foreign Direct Investment and Opportunities for Developing Economies in the World Market’. This book outlined the doctrines established relating to FDI and discussed the newer ideology to trace the nature and direction of desirable policy parameters that are relevant to the present scenario in the ever-changing dynamics in the world economies.

I strongly believe that this book is quite useful to students, researchers, academicians and policy makers who are in the fields of Commerce, Economics, and Management.

Jawahar Babu
Vikrama Simhapuri University, India

Preface

Developing countries, emerging economies and countries in transformation are seeing Foreign Direct Investments (FDI) as a source of economic development in a country in terms of modernization, mass infrastructure creation, growth in Gross Domestic Development (GDP) and rapid growth in employment creation. In order to reap the fruits of globalization, most of the countries in the world have liberalized their policies towards the FDIs to attract massive investment across various sectors of the economy. These policies primarily intended to address the issue of how best to pursue indigenous policies to optimize the benefits of the foreign presence in terms of their investment in the host country. Existing literature in the FDI clues us that FDI activates technology spillovers, assists human capital formation, contributes to more integration of international trade and helps to create the conducive business environment. The inquiry about FDI and its opportunities for developing countries to reach out their socio-economic goals is a flagship program for every government in the 21st century. The overall development took over a period of time in terms of FDIs inflows and outflows across developing and transitional economies, a variety of opportunities available therein, challenges posed and encountered around policy making and implementation, outcomes out of the FDI policies are intended to discuss in the present book. The present book does not focus merely on the positive effects of FDI for the development and growth of an economy but it also addresses the concerns of potential drawbacks for host countries including economic as well as non-economic.

ORGANIZATION OF THE BOOK

The book is organized into 12 chapters. A brief description of each of the chapters follows under.

Chapter 1 deals FDI, technological innovation and export performance with empirical evidence from developing Asia. The primary objective of the chapter is to explore the effects of FDI inflows and technological innovations on export performance in the development of Asian countries during 1990-2015. The empirical results ravel that there is a co-integration among the variables and have the positive impact on export performance and FDI in developing Asian countries.

Chapter 2 proposes that in order to compete with other countries to attract more FDI, the country should make the investment climate much better and conducive to foreign players. This requires a critical examination of the firm-specific motivations that make them indulge in FDI. This study observes that there is a need to increase the productive efficiency which is possible only if the infrastructure bottlenecks are properly addressed and the wages and other relative costs are kept low.

Chapter 3 talks about the role of FDI in the least developing countries. This paper concludes that the Least Developing Countries (LDCs) have faced many problems including financial fragility, lack of good institutions, and civil conflict. One possible way to mitigate these problems is to rely on the importance of attracting inward FDI. However, it has taken a long and often humpy road, especially over the past decade for LDCs to attract and utilize FDI inflows.

Chapter 4 reviews the socio-economic impact of Foreign Direct Investment in developing countries. This paper investigated from an empirical point of view, the determinants and impact of socioeconomic factors on FDI flow to African countries. The results indicate that openness, GDP, direct credit to the private sector and regulatory quality, have a positive impact on FDI flow to African countries.

Chapter 5 ravels that Global trends in the movement of capital, as well as the value of realized investments, indicate great importance of FDI, which is reflected in the development of the national economy of each country. For this reason, the goal of every country is to attract more FDI, given that they are one of the factors of success of the national economy in the global market. Attracting FDI is a necessary condition for the stable growth of most countries.

Chapter 6 investigates the relative strength of the contributions of trade openness and FDI inflows towards the economic growth of Thailand. The study finds significant evidence of the complementarities between domestic investment and trade openness, providing support for import-led growth. In contrast, direct support for FDI-led growth is relatively weak, which implies that trade openness has played a more significant role than FDI in influencing Thai economic growth.

Chapter 7 opined that FDI flows overpowered other capital flows since the decade that marked notable liberalization and heavy relaxations in foreign investments and trade regimes. The study concludes that Foreign Direct Investment Inflows pouring into the host economies of BIMSTEC causes Current Account Balance in the region. This outcome is in perfect conformity with the existing empirical works that reckons that Foreign Direct Investment causes Current Account. However, the causality is deduced to be Unidirectional.

Chapter 8 made a comparative study of FDI between India and China. The study clues that underdeveloped retail market of India and China has witnessed growth over the years. These markets have been taken by the retailers as the function of experimentation. Both will grow rapidly taking a much larger share of GDP. In both countries, the domestic market will become increasingly attractive to global companies. Both countries will create new world-class companies that will be competitive with companies based in the west.

Chapter 9 reviews the choice between M&A and Greenfield Investment. The study opined that both modes have their advantages and disadvantages. It says the choice depends on the circumstances faced by the firm. If the firm is seeking to enter a market where there are already well-established incumbent enterprises, and where global competitors are also interested in establishing a presence, it may pay the firm to enter via an acquisition. In such circumstances, Greenfield Investment may be too slow to establish a sizeable presence.

Chapter 10 suggests that the activities of MNEs are difficult to assess as markets are more volatile than over. However, it would be important if public policy could address FDI from a more holistic perspective taking into account not only initial conditions to attract FDI but also to consider sequential investments that are tuned to efficiency-seeking activities with local suppliers, which would allow local firms to augment and explore their core competencies creating endogenous condition for sustainable economic development.

Chapter 11 presents that improvement in each aspect of governance structure attracts more FDI inflows in all country clusters except political stability in less developed countries. Following policies to increase GDP growth attract the higher amount of FDI inflows in advanced and developing countries.

Chapter 12 explains the trend lines, random walk, stationarity, structural breaks and volatility of FDI inflows in India during 1971-2015.Both log-linear and exponential trends are significant. FDI inflows are stationary and showed four structural breaks in 1985, 1994, 2000, and 2006. Author found the relation among FDI inflows, growth rate, interest rate, inflation rate, exchange rate, fiscal deficit, external debt, and trade openness with the help of Granger causality, Johansen co-integration test, and vector error correction models.

Venkataramanaiah Malepati
University of Gondar, Ethiopia

C. Mangala Gowri
University of Gondar, Ethiopia

Chapter 1
Foreign Direct Investment, Technological Innovation, and Export Performance:
Empirical Evidence From Developing Asia

Arzu Tay Bayramoglu
Bulent Ecevit University, Turkey

Tezcan Abasız
Bulent Ecevit University, Turkey

ABSTRACT

This chapter's objective is to explore the effects of foreign direct investment inflows and technological innovations on export performance in developing Asian countries (Hong Kong, China, Indonesia, Singapore, India, Turkey, Malaysia, Vietnam, United Arab Emirates, and Thailand) in the period of 1990-2015 by using the panel cointegration technique. The empirical results reveal that there is a cointegration among the variables, and cointegration regression shows that the foreign direct investments, per income and patent applications, have a positive and statistically significant impact on export performance in developing Asian countries. The results reveal that the impact of patent applications is greater than the foreign direct investments on exports. Then, technological development affects exports positively in all countries in the sample, except for India and the United Arab Emirates.

DOI: 10.4018/978-1-5225-3026-8.ch001

INTRODUCTION

The aggregation of knowledge and the development of technological capabilities are the key elements for the economic growth and competitiveness building in emerging countries. One of the most important ways of getting technology in developing economies is to attract foreign direct investment (Fu, 2007; Sılovagathasan & Wuu, 2014).

Foreign Direct Investment (FDI) is a form of the large multinational enterprises (MNEs). It is widely believed that multinational exporter corporations have higher productivity than domestic non-exporters (Helpman et al., 2004). Also, MNEs activities carry the technology to the host country due to having knowledge of new technologies and materials, production process, or management experience (Barios et al., 2005).

In the economic growth perspectives, the Solow's neoclassical growth (1956) model, suggest that technology is exogenous, and capital increases are the engine of economic growth. Since the mid-1980s the new endogenous growth theories have emerged and focused on the technological knowledge and its transmission. It exclaims that the accumulation of innovation and human capital are the critical elements in economic growth. Grossman and Helpman (1991), Lucas (1988), and Romer (1990) emphasize the role of technology, human capital improvement and the impact of their externalities on economic growth. In that, FDI can affect positively domestic production through spillovers benefits (Fan, 2002:7). Such benefits could be in the type of technology expansion, productivity advancement, transfer of skills, increased competition, and market access effects (Görg & Greenaway, 2004).

It is believed that China, Hong Kong, Singapore, South Korea, India, Malaysia, and had a strong economic growth and enhanced their competitiveness over the past twenty years. After they had produced high-tech products by FDI inwards, they exported them in the global competitive market (Erdal & Göçer, 2015:750).

FDI's effects on technological improvement and economic growth in emerging countries have been studied extensively in the literature. Also, there are many studies investigate the FDI impact on export in developing and developed countries. This study is one of the few studies which have explored the matter of both foreign direct investment and technological innovations on export performance in developing countries.

The purpose of this chapter is to determine the impacts of the foreign direct investments and technological investments on export performance in ten host developing Asian economies between 1990-2014.

GLOBAL TRENDS IN FDI AND DEVELOPING ASIAN ECONOMIES

Since 1980's, foreign direct investment is an attracting issue for the economies all around the world. Developed and developing countries attempt to get much FDI for the economic growth and development strategy. Global foreign direct investment inflows increased to $1,762 billion in 2015, from $1,277 billion in 2014, with changing between countries and regions. In 2015, inward FDI to developing economies was $765 billion, and Developing Asia stayed the largest FDI host in the world with inward FDI half a trillion dollars. East and South Asian economies have a good performance to attract the FDI inflows. FDI inflows to Hong Kong (China) increased by 53 percent from in 2015 and reached to $175 billion. Inflows of FDI to India increased 28 percent and to Turkey increased by 33 percent in 2015, in the same time flows to China was $136 billion with a 6 percent increase as seen in Table 1 (UNCTAD 2016:43-45).

Developing Asia is the most important host location for FDI inflows in the world, but the main part of FDI inflows are going to large and high-income economies in the region. In 2015, FDI inflows to Developing Asia were $541 billion, and the percentage share is 11% in world FDI flows. The leading four host country, namely Hong Kong (China, ($175 billion), China ($136 billion), Singapore ($65 billion), and India ($44 billion). Moreover, there is a significant amount of FDI inward to the other developing Asian countries such as Turkey ($17 billion), Indonesia ($16 billion), and Viet Nam ($12 billion). Also, Malaysia, United Arab Emirates (UAE), and Thailand received 11billions of dollars FDI in 2015 (Figure 1).

Figure 1. FDI inflows: Top 10 host economies in developing Asia
Source: *UNCTAD, FDI / MNE database (www.unctad.org/fdistatistics).*

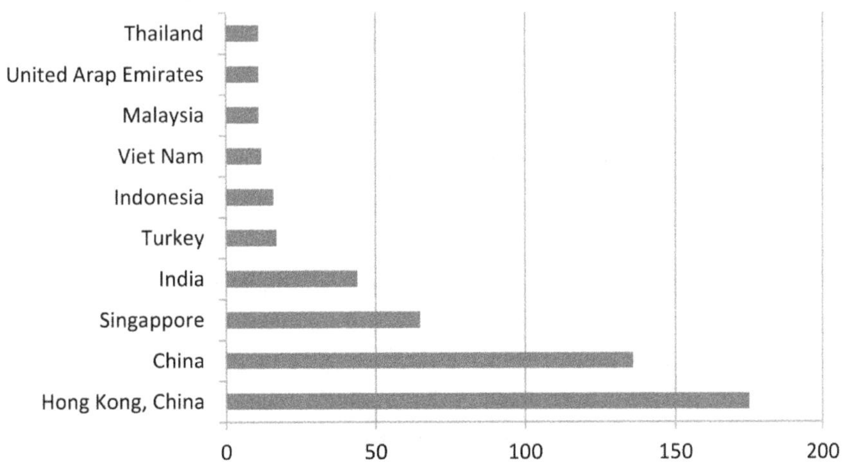

Table 1. FDI inflows, by region, 2013-1015 (billions of dollar)

Region	2013	2014	2015
World	1,427	1,277	1,762
Developed Economies	680	522	962
Europe	323	306	504
North America	283	165	429
Developing Economies	662	698	765
Africa	52	58	54
Asia	431	468	541
East and South-East Asia	350	383	448
China	123.9	128.5	135.6
Hong Kong,China	74.5	114	174.8
Indonesia	18.8	21.8	15.5
Malaysia	12.1	10.8	11.1
Singapore	66	68.4	65.2
Thailand	16.6	3.5	10.8
Vietnam	8.9	9.2	11.8
South Asia	36	41	50
India	28.1	34.5	44.2
West Asia	46	43	42
Turkey	12.2	12.1	16.5
UAE	9.4	10.8	10.9
Latin America and Caribbean	176	170	168
Transition economies	85	56	35
Structurally weak, vulnerable and small economies (LDC, LLDC, SIDS)	52	55	56

Source: UNCTAD, FDI/MNE database (www.unctad.org/fdistatistics).
Note:LDCs = least developed countries, LLDCs = landlocked developing countries, SIDS = small island developing States.

BACKGROUND OF FDI-EXPORT LINKS IN THEORETICAL AND EMPIRICAL LITERATURE

Foreign direct investments are the form of the multinational firms (MNE), integrated horizontally and vertically. Different part of the production steps are performed in the different countries to get low costs for vertical integration. In horizontal integration, the MNE try to avoid trade barriers or high transport costs when producing the same product in different locations and countries, (Markusen & Venables, 1998; Kutan &

Vuksic, 2007). More recently, some papers have investigated a type of FDI entitled *export-platform FDI,* MNE set up a production platform in a host country for exports to neighboring host countries (Ekholm et al., 2003). Furthermore, exports and FDI outward may move as substitutes or complements of each other (Martínez-Martín, 2010:8).

There is a consensus regarding the direct and indirect impacts of MNE on the export of host country. According to the *Theory of Multinational Enterprise*, Ownership advantage, location advantage and general benefits which suggest that the MNE has a motivation to produce or to sell internationally (Dunning, 1993). It is suggested that FDI effects on host country's exports positively, in vertically integrated FDI, as typically intermediate products produced by MNEs in the invested economy is sent back to the investing economy (Markusen 2002). Also, MNEs affect the amount of trade by way of interfirm and inter-industry relations in a host country with integrating exports (Ciruelos & Wang, 2005).

The indirect effects are consists of some transfers from foreign to domestic firms. When MNE conveys managerial and production methods, the human capital, or innovative product or service (Markusen, 2002) to its affiliate company in the host economy, some spillovers occur in the host economy.

One of the indirect effects of FDI is that domestic company's export may rise by detecting the MNEs export operations and using the framework of MNEs communications (Haddad & Harrison, 1993). Addition to that FDI inward impact on the competitive power of the invested country company and spread of advanced technologies. MNEs have critical advantages in management skills, marketing, and advanced technology may influence the host economy's structure and local firms' performance. By transferring their firm-specific assets to the local firms, MNEs may affect competition in domestic markets positively and, enforce to follow more effective forms in local firms (Markusen, 2002).

On the other hand, MNEs may ease to entry to international markets for the local firms by giving knowledge about the home country (UNCTAD 1999:240). Addition to that, when exporting foreign affiliates buy the inputs from the domestic companies, trade account of the host country recover (Din 1994). Technology spillovers occur by way of such relationship between a foreign affiliate and its domestic suppliers.

The connection between FDI inward and export performance has been long acknowledged in the literature see Markusen (1995). There are indications in the literature that supports FDI boost the exports of invested countries. Zhang and Song (2002) explore the impact of FDI on the export of provincial level of China during 1986-1997. The findings reveal that FDI effects on provincial manufacturing export performance positively. Zhang (2005) indicates that FDI effect on the export performance of China positively, and the exporting effect is higher effect in labor-intensive industries. Goswami and Saikia (2012) show that FDI effects on manufactured export positively, and export-led growth stimulates the FDI inflow. Prasanna (2010) show that inward FDI has significantly contributed to better the export performance of India. Sultan (2013) analyze the connection between export and FDI in India between 1980-2010 by using Johansen cointegration technique. The results indicate that there is a unidirectional causality run from export to FDI inflow.

Kutan and Vuksic (2007) show that FDI has increased the supply and exports in 12 Central and Eastern European economies during 1996-2004. Martínez-Martín (2010) examines the causality relationship between exports and outward FDI by using multivariate cointegrated model (VECM) in Spain. The findings expose that a strong causality from outward FDI to goods exports and a weak causality from FDI to exports of services in the short term. In the long term, outward FDI effect on goods exports positively.

Temiz and Gökmen (2011) examine the connection between FDI and export in Turkey during 1991-2010. Cointegration and Granger causality tests demonstrate that one-way causality is from export to foreign direct investment in Turkey.

BACKGROUND OF TECHNOLOGY SPILLOVERS FROM FDI IN THEORETICAL AND EMPIRICAL LITERATURE

FDI and MNEs perform a lot of research and development operation around the world; they have the most advanced technology. In that way, technology diffusion may occur in the host countries with complimentary of advanced technologies, and management skills.

Technology spillovers from FDI are classified into three types: labor, vertical, and horizontal spillovers. Horizontal Spillovers occur between companies working in the same industry or the same location while vertical spillovers occur in vertically-related industries, the form of forward linkages-foreign suppliers to domestic users- or the form of backward linkages -from foreign users to domestic suppliers-. Labor spillover occurs when employees who worked previously in foreign companies pass on to a local company (Sönmez & Pamukçu, 2011:7-8).

Das (1987) and Wang and Blomström (1992) suggest that copying of MNEs by domestic companies is the most appear spillover channel. Domestic entrepreneurs may try to imitate and copy the innovation technics, organizational practices and new types of production, and to adapt the product innovation to the local circumstances. Hence, the introduction of a new technology becomes less costly and risky. Imitation of the technology mentioned as intra-industry spillovers and worked primarily among firms inside same industries (Saggi, 2002).

Cheung and Ping (2004) imply domestic companies become efficient in leading their innovation operations by analyzing and imitating the MNEs past Research and

Development (R&D) operations. They also mention the FDI's crowding-out effect and suggest that local companies may favor participation of foreign investors, to purchase technologies from abroad instead of building an innovative environment. Al Azzawi (2012) reports the outcome of the spillover impacts of R&D on the further innovation of outward and inward FDI. The report concludes that followers of technology have much to benefit from FDI-induced R&D spillovers, that governments want to attract foreign MNEs.

The second channel of technology spillover is the human capital. The entry of FDI can also enhance the human capital in the invested economy by training domestic labor. The labor learns how to manage the leading technology and management procedure used by MNEs. These learnings may be conducted to the domestic economy by these workers help grow the domestic economy's productivity and promote the technology transfer.

Third, FDI may impact on innovation ability by way of competition. When domestic firms compete with MNEs, it may force to advance their competitiveness. Technological improvement may force the inter-industries spillovers in that foreign partner's trade; then forward linkages may occur (Kutan & Vuksic, 2007; Sönmez & Pamukçu, 2011).

When MNEs with advanced technologies have a lower marginal cost production, the condition of domestic companies may also face negativity by the competition. MNEs may increase its share in the market and force the domestic firms to perform on an inefficient scale, cause to increase their average costs. Thus, MNEs may cause to decrease the local firm's productivity (Aitken & Harrison, 1999). Even, many local firms have to close (Markusen & Venables, 1998; Barrios et al., 2005).

MNEs R&D operations can negatively affect local firms because they pull the most successful researchers to themselves, and they strongly compete with the domestic firms in the innovation products markets (Aghion et al., 2005; Fu, 2007, 2008). Hu and Jefferson (2002) show that FDI effect on domestic electronics firms in China negatively.

The fourth channel of technology spillover is backward and forward linkages. The trade operations of domestic firms by MNE establish intrafirm and intraindustry connections by increasing the demand from the world. The demand from the host country to home country-backward effect- and from home country to host country-forward effect- would increase the international trade and export quantity of countries (Zheng et al., 2004; Ciruelos & Wang, 2005). The initial MNEs investments emerged backward linkage impacts to domestic suppliers, improved their quality and productivity in developing East Asia, such as athletic shoes, personal computers, computer keyboards, sewing machines, and bicycles in Taiwan (Markusen and Venable 1999:338). Gorodninchenko et al. (2007) examine the forward and backward linkages of FDI with firm-level data in 17 transition economies over the 2002-2005.

The findings indicate that backward spillovers are always positive in all sectors, while forward spillovers positive in service sector firms.

FDI impact on innovation capacity is determined the result of an interrelation R&D workforce, R&D investment, institutional factors such as technical infrastructure (Aghion & Tirole, 1994; Braczyk et al., 1998). The terms of absorptive capacity impact the power of spillovers from FDI in that sense. The absorptive capability is decided by some factors, such as variations in technology level between the invested and investing companies, invested company's R&D capabilities, and human capital worked in invested firms. Additionally, supplementary elements may play a major role to realize technological opportunities into the advantage of innovative products and competitive market (Cosh et al. 2005). Supplementary elements are the mix of some factors like a country's adoption of a new idea, entrepreneurial power, the competition in business, the infrastructure of information and communication which determine the business environment. To summarize, the business environment determines the feature of FDI performance in a country and the effects of spillovers.

There are some studies conclude that spillovers have a positive impact on competition environment in the market. For example, Blalock and Gertler (2004) and Abraham et al. (2006) reveal that spillovers have an impact on the competitive sectors in Indonesia and China positively. Also, Sabirianova et al. (2005) suggest that spillovers are a favor to be positive in markets indicated by competitive business environment, such as openness to foreign investment and legal framework.

Foreign affiliates are a favor to bring better technology in advanced business environments as they may have high profits, then have many spillovers. Moran et al. (2005) show that domestic firms as foreign affiliates are often in subscale and inefficient in operation in protected markets. Javorcik and Saggi (2004) claim that MNEs that have an advanced technology try to protect their proprietary asset, so prefer to have full ownership, rather than joint ventures. Sönmez and Pamukçu (2011) examine the effects of MNEs horizontal technology spillovers in term of ownership in the Turkish manufacturing industry between 2003-2006. The evidences suggest that horizontal spillovers occur in case of majority or full ownership, while no such effect occurs in minority ownership.

There are many studies in literature, examine the impact of FDI on the capacity of innovation in the host country. Girma et al. (2007) uncover microeconomic indications on technology spillover by FDI in United Kingdom manufacturing sector. They show that FDI is an essential channel of technology transmission. Fu (2008) and Fan (2002) also find that FDI effect on the regional innovation in China positively.

Loukil (2016) investigate the impact of the FDI on technological innovation in developing economies. They used the panel threshold model covers 54 developing countries and the period of 1980-2009. The results confirm the non-linear relationship between FDI and innovation, and FDI's impact on innovation depends upon the threshold value of technological development. The study concludes that when the technological development is below the threshold value, FDI impact on innovation negatively, and technical development is higher the threshold value, FDI impact on innovation positively.

Dhrifi (2015) analyze the interrelationship between economic growth, technological innovation, and foreign direct investment with simultaneous equations model for 83 developed and developing countries during 1990–2012. The empirical findings reveal that FDI has a significant and positive impact on economic growth in high and middle -income economies, while foreign direct investment has not a positive impact on low-income economies.

Erdal and Göçer (2015) investigate the impact of FDI on innovation and R&D activities and in 10 developing economies (Iran, Malaysia, China, India, South Korea, Turkey, Saudi Arabia Pakistan, Thailand and Singapore) between 1996-2013. According to the panel causality and cointegration analysis, FDI inflows effect on innovation and R&D activities positively, in invested countries.

Falvey et al. (2004) investigate FDI effects on imports and exports of OECD countries during 1975–1990. They conclude that import spillovers are higher than the export spillovers. Sılovagathasan and Wuu (2014) examine the effect of MNEs on domestic innovation activities in South Asian countries between 2000-2010. The findings support the hypothesis that FDI inward brings advanced and technologies into the invested country and improve innovation activities of domestic firms in South Asian countries.

MAIN FOCUS OF THE CHAPTER

The primary purpose of this chapter is to explore the impact of FDI inflows and technological innovations on export performance, by using a panel cointegration model. The sample is composed of 10 host developing countries (Hong Kong, China, India, Malaysia, Turkey, Indonesia, Viet Nam, Singapore, United Arab Emirates, and Thailand) over the period 1990–2014.

Data Set, Econometric Method, and Empirical Results

The effects of FDI inflows and technological innovation on export performance of 10 host countries by panel cointegration technique for Developing Asian Countries as the following:

$$EXP_{it} = \alpha_0 + \alpha_1 \sum_{i=1}^{n} FDI_{it} + \alpha_2 \sum_{i=1}^{n} PN_{it} + \alpha_3 \sum_{i=1}^{n} GDP_{it} + \mu_{it} \quad (1)$$

In equation (1), export (EXP) is dependent variable; inward foreign direct investment (FDI), patent applications (PN), and Gross Domestic Product per Capita (GDP) are the independent variables. (t) is the time; (i) is the cross dimension of the model. The number of patent applications (PN) represents R&D activities, proxy as innovation capability in a country. FDI investments are expected to have a positive impact on the patent application because of the assumption that MNEs transfer advanced technologies into the host country and improve domestic companies innovation activities. Then, it is expected that FDI inflows and GDP growth's impact on export positively, due to the trade-induced effect of foreign direct investment.

Data Set

In this model, the dependent variable is an inward foreign direct investment (FDI), independent variables are patent applications (PN), export (EXP) and Gross Domestic Product per Capita (GDP). The annual data for a 1990-2015 period for 10 Developing Asia countries were used in the analysis. The top host economies in developing Asia were selected base on UNCTAD 2016. Table 2 shows the definitions of variables in the logarithmic form and sources. Table 3, demonstrate the summary of the descriptive statistics.

Panel Data

Panel data analysis method which has significant advantages compared to other techniques was chosen in the chapter. The most important feature of this analysis is that it allows building a data set with both time and cross-section dimensions, by

Table 2. Definition and source of variables

Variable	Definition	Source
FDP	FDI inwards, US Dollars	IMF-IFS (International Monetary Fund, International Financial Statistics)
EXP	Export of goods and services, US Dollars	IMF-DOTS (Direction of Trade Statistics)
PN	Residents and Nonresidents patent applications	World Bank WDI (World Development Indicators)
GDP	Real Gross Domestic Product per capita (US Dollars)	World Bank WDI

Table 3. Descriptive statistics

Statistic	EXP	GDP	PT	FDI
Mean	25.52333	8.202687	8.293451	22.94821
Median	25.58587	8.079558	8.465268	22.84768
Maximum	28.40035	10.93324	11.75227	26.39634
Minimum	23.06248	5.76169	2.833213	18.55752
Std. Dev.	1.031574	1.416195	1.669949	1.544628
Skewness	0.281528	0.197521	-0.85741	0.158251
Kurtosis	3.207056	2.045682	4.769762	2.761248

compounding cross-section and time series. Panel data analysis seems to have various advantages when examined in contrast with cross-section and time series analysis. At first, by compounding cross-section with time series observations, means that large observation provides a high degree of freedom, and reduces the likelihood of high linear correlation between explanatory variables. Then, panel data can better observe and determine impacts, easily cannot be determined in a cross-section or a time series data.

Another benefit of panel data analysis is that it provides the establishment and examining of more complex behavioral models than cross-section or time series. This advantage does not cause any significant problem in the panel data analysis of excluded variables leading to significant deviations in estimation results in studies using time series or cross-section data (Baltagi, 2008:295).

Cross-Section Dependence

Regarding econometrics, cross-section independence refers that there is no connection between individuals forming the panels and error terms in the model, see in Equation (2). According to the economics perspective, it could be inferred that in a situation in which the panel units are forming the panel are not influenced by a shock; the other panel units will be influenced too (Akbaş et al., 2013).

$$y_{it} = \alpha_i + \beta_i x_{it} + \varepsilon_{it} \qquad (2)$$

$$Cov(\varepsilon_{it}, \varepsilon_{ij}) \neq 0$$

Then, traditional Ordinary Least Square (OLS) based estimations are inefficient, biased and inconsistent in case of cross-section dependence. Hence, the existence of cross-section dependence in the panel should be tested before proceeding to the panel analyses (Pesaran, 2004; Breusch & Pagan, 1980). Pesaran et al. (2008) added the mean and the variance to the test statistics to the adjusted Breusch-Pagan (1980) Lagrange Multiplier test and Cross Dependence test advanced by Pesaran (2004). Then, this test is known the *LM* test adjusted according to the bias method (LM_{adj}), is in below:

$$CD = \sqrt{\frac{2T}{N(N-1)}}\left[\sum_{i=1}^{N-1}\sum_{j=i+1}^{N}\hat{\rho}_{ij}\right] \mathrm{N}(0,1) \tag{3}$$

In Equation (3), $\hat{\rho}_{ij}$ represents the correlation coefficient between the residuals acquired from each regression by using Ordinary Least Square (OLS). Test hypotheses are;

H_0: no cross-section dependence

H_1: cross-section dependence

From the test results, if the H_0 is not rejected, the analysis is needed to be continued with the first generation of panel unit root tests. However, if the $H0$ is rejected and there is a cross-section dependence among panel units, then the analysis should be continued with second-generation of panel unit root tests (Baltagi, 2008:284).

The cross-section dependency in the series was checked by Pesaran (2004) CDLM test and the outcome is shown in Table 4. As seen in Table 4, there is a

Table 4. Cross-sectional dependency and homogeneity

CD Tests	Stat.	Prob.
CD_{Lm1}	55.714	0.1310
CD_{LM2}	1.129	0.1290
CD_{LM}	1.858	0.0320
$CD_{adjusted}$	96.979	0.0020
CD test for cointegration	2.8330	0.0020
Delta tilde ($\hat{\Delta}$)	-0.0446	0.5178
Adj. Delta tilde ($\hat{\Delta}_{adj}$)	-0.0151	0.5060

significant relationship between the cross-sectional units. Hence, it is rejected the null hypothesis (H_0) assuming that the series are independent of each other, and it is revealed that there is a cross-sectional dependence in the panel data model. From here it is concluded that the shocks of the variables in one of the country also affect other countries.

Then, ($\hat{\Delta}$) and ($\hat{\Delta}_{adj}$) test statistics are not significant as seen in Table 3. Accordingly, the null hypothesis (H_0) is not rejected, and it is exposed that the slope coefficients are not changing among the cross-sectional units. Namely, variables in the panel dataset are homogenous.

Panel Unit Root

Panel-based unit root tests, which are called first generation tests, are devised under the hypothesis that the panel individuals are independent of each other, while panel-based unit root tests called second generation tests are build on the assumption that the individuals are not independent of each other.

Cross section dependence influence the test structures used in statistical analysis. It needs to apply second generation panel unit root tests due to the existence of cross-sectional dependence in the model. Therefore, it was used the one of the second generation unit root test by Pesaran (2007) CADF (Cross-Sectionally Augmented Dickey-Fuller) test for the analysis of stationary. Second generation tests are applied as CADF, and CIPS (Cross section Im, Pesaran, and Shin) unit root test process can be considered as follows:

$$\Delta y_{it} = \alpha_i + b_i y_{i,t-1} + c_i \bar{y}_{t-1} + d_i \Delta \bar{y}_t + u_{it} \tag{4}$$

In equation (4), α_i is constant, $\Delta \bar{Y}_{t-1}$ is the differences' a lag and $\bar{Y}_{t-1}$ is the one lag of $\bar{Y}_t$. The hypotheses of null and alternative for CADF testing are in below:

$H_0 = \beta 1 = \beta 2 = \ldots.. \beta n = 0$ (series contains a unit root)

$H_A = \beta 1 \neq \beta 2 \neq \ldots.. \beta n \neq 0$ (series are stationary).

The CADF test cannot analyze the stationarity of all panels; thus, the CIPS test developed by Pesaran (2007) fills a gap of the CADF test. This test can analyze for all panels which series is stationary under the null hypothesis and use the Pesaran critical value. Equation (13) stability analysis is tested in CADF by comparing the statistical values of the t values for the b_i coefficients with of the Pesaran (2007) table critical values obtained from the Monte Carlo simulations. Unit root test outcomes are shown in Table 5.

According to the unit root results obtained from the CIPS statistics in Table 5, EXP variable has a unit root at the level, and GDP, EXP and PN variables have not a unit root at level.

Westerlund Cointegration

To determine if there is a stable long-term relationship between the non-stationary series is investigated using cointegration analyzes. In this study "Durbin Hausman Cointegration Test" developed by Westerlund (2008) is used. This test takes into account both the cross-section dependency and allows the slope coefficients to be heterogeneous. This test contains two statistics. These are Durbin Hausman group and Durbin Hausman panel statistics. The Durbin Hausman group statistic DH_g assumes that the autoregressive parameter (φ) is heterogeneous and it produces results under this assumption. This test statistic is calculated as follows:

$$DH_g = \sum_{i=1}^{n} \tilde{S}(\tilde{\varphi}_i - \hat{\varphi}_i)^2 \sum_{t=2}^{T} \hat{e}_{it-1}^2 \tag{5}$$

Table 5. CADF test stat value

Countries	Variables							
	EXP		FDI		PN		GDP	
	level	I(1)	level	I(1)	level	I(1)	level	I(1)
Hong Kong	-3.6552***	-7.3043*	-4.0792**	-8.3743*	-2.2168	-9.8143*	-1.8694	-8.5494
China, Mainland	-2.5353	-7.9123*	-3.0632	-7.2614*	-5.2103*	-11.1735*	-5.9859*	-8.9847
India	-2.3081	-6.2172*	-4.3161**	-3.8869**	-3.241	-5.2717*	-3.3347	-4.0802
Indonesia	-2.4254	-3.114	-2.3389	-3.7942**	-3.1933	-6.8351*	-2.9947	-4.5532
Malaysia	-1.828	-2.8195	-3.2285	-4.9017*	-2.6567	-5.6939*	-1.2307	-4.283
Singapore	-2.9746	-4.0568**	-3.2067	-3.8314**	-3.2585	-4.0146**	-2.173	-4.1856
Thailand	-0.3634	-2.2525	-1.5276	-3.062	-1.6237	-5.0609*	-1.4097	-4.4141
Turkey	-3.7114***	-2.9114	-3.4904***	-6.0763*	-2.9044	-2.6428	-3.4165	-4.0623
UAE	-2.983	-6.8276*	-2.8957	-5.4626*	-2.2762	-5.9075*	-3.7203***	-4.3951
Vietnam	-3.688***	-11.8043*	-3.6233***	-12.4091*	-6.6243*	-13.0157*	-6.9467*	-17.9896
CIPS	**-2.6473**	**-5.4988***	**-3.177***	**-5.6060***	**-3.3205***	**-6.5017***	**-3.3081***	-6.1779*

Note: " * ", " ** ", and " *** " are implied that provided stationary in 1%, 5%, and 10% according to the Pesaran (2007:274,281) critical values of constant and trend models.

The Durbin Hausman panel statistic DH_p assumes that autoregressive parameters are homogeneous and produces results under this assumption. This test statistic is as follows:

$$DH_p = \hat{S}_n(\tilde{\varphi} - \hat{\varphi})^2 \sum_{i=1}^{n} \sum_{i=1}^{T} \hat{e}_{it-1}^2 \tag{6}$$

Both test statistics indicate the presence of cointegration for the panel in the rejection of the hypothesis H_0 (Westerlund, 2008: 196-203).

In that sense, The Westerlund (2008) cointegration test is used in the presence of cross-section dependence and series with I(0) and I(1). The statistical values obtained from the Durbin-Hausman cointegration test results show that on Table 6 there is a long-run relationship between variables.

Estimation of Long-Run Coefficient by Panel Dynamic Ordinary Least Square (PDOLS)

After the unit root and cointegration tests have been applied, it is possible to estimate the final unbiased coefficient of this relationship with Panel Dynamic Ordinary Least Square Methodology developed by Pedroni (2001). The group mean panel DOLS method developed by Pedroni (2000) is based on the following panel regression model:

$$y_{it} = \alpha_i + \beta x_{it} + \varepsilon_{it} \tag{7}$$

$$x_{it} = x_{it-1} + \mu_{it} \tag{8}$$

In this equation, y_{it} denotes the dependent variable x_{it} denotes the independent variables and α_i denotes constant effects; it is assumed that there is no dependency between the sections forming the panel. Error in Equation (8) is a stationary process,

Table 6. Durbin-Hausman cointegration test results

Stats	Value	Prob	Decision
Durbin-Hg	27.35	0.0000	Cointegrated
Durbin-Hp	147.414	0.0000	Cointegrated

if there is a long-term cointegration relationship between the two integrated in the first order y_{it} and x_{it}. Thus, β represents the required estimated long-term cointegration vector in Equation (7).

The estimator of group mean panel DOLS suggested by Pedroni (2001) requires the estimation of the following regression model.

$$y_{it} = \alpha_i + \beta x_{it} + \sum_{k=-K_i}^{K_i} \gamma_{ik} \Delta x_{it} + \varepsilon_{it} \tag{9}$$

In this regression model, $-K_i$ and K_i show the number of premise and lag. When the cointegration vector is obtained in this model, which assumes no dependency between the cross sections forming the panel, the model in Equation (9) is obtained at first. The Newey-West method is used to get the panel DOLS estimator. In the second stage, the mean of the cointegration coefficients obtained from the DOLS estimate, and the panel cointegration coefficient is computed as follows.

$$\hat{\beta}^{*}_{GD} = N^{-1} \sum_{i=1}^{N} \beta^{*}_{D,i} \tag{10}$$

where $\hat{\beta}^{*}_{GD}$ is the cointegration coefficient obtained from the DOLS estimate for each cross section the t-statistics for group average of panel DOLS estimators are calculated as follows:

$$t_{\hat{\beta}_D} = N^{-1/2} \sum_{i=1}^{N} t_{\hat{\beta}^{*}_{D,i}} \tag{11}$$

Where $t_{\hat{\beta}_{D=1}}$ is the t-statistic for the cointegration coefficient obtained from the DOLS estimate for each horizontal section.

Because of the existence of cross-section dependency and the slope parameters being homogeneous in cross-sectional dimension, the effect of foreign direct investment, per income and patent applications on export performance was analyzed using PDOLS technique. Table 7 gives the estimation results obtained. The PDOLS regression in our case is given as follows:

$$EXP_{it} = \alpha_0 + \alpha_i FDI_{it} + \beta_i PN_{it} + \lambda_i GDP + \sum_{j=-ni}^{ni} \alpha_{1j} \Delta FDI_{it-j} + \sum_{j=-ni}^{ni} \alpha_{2j} \Delta PN_{it-j} + \sum_{j=-ni}^{ni} \alpha_{3j} GDP_{it-j} + \varepsilon_{it} \tag{12}$$

Table 7. Panel DOLS estimation results

Dependent Variable: Export		
Variables	**Coefficient**	**Prob. Value**
FDI	0.064672	0.0358
GDP	0.346595	0.0004
PT	0.128843	0.0207
Diagnostic Test Results		
R-squared	0.993699	
Long-run variance	0.010563	
Lead and lag length (p):1		
Long-run variance weights (Bartlett kernel, Integer Newey-West fixed bandwidth)		

In Equation (12) subscript *i* represents countries, *t* represents the period, and *p* denotes a lead and lag length in the regression.

According to the results obtained from Table 7, it can be said that the foreign direct investments, per income and the number of patents have a statistically significant and positive effect on export performance. Moreover, the effect of the patent application variable on exports is higher than the effect of the foreign direct investments on exports. When the model is estimated under the assumption that the slope coefficients of the variables are different, the slope coefficients are estimated as in Table 8.

According to the Table 8, it is observed that FDI has a positive impact on export performance in all of the country groups. India, Vietnam, China, Turkey, Indonesia, and Thailand are more likely to have a greater impact on exports compared to other countries in the group. However, it has been observed that the number of patents has different effects on the export performance of host countries. In Turkey and Indonesia, the number of patents appears to have a significant impact on export performance compared to the rest of the country groups. However, in India and the United Arab Emirates, technological innovations have a negative effect on export performance.

Table 8. Slope heterogeneity and individual coefficient effect on export performance

Variables	China, P.R.: Hong Kong	China, P.R.: Mainland	India	Indonesia	Malaysia	Singapore	Thailand	Turkey	UAE	Vietnam
FDI	0.2157	0.6643	0.8592	0.5450	0.4689	0.3952	0.5183	0.6922	0.1996	0.8919
GDP	0.6296	1.4301	0.0993	-0.2931	0.1273	0.9307	0.1172	-0.2082	0.0104	0.9539
PATENT	0.1784	0.1098	-0.0609	0.2083	0.1299	0.1972	0.0148	0.2217	-0.0940	0.0577

CONCLUSION

This chapter has examined the impacts of FDI inward and technological innovations on export performance in Developing Asian countries by using panel cointegration technique. The empirical results show that inward FDI, per income and patent application, have a positive impact on export performance in Developing Asian countries. More specifically, a patent application has a higher effect than foreign investments on host country exports. According to the individual coefficient effect on export performance, foreign direct investments have a positive impact on export in the sample. Addition to that, technological development affects exports positively in the Turkey, Indonesia, Hong Kong, Singapore, Malaysia, China, Vietnam, Thailand, negatively in India and the United Arab Emirates. From the results of the empirical analysis, it is concluded that the trade-induced effect of foreign direct investment and technological spillover effects are valid in Developing Asian Countries. In other words, foreign direct investment and technological innovations positively affect the balance of payments and economic growth in host countries.

REFERENCES

Abraham, F., Konings, J., & Slootmaekers, V. (2006). *FDI spillovers, firm heterogeneity and degree of ownership: evidence from Chinese manufacturing* (Unpublished Paper). Department of Economics, Catholic University of Leuven.

Aghion, P., Bloom, N., Blundell, R., Griffith, R., & Howitt, P. (2005). Competition and innovation: An inverted-U relationship. *The Quarterly Journal of Economics*, *120*(2), 701–728.

Aghion, P., & Tirole, J. (1994). The management of innovation. *The Quarterly Journal of Economics*, *109*(4), 1185–1209. doi:10.2307/2118360

Aitken, B. J., & Harrison, A. E. (1999). Do domestic firms benefit from direct foreign investment? Evidence from Venezuela. *The American Economic Review*, *89*(3), 605–618. doi:10.1257/aer.89.3.605

AlAzzawi, S. (2012). Innovation, productivity and foreign direct investment-induced R&D spillovers. *The Journal of International Trade & Economic Development*, *21*(5), 615–653. doi:10.1080/09638199.2010.513056

Alper & Teoman. (2011). *Foreign Direct Investment and Technology Spillovers in the Turkish Manufacturing*. Industry, Science and Techonology Policies Research Center TEKPOL Working Paper series, 11/3.

Barrios, S., Görg, H., & Strobl, E. (2005). Foreign direct investment, competition and industrial development in the host country. *European Economic Review*, *49*(7), 1761–1784. doi:10.1016/j.euroecorev.2004.05.005

Blalock, G., & Gertler, P. (2004). *Firm capabilities and technology adoption: Evidence from foreign direct investment in Indonesia* (Working Paper). Department of Applied Economics and Management, Cornell University.

Braczyk, H. J., Cooke, P. N., & Heidenreich, M. (1998). *Regional innovation systems: the role of governances in a globalized world*. Psychology Press.

Breusch, T. S., & Pagan, A. R. (1980). The Lagrange multiplier test and its applications to model specification in econometrics. *The Review of Economic Studies*, *47*(1), 239–253. doi:10.2307/2297111

Cheung, K. Y., & Ping, L. (2004). Spillover effects of FDI on innovation in China: Evidence from the provincial data. *China Economic Review*, *15*(1), 25–44. doi:10.1016/S1043-951X(03)00027-0

Ciruelos, A., & Wang, M. (2005). International technology diffusion: Effects of trade and FDI. *Atlantic Economic Journal*, *33*(4), 437–449. doi:10.100711293-005-2871-1

Cosh, A., Fu, X., & Hughes, A. (2005). *Management characteristics, collaboration and innovative efficiency: Evidence from UK survey data*. Cambridge, UK: Centre for Business Research, University of Cambridge.

Das, S. (1987). Externalities, and technology transfer through multinational corporations A theoretical analysis. *Journal of International Economics*, *22*(1-2), 171–182. doi:10.1016/0022-1996(87)90028-6

Dhrifi, A. (2015). Foreign direct investment, technological innovation and economic growth: Empirical evidence using simultaneous equations model. *International Review of Economics*, *62*(4), 381–400. doi:10.100712232-015-0230-3

Din, M. U. (1994). Export processing zones and backward linkages. *Journal of Development Economics*, *43*(2), 369–385. doi:10.1016/0304-3878(94)90014-0

Dunning, J. H. (1993). *Multinational Enterprises and the Global Economy*. Addison-Wesley Publishing Company.

Ekholm, K., Forslid, R., & Markusen, J. R. (2003). *Export-Platform Foreign Direct Investment*. NBER Working Paper, No 9517.

Erdal, L., & Göçer, I. (2015). The Effects of Foreign Direct Investment on R&D and Innovations: Panel Data Analysis for Developing Asian Countries. *Procedia: Social and Behavioral Sciences*, *195*, 749–758. doi:10.1016/j.sbspro.2015.06.469

Falvey, R., Foster, N., & Greenaway, D. (2004). Imports, exports, knowledge spillovers and growth. *Economics Letters*, *85*(2), 209–213. doi:10.1016/j.econlet.2004.04.007

Fan, E. X. (2002). *Technological spillovers from foreign direct investment: A survey (No. 33)*. Manila, Philippines: Asian Development Bank.

Fu, X. (2007). Trade-cum-FDI, Human Capital Inequality and the Dual Economy in China: The Signer Perspective. *Journal of Economic Change and Restructuring*, *2*(1), 55–71.

Fu, X. (2008). Foreign direct investment, absorptive capacity and regional innovation capabilities: Evidence from China. *Oxford Development Studies*, *36*(1), 89–110. doi:10.1080/13600810701848193

Girma, S., Kneller, R., & Pisu, M. (2007). Do exporters have anything to learn from foreign multinationals? *European Economic Review*, *51*(4), 993–1010. doi:10.1016/j.euroecorev.2006.07.003

Görg, H., & Greenaway, D. (2004). Much ado about nothing? Do domestic firms really benefit from foreign direct investment? *The World Bank Research Observer*, *19*(2), 171–197. doi:10.1093/wbro/lkh019

Gorodnichenko, Y., Svejnar, J., & Terrell, K. (2007). *When Does FDI Have Positive Spillovers? Evidence from 17 Emerging Market Economies.* IZA Discussion Paper No. 3079.

Goswami, C., & Saikia, K. K. (2012). FDI and its relation with exports in India, status and prospect in north east region. *Procedia: Social and Behavioral Sciences*, *37*, 123–132. doi:10.1016/j.sbspro.2012.03.280

Grossman, G. M., & Helpman, E. (1991). Trade, knowledge spillovers, and growth. *European Economic Review*, *35*(2-3), 517–526. doi:10.1016/0014-2921(91)90153-A

Haddad, M., & Harrison, A. (1993). Are there positive spillovers from direct foreign investment?: Evidence from panel data for Morocco. *Journal of Development Economics*, *42*(1), 51–74. doi:10.1016/0304-3878(93)90072-U

Helpman, E., Melitz, M. J., & Stephen, R. Y. (2004). Exports Versus FDI with Heterogenous Firms. *The American Economic Review*, *94*(1), 300–316. doi:10.1257/000282804322970814

Hu, A. G., & Jefferson, G. H. (2002). FDI impact and spillover: Evidence from China's electronic and textile industries. *World Economy*, *25*(8), 1063–1076. doi:10.1111/1467-9701.00481

IMF (International Monetary Fund). (n.d.). *DOTS (Direction of Trade Statistics), IFS (International Financial Statistics)*. Retrieved from https://www.imf.org/external/pubs/cat/longres.aspx?sk=19305.0

Javorcik Smarzynska, B., & Saggi, K. (2004). *Technological asymmetry and the mode of foreign investment*. World Bank Policy Research Working Paper, 3196.

Kutan, A. M., & Vukšić, G. (2007). Foreign direct investment and export performance: Empirical evidence. *Comparative Economic Studies*, *49*(3), 430–445. doi:10.1057/palgrave.ces.8100216

Loukil, K. (2016). Foreign Direct Investment And Technological Innovation In Developing Countries. *Oradea Journal of Business and Economics*, *1*(2), 31–40.

Lucas, R. E. Jr. (1988). On the mechanics of economic development. *Journal of Monetary Economics*, *22*(1), 3–42. doi:10.1016/0304-3932(88)90168-7

Markusen, J. R. (1995). The boundaries of multinational enterprises and the theory of international trade. *The Journal of Economic Perspectives*, *9*(2), 169–189. doi:10.1257/jep.9.2.169

Markusen, J. R. (2002). *Multinational Firms and the Theory of International Trade*. Cambridge, MA: MIT Press.

Markusen, J. R., & Venables, A. J. (1998). Multinational firms and the new trade theory. *Journal of International Economics*, *46*(2), 183–203. doi:10.1016/S0022-1996(97)00052-4

Markusen, J. R., & Venables, A. J. (1999). Foreign direct investment as a catalyst for industrial development. *European Economic Review*, *43*(2), 335–356. doi:10.1016/S0014-2921(98)00048-8

Martínez-Martín, J. (2010). *On the dynamics of exports and FDI: the Spanish internationalization process*. IREA–Working Papers, 2010, IR10/010.

Moran, T. H., Graham, E. M., & Blomström, M. (2005). *Does Foreign Direct Investment Promote Development?* Washington, DC: Institute for International Economics, Center for Global Development.

Pesaran, M. H. (2004). *General diagnostic tests for cross section dependence in panels*. University of Cambridge Working Papers in Economics, No 0435.

Pesaran, M. H. (2007). A simple panel unit root test in the presence of cross-section dependence. *Journal of Applied Econometrics*, *22*(2), 265–312. doi:10.1002/jae.951

Pesaran, M. H., Ullah, A., & Yamagata, T. (2008). A bias-adjusted LM test of error cross-section independence. *The Econometrics Journal*, *11*(1), 105–127. doi:10.1111/j.1368-423X.2007.00227.x

Pesaran, M. H., & Yamagata, T. (2008). Testing slope homogeneity in large panels. *Journal of Econometrics*, *142*(1), 50–93. doi:10.1016/j.jeconom.2007.05.010

Prasanna, N. (2010). Impact of foreign direct investment on export performance in India. *Journal of Social Science*, *24*(1), 65–71.

Romer, P. M. (1990). Endogenous technological change. *Journal of Political Economy*, *98*(5, Part 2), S71–S102. doi:10.1086/261725

Sabirianova Peter, K., Svejnar, J., & Terell, K. (2004). *Distance to the Efficiency Frontier and FDI Spillovers*. William Davidson Institute Working Paper Number, No 721.

Saggi, K. (2002). Trade, foreign direct investment, and international technology transfer: A survey. *The World Bank Research Observer*, *17*(2), 191–235. doi:10.1093/wbro/17.2.191

Sivalogathasan, V., & Wu, X. (2014). The effect of foreign direct investment on innovation in south asian emerging markets. *Global Business and Organizational Excellence*, *33*(3), 63–76. doi:10.1002/joe.21544

Solow, R. M. (1956). A contribution to the theory of economic growth. *The Quarterly Journal of Economics*, *70*(1), 65–94. doi:10.2307/1884513

Sultan, Z. A. (2013). A causal relationship between FDI inflows and export: The case of India. *Journal of Economics and Sustainable Development*, *4*(2), 1–9.

Temiz, D., & Gökmen, A. (2011). Foreign direct investment (FDI) and export relation in Turkey: 1991–2010. *Journal of Transnational Management*, *16*(3), 157–180. do i:10.1080/15475778.2011.596779

UNCTAD. (1999). *World Investment Report 1999: foreign direct investment and the challenge of development*. UNCTAD.

UNCTAD. (2016). *World Investment Report (Chapter II Regional Investment Trends).* Retrieved from http://unctad.org/en/pages/PublicationWebflyer.aspx?publicationid=1555

Wang, J. Y., & Blomström, M. (1992). Foreign investment and technology transfer: A simple model. *European Economic Review, 36*(1), 137–155. doi:10.1016/0014-2921(92)90021-N

Westerlund, J. (2008). Panel cointegration tests of the Fisher effect. *Journal of Applied Econometrics, 23*(2), 193–233. doi:10.1002/jae.967

World Bank. (n.d.). *World Development Indicators.* Retrieved from http://data.worldbank.org/data-catalog/world-development-indicators

Zhang, K. H. (2005). How does FDI affect a host country's export performance? The case of China. *International Conference of WTO, China and the Asian Economies.*

Zhang, K. H., & Song, S. (2002). Promoting exports: The role of inward FDI in China. *China Economic Review, 11*(4), 385–396. doi:10.1016/S1043-951X(01)00033-5

Zheng, P., Siler, P., & Giorgioni, G. (2004). FDI and the export performance of Chinese indigenous firms: A regional approach. *Journal of Chinese Economic and Business Studies, 2*(1), 55–71. doi:10.1080/14765280310001631381

KEY TERMS AND DEFINITIONS

Developing Asia: It represents developing economies located on the Asian continent.

Export: Sale of goods and services to foreign countries.

Foreign Direct Investments: Investors who are outside the borders of a country by making production facilities such as factories, opening branches, acquiring immovables, or purchasing an existing company wholly or partly.

Innovation: Innovation is developing new ideas and applying them. It can be different shapes as to produce a new product or to make it more useful by developing an existing product.

Panel Cointegration: The econometric methodology analyzing the long-run relationship between the non-stationary series in panel data.

Patent Application: The application of the document that gives the inventor the right to produce, use, sell, or import the product of the invention subject for a certain period. It emerges as a result of research and development activities and serves as a model for innovation.

Research and Development: It defines the systematically creative work to increase the knowledge circulation and the use of this information to create new applications.

Technology Spillover: It refers to the widespread use of advanced technology products and methods.

Chapter 2
Determinants of FDI Inflows in Developing Countries:
A Dynamic Panel Approach

Dinesh Kumar Choudhury
Sri Sathya Sai Institute of Higher Learning, India

Prabhakara Rao
Sri Sathya Sai Institute of Higher Learning, India

ABSTRACT

In the era of globalization, FDI plays an important role as it intensifies the interaction among the countries, regions, and firms. FDI is playing a crucial role in improving the infrastructural facilities of countries and enhancing economic situation especially in the developing countries. Another important aspect of FDI is it increases employment in domestic economies, which in turn reduces the poverty level and also promotes the competition in domestic markets. With these activities, the government earns more revenue, which can be used for developmental activities. In this context, the chapter makes an attempt to identify the determining factors of FDI inflows into developing economies by selecting nine developing countries for the time period 2000-2015. Due to the different characteristics of each of these countries, there is a lot of heterogeneity in the data. To reduce the heterogeneity among the selected economies, the authors propose employing a panel data approach to identify the factors that influence the FDI inflows.

DOI: 10.4018/978-1-5225-3026-8.ch002

INTRODUCTION

In the era of globalization, Foreign Direct Investment (FDI) has witnessed tremendous increase across the countries in the world. Now, FDI is an integral part of an open and effective international economic system and a major catalyst to economic development. These FDI flows are most important to the developing economies in achieving their growth and development as these countries do not have enough national savings to finance their investments. Initially they borrowed the loans from international agencies and during the 1980's the lending of commercial banks decreased due to debt crises, forced many countries to reform their investment policies so as to attract more stable forms of foreign direct investments.

Developing countries, emerging economies and countries in transition have come increasingly to see FDI as a source of economic development. They believe that in addition to foreign capital, FDI brings with it employment, managerial skills and technology and therefore it accelerates growth and development. The role of FDI as a source of capital has become increasingly important in the modernization, income growth and employment of these developing economies and hence, they have liberalized their FDI regimes.

There has been a long debate over issue of the role of FDI's and economic development of a country. It is widely believed that FDI provides a stronger stimulus to economic growth in host countries than other types of capital inflows. The underlying argument is that FDI is more than just capital, as it offers access to internationally available technologies and management knowhow (The Economist, 2001). However, Townsend (2003) observed that there is no clear evidence of the relationship between foreign direct investment and economic growth. Lall (2002) concluded that the contribution of FDI to economic growth depends on many factors and it varies over time and from one host country to another. Some see FDI as a very important tool for economic growth especially in the less developed countries (LDCs) but some scholars claimed that the contribution of FDI to economic development is not as pronounced as most people believe.

It is well known that countries which offer profitable investment opportunities in the global competition can attract capital. Indeed, most of foreign direct investment (FDI) in world took place among the developed economies. However, in recent times capital flows to developing countries is also increasing. Developing countries from Asia, Africa and Latin America are successful in opening up their economies to FDI flows by implementing the liberalized policies. Most countries are creating favorable environment to attract more FDI inflows in modern managerial, production and marketing technologies which are necessary for development of an economy.

Foreign investors seeking rates of return on their funds may be attracted to invest in developing countries with low capital stock and hence a high marginal productivity rate of capital provided that investment in those economies is not viewed to be too risky. Also, the availability of human capital at lower cost is another attracting feature of the investments. Investment in developing countries can take place through three main financial channels: Loans, equity investment and FDI. Among these the least desirable form of capital flows is debt financing (loans) as debt- financed activities may produce insufficient returns to cover the debt service payments (i.e. interest). If we consider equity financing like portfolio investment can be destabilizing factor, especially in countries with emerging financial sectors. Moreover, they are very volatile in nature. Given these conditions, FDI is most likely form of capital flows to exhibit long term investment intentions due to large fixed costs of setting up and dismantling subsidiaries for multinational enterprises.

FDI is important for any developing country because it facilitates the transfer of technology, increase employment in the domestic economy, reduces poverty, and strengthens the links with international markets. It also promotes competition in the domestic market, contributes to human capital development through employee training, and to maximize corporate tax revenues. It is useful in bridging the gap between domestic savings and investments.

However, these FDI flows will depend on the major factors such as Growth, Infrastructure, market size, trade openness and availability of low cost human capital etc. of an economy. Lucas (1990) conjectures that lack of human capital discouraged foreign investment in less-developed countries. Wheeler and Mody (1992) have shown that a "well developed infrastructure" as a key determinant of capital investment by multinationals. The World Investment Report of 1998 states that infrastructure definitely exerts its influence on the inflow of FDI. Dunning (1988) highlighted that the skill and education level of labor can influence the volume of FDI inflows. According to World Investment Report, UNCTAD (1998) has analyzed the determinants of FDI and host country determinants have been classified into the three groups. These are political factors, business facilitation and economic factors. Zhang and Markusen (1999) also emphasized that the availability of skilled labor in the host country is a direct requirement of transnational companies (TNC) and affects the volume of FDI inflows.

According to Asian Development Bank Outlook (ADB, 2004), it is stated that in recent years FDI has substantially accelerated as a result of many factors, such as rapid technological progress, emergence of globally integrated production and marketing networks, existence of bilateral investment treaties, recommendations from multilateral development banks, and positive evidence from developing countries that have opened their doors to FDI. Chakrabarti (2001) found that there is high correlation between FDI and openness. Artige and Nicolini (2006) found that the market size as measured by GDP or GDP per capita seems to be the most robust FDI determinant in econometric studies. Pravakar Sahoo (2006) conducted a study to identify the determinants of FDI in South Asian countries over the period 1975-2003. The empirical results of this study reflect that major determinants of FDI were market size, labor force growth rate, and infrastructure index and trade openness.

Recently there are some studies for a group of economies like BRICS and EU regions to identify the determinants of FDI inflows. Vijayakumar, N. et al., (2010) observed that the market size, labor cost, infrastructure, currency value and gross capital formation as the potential determinants of FDI inflows among the BRICS countries. Pravin Jadhav (2012) highlighted that the role of economic, institutional and Political factor in attracting FDI in BRICS economies. Hunady and Orviska (2014) analyzed the determinants of FDI in EU, where they found labor cost, trade openness, GDP per capita and Public Debt as significant factors. Nawal Kishor and Raman Preet Singh (2015) in their study found that GDP, market capitalization and infrastructure are significant variables for FDI inflows into BRICS economies.

So, it appears that there is no consensus among the researchers on the determinants of FDI inflows as these variables vary across time and countries. In this paper the authors are making an attempt to identify the determinants of FDI flows into the nine developing countries by selecting a sample period of 2000 to 2015, as these nine countries attracted major shares of global FDI inflows in recent times. The rest of the paper is organized as follows. Section II deals with the theoretical background. Section III describes the data and methodology adopted in this study. Section IV presents the empirical results. Section V provides summary and conclusions.

THEORETICAL BACKGROUND

In theory we expect capital to flow from capital rich to capital poor countries and likewise technology should also flow from technology rich to technology poor countries. However, in practice the bulk of foreign direct investments (FDI) flows to developed countries. The flow of FDI varies from one country to another. This limits the potential for growth; therefore it is important to understand the reasons behind this. One of the explanations for this could be the country specific characteristics. The ultimate goal of foreign direct investment is to make profit from investment.

There are many theories regarding FDI inflows such as product life cycle hypothesis (Vernon (1966)), Kindleberg (1969), Aliber (1970), Caves (1971), Buckley and Casson (1976) to explain the determinants of FDI. These theories are significant steps towards the development of a systematic framework for the emergence of FDI models.

The theory of capital movements was the earliest explanation for FDI, which was viewed as a part of portfolio investments. Hymer's (1960) pioneering contribution was the first explanation of FDI in the industrial organization tradition. Hymer further explains that MNCs indulge in FDI only if they possess some monopolistic advantages or have an edge over local firms arising from intangible assets such as well-known brand name, patent- protected technology, managerial skills, and other firm specific factors.

Currently, the framework developed by Dunning (1980, 1981, 1993) namely Ownership- Location –Internalization (OLI) paradigm is extensively used to analyze the determinants of FDI inflows. The paradigm argues that when a multinational enterprise (MNE) invests and decide to manufacture in a foreign location, it faces both advantage and disadvantage. The advantage may arise out of ownership of intangible assets like technology, brand name and goodwill. It also faces disadvantages like its lack of familiarity with the legal and other framework of host country, customs, language and attitude of local population. However, the advantages can outweigh the disadvantages. The paradigm emphasis the ownership advantage of intangible assets. These assets include technology, Research and Development and patents held, brand name, goodwill, specialized skills like marketing and management skills. These ownership advantages could be exploited through exports, market transfer i.e transfer of patents against royalty and technical fee payments to third parties, licensing of brand name and FDI.

The choice between market transfer and FDI for taking advantage from ownership of intangible assets will depend on the internalization advantage. If these advantages are large and substantial, then FDI would be the preferred mode. On the other hand, if there are not much internalization advantages then licensing to third parties would be preferred. The internalization advantages in turn depend on the transaction costs. Information asymmetry is an important cause of high transaction cost. In several cases there could be information gap between the technology creator and the enterprise buying the technology. Sometime the technology owned by the MNE could be new and still evolving and therefore could not be codified.

If the possession of ownership advantages offers internalization incentives across countries, and there are additional location advantages like access to natural endowments, lower factor costs, cheap labor and so on which favor overseas production over production at home, then the three conditions for FDI are satisfied.

Table 1. Mode of foreign services

Mode of Foreign Market Services	Ownership Advantage	Internalization Advantage	Locational Advantage
FDI	Yes	Yes	Yes
Exports	Yes	Yes	No
Licensing	Yes	No	No

Source: Dunning (1981)

Dunning's approach which combines elements of different theories, successfully explains 'why', 'how' and 'where' international production should be taking place. It is still regarded as the most comprehensive FDI framework that has emerged till date.

The determinants of FDI are multidimensional, as there are different motives which the multinational corporations consider before investing in foreign countries. The motives can be broadly divided into three categories

1. Market seeking FDI
2. Resource seeking FDI
3. Efficiency seeking FDI

The first type of FDI is called market-seeking FDI, whose aim is to serve local and regional markets. It is also called horizontal FDI, as it involves replication of production facilities in the host country. Tariff-jumping or export-substituting FDI is a variant of this type of FDI. Because the reason for horizontal FDI is to better serve a local market by local production, market size and market growth of the host economy play important roles. Obstacles to accessing local markets, such as tariffs and transport costs, also encourage this type of FDI. A second type of FDI is called resource-seeking: when firms invest abroad to obtain resources not available in the home country, such as natural resources, raw materials, or low-cost labor. Particularly in the manufacturing sector, when multinationals directly invest in order to export, factor-cost considerations become important. In contrast to horizontal FDI, vertical or export-oriented FDI involves relocating parts of the production chain to the host country. Availability of low-cost labor is a prime factor for export-oriented FDI. Naturally, FDI in the resource sector, such as oil and natural gas, is attracted to countries with plentiful natural endowments. The third type of FDI, called efficiency-seeking, takes place when the firm can gain from the common governance of geographically dispersed activities in the presence of economies of scale and scope.

DATA AND METHODOLOGY

Data and Variable

In accordance with the scope and objective of this study, the panel data has been obtained from the nine countries which include India, Indonesia, Mexico, Malaysia, Nigeria, South Africa, Thailand, Turkey and Vietnam for the period 2000 to 2015.

Countries are chosen from the list of developing countries from UNCTAD who happens to receive larger share of FDI in recent years among the developing countries.

In this study, variable FDI inflows per capita(FDIPC) is considered as a dependent variable and following variables are chosen as explanatory variables, namely, GDP growth(GDPGR), Human Capital(HC), Electric Power Consumption(ELEC), GDP per capita(GDPPC), Trade(TR), Inflation(INF). Annual Data for all variables except human capital are collected from World Bank database. Human Capital Data is compiled from Penn World Table (PWT 9.0).

Foreign Direct Investment Per Capita (FDIPC)

Foreign direct investment refers to direct investment equity flows into the reporting economy. It is the sum of equity capital, reinvestment of earnings, and other capital. Data are in current U.S. dollars. This series shows net inflows (new investment inflows less disinvestment) in the reporting economy from foreign investors and is measured in current US$. These net inflows were divided by its population to get per capita FDI.

GDP Growth Rate (GDPGR)

Annual percentage growth rate of GDP at market prices based on constant local currency. Aggregates are based on constant 2005 U.S. dollars. GDP is the sum of gross value added by all resident producers in the economy plus any product taxes and minus any subsidies not included in the value of the products. In general, the countries with higher economic growth will attract higher FDI.

Trade (% of GDP) (TR)

Trade is the sum of exports and imports of goods and services measured as a share of gross domestic product. Trade is generally expected to be positive and significant determinant of FDI.

Electric Power Consumption (ELEC)

Electric power consumption measures the production of power plants and combined heat and power plants less transmission, distribution, and transformation losses and own use by heat and power plants. It is a proxy variable for infrastructure. Sound infrastructure is positive and significant variable in determinants of FDI inflows.

GDP per Capita (GDPPC)

GDP per capita is gross domestic product divided by midyear population. GDP is the sum of gross value added by all resident producers in the economy plus any product taxes and minus any subsidies not included in the value of the products. It is calculated without making deductions for depreciation of fabricated assets or for depletion and degradation of natural resources. Data are in constant 2010 U.S. dollars. Countries with greater per capita GDP can attract more FDI as it signifies the market size.

Inflation (INF)

Inflation as measured by the consumer price index reflects the annual percentage change in the cost to the average consumer of acquiring a basket of goods and services that may be fixed or changed at specified intervals, such as yearly. It is a proxy of economic stability. Effect of Inflation rate on the flow of FDI can be positive or negative.

Human Capital (HC)

Index of human capital per person, based on years of schooling (Barro/Lee, 2012) and returns to education (Psacharopoulos, 1994). Human Capital can lead to higher productivity and profitability as a direct result of the increased capacity of the employees to perform their tasks. Human capital signifies the productivity of labor force which helps in attracting FDI inflows.

Methodology

In any econometric modeling, one need to select a proper model to have valid inferences. Here, in this study the authors consider panel data model to identify the determinants which can influence the FDI flows into developing countries. There are several versions of panel data models are available in the literature to model the data. Simple panel data linear regression models suffer from few drawbacks. Firstly, it is common for panel data models, consisting of cross sections observation for time span to exhibit both characteristics of heteroscedasticity and autocorrelation. Countries with different characteristics may distort very assumption of constant variance of regression disturbances. Similarly, potential endogeneity problem among explanatory variables may lead to the issues regarding OLS estimation in presence of autocorrelation and it gives biased and inconsistent estimator. Owing to all these limitations of linear regression models, system GMM (Generalized Method of Moments), as suggested by Blundell and Bond (1998) is employed here for empirical analysis. This method has some advantage over GMM estimators of Arellano and Bond (1991).

System GMM approach of Blundell and Bond has the advantage of avoiding biases related to omission of specific individual effects and it also controls for endogeneity problem arising from dependence among explanatory variables. This can be achieved by incorporating differences of dependent variable as instruments for equations in first differences. In addition, GMM estimator does not require a priori assumption regarding any distributions of error term. Hence, even in the presence of heteroscedasticity, the estimator produces consistent and efficient estimators. In presence of unit roots in variables at level, first difference GMM estimation will not produce an efficient estimator. Same reason restricts use of lagged level variables as a suitable instrument. Owing to all these shortcomings associated with first difference GMM method, the authors prefer system GMM method in this study.

The system GMM approach of Blundell and Bond (1998) can be represented as

$$\Delta \text{ FDIPC } (i, t) = \beta_0 + \beta 1 \,\Delta \text{ FDIPC } (i, t\text{-}1) + \beta 2 \,\Delta \text{ HC}(i,t) + \beta 3 \,\Delta \text{ELEC}\left(\text{i}, \text{t}\right) + \beta 4 \,\Delta \text{GDPGR}\left(\text{i}, \text{t}\right) + \beta 5 \,\Delta \text{GDPPC}\left(\text{i}, \text{t}\right) + \beta 6 \,\Delta \text{TR}\left(\text{i}, \text{t}\right) + \beta 7 \,\Delta \text{ INF}(i,t) + \Delta vi, t \ldots\ldots\ldots\ldots \quad (1)$$

i=1, 2, 3…..9 and t= 2000, 2001…2015.

Δ is a difference operator and

β_0 is the constant term.

Similarly βj are coefficients of respective explanatory variables. Lagged dependent variables Δ FDIPC (i, t-1) is included as instrument. Inclusion of this instrument variable is validated later. Levin- Lin- Chu or LLC (2002) test is employed to check the panel unit roots of all the variables.

EMPIRICAL RESULTS

In this section, the researchers present the data analysis and estimation results of FDI inflows for the selected developing countries during the period 2000-2015.

Trend Analysis

The total FDI flows across the countries are shown in Figure 1 and also various groups of economies viz., developing, developed and transition economies in the world during the period 2000 – 2015 in terms of US dollars were given in the Table 1.

From the Figure 1 it is evident that after the year 2000 the inflows of global FDI are slowly deceasing. This may be due the fact that the effect of European crisis which continued till 2003. Later it was picked up after the year 2003 and reaches its maximum in the year 2007. After 2007 there were some fluctuations in global FDI. This can be attributed to global financial crisis. But it is showing an increase in the year 2015.

The percentage share of Global FDI's for these three groups of economies viz., developing, developed and transition economies are given in Table 2 and shown in Figure 2. From this it can be observed that the percentage shares of developing countries are increasing from 17.10% to 43.39%. Similarly, the percentage share of developed countries are decreasing from 82.46% to 54.62%, whereas the percentage share of transitional countries are more or less stable during the period 2000-2015.

From the Figure 2 it can be seen clearly that FDI inflows in developing countries are rising continuously after 2009 global meltdown. After 2013 FDI inflows in developing economics overtook FDI inflows in developed economies for the first time which shows that all developing economies are really trying to attract FDI inflows which will boost their economies.

By comparing the above two Figure 3 and Figure 4, it is clear that in year 2000 developing countries gets 17% of Global FDI Inflows whereas Developed countries attracted a large chunk of FDI inflows as high as 82%. But the scenario is different

Figure 1. Global FDI inflows during 2000-2015

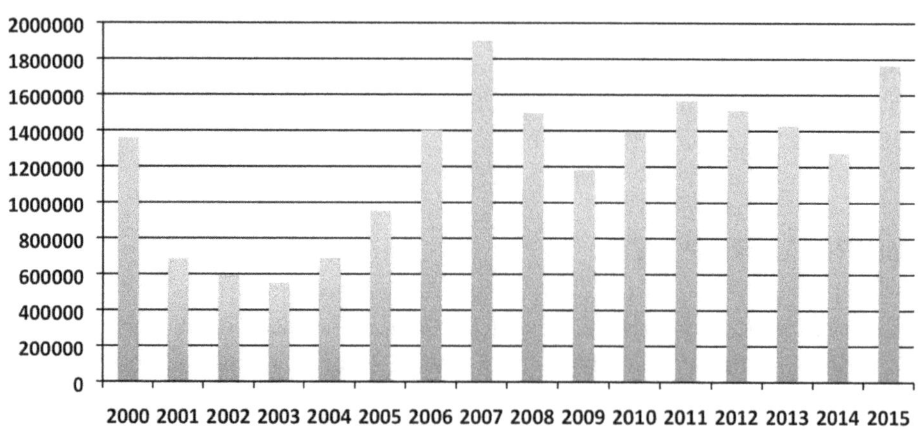

Table 2. Total FDI inflows from 2000 to 2015 (in US $)

Year	Global FDI Inflows	Developing Economies	Developed Economies	Transition Economies
2000	1358820.38	232390.26 (17.10)	1120507.63 (82.46)	5924.34 (0.44)
2001	683765.38	215793.85 (31.56)	459714.78 (67.23)	8257.96 (1.12)
2002	589808.93	166738.99 (28.27)	413024.48 (70.03)	10045.55 (1.70)
2003	550588.79	195584.23 (35.52)	337172.02 (61.24)	17832.53 (3.24)
2004	688233.04	263718.33 (38.32)	395517.74 (57.47)	28996.98 (4.21)
2005	950125.01	331752.13 (34.92)	587709.79 (61.86)	30668.09 (3.23)
2006	1402125.86	402982.75 (28.74)	940318.37 (67.06)	58824.76 (4.20)
2007	1902244.48	525525.04 (27.63)	1289493.50 (67.79)	87225.94 (4.59)
2008	1497788.14	578482.16 (38.62)	801909.21 (53.54)	117396.77 (7.84)
2009	1181412.19	465306.64 (39.39)	654366.69 (55.39)	61738.87 (5.23)
2010	1388821.03	625330.31 (45.03)	699889.23 (50.39)	63601.49 (4.58)
2011	1566838.97	670149.29 (42.77)	817414.80 (52.17)	79274.88 (5.06)
2012	1510918.31	658773.74 (43.60)	787358.83 (52.11)	64785.73 (4.29)
2013	1427180.95	662405.60 (46.41)	680275.02 (47.67)	84500.33 (5.92)
2014	1276999.29	698493.63 (54.70)	522042.92 (40.88)	56462.74 (4.42)
2015	1762155.04	764670.44 (43.39)	962496.29 (54.62)	34988.31 (1.99)

*The figures in the parenthesis represent the % share of FDIs.

Figure 2. Percentage Share of FDI Inflows into various groups of economies

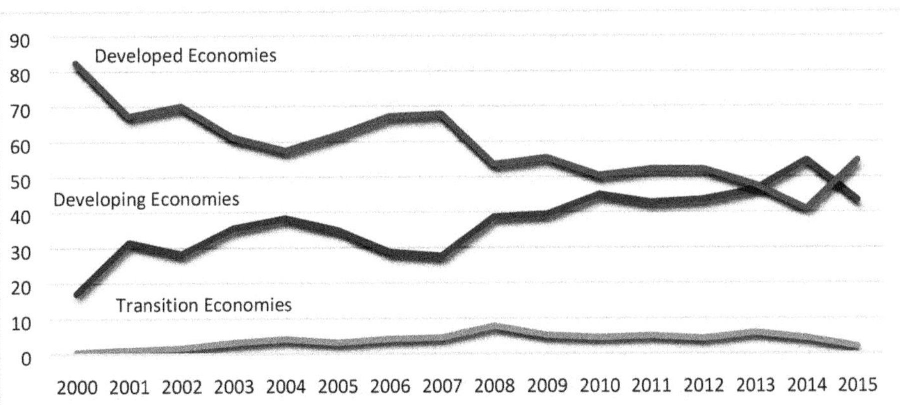

Figure 3. FDI inflows in 2000

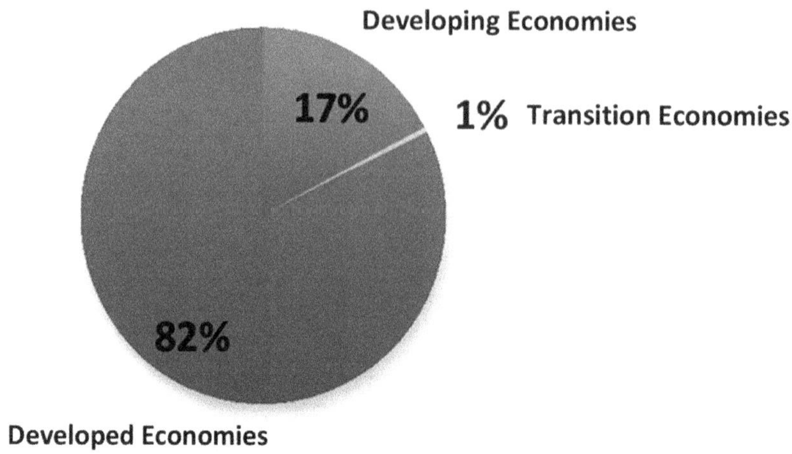

Figure 4. FDI inflows in 2015

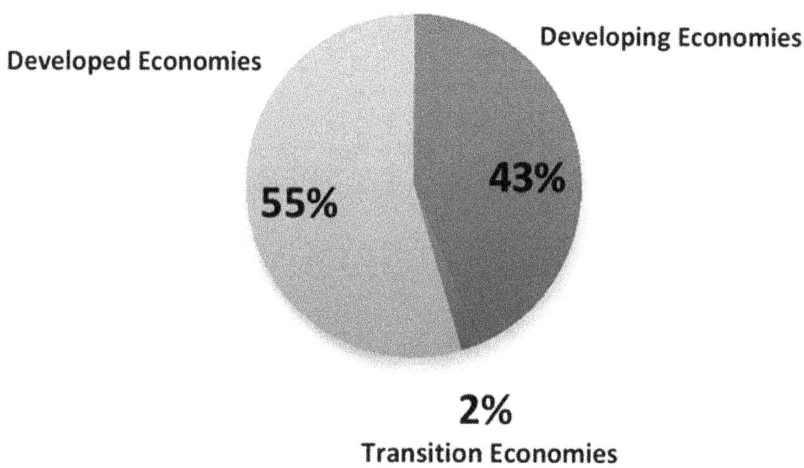

in year 2015 as share of developing countries have increased to 43% and share of developed countries has reduced to 55%. This clearly shows that developing countries have made favorable condition to attract FDI inflows and use that for their development.

Recently, World Investment Report observed that the nine developing countries viz. India, Indonesia, Mexico, Malaysia, Nigeria, South Africa, Thailand, Turkey and Vietnam received larger share of global FDI's among the developing countries. This study analyses the FDI inflows of these developing countries during the period 2000 to 2015, according to objectives of this study the authors have provided the data of FDI inflows of each country given in Table 3 and the percentage share of total FDI's in each of these countries are shown in Figure 5.

Among the selected countries from the above Figure 5 it can be observed that Mexico (27%) attracted larger share of FDI inflows in the period 2000 to 2015, followed by India (22%), Turkey (11%), Indonesia (10%), Thailand (8%), Malaysia (7%), Vietnam (6%), Nigeria (5%), South Africa (4%).

Table 4 provides the summary statistics of the dependent variable of this study that is FDI per capita of these selected developing countries in US dollars. Average per capita FDI inflows of Malaysia is 250.47 US dollars which is highest followed by Mexico 225.88 and Average per capita FDI inflows of India is 17.751 which is minimum among the selected countries. Though the India's share of total FDI's is 22%, the lowest average per capita can be attributed to its large population. However, the standard deviation of FDI per capita is lowest for India 11.648 which indicates the steady flow of these FDI's whereas Turkey has a standard deviation of 100.055

Figure 5. Total FDI inflows of selected economies during 2000-2015

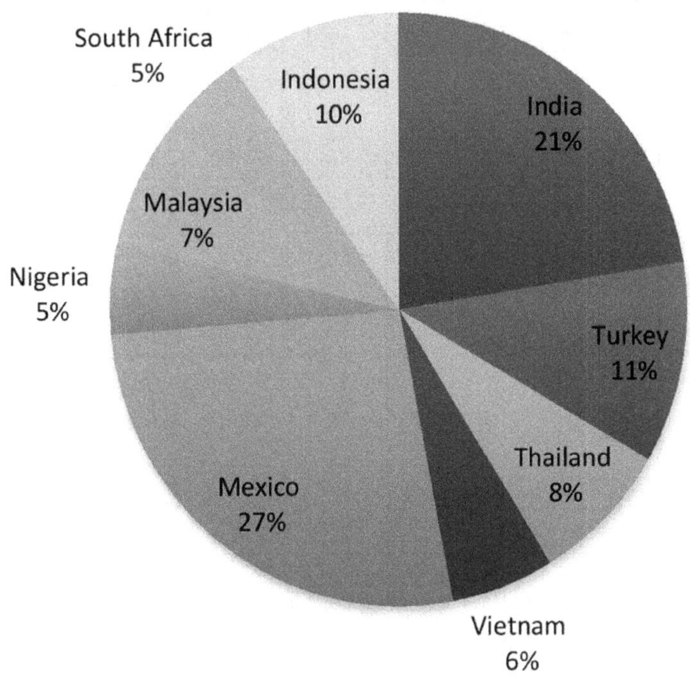

Table 3. Total FDI inflows of selected economies (in US $)

Year	India	Turkey	Thailand	Vietnam	Mexico	Nigeria	Malaysia	South Africa	Indonesia
2000	3584217307	982000000	3365987583	1298000000	18314697208	1140137660	3787631579	968831356	-4550355286
2001	5128093562	3352000000	5067170388	1300000000	30055344733	1190632024	553947368.4	7270344986	-2977391857
2002	5208967106	1082000000	3341612007	1400000000	24047891415	1874042130	3192894737	1479804589	145085548.7
2003	3681984671	1702000000	5232270340	1450000000	18221148211	2005390033	3218947368	783136092	-596923828
2004	5429250990	2785000000	5860255943	1610000000	24913521737	1874033035	4376052632	701422008	1896082770
2005	7269407226	10031000000	8222768955	1954000000	25971074832	4982533943	3924786635	6522098178	8336257208
2006	20029119267	20185000000	8926154246	2400000000	21109968232	4854416867	7690731246	623291744	4914201435
2007	25227740887	22047000000	8620806614	6700000000	32407302149	6034971231	9071369835	6586792253	6928480000
2008	43406277076	19851000000	8566235387	9579000000	29078447750	8196606673	7572512432	9885001293	9318453650
2009	35581372930	8585000000	6427288799	7600000000	17899614356	8554840769	114664434.6	7624489974	4877369178
2010	27396885034	9099000000	14714893498	8000000000	26431284197	6026232041	10885614182	3693271715	15292009411
2011	36498654598	16182000000	2468144240	7430000000	23649208420	8841113287	15119371191	4139289123	20564938227
2012	23995685014	13284000000	12894549139	8368000000	20436852838	7069934205	8895774251	4626029122	21200778608
2013	28153031270	12384000000	15822132057	8900000000	45854568760	5562873606	11296278696	8232518816	23281742362
2014	33871408468	12523000000	3718726247	9200000000	25675440122	4655849170	10619431770	5791659020	26277377236
2015	44208019072	16819000000	8003235491	11800000000	30284595503	3064170000	10962721673	1575170030	15508160000

Table 4. Summary statistics of FDI per capita of selected countries (US $)

Country	Mean	Median	Std.Dev	Kurtosis	Skewness	Minimum	Maximum
India	17.751	20.188	11.648	-1.485	0.016	3.322	36.260
Turkey	148.399	154.678	100.055	-1.045	0.177	15.528	317.152
Thailand	114.245	107.173	59.503	-0.098	0.796	36.891	234.571
Vietnam	63.853	82.061	41.394	-1.818	-0.039	16.535	128.675
Mexico	225.881	225.300	55.507	1.795	1.146	153.230	370.572
Nigeria	30.694	33.031	16.185	-1.314	0.149	9.279	55.119
Malaysia	250.473	285.631	145.093	-0.561	-0.057	4.145	529.149
South Africa	88.747	84.327	62.754	-1.378	0.204	13.006	200.522
Indonesia	38.007	33.335	39.631	-1.177	0.203	-21.511	103.269

which is highest among the chosen countries having more fluctuations in their FDI inflows.

Results of System GMM Estimation

Since system GMM estimator suffers from downward bias due to presence of unit root in the variables of the model, it is necessary to check the stationary property of all the series. The results of panel unit root test of Levin- Lin- Chu or LLC (2002) were provided in Table 5.

The null hypothesis of LLC test is that there is a presence of unit root in the chosen variable i.e the variable is non-stationary. In Table 5, the figures in the parentheses () indicate the *p*- values. From the Table 5 it is evident that null hypothesis of non-stationarity of some variables like HC, ELEC, GDPPC, TR at level (without trend) cannot be rejected at 5% level of significance. However, after first difference LLC test confirms the stationarity of all variables Δ

Since in addition to first differences of the variables in the equation representing system-GMM, it also includes the lagged differences of dependent variable as instruments in the equation, that there is a risk of over-identifying restrictions as a range of moment conditions are identified. The suitable test for the validity of the instruments for system GMM is the Sargan test which follows $\chi 2$ distribution and the null hypothesis of this test is validity of the instrument.

It is evident that instruments used for system GMM estimation of Equation 1 is appropriate since p-value for Sargan $\chi 2$ test statistics is 0.0318. It implies that at 1% level of significance, the null hypothesis of valid instrument cannot be rejected. Since the validity of the system-GMM model, as represented by equation 1 is verified with Sargan Test, impact of different explanatory variables can be analyzed.

Table 5. The panel unit root tests

Variables	LEVEL		FIRST DIFFERENCE	
	Trend	Without Trend	Trend	Without Trend
FDIPC	-2.8603 (0.0021)	-2.3678 (0.0089)	-6.2120 (0.0000)	-6.9996 (0.0000)
HC	-2.2516 (0.0122)	-1.5624 (0.0591)	-4.7049 (0.0000)	-1.3463 (0.0891)
ELEC	-2.3853 (0.0085)	2.9841 (0.9986)	-5.1101 (0.0000)	-4.1578 (0.0000)
GDPGR	-3.8084 (0.0001)	-4.3786 (0.0000)	-5.1017 (0.0000)	-6.2828 (0.0000)
GDPPC	-2.3933 (0.0083)	2.4303 (0.9925)	-5.0275 (0.0000)	-3.7013 (0.0001)
TR	-3.4365 (0.0003)	-0.8876 (0.1874)	-5.2626 (0.0000)	-6.4884 (0.0000)
INF	-3.2659 (0.0005)	-4.5609 (0.0000)	-6.2638 (0.0000)	-5.8751 (0.0000)

Table 6. Results of system GMM estimation

Variables	Coefficient	Std. Error	Z-statistics	Probability>|Z|
ΔFDIPC	0.197091	0.074882	2.63	0.008
ΔHC	21.93509	55.66263	0.39	0.694
ΔELEC*	0.047886	0.020513	2.33	0.02
ΔGDPGR*	5.144029	1.719231	2.99	0.003
ΔGDPPC	0.009643	0.008697	1.11	0.268
ΔTR*	0.851603	0.33997	2.5	0.012
ΔINF	-0.54102	1.21093	-0.45	0.655
CONST	-192.111	98.61113	-1.95	0.051

From Table 6, it can be noticed that the nature and size of effect of each of explanatory variables. FDI inflows per capita is positively related to variables like electricity, GDP growth and Trade which are found to be statistically significant since the probability of Z statistic is less than 0.05. Electric power consumption which is a proxy for infrastructure is also one of the main determinants of FDI as revealed by the empirical results of many studies (see for example Wheeler and Mody (1992), Pravakar Sahoo (2006), Vijayakumar, et al., (2010)). This implies countries with better and improved infrastructure facilities out-compete others in attracting the foreign investment. Infrastructure facilities increase the productivity of the investments and therefore may stimulates FDI inflows into the country. GDP growth signifies the economic growth. Stable macro-economic conditions are shown by the high and sustained growth rates. Countries which are economically stable receive more FDI. Trade variable signifies trade openness which is computed as ratio of imports and exports of goods and services to GDP, plays a major role in attracting FDI. An increase in Trade will lead to increase in FDI inflows. Inflation turns out to be insignificant, but the negative sign shows that an increase in inflation will lead to decrease in FDI inflows.

SUMMARY AND CONCLUSION

In the context of growing importance of FDI in growth and development of a country, many countries try to attract the FDI inflows to give impetus to their economy. It is observed that in recent times developing economies receiving large share of global FDI's. It is of interest of policy makers to know the major determinants of FDI's to attract more and more FDI investments into their country.

In this study the authors made an attempt to identify the factors determining overseas investment in some chosen developing countries viz. India, Indonesia, Mexico, Malaysia, Nigeria, South Africa, Thailand, Turkey and Vietnam for the period 2000 to 2015. System Dynamic panel data model of Blundell and Bond (1998) has been used to avoid plausible fallacy and shortcomings of simple linear regression model of panel data framework. Empirical results suggest there is strong and positive relation between FDI and the GDP growth. It implies that the countries with higher economic growth are getting a large amount of overseas investments. The result commensurate with the Dunning's OLI Paradigm according to which a great deal of market-seeking investment flows into the countries with higher economic growth. Apart from that, electric consumption, a proxy for infrastructure is found to exert positive impact on FDI flows. A strong impact of trade flow on FDI inflows is also found.

The study proposes that in order to compete with other countries to attract more FDI, the country should make the investment climate much better and conducive to foreign players. This requires a critical examination of the firm-specific motivations that make them to indulge in FDI. This study observes that there is a need to increase the productive efficiency which is possible only if the infrastructure bottlenecks are properly addressed and the wages and other relative costs are kept low. The findings of the present study suggest that in order to attract more inflows of FDI and to maximize the gains from it, the improvement in infrastructure, trade and growth of GDP should be the key agenda of the foreign policy of developing countries.

REFERENCES

ADB. (2004). *Asian Development Outlook 2004*. Retrieved from http://www.adb.org/Documents/Books/ ADO/2004/default.asp

Agarwal, J.P. (1980). Determinants of Foreign Direct Investment: A Survey. *Weltwirtschaftliches Archive, 116*, 739-773.

Aliber, R. Z. (1970). A theory of direct foreign investment. In C. P. Kindleberger (Ed.), *The International Corporation*. Cambridge, MA: MIT Press.

Arellano, M., & Bond, S. (1991). Some tests of specification for panel data: Monte Carlo Evidence & an application to employment equations. *The Review of Economic Studies*, *58*(2), 277–297. doi:10.2307/2297968

Artige, L., & Nicolini, R. (2006). *Evidence on the determinants of foreign direct investment. The case of three European regions*. CREPP working paper.

Asiedu, E. (2002). On the Determinants of Foreign Direct Investment to Developing Countries: Is Africa Different? *World Development*, *30*(1), 107–119.

Baltagi, H. (2005). *Econometric Analysis of Panel data*. New York: John Wiley and Sons.

Barro, R. J., & Lee, J. W. (2013). A net data set of educational attainment in the world, 1950-2010. *Journal of Development Economics*, *104*, 184–198. doi:10.1016/j.jdeveco.2012.10.001

Blundell, R., & Bond, S. (1988). Initial conditions & moment restrictions in dynamic panel data models. *Journal of Econometrics*, *87*(1), 115–143. doi:10.1016/S0304-4076(98)00009-8

Buckley, P., Clegg, J., & Wang, C. (1995). The impact of inward FDI on the performance of Chinese manufacturing firms. *Journal of International Business Studies*, *33*(4), 637–655. doi:10.1057/palgrave.jibs.8491037

Buckley, P. J., & Casson, M. (1976). *The Future of Multinational Enterprise*. London: MacMillan. doi:10.1007/978-1-349-02899-3

Caves, R. E. (1971). International Corporations: The Industrial Economics of Foreign Investment. *Economica*, *38*(149), 1–27. doi:10.2307/2551748

Caves, R. E. (1974). 'Causes of Direct Investment: Foreign Firms' Share in Canadian and UK Manufacturing Industries'. *The Review of Economics and Statistics*, *56*(3), 272–293. doi:10.2307/1923965

Chakravati, A. (2001). The Determinants of Foreign Direct Investments: Sensitvity Analysis of Cross- Country Regressions. *International Review for Social Sciences, 54*(1), 89–114.

Dabour, N Md. (2000). The Role of Foreign Direct Investment in Development and Growth in OIC Member Countries. *Journal of Economic Cooperation, 21*(3), 27–55.

Demirhan, E., & Masca, M. (2008). Determinants of Foreign Direct Investments to Developing Countries: A Cross – Section Analysis. *Prague Economic Papers, 4*(4), 356–369. doi:10.18267/j.pep.337

Dunning, J. H. (1980). Toward an Eclectic Theory of International Production. *Journal of International Business Studies, 11*(1), 9–31. doi:10.1057/palgrave.jibs.8490593

Dunning, J. H. (1981). *International Production and the Multinational Enterprise*. London: Allen & Unwin.

Dunning, J. H. (1993). *Multinational Enterprises and the Global Economy*. Reading, UK: Addison-Wesley Publishing Company.

Dunning John, H. (1988). The Eclectic Paradigm of International Production: A Restatement and Some Possible Extensions. *Journal of International Business Studies, 19*(1), 1–31. doi:10.1057/palgrave.jibs.8490372

Hunady, J., & Orviska, M. (2014). Determinants of Foreign Direct Investment in EU Countries- Do Corporate Taxes Really Matter? *Procedia Economics and Finance, 12*, 243–250. doi:10.1016/S2212-5671(14)00341-4

Hymer, S. H. (1960). *The International Operations of National Firms: A Study of Direct Investment* (Ph.D. Thesis). MIT.

Jadhav, P. (2012). Determinants of foreign direct investment in BRICS economies: Analysis of economic, institutional and political factor. *Procedia: Social and Behavioral Sciences, 37*, 5–14. doi:10.1016/j.sbspro.2012.03.270

Khondoker, A. M., & Kalirajanb, K. (2010). *Determinants of Foreign Direct Investment in Developing Countries: A Comparative Analysis*. ASARC working paper 2010/13.

Kindleberger, C. P. (1969). American Business Abroad. *The International Executive, 11*(2), 11–12. doi:10.1002/tie.5060110207

Kishor, N., & Singh, R. P. (2015). Determinants of FDI and its Impact on BRICS Countries: A Panel Data Approach. *Transnational Corporations Review, 7*(3), 269–278. doi:10.5148/tncr.2015.7302

Lall, S. (2002). *FDI and development: research issues in the emerging context* (B. Bora, Ed.). Routledge. doi:10.4324/9780203469699.ch19

Lall, S., & Streeten, P. (1980). *Foreign Investment Transnational's and Developing countries*. London: Macmillan Press Ltd.

Levin, A., Lin, F., & Chu, C. (2002). Unit root tests in panel data: Asymptotic and finite sample properties. *Journal of Econometrics*, *108*(1), 1–24. doi:10.1016/S0304-4076(01)00098-7

Lucas, R. (1990). Why doesn't capital flow from Rich to Poor countries? *The American Economic Review*, *80*(2), 92–96.

Nunnenkamp, P., & Julius, S. (2002). *Determinants of FDI in Developing Countries: Has Globalization Changed the Rules of the Game?* (Vol. 11). Transactional Corporations.

Psacharopoulos, G. (1994). Returns to investment in education: A global update. *World Development, Elsevier*, *22*(9), 1325–1343. doi:10.1016/0305-750X(94)90007-8

Sahoo, P. (2006). *Foreign Direct Investment in South Asia: Policy, Trends, Impact and Determinants*. ADB Institute Discussion Paper No. 56.

Satguru, Y. S., & Satsangi, P. (2013). FDI & Developing Countries, Role of World Bank. *Global Journal of Management and Business Studies*, *3*(8), 929–934.

The Economist. (2001, February 24). The Cutting Edge. *The Economist*, 90.

Townsend, I. (2003). *Does Foreign Direct Investment Accelerate Economic Growth in Less Developed Countries?* (Working Paper). St. Olaf College.

UNCTAD. (1998). World Investment Report (WIR) 1998: Trends and Determinants. New York: UNCTAD.

UNCTAD. (2011). *Foreign Direct Investment in LDCs: Lessons Learned from the Decade 2001-2010 and the Way Forward*. New York: United Nations.

Vernon, R. (1966). International investment and international trade in the product cycle. *The Quarterly Journal of Economics*, *80*(2), 190–207. doi:10.2307/1880689

Vijayakumar, N., Sridhran, P., & Rao, K.C.S. (2010). Determinants of FDI in BRICS Countries: A Panel Analysis. *International Journal of Business Sciences and Applied Management, 5*.

Wheeler, D., & Mody, A. (1992). International Investment Location Decisions: The Case of US Firms. *Journal of International Economics*, *33*(1-2), 57–76. doi:10.1016/0022-1996(92)90050-T

Zhang, K., & Markusen, J. (1999). Vertical multinationals and host-country characteristics. *Journal of Development Economics*, *59*(2), 233–252. doi:10.1016/S0304-3878(99)00011-5

Chapter 3
The Role of Foreign Direct Investment in Less-Developed Countries

Chengchun Li
Changzhou University, China

Sailesh K. Tanna
Coventry University, UK

ABSTRACT

This chapter analyses a number of economic and developmental issues in less-developed countries (LDCs), reviewing the related literature and outlining the challenges ahead for LDCs. The issues considered include foreign direct investment (FDI) policies, recent trends on growth, civil conflict, institutional development, financial sector development, external debt, and other macroeconomic factors. These are identified as pertinent areas where LDCs have faced major challenges in their endeavours to improve economic welfare since they are related to the absorptive capacities, which are important for accruing growth benefits from inward FDI in LDCs. It is anticipated that coverage of these issues will enlighten the issues that these countries face in order to attract and utilise inward FDI. Additionally, it is argued that LDCs can avoid the risk of civil conflict by adopting proactive policies to attract FDI.

DOI: 10.4018/978-1-5225-3026-8.ch003

INTRODUCTION

The less developed countries (LDCs) have implemented significant economic reforms over the past few decades by moving away from previously inward-looking import substitution policies towards more outward-looking, market-oriented trade strategies. However, the liberalisation of these economies has not just been confined to trade openness since host countries have also exercised greater openness to foreign direct investment (FDI) as a means for obtaining new technologies and skills, and consequently there has been a significant growth in the volume of FDI inflows to LDCs over the past two decades. By attracting FDI and with it the embedded technologies that multinational enterprises (MNEs) bring to the host countries, domestic firms have been able to reap spill over benefits in terms of technology transfer through interaction with MNEs.

MNEs have played an important role in bringing new capital and technology to the host countries, especially to countries with natural resources which lacked capital and innovation capabilities. Realising the potential benefits from inward FDI, most governments in LDCs have progressively removed restrictions on inward FDI. Over time MNEs have tended to dominate the technology innovation space in LDCs and have also become increasingly mobile seeking to invest in new markets and locations that are more efficient with lower cost production (Lall & Narula, 2004). However, the increased inward FDI has not always contributed to the growth and development of LDCs. As discussed later in this chapter, we shall see that the main concern has been that of meeting the economic pre-conditions (or thresholds) for effectively utilising inward FDI to enhance economic growth.

Another concern is whether and how globalisation (which in a narrower sense entails greater ability for countries to attract FDI) represents a pathway to peace and economic stability (Bussmann & Schneider, 2007; Blanton & Apocada, 2007). In the context of LDCs, where the incidence of civil conflict in the recent past has been higher than the world average, this relates to the important question of whether FDI contributes to the possibility of reducing the incidence of civil conflict (Polachek, Seiglie, & Xiang, 2005; 2007; 2011). Historically, records show that LDCs have a higher likelihood of experiencing conflict or war compared to other developing and developed countries (Themnér & Peter, 2013). Hence, the importance of FDI for LDCs has to be seen not only in terms of its effect on economic growth but also in terms of its ability to reduce the potential for conflict or war as evidence shows that the latter can significantly affect FDI inflows (Li, Murshed, & Tanna, 2017).

Against this backdrop, our aim in this chapter is to provide an overview of the role of FDI and associated issues facing LDCs along with the relevant development trends and indicators that are important for attracting FDI. We then discuss the related literature emphasising the economic conditions and the challenges that LDCs face in terms of yielding gains from inward FDI.

THE ROLE AND CONCERNS OF FDI IN LDCS

Increasing FDI Inflows and a Promising Outlook

In 2001, a consensus was reached at the United Nations Conference on Trade and Development (UNCTAD) to help LDCs which led to the initiation of so-called 'The Programme of Action of LDC for the Decade 2001-2010'. According to the programme, the member countries of UN realised that FDI would be a very important source for LDCs to obtain capital formation, technological and knowledge know-how, employment creation, and trade opportunities. Since the conference, LDC governments and partner countries have indeed promoted FDI inflows into LDCs. There has been around 15% growth rate per year of FDI inflows into LDCs (the UN definition for the 50 poorest countries) in the past decade starting from 7.1 billion USD in 2001 to 24 billion USD in 2010, and the ratio of LDCs inflows over total amount worldwide increased from 0.9% to more than 2% (UNCTAD, 2011). From Figure 1, it is clear that the amount of FDI inflows into LDCs had been even larger – with around 110 billion USD in 2010. However, this is still below the global average.

Figure 1. Total volume of FDI inflows to LDCs
Source: The World Bank (2016)

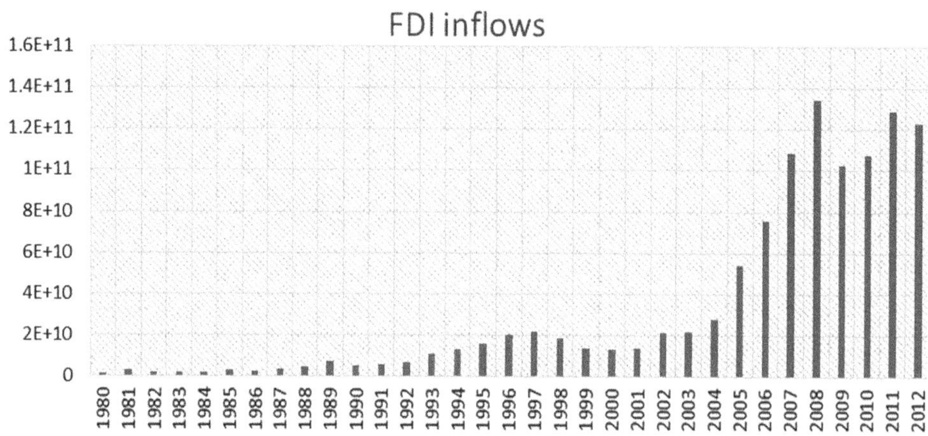

FDI Inflows to LDCs Still Remain Marginal Compared to Global FDI Inflows

Due to technological developments and improvements in production and management in the global economy, MNEs have fundamentally changed the way of goods and services production in LDCs. The modern norm in global value chains requires a high degree of specialisation in production; and outsourcing has become an important part of MNEs' production in order to increase cost efficiency and strength the competitiveness. This implies that outsourcing some parts of production to low-cost manufacturers especially those in LDCs is one of the best options for MNEs to lower costs of production.

However, participation in MNEs' outsourcing requires capacities to produce relatively high quality and quantity of specialised goods or services. It is quite difficult for most LDCs to achieve this requirement. Most LDCs still remain low-level suppliers of raw materials. The problem could be potentially mitigated by increasing infrastructure development, human capital and other kinds of capabilities that LDCs possess. But the present status of LDCs, which has focussed on engaging in low-skilled and labor-intensive methods of production, is far from enough to realise benefits from global value chains.

The Share of FDI Inflows in Natural Resource Extraction Has Been Too Large

Another problem is that most FDI flows to LDCs have gone into countries with abundant natural resources. According to UNCTAD (2011), while the number of FDI projects in primary sector represents a small percentage of the entire amount of projects in LDCs, the amount of capital invested by MNEs is quite high. The main target of MNEs is oil and mining in LDCs. For example, in 2009, Madagascar received above 80% of FDI inflows into the mining sector. In general, inflows into the primary sector in LDCs have tended to lumpy and unstable.

The Good News Is That LDCs Have Been Successful in Attracting Other Forms of FDI

Fortunately, LDCs are now increasingly attracting large projects which do not engage in natural resources, although the amount of capital is relatively less. FDI in telecommunication, tourism, food and beverages, banking and other industries are always under-rated because of their small scale; but they are now regarded as more important than large-scale FDI in the natural resource as they truly generate better job opportunities, bring closer linkages with local firms, and transfer technology and skills to local firms. For instance, in Mozambique, while FDI in the mining sector represents only 5% of FDI-related jobs, the issue is that these 'better forms' of FDI have created supply chains which have often been neglected by LDC policymakers.

Very Limited FDI Contributes to Infrastructure Development

Most LDCs lack proper infrastructure and developing that capability would be the most efficient way to increase productivity growth. Unfortunately, few MNEs have contributed to building the infrastructure in LDCs, and this is partly due to the complexity of obtaining concession agreements in infrastructure (which is a heavily regulated sector). As a consequence, most LDCs remain weak in infrastructure development.

Weak Linkages With Domestic Firms in LDCs: FDI Tends to Crowd Out Domestic Investment

Another issue is that many businesses in LDCs are categorised as small or micro-scale, while affiliates of MNEs usually occupy a significant share of the private sector and they are the largest corporate taxpayers. Most of those affiliates in LDCs are market-seeking companies. This raises the concern that FDI can negatively impact on domestic firms' productivity via horizontal linkages. It is difficult to create backward or forward linkages from FDI in natural resource extraction since these industries do not have adequate domestic suppliers or consumers. The main concern for LDC policymakers is that, owing to weak linkages of MNEs with domestic firms, FDI may crowd out domestic investment rather than foster the productivity growth of domestic firms.

DEVELOPMENT TRENDS IN LDCS

Having addressed the importance of FDI and some of concerns that LDCs face in realising the benefits, it is now appropriate to highlight some of the broader economic and institutional trends to provide a backdrop for an assessment of the economic pre-conditions that could yield potential gains from inward FDI and the challenges that LDCs face in this regard.

Economic Growth and Income

Economic growth in LDCs, on average, has been strong over the past 15 years, indeed much faster than in the last 15 years of the 20th century (see Figure 2). The

Figure 2. Total GDP volume of LDCs
Source: The World Bank (2016)

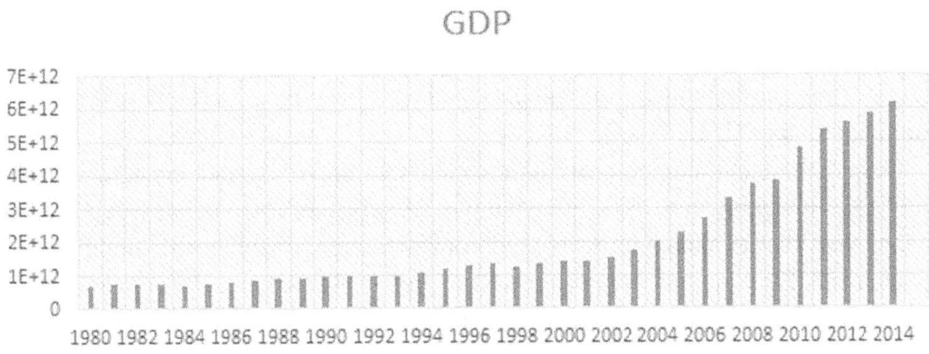

good performances were helped by external factors such as globalisation along with sound macroeconomic management and domestic market-oriented reforms. The issue that hides behind the apparently good-looking performance is that around 20% of LDCs experienced failure in terms of output level per capita since they were adversely affected by civil conflict, problematic policies and weak institutional development. Thus growth is not fast enough and there is still a large amount of population trapped in poverty.

Financial Sector

Financial Development

According to the IMF's 2014 report on Macroeconomic Developments in low-income countries, financial systems in LDCs are dominated by banks and insulated from international financial developments. LDCs, in general, lack internal capital and tend to rely on external funding; however, they have limited access to external capital and there have been frequent episodes of capital controls in place. In LDC financial systems, state-owned banks (SOBs) play an important role in intermediating domestic savings from resident deposits. However, the financial systems have been vulnerable because of the erosion of asset quality. The erosion of assets has been severe when (a) there is a rapid credit expansion with weak supervisory controls (e.g. in Nigeria, 2008-2009); (b) there is an excessive exposure to specific economic sectors by large firms – a common issue in LDCs; (c) banks that belonged to large financial conglomerates issued significant amount of loans to one specific debtor like a state owned entity (e.g. Cameroon 2010-2011); (iv) domestic financial systems are insulated from external developments and inefficient in export and exchange rate management where there is a global financial crisis (e.g. Zambia).

However, the last two decades have witnessed greater financial development in LDCs. Many LDCs are now seriously engaging in financial deepening and attracting foreign investors to invest in domestic financial markets. Some of their governments have issued sovereign bonds in the international financial market and started to use new financial instruments such as salary-based lending and mobile banking services (IMF, 2014).

Despite this technological progress, the vulnerabilities of financial systems remain and LDCs are facing new risks. For example, the profitability of banks is reportedly higher than that of banks in developed countries, implying that the oligopolistic financial market structure brings a high risk of credit enforcement. The vulnerabilities also relate to the country-specific historical experience. IMF (2014) claims that the abnormal Z-score of LDCs' banks compared to stable financial systems is high, implying that a boom in credit growth causes cross-border exposures and pressure in high loan-deposit ratios.

Financial Repression

LDCs historically are highly financially repressed – there are distortions in foreign exchange rates, interest rates, and other aspects of financial markets. The pursuit of financial repression facilitated LDCs governments to reap seigniorage gains from financial markets (i.e. reducing the real burden of debt by extracting resources through repressive controls). Most LDCs enforced a high level of bank reserve requirements and forced financial institutions holding governments bonds to obtain savings at a low or even negative real interest rate. Governments also suppressed private bond and equity markets by implementing high taxation on private capital transactions, expropriating special taxes on incomes of capital, and creating laws and regulations to claim charges and taxes on private holders' assets. The authorities also imposed foreign exchange controls and interest rate ceilings (Nafziger, 2012, p. 475). The controls on interest rates was a means of maintaining cheap credit for governments to enforce preferential lending to priority sectors. As a consequence, low deposit interest rates reduced savings which hindered financial development; low lending rates deprived bank profits leading to a discouraged effect of private sector participation in the financial markets; and the distortions of capital allocation between savers and investors also made credit difficult to be distributed to efficient users.

Since the 1980s, however, LDCs have embarked on a process of financial liberalisation. Most of LDCs initiated policies to abolish credit controls, liberalise interest rates, restructure banks, privatise stated-owned enterprises, enhance financial regulation and supervision, and lower the entry threshold for the banking sector.

The expected effect of financial liberalisation was to improve savings and investments and therefore accelerate economic growth. Fowowe (2013) concludes that many LDCs increased deposit interest rates immediately following liberalisation; however, lending rates also increased faster than deposit rates. Consequently, there has been a high level of interest rate spread in LDCs, indicating that the expected effect of increased savings for investments could not be realised.

External Debt

Most LDCs have significantly increased their level of indebtedness since the 1970s. While some LDCs borrowed foreign money for domestic investment, others borrowed to finance domestic consumption. Figure 3 shows that from 1980 to 2012 LDCs increased their indebtedness level by sevenfold. Over the same period, as observed from the World Bank database, the indebtedness level in African countries soared by more than 10 times. The indebtedness level in Asian LDCs also had a consistently rising trend. There were two-time periods of sharp adjustment – the first one was at the end of the 1980s and the second around 1998 after the Asian financial crisis. The situation in Africa was the most serious and worsened alarmingly in the 1990s.

Under the Heavily Indebted Poor Countries / Multilateral Debt Relief Initiative (HIPC/MDRI), 34 LDCs were helped by external debt relief to reduce their indebtedness risk from high level to low/moderate level. However, still more than one-third LDCs have increased their indebtedness level significantly in recent years (IMF 2014).

Figure 3. Total external debt volume of LDCs
Source: The World Bank (2016)

Other Macroeconomic Indicators

Inflation

LDCs have historically suffered from high level of inflation. The average inflation rate has been around 10% (based on the calculation of the data collected from the World Bank). Some counties, for example Zimbabwe, experienced episodes of hyperinflation. There are underlying factors behind such high inflation levels – such as weak institutions, ineffective macroeconomic management, political instability, and civil conflict - leading to the fragile states of economies.

Because of improved macroeconomic management, LDCs have been more effective in reducing inflation. The relief of foreign debt from international relief initiatives and a great amount of trade and investment from China also contributed to lower growth volatility and inflation. Some LDCs also have embarked on a wide range of reforms towards market-orientation which have contributed to the robust decline in inflation (Dabla-Norris, Ho, Kochhar, & Kyobe, 2014). However, according to the World Economic Outlook, at least 11 LDCs have failed in reducing inflation after 2000.

Trade

Prior to 2000, LDCs had a low volume of trade in terms of both imports and exports, because of poverty. Almost 50% the population in the poorest 50 countries lived in poverty - below one dollar per day - before 2000 (Bowles, Durlauf, & Hoff, 2006). Most of the trade volume was, in fact, related to the demand from the subsidiaries of MNEs. The exports from those 50 countries were only 0.6% of the world exports (Bowles et al., 2006).

However, there has been a significant change since 2000. The trade volume has started to grow fast – the average growth rate of trade is around 6%. The trade links have steadily shifted from developed countries ("North-South" trade) to both developed countries and developing and emerging countries ("South-South" trade). China has become one of the important export destination countries for LDCs. The export share to China has tripled from below 5% in 2000 to around 15% in 2010. The export merchandise has changed from only primary sector products to fuel, cruel material, and manufacturing products (IMF, 2014).

Institutional Factors

It is now generally accepted that the most fundamental factor supporting economic growth is the role of institutions. As argued by a famous political economist Francis

Fukuyama, "Economics… is powerful at explaining markets, but not institutions…" His words suggest that the basic ingredients for economic growth are institutional factors, not markets and other pure policy-based factors. This argument has been supported by Fergusson (2006) and Rodrik (2006). Fergusson (2006) emphasises that institutions are fundamental to policies and regulations, financial development, and other factors. Referring to the importance of institutions underlying the failure of the Washington Consensus, which advocated liberalisation for LDCs, Rodrik (2006) explains the practitioners view that the reforms did not go deep and far enough. According to the practitioners, the prescribed policy reforms for LDCs could not have lasting effects if the policies are not embedded in solid institutions.

According to Mishkin (2009), sound institutions maintain strong property rights, an effective legal system, trades openness and a sound and efficient financial systems. However, as Mishkin (2009) argues, it takes time for institutions to evolve and adapt to local circumstances.

Law

The legal system provides protection for people from exploitation by those who are more powerful, and therefore access to justice is not merely for the realisation of the constitutional and guaranteed rights but also the aim of development and poverty reduction (Anderson, 1999). However, the circumstances in most LDCs are that there is little access to the legal system; and sometimes people in LDCs face various kinds of illegality. The primary weaknesses of the legal system in LDCs were aptly summarised by Anderson (1999):

- There are abuses of political power in LDCs, especially political restriction on the press which has significantly suppressed the freedom of expression and thus becomes the main threat to human lift.
- Unchecked violence by public officials including police, prison officers, etc. The violence can directly lead to injury, disability, and even death.
- Corruption among officials is always interacting with weak legal capability in LDCs. It is common that individuals have to pay a premium for use of public goods and basic services (e.g. water and electricity, access to health care and medicines, public transportation, education) because of corruption.
- In some LDCs, there is an extreme abuse of human rights. Their culture of fear might even worsen the problem, which discourages the productive activity and make the poor devote their income to pay bribes for living or purchase weapons for defence.
- There is a high level of risk of losing the ownership of the property by public expropriation or private theft.

- The poor in society easily suffer from arbitrary treatment, intimidation, and humiliation by officials.
- Investments and individual economic decision makings are more likely to be short-term, as there is a weak level of security from the law.

Although some LDCs have started to reform and improve their legal systems, and there is a greater degree of transparency than before, enforcement of law and order and accountability remains generally poor.

Corruption

Apart from poor enforcement of law and order, corruption is a recurrent phenomenon in most LDCs and significantly hampers their development. Most LDCs have been listed at the bottom of Corruption Perception Index with very low scores by Transparency International (www.transparency.org).

In order to deal with high corruption, WTO tends to provide help to LDCs. The Agreement on Transparency in Government Procurement (ATGP) requires signatories to show the specified areas of government procurement to the signatories in order to maintain transparent producers of government procurement. This could be a good way to control corruption if LDCs are able to take advantage of having better access to international markets through negotiations with WTO and increase their volume of trade with advanced nations (Appleton & Plummer, 2007).

Democracy

The United Nations first report on the governance of LDCs by Welch and Nuru (2005), "Governance for the Future: Democracy and Development in LDCs", highlights that good institutional development cannot lack good national leadership and power relations. Democratic regimes have been widely regarded as being good for national leadership since the Cold War. Democratic nations always have principles of efficiency, transparency, and accountability and indicate there are good leaderships which can guide governments to focus on policies in line with the needs of the domestic citizen, give priority on conducting a functioning rule of law, and generate a good framework for economic growth.

Many LDCs have been focusing on developing a new type of leadership. For example, according to the Bamako Declaration, 15 African countries declared the call for democracy and peaceful power transfer in 2005. The declaration aimed to create constitutional rules and democratic regimes, and also to address the issue of conflict.

Welch and Nuru (2005) consider that most LDCs need to make greater efforts towards establishing democracy, although there are existing multiparty democracies in LDCs with the progress made in electoral selections. In LDCs, the executive departments often have much more power than legislative and judicial departments, because there is still a lack of separation and independence for the departments of governments.

Human Capital

While human capital cannot be strictly regarded as a formal institutional factor, the purpose of developing institutions is to enhance the growth of human capital, and therefore the issue of human capital is discussed here. Since the 1990s, human capital has been regarded as a fundamental factor in explaining the long-term growth of advanced economies. LDCs also have focused on the development of human capital and have received a considerable amount of donations, increasing from 2 billion USD in 1995-1996 to 7.8 billion USD in 2010-2011 (UNCTAD, 2013). The increased amount of resources available for education has improved human capital development in LDCs. The average ratio of primary school enrolment in LDCs is now quite close to the ratio of developing countries. The secondary and tertiary levels of education have also improved but still fall behind those in developing countries. The training for better-skilled workers has also improved to create decent employment opportunities which cater for the development of modern production techniques in the private sector.

Many families, especially from the poor, in LDCs invest a large number of their resources to obtain the better education. One of the problems is that private institutions always require high tuition fees for education. Another problem is that there are mismatches of job opportunities in some industries – the labour demand is high in some industries but there is often a shortage of skilled workers; while there is a surplus of labour in other industries. This is because higher educational institutions sometimes lag in response to the actual demands in labour markets and young people in LDCs are more likely to choose jobs which have low skills requirement (UNCTAD, 2013).

Civil Conflict

As noted earlier, LDCs have a higher propensity to experience civil conflict compared to the rest of the world. According to data from the Uppsala Conflict Data Program (UCDP) of Uppsala University, 72 LDCs (classified as low income or lower middle income by the World Bank) have recorded several onsets of civil conflict since the1970s. For these countries as a whole, between 1970 and 2012, there were 424 recorded incidences of minor civil conflicts (between 25-999 deaths per year); and 229 were categorised as violent, associated with civil wars (resulting in more than 1000 deaths per year) (see Figure 4 and Table 1). These figures suggest that the possibility of civil conflict onset in the 72 LDCs was around 23.27% (given 2806 observations of country-years) between 1970 and 2012 – implying that, on average, there was a conflict around every four years. In contrast, the possibility of conflict onset worldwide (see Figure 5 and Table 2) was about 42% (2806/6681 x 100); indicating that there was 6.69% (83.42%-76.73%) higher possibility of conflict onset in LDCs than worldwide. This suggests that civil conflicts outbreaks are more common in LDCs.

RELATED LITERATURE

Following the above perspective of past and emerging trends in LDCs, we now highlight the nature of academic research in FDI and point to the challenges ahead. Two main strands of the literature are relevant in this regard and relate to the importance

Figure 4. Possibility of conflict in LDCs
Source: The Uppsala Conflict Data Program, 2016

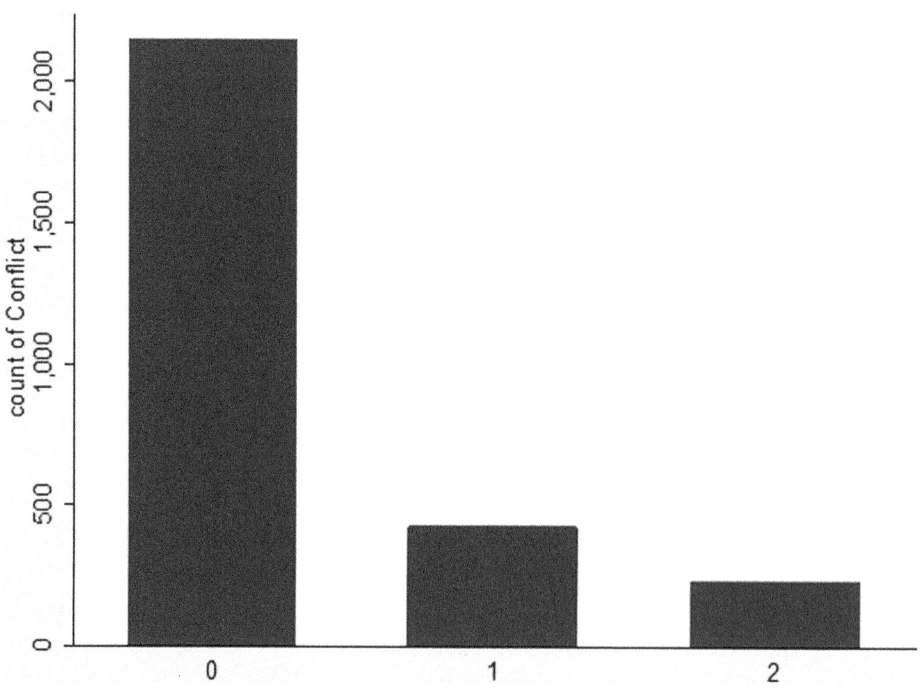

Table 1. Possibility of conflict in LDCs

Conflict	Frequency	Percent
0 (None)	2153	76.73
1 (Minor)	424	15.11
2 (Major)	229	8.16
Total:	2806	100.00

Source: the Uppsala Conflict Data Program, 2016

Figure 5. Possibility of conflict in the world
Source: The Uppsala Conflict Data Program, 2016

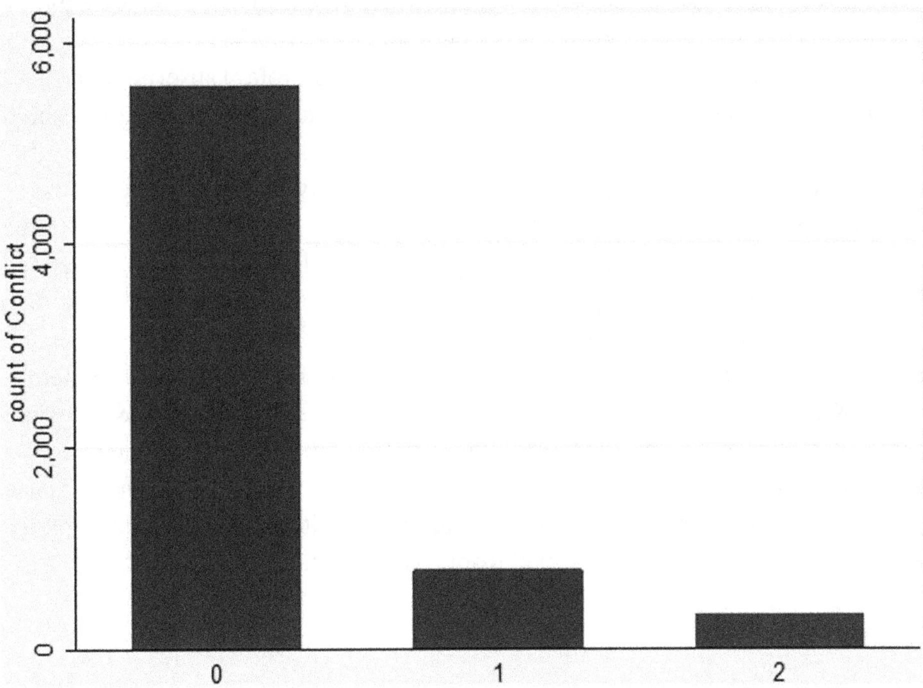

Table 2. Possibility of conflict in the world

Conflict	Frequency	Percent
0 (None)	5573	83.42
1 (Minor)	769	11.51
2 (Major)	339	5.07
Total:	6681	100.00

Source: the Uppsala Conflict Data Program, 2016

of: (a) achieving the minimal threshold conditions for FDI to have a positive impact on economic growth in LDCs; and (b) attracting FDI inflows to LDCs to reduce the risk of conflict in LDCs and thereby preserve economic stability.

FDI and Local Capability of Host Countries

It has been recognised, as argued earlier, that host countries gains from FDI and the scope for technology transfer from MNEs requires local capabilities – given that foreign investors always focus on countries with strong local capabilities as good external environments for their business expansion. As Lall and Narula (2004) state, FDI is 'vigorous in host countries with strong local capabilities and feeblest in those with weak capabilities' (p. 3). This suggests that policies to attract FDI should be accompanied by improving local absorptive capacity in LDCs.

Table 3 summarises the relevant literature outlining the role of absorptive capacity in relation to different economic conditions. Empirical research using threshold estimation methods on data for developing countries has sought to quantify the importance of absorptive capacity in terms of a variety of explicit thresholds (or economic conditions) that host countries need to achieve in order to realise the benefits from inward FDI. As Table 3 highlights, the literature has characterised the importance absorptive capacity using thresholds for variables such as human capital (Borensztein, De Gregorio, & Lee, 1998), economic freedom (Azman-Saini, Baharumshah, & Law, 2010a), financial development (Alfaro, Chanda, Kalemli-Ozcan, & Sayek, 2004; Azman-Saini, Law, & Ahmad, 2010b; Hermes & Lensink, 2003), institutional quality (Slesman, Baharumshah, & Wohar, 2015), corruption (Okada and Samreth, 2014), and external debt (Tanna & Li, 2017). Thus, the evidence clearly points to the importance of achieving these criteria as a pre-condition for economic growth gains to be accrued from inward FDI.

FDI and Conflict

On research relating to the FDI-conflict nexus, there are a few studies which provide supportive evidence to illustrate how FDI can reduce the risk of conflict, at both domestic (civil) and inter-state (dyadic) levels. Polachek et al. (2005; 2007; 2011) argue that, in order to protect gains from FDI, governments of both countries (home and host) will tend to reduce international conflict and increase cooperation, similar to the reason why governments of trading partners maintain peaceful relations. Furthermore, they argue that FDI has a stronger effect on increasing peace than trade because FDI carries certain attributes that trade does not. For instance, FDI has a long-term trait that differentiates it from trade. Moreover, in terms of trade, countries can switch partners more easily and frequently during adverse circumstances. For

Table 3. Evidence from selected literature related to FDI and absorptive capacity

Study	Thresholds (absorptive capacity)	Findings
Alfaro *et al.* (2004)	Financial development	They use cross-country data covering up to 71 countries over the period 1975-1995 to argue that the relationship between FDI and economic growth is ambiguous. After considering the threshold effect of financial development, however, the FDI effect on growth turns out to be significant and positive.
Azman-Saini *et al.* (2010a)	Financial development	They apply threshold estimation using cross-country data for 91 countries from 1975 to 2005 to confirm that the positive effect of FDI on economic growth "kicks in" only if financial development is above a certain threshold.
Azman-Saini *et al.* (2010b)	Economic freedom	Using system GMM estimation with interaction effects in cross-country growth regressions for 85 countries from 1976 to 2004, their findings reveal that a country can gain significantly from FDI when it has a sufficiently high degree of economic freedom
Borensztein *et al.* (1998)	Human capital	They examine the importance of human capital in the FDI-GDP growth nexus using data for 69 developing counties over the period 1970-1989 and conclude that FDI contributes to growth only when the host country meets a minimum threshold level of human capital.
Hermes and Lensink (2003)	Financial development	Their empirical evidence, using cross-section and panel data for 67 developing countries, suggests that FDI has a positive growth impact if the financial system is sufficiently developed.
Okada and Samreth (2014)	Corruption	Using data for 130 countries over the period 1995-2008, they investigate the influence of corruption in the estimation of the FDI-growth regression using interaction effects and find that the impact of FDI on economic growth is negative if corruption level is below a threshold but positive otherwise. In other words, a high level of corruption has a positive impact of FDI on growth. They rationalise this counter-intuitive result by arguing that profit-seeking MNEs engage in foreign investments in countries with weak regulations or poor law enforcement.
Slesman *et al.* (2015)	Institutional quality	They present evidence that FDI has a positive impact on economic growth only in countries with high-quality institutions, using data for 80 developing and developed countries over the period 1975-2005.
Tanna and Li (2018)	External debt	Applying threshold estimations using panel data for 39 developing countries over the period 1984-2010, they find that the FDI-induced growth effect is dependent on a country's level of external debt. High indebtedness can restrict growth benefits from FDI as countries seek reduce their debt although this is offset by higher levels of financial development.

example, if an international conflict breaks out between two countries, the goods for trade can be held or delayed, or even traded via another destination. The losses from ending trade can be minimised. However, when FDI is created, firms cannot withdraw their investments arbitrarily. The losses due to conflict can remain for a long period with the huge cost that may not be recovered. Therefore, MNEs might use their power to push governments to make cooperative policies rather than being drawn into conflict. Additionally, the host country's government may adopt cooperative policies to present a friendly image for FDI in order to attract more FDI from other countries. Hence, the presence of FDI is likely to bring the cooperative relationship between countries.

Focussing on military conflict, Bussmann (2010) suggests that FDI has a similar rationale as trade, thus reducing the likelihood of conflict. He finds empirical evidence using global FDI and conflict data over the period 1980-2000 to suggest that a highly integrated world economy is less likely to trigger a militarised conflict.

Blanton and Apodaca (2007) also support the view that FDI can alleviate the risk of conflict. Their arguments are based on bargaining theories of conflict. According to their view, the functions of the global marketplace are like an "audience" that rewards or punishes the attitude and policies towards conflict. Countries act as actors communicating their intentions and resolving conflict through 'costly signalling' devices including policy statements, sanctions and military mobilisation. These signals are meant to represent the strength of the actors' preferences for consequences associating with the 'costs' that they are willing to bear, and the ability to achieve such a consequence. Signals ideally enhance the ability of countries to resolve disputes through means short of warfare. The 'audience' in the global marketplace responds to signals in different ways. For example, countries that send adverse signals to the marketplace may face increasing costs such as currency depreciation, loss of FDI and trade, or failure to find international financial assistance. Actors generally are less willing to suffer from more expensive 'audience costs'. As a result, countries tend to avoid conflict by eliminating potential costs of losing FDI.

CONCLUSION: THE CHALLENGES AHEAD

In concluding, we consider that LDCs have faced many problems including financial fragility, economic instability, weak institutions and high risk of conflict. It is generally acknowledged that a possible way to mitigate these problems is to rely on the importance of attracting FDI inflows. Fortunately, after decades of low inward investment growth and there is now a rising trend in FDI inflows to LDCs and the challenge is to utilise the underlying capacities for domestic firms to benefit from inward FDI with the aim of improving economic growth and productivity. Although it has taken a long and bumpy ride to achieve these goals, the outlook is now positive.

LDCs have indeed experienced faster inflows of FDI especially since 2000. The main challenges ahead can be summarised as follows: (i) LDCs need to continue attracting more FDI inflows since the volume of FDI is still marginal compared to the rest of the world; (ii) LDCs must improve their absorptive capacities to accrue benefits from FDI in ways discussed above; (iii) there should be greater diversity in attracting the quality of FDI, since relying on primary sector FDI as traditionally been the case is likely to increase the risk of conflict; and (iv) the expected productivity gains for domestic firms from FDI can take time to realise as these are mainly accrued through exploiting the potential linkages with MNEs.

REFERENCES

Alfaro, L., Chanda, A., Kalemli-Ozcan, S., & Sayek, S. (2004). FDI and economic growth: The role of local financial markets. *Journal of International Economics*, *64*(1), 89–112. doi:10.1016/S0022-1996(03)00081-3

Anderson, M. (1999). *Access to justice & legal process: making legal institutions responsive to poor people in LDCs.* Discussion Paper at WDR 2000 Conference.

Appleton, A. E., & Plummer, M. G. (2007). *The world trade organization: Legal, economic and political analysis.* Berlin, Germany: Springer Science & Business Media.

Azman-Saini, W., Law, S. H., & Ahmad, A. H. (2010a). FDI and economic growth: New evidence on the role of financial markets. *Economics Letters*, *107*(2), 211–213. doi:10.1016/j.econlet.2010.01.027

Azman-Saini, W., Baharumshah, A. Z., & Law, S. H. (2010b). Foreign direct investment, economic freedom and economic growth: International evidence. *Economic Modelling*, *27*(5), 1079–1089. doi:10.1016/j.econmod.2010.04.001

Blanton, R. G., & Apodaca, C. (2007). Economic globalization and violent civil conflict: Is openness a pathway to peace?'. *The Social Science Journal*, *44*(4), 599–619. doi:10.1016/j.soscij.2007.10.001

Borensztein, E., De Gregorio, J., & Lee, J. (1998). How does foreign direct investment affect economic growth? *Journal of International Economics*, *45*(1), 115–135. doi:10.1016/S0022-1996(97)00033-0

Bowles, S., Durlauf, S. N., & Hoff, K. (2006). *Poverty traps.* Princeton, NJ: Princeton University Press.

Bussmann, M. (2010). Foreign direct investment and militarized international conflict. *Journal of Peace Research*, *47*(2), 143–153. doi:10.1177/0022343309354143

Bussmann, M., & Schneider, G. (2007). When globalization discontent turns violent: Foreign economic liberalization and internal war. *International Studies Quarterly*, *51*(1), 79–97. doi:10.1111/j.1468-2478.2007.00440.x

Dabla-Norris, E., Ho, G., Kochhar, K., Kyobe, A., & Tchaidze, R. (2014). Anchoring Growth: The Importance of Productivity-Enhancing Reforms in Emerging Market and Developing Economies. *Journal of International Commerce Economic Policy, 5*(02), 1–29.

Fergusson, L. (2006). Institutions for financial development: What are they and where do they come from? *Journal of Economic Surveys, 20*(1), 27–70. doi:10.1111/j.0950-0804.2006.00275.x

Fowowe, B. (2013). Financial liberalization in Sub-Saharan Africa: What do we know? *Journal of Economic Surveys, 27*(1), 1–37. doi:10.1111/j.1467-6419.2011.00689.x

Hermes, N., & Lensink, R. (2003). Foreign direct investment, financial development and economic growth. *The Journal of Development Studies, 40*(1), 142–163. doi:10.1080/00220380412331293707

IMF. (2014). *Macroeconomic developments in low-income developing countries.* Washington, DC: International Monetary Fund.

Okada, K., & Samreth, S. (2014). How does corruption influence the effect of foreign direct investment on economic growth? *Global Economic Review, 43*(3), 207–220. doi:10.1080/1226508X.2014.930671

Lall, S., & Narula, R. (2004). Foreign direct investment and its role in economic development: Do we need a new agenda? *European Journal of Development Research, 16*(3), 447–464. doi:10.1080/0957881042000266589

Li, C., Murshed, S. M., & Tanna, S. (2017). The impact of civil war on foreign direct investment flows to developing countries. *The Journal of International Trade & Economic Development, 26*(4), 488–507. doi:10.1080/09638199.2016.1270347

Mishkin, F. S. (2009). Globalization and financial development. *Journal of Development Economics, 89*(2), 164–169. doi:10.1016/j.jdeveco.2007.11.004

Nafziger, W. (2012). *Economic development* (5th ed.). New York, NY: Cambridge University Press. doi:10.1017/CBO9781139028295

Polachek, S., Seiglie, C., & Xiang, J. (2007). The impact of foreign direct investment on international conflict. *Defence and Peace Economics, 18*(5), 415–429. doi:10.1080/10242690701455474

Polachek, S., Seiglie, C., & Xiang, J. (2005). *Globalization and international conflict: can fdi increase peace? (*Department of Economics Working Paper). Rutgers University.

Polachek, S. W., Seiglie, C., & Xiang, J. (2011). Globalization and international conflict: Can FDI increase cooperation among nations? In M. R. Garfinkel & S. Skaperdas (Eds.), *The Oxford Handbook of the Economics of Peace and Conflict* (pp. 733–762). New York, NY: Oxford University Press.

Rodrik, D. (2006). Goodbye Washington Consensus, Hello Washington Confusion? A Review of the World Bank's Economic Growth in the 1990s: Learning from a Decade of Reform. *Journal of Economic Literature*, *44*(4), 973–987. doi:10.1257/jel.44.4.973

Slesman, L., Baharumshah, A. Z., & Wohar, M. E. (2015). Capital inflows and economic growth: Does the role of institutions matter? *International Journal of Finance & Economics*, *20*(3), 253–275. doi:10.1002/ijfe.1514

Tanna, S., & Li, C. (2018). *FDI and economic growth: An external debt threshold effect.* Paper presented at the Annual Conference of the American Economic Association (AEA) in conjunction with the Allied Social Sciences Associations (ASSA), January 2018, Philadelphia, PA.

Themnér, L., & Wallensteen, P. (2013). Armed conflicts, 1946–2012. *Journal of Peace Research*, *50*(4), 509–521. doi:10.1177/0022343313494396

UNCTAD. (2011). *Foreign direct investment in LDCs: Lessons learned from the decade 2001-2010 and the way forward.* New York: United Nations.

UNCTAD. (2001). *Host country operational measures*. New York: United Nations.

UNCTAD. (2013). *The least developed countries report 2013: Growth with employment for inclusive and sustainable development*. New York: United Nations.

Welch, G., & Nuru, Z. (2005). *Governance for the future: Democracy and development in the least developed countries*. New York, NY: UN-OHRLLS.

World Bank. (2016). *Indicators.* Retrieved January 26, 2017, from http://data.worldbank.org/indicator

Chapter 4
Socio-Economic Impact of Foreign Direct Investment in Developing Countries

Christopher Boachie
Central University, Ghana

Eunice Adu-Darko
Central University, Ghana

ABSTRACT

The purpose of this chapter is to empirically examine the impact of socio-economic determinate of foreign direct investment in developing economies. FDI is an important part of the massive private investment that is driving economic growth around the world, particularly in the past two decades. This was achieved by examining 10 African countries using data from world development indicators on FDI and socio-economic parameters ranging from 1990 to 2015. A panel regression model was applied to 260 samples. The results showed openness, exchange rate, domestic credit to private sector, and regulatory quality have a significant effect on FDI. Policy makers in African countries need to adopt institutional reforms that could contribute to improving their state of governance, promote their investment climate, and help in attracting more FDI.

DOI: 10.4018/978-1-5225-3026-8.ch004

INTRODUCTION

Policy makers in recent years, especially in the developing countries, have noted that foreign direct investment (FDI) is necessary to boost socioeconomic growth in their economic environment. Over the years, FDI inflows have acted as strong determinants of economic development across countries (Mckinney, 2014; Jensen, 2003; Li & Resnick, 2003). FDI is the net inflows of investment to acquiring long lasting management interest in an enterprise operating in an economy other than that of the investor (World Bank, 2016). It serves as an important source of supply funds for domestic investment thus, promoting capital formation in the host country (Omisakin et al., 2009). FDI inflows can assist an economy by giving opportunities for improving the level of the service sector. There have been different strands in the empirical and theoretical literature aimed at investigating the relationship between FDI inflows and their determinants in developed and developing markets. Many developing countries, including the least developed ones, have attracted only small amounts of FDI inflows despite their efforts towards economic liberalization in an increasingly globalizing world (UNCTAD, 2009).

Many reasons have been given for the importance of FDI inflows, including employment creation, foreign exchange, technology transfer, easier access to foreign markets, enhanced competition as well as the transfer of skills through training (Crespo & Fontura, 2007). For these reasons, strong recommendations have been made for developing countries to use foreign direct investment as a source of external finance. Accordingly, efforts have been made by many governments to develop policies to encourage inward FDI flows. Furthermore, FDI gives developing countries the opportunity to reduce dependence on foreign aid, thereby boosting the state's sovereignty from donor policies. Many African countries have been committed to reaching the millennium development goals. As pointed out by Adewumi (2006), most developing countries across Sub-Saharan Africa are off track and this has left them desperate for significant levels of foreign investments to restore them to their earlier economic status. It is believed that most of these developing countries are lagging because of inadequate resources to finance long-term investments and this has proved to be a big setback to economic growth. According to Adams (2009), the direction and volume of FDI across countries and regions suggest that its attractiveness depends on institutional and country-specific factors. Some of these factors include the host country's openness to trade as well as macroeconomic, political and social stability. Due to political and socioeconomic differences across developing countries, the growth effects of FDI varies from country to country.

According to Nunnenkamp et.al. (2004), recipient countries with a better endowment of human capital are more likely to benefit from FDI-induced technology transfer, as spillover from foreign affiliates to a local enterprise is more likely. This is also known as the host country's absorptive capacity. Likewise, institutional development such as the rule of law, the level of corruption, protection of property rights, the quality of public management and unrestricted government interference are crucial factors that determine the volume of FDI and technological know-how transfer from foreign affiliates to domestic firms. A number of multinational corporations from developing economies are becoming key players in the global economy (Ogutu, 2010). With the development of infrastructure across West Africa such as improvement of the transport network as well as the establishment of the undersea fibre optic cable, foreign investment has significantly improved (). These African countries depend on Foreign Direct Investment (FDI) for capital and employment. Also, remittances are the single largest source of foreign exchange to most Sub-Saharan African countries. So, what are the determinants and socioeconomic impact of FDI in Africa?

Limited access to finance and poor institutional framework have affected the performance of the manufacturing sector resulting in limited FDI into these developing countries (KNBS, 2013; UNCTAD, 2012). The challenge facing developing countries is how to attract more FDI in dynamic products and sectors with high-income elasticities of demand away from the primary sector. Although institutional indexes for these countries have been worsening over the years, FDI inflow though sluggish has been on the rise (TI, 2012; UNCTAD, 2012). This evidence posed a problem and necessitated an examination of what determines the growth of FDI and its socioeconomic impact in West Africa.

While the literature on the determinants and socioeconomic impact of FDI is not fully conclusive, with companies, increasingly able to capitalize on differentials in labor costs and increasingly interested in providing goods or services directly in often protected emerging markets, these flows are likely to continue increasing. It remains an open question, however, as to what pulls FDI into countries. With the increasing level of corruption, terrorism, lack of proper infrastructure and dictatorship in some African countries, one would wonder why FDI flows into this parts of the world. It is intuitive that FDI should flow into countries with relatively stable economic conditions and strong institutions, and that investors should be concerned about political instability, inflexible regulations, and poor development indicators among prospective workers. But there is strangely little evidence to support these arguments.

This chapter, therefore, tries to address this question by studying the socioeconomic impact of FDI, focusing on West African countries where terrorism and political instability are rampant. The purpose of this chapter is to analyze the determinants and socioeconomic impact of FDI. The rest of this chapter is organized as follows. In the next section, we carry out a review of the relevant literature, including the theoretical framework. We then outline the model and the methodology employed to answer the research question. The results are presented in the penultimate section, and the final section contains a discussion of the findings and conclusions.

LITERATURE REVIEW

The impact of FDI has been largely debated in the literature as empirical research has yielded various contrasting outcomes (Ezehohe & Cattaneo, 2012; Heizer, 2012; Morrissey, 2012; Adams 2009; Ndikumani & Verick, 2008; Ahmed, Cheng & Messinis, 2011; Adeniyil & Omisakin, 2012). Conceptually FDI is hypothesized to promote both economic and social benefits to host economies, all things being equal (Mckinney, 2014; Jensen, 2003; Li & Resnick, 2003). The main assertion in the literature is that through technology spillovers, the growth promoting effects of FDI is evident when productivity levels rise and employment levels and quality increase, capital formation, technology transfer, improved balance of payment (BOP), and transfer of managerial skills (Piggott & Cook, 2006 pp 215-219; Lipsey, 2004; Anfofum, Gambo & Suleiman, 2013; de Mello, 1999). FDI has indeed played a major role in the process of globalization due to its characteristics and rapid growth leading to economic, political and social integrations in many regions of the world (Lipsey, 2004; Borensztein, Gregorio & Lee, 1998). The principal characteristic of FDI is the control over operations exercised by the investing entity due to ownership of equity. The determinants and impact of FDI however, cannot be dissociated from the social lives of the host economies (McKinney, 2014; Piggott & Cook, 2006; Lipsey, 2004). This brief review discusses some of the main theoretical frameworks and empirical evidence provided by existing literature on how FDI affects the socio-economy of host countries.

Theories of Foreign Direct Investment

FDI in its very make-up proves a difficult phenomenon for a single theory. Due to the fact that it is closely linked to welfare and economic growth, many economists find that explaining FDI within the context of theories of economic growth is important. Piggott and Cook (2006) state that FDI has several theories including the traditional, modern and radical. Indeed, several theories have tried to explain the activities of MNE's. Recent explanations of FDI usually refer to three different types of advantages that are assumed by some to be the backbone of theories used to explain why firms engage in FDI. There is the ownership-specific advantages (OSA) such as by Hood and Young, (1979) which answer why a firm will favor foreign direct foreign market when exporting and licensing are available. The question is an important one because FDI may be both expensive and risky. FDI is expensive because a firm must establish production facilities in a foreign country or acquire a foreign establishment. It is risky because of the problems associated with doing business in a different country where the "rules of the game" may be very different. However, the viability of an export strategy is often constrained by transportation cost and trade barriers. When transportation cost is added to production cost, it becomes unprofitable to ship a product over a long distance. Again, a branch of economic theory known as internationalization theory seeks to explain why firms often prefer FDI to licensing as a strategy for entering a foreign market (See Hymer, 1976). According to this theory, licensing may result in a firm giving away valuable technological know-how to a potential foreign investor. A second problem is that licensing does not give a firm the tight control over manufacturing, marketing and strategy in a foreign country that may be required to maximize its profitability. With licensing, control over manufacturing, marketing, and strategy is granted to a licensee in return for a royalty fee. However, for both strategic and operational reasons, a firm may want to retain control over these functions.

Second to OSA is location-specific advantage theories (LSA) also attributable to researchers like Dunning (1998) and Erramilli, Agarwal, and Kim (1997) which explain the pattern of FDI. Why do firms in the same industry often undertake FDI at the same time and why are some locations preferred as a target FDI location? Conceptualizations that attempt to explain the pattern of FDI include firms following Competitors, where FDI pattern is based on the idea that firms follow their domestic competitors overseas. First expounded by Knickerbocker (1973), the theory is based on Oligopolistic industries. A critical competitive feature of such industries is interdependence of the major players. These firms tend to imitate each other's FDI strategy and secondly, the product life cycle hypotheses propounded by Raymond Vernon (1966). Here, firms undertake FDI at particular stages in the life cycle of the product they pioneered. They invest in other advanced countries when local demand in those countries grows large enough to support local production. They subsequently shift production to developing countries when product standardization and market saturation give rise to price competition and cost pressures. Investment in developing countries is seen as the best way to reduce cost. (See also Pinho, 2007; Chen & Chen, 1998; Outreville, 2008)

The third strand of theories termed Internalization – specific advantage (ISA) seeks to combine the previous two advantages and is projected within the framework of the eclectic paradigm originally postulated by Dunning (1988). The eclectic paradigm holds the view that in addition to the various factors discussed above, location specific advantages are also of considerable importance in explaining both the rationale for and the direction of foreign direct investment. By location-specific advantages, Dunning (1998) means the advantages that arise from utilizing resource endowments or assets that are tied to a particular foreign location and that a firm finds valuable to combine with kits own assets (such as the firm's technological, marketing and management capabilities). Dunning accepts the argument of internalization theory that it is difficult for a firm to license its own unique capabilities and know-how. Therefore, he argues that combining location-specific assets or resource endowment and the firm's own unique capabilities often require foreign direct investment. That is, it requires the firm to establish production facilities where those foreign assets or resources are located. Finally, Dunning (1993, 2002) provides four motives for FDI which are market-seeking, resource-seeking, efficiency-seeking and strategic-asset- seeking FDIs. Chesnais, Ietto-Gillies and Simonetti (2000) provide a seminal and thorough insight into these four motives.

Theoretically, the impact of FDI inflows include but is not limited to increase in employment which in turn increases real wages, superior wages, conditions of work and benefit than local firms (Jensen & Rosas, 2007; Greenhill, Mosley & Prakash, 2009) increase in efficiency through lower costs and selling prices through mass markets since the introduction of new technology from FDI has been seen as a way of encouraging technological change where the effect of technology could be direct through transfer of technology to a local affiliate or indirect through technology spill-overs (Borenszteina, De Gregoriob, Lee, 1998; de Melo, 1997; Ford et al., 2008). Better access to capital markets (Anfofum, Gambo & Suleiman, 2013), improved management styles and a favourable balance of payments of host countries are also positively affected with FDI (Heizer, 2012). It must be emphasized that the impact of FDI may not always be positive as proposed by theory. Ethical, human rights and environmental challenges have been named among the impacts of FDI in certain instances (Trakman, 2010; Dutt, 1998; Reis, 2001 and Aitken and Harrison,1999)

The impact of FDI ultimately manifests in welfare changes and these are embedded in higher levels of output or economic growth at the aggregate level. FDI followed or accompanied by productivity level and rate increases as well as improved capital formation, holding all other factors constant would imply better living standards for people. Both the neoclassical and endogenous growth theorists have underscored FDI as an important factor for achieving economic growth and development (Balasubramanyam, Salisu & Sapsford, 1996; Li & Liu, 2005; Calvet, 1981). Herzer (2012) finds from a panel of 44 countries that cross-country variations in the growth effects of FD can be explained primarily by cross-country differences in freedom from government intervention, business freedom, FDI volatility, and primary export dependence (Asiedu, 2006).

However, implicit in these factors affected by FDI are social factors (Kumar & Waheed, 2007; Trackman, 2010; Abdou & Zazoou, 2013) and this is the main hypothesis of this paper. That the impact of FDI is not only economic but has a socioeconomic make-up is what we seek to test for these five sub-Saharan African countries. As observed by Abdou and Zazoou (2013), developing countries have been burdened with increasing levels of social inequality, weak public corporate governance, limited competition, lack of a well-structured public sector, and pervasive corruption and a well-placed implementable policy of FDI inflows is likely to mitigate these challenges. Although there's a plethora research finding on the impact of FDI in SSA, very few of these, place emphasis on the socio-economic impact of inward FDI. Measures such employment variability, government effectiveness, rule of law, education, macroeconomic stability, political stability and absence of violence are a few of such socio-economic factors that need to be considered in conjunction with the conventional studies of FDI. The emphasis has mainly been on the macroeconomic impacts of FDI. Socio-economic factors have been viewed mostly in the light of factors that influence FDI flows. The main goal of this paper is to stir a debate on the role of socioeconomic factors in FDI and the effect of FDI on both social and economic development in Africa, specifically sub-Saharan Africa.

METHODOLOGY

To estimate the determinants and economic impact of FDI flows to Africa, a panel regression model for 10 African countries for the period 1990-2015 is employed. The following economic model guided by the empirical literature and based on data availability is formulated:

$$FDI_{it} = b_0 + b_1 GDPG_{it} + b_2 OP_{it} + b_3 IFL_{it} + b_4 EXR_{it} + b_5 LGDP_{it} + u_{it} \quad (1)$$

where FDIit, percentage of FDI flows to GDP in country i and in year t; GDPGit, GDP growth in country i and year t; OPit, openness index estimates in country i and year t; IFit, inflation in country i and in year t; EXRit, exchange rate in country i and in year t; LGDPit, log of GDP in country i and in year t.

The dependent variable in the specifications below is the inflow of FDI as a share of nominal GDP. A first pass of the data looks at which macroeconomic variables are associated with higher FDI flows. The variables include real GDP growth proxy for host countries' market size and growth potential, openness, inflation, exchange rate, and log level of GDP. Openness is measured as the share of goods and services trade in GDP.

The next set of regressions includes each of the qualitative variables successively in the specification. The qualitative variables included in this set of regressions represent a range of institutional and development factors that might be expected to affect the willingness of investors to locate foreign investment in the target country. The

Table 1. Averages (for years 2002-2014) of the six economic indicators for African countries

Country	OP	IFL	FDI	LGDP	GDPG	EXR
Ghana	2042.527	630.726	103.150	262.376	142.748	22.997
Nigeria	1465.742	582.740	87.320	284.294	144.049	2477.960
Kenya	1467.079	290.581	16.757	227.105	93.916	1769.555
Guinea	1603.550	302.135	73.590	249.239	80.342	83036.328
Cote D'Ivior	2037.663	126.872	40.251	216.463	66.396	13216.131
Mali	1423.902	138.764	51.659	202.479	115.426	13216.131
Niger	1246.168	96.568	98.825	200.236	93.623	13216.131
Senegal	1727.892	79.689	46.865	209.540	91.902	13216.131
Burkina Faso	1076.367	70.431	22.419	189.788	139.374	13216.131
Guinea-Bissau	1311.110	2036.670	37.809	171.825	59.412	11781.815

Source: World Bank (2016)

variables included are a measure of domestic credit to the private sector, government effectiveness, regulatory quality, and corruption control. A panel regression model for 11 African countries for the period 2002-2014 is employed. The model below, guided by the empirical literature and based on data availability is formulated:

$$LFDI_{it} = \beta_0 + \beta_1 GDPG_{it} + \beta_2 GE_{it} + \beta_3 RQ_{it} + \beta_4 CC_{it} + \varepsilon_{it} \quad (2)$$

where LFDIit, log of the percentage of FDI flows to GDP in country i and in year t; DCPSit, domestic credit to the private sector in country i and in year t, GEit, government effectiveness in country i and in year t, RGit, regulatory quality in country i and in year t, and CCit, control of corruption index in country i and in year t.

Different data sources are used in this chapter. FDI flows measured in millions of US dollars is obtained from the database of the UNCTAD. Data for the four social indicators' is obtained from the World Bank's World Governance Indicators (EGI). The estimation of the model for random and fixed effect produces the results in Table 3.

ANALYSIS OF RESULTS

This section determines how location factors determine and impact flows of FDI. Table 3 reports the random and fixed effect estimations.

Table 2. Social indicators

Country	LFDI2	DCPS	GE	RQ	CC
Ghana	116.432	11.449	-1.028	-0.885	-1.327
Nigeria	125.847	-1.900	-13.411	-11.415	-14.717
Kenya	105.112	1.956	-7.169	-2.909	-12.493
Cote D'Ivior	110.803	187.175	-14.473	-10.608	-12.891
Mali	107.770	196.115	-10.054	-5.857	-7.273
Gambia	99.352	168.239	-8.011	-5.032	-7.916
Niger	106.723	106.798	-9.480	-7.154	-9.722
Senegal	108.900	307.397	-4.346	-3.007	-3.677
Burkina Faso	100.824	209.522	-7.963	-2.931	-4.059
Togo	103.569	275.944	-18.632	-11.138	-12.389
Guinea-Bissau	91.391	68.434	-16.001	-14.437	-14.552

Source: World Bank (2016)

SUMMARY OF RESULTS

This study has found that two of the economic variables have a statistically significant relationship with FDI in the 10 different countries studied in Africa. The relationship between openness and FDI was a significant and positive factor in attracting FDI. The coefficient estimate of 0.0818 indicates that foreign direct investment is very responsive to openness. The volume of trade as a percentage of GDP is a proxy for openness. This is consistent with FDI theory. International trade theory explains that trade, which represents the sum of exports and imports of goods and services, measured as a share of gross domestic product is has a direct effect in attracting FDI. This confirms Dunning (1988) and Erramilli et al (1997)'s assertion on location specific advantages as reasons or determinants of FDI. Also, the relationship between GDP measured in US$, was a significant and positive factor in attracting FDI. The coefficient estimate of 1.00137 indicates that foreign direct investment is very responsive to the sum of gross value added by all resident producers in the economy plus any product taxes and minus any subsidies not included in the value of the products. This finding confirms the theory and supports the hypothesis that the market demand and size as well as the general level development of a country, have a positive impact on attracting FDI. This is consistent with findings of Li and Liu (2004) as well as Borenszteina and Lee (1998). GDP growth has a positive relationship with FDI flows into Africa. Consistent with the theory, the expansion of the economy creates jobs and opens up other opportunities for investors. With the help of globalization, firms have started exploring new markets, especially in

Table 3. Panel regression analysis

	Fixed Effects		Random Effects	
	Coef.	**P(Sig)**	**Coef.**	**P(Sig)**
Observation	260			
No. of groups	10			
GDPG	0.0467203	0.2060		
OP	0.0818053	0.0000		
IFL	0.00387	0.6170		
EXR	-7.35E-10	0.0640		
LGDP	0.0005985	0.0040		
Cons	-3.232804	0.1660		
R^2	0.1618			
F-statistic (P-value)	0.0000			
Hausman Statistic (p-value)	0.0014			
Second Panel				
Observation	143			
No. of groups	11			
DCPS			0.0283328	0.0000
GE			0.2572807	0.4090
RQ			0.9135008	0.0020
CC			-0.3003007	0.2500
Cons			8.393752	0.0000
R^2			0.0046	
Wild $\chi 2$-statistic (P-value)			0.0000	
Hausman Statistic (p-value)			0.4871	

economies that are growing. Most of the developed areas such as euro area have stagnated growth while the developing economies such as those in the Sub-Sahara Africa have been enjoying growth. One percent increase in GDP is estimated to lead to a 0.04672 percent increase in FDI. The exchange rate had an inverse relationship with FDI. Depreciation in domestic currency has been a major problem in most countries in African. This introduces uncertainty and jeopardizes future planning. Official exchange rate refers to the exchange rate determined by national authorities or to the rate determined in the legally sanctioned exchange market. One percent increase in the exchange rate is estimated to lead to a 7.35e-10 percent decrease in FDI. Finally, the relationship between inflation measured by the annual growth rate of the GDP implicit deflator was statistically insignificant and positive factor in attracting FDI. The coefficient estimate of 0.00387 indicates that foreign direct investment is responsive to changes in inflation levels. This finding does not support the hypothesis that the FDI flows to an environment with low inflation levels. Practically, this is not the case in most African countries.

The estimation of the model for random effect produces the results in Table 2. The results show that domestic credit to private sector and regulatory quality are statistically significant variables that affect FDI flow to African countries. These factors have a positive impact on FDI flows to African countries. This finding agrees with the theory. Domestic credit to private sector refers to financial resources provided to the private sector, such as through loans, purchases of nonequity securities, and trade credits and other accounts receivable, that establish a claim for repayment These facilities are needed to finance investment opportunities. For some countries, these claims include credit to public enterprises.

Regulatory quality has a direct and significant relationship with FDI. This confirms the hypothesis which states that regulatory quality captures perceptions of the ability of the government to formulate and implement sound policies and regulations that permit and promote private sector development. Multinational companies thrive in an environment with sound and solid regulatory quality and rule of law.

While the other two governance indicators (i.e. government effectiveness and control of corruption are statistically insignificant. The independent variable jointly within the sample explains approximately 48 percent of the variation of FDI flows to African countries.

CONCLUSION

Research on African, particularly small West African, economies have been largely neglected. Given their vulnerability and special economic characteristics, empirical results derived from them are believed to supplement the existing literature and help similar countries to enhance understanding in FDI phenomenon and in policy implementation. This paper investigated from an empirical point of view, the determinants and impact of socioeconomic factors on FDI flows to African countries. The results indicate that openness, GDP, direct credit to the private sector and regulatory quality, have a positive impact on FDI flow to African countries. In recent years, many development countries around the world have launched initiatives designed to improve competitiveness and have shown that improving institutional structures can yield significant benefits. Policy makers should strengthen socioeconomic variables by ensuring a stable financial environment, to effectively deliver stable low inflation conducive for sustainable and balanced long-term growth. While GDP growth, inflation, exchange rate government effectiveness and corruption control have a statistically insignificant effect on FDI flows to Africa. Thus, we can conclude that beside economic reforms African countries need to adopt institutional reforms that could contribute to improving their state of governance, promote their investment climate and help in attracting more FDI.

In recent years, many development banks around the world have launched initiatives designed to improve competitiveness and have shown that focusing a limited quantity of resources on a group of high-potential entrepreneurs can yield significant benefits. These institutions have also found that non-financial solutions can be highly useful. Globally, the outlook for financial services is solid. But the rise of disrupters in the market, especially from unexpected places, has provoked the need for financial services entities to rethink their strategies. It also means that innovation and technology have moved a few notches up on their agenda. This is particularly true for Africa where the market is less mature or saturated, giving rise to opportunities for new entrants to challenge the status quo.

The study is not without limitations. Although African countries are important in attracting FDIs, our results may be peculiar to the countries studied due to marked institutional and organizational differences. The availability of data has affected the representativeness of the data. This undoubtedly will impact the universal applicability of our findings to other African countries sectors, countries and markets. Future research may examine a relatively more countries with longer horizon time scale provided supportive data is available.

REFERENCES

Abdou, D. S., & Zaazou, Z. (2013). The Egyptian revolution and post socio-economic impact *Topics in Middle Eastern and African Economies, 15*(1), 91-115.

Adams, S. (2009). Foreign direct investment, domestic investment, and economic growth in Sub- Saharan Africa. *Journal of Policy Modeling, 31*(6), 939–949. doi:10.1016/j.jpolmod.2009.03.003

Adewumi, S. (2006). *The impact of foreign direct investment on growth in developing countries: An African Experience.* Jönköping International Business School Jönköping University Jonkoping University.

Ahmed, A. D., Cheng, E., & Messinis, G. (2011). The role of exports, FDI and imports in development: Evidence from Sub-Saharan African countries. *Applied Economics, 43*(26), 3719–3731. doi:10.1080/00036841003705303

Anfofum, A. A., Gambo, J. S., & Suleiman, T. (2013). Estimating the impact of foreign direct investment in Nigeria. *International Journal of Humanities and Social Science*, *3*(17), 138–145.

Atique, Z., Ahmad, M., Azhar, U., & Khan, A. (2004). The Impact of FDI on economic growth under foreign trade regimes: A case study of Pakistan. *Pakistan Development Review*, *43*(4), 707–718.

Balasubramanyam, V. N., Salisu, M., & Sapsford, D. (1996). Foreign direct investment and growth in EP and IS countries. *Economic Journal (London)*, *106*(434), 92–105. doi:10.2307/2234933

Borensztein, E., De Gregorio, J., & Lee, J. W. (1998). How does foreign direct investment affect economic growth? *Journal of International Economics*, *45*(1), 115–135. doi:10.1016/S0022-1996(97)00033-0

Calvet, A. L. (1981). A synthesis of foreign direct investment theories and theories of the multinational firm. *Journal of International Business Studies*, *12*(1), 43–59. doi:10.1057/palgrave.jibs.8490570

Carlos Pinho, J. (2007). The impact of ownership: Location-specific advantages and managerial characteristics on SME foreign entry mode choices. *International Marketing Review*, *24*(6), 715–734. doi:10.1108/02651330710832676

Chesnais, F., Ietto-Gillies, G., & Simonetti, R. (Eds.). (2003). *European integration and global corporate strategies*. London, UK: Routledge.

Crespo, N., & Fontoura, M. P. (2007). Determinants factors of FDI spillovers – what we really know? *World Development*, *35*(3), 410–425. doi:10.1016/j.worlddev.2006.04.001

De Mello, L. R. (1999). Foreign direct investment-led growth: Evidence from time series and panel data. *Oxford Economic Papers*, *51*(1), 133–151. doi:10.1093/oep/51.1.133

Dunning, J. H. (1998). Location and the multinational enterprise: A neglected factor? *Journal of International Business Studies*, *29*(1), 45–66. doi:10.1057/palgrave.jibs.8490024

Erramilli, M. K., Agarwal, S., & Kim, S. S. (1997). Are firm-specific advantages location-specific too? *Journal of International Business Studies*, *28*(4), 735–757. doi:10.1057/palgrave.jibs.8490117

Greenhill, B., Mosley, L., & Prakash, A. (2009). Trade-based diffusion of labor rights: A panel study, 1986–2002. *The American Political Science Review*, *103*(04), 669–690. doi:10.1017/S0003055409990116

Herzer, D. (2012). How does foreign direct investment really affect developing countries' growth? *Review of International Economics*, *20*(2), 396–414. doi:10.1111/j.1467-9396.2012.01029.x

Hood, N., & Young, S. (1979). *The economics of multinational enterprise*. London, UK: Longman.

Jensen, N. M. (2003). Democratic governance and multinational corporations: Political regimes and inflows of foreign direct investment. *International Organization*, *57*(3), 587–616. doi:10.1017/S0020818303573040

Jensen, N. M., & Rosas, G. (2007). Foreign direct investment and income inequality in Mexico, 1990–2000. *International Organization*, *61*(03), 467–487. doi:10.1017/S0020818307070178

Kaplinsky, R., & Morris, M. (2009). Chinese FDI in Sub-Saharan Africa: Engaging with large dragons. *European Journal of Development Research*, *21*(4), 551–569. doi:10.1057/ejdr.2009.24

Kerner, A. (2014). What we talk about when we talk about foreign direct investment. *International Studies Quarterly*, *58*(4), 804–815. doi:10.1111/isqu.12147

Knickerbocker, F. T. (1973). Oligopolistic reaction and multinational enterprise. *Thunderbird International Business Review*, *15*(2), 7–9.

Lipsey, R. E. (2004). Home-and host-country effects of foreign direct investment. In *Challenges to globalization: Analyzing the economics* (pp. 333–382). University of Chicago Press. doi:10.7208/chicago/9780226036557.003.0010

Lipsey, R. E., & Sjöholm, F. (2004). FDI and wage spillovers in Indonesian manufacturing. *Review of World Economics*, *140*(2), 321–332. doi:10.1007/BF02663651

Li, Q., & Resnick, A. (2003). Reversal of fortunes: Democratic institutions and foreign direct investment inflows to developing countries. *International Organization*, *57*(01), 175–211. doi:10.1017/S0020818303571077

McKinney, L. A. (2014). Foreign direct investment, development, and overshoot. *Social Science Research*, *47*, 121–133. doi:10.1016/j.ssresearch.2014.04.003 PMID:24913949

Morrissey, O. (2012). FDI in Sub-Saharan Africa: Few linkages, fewer spillovers. *European Journal of Development Research*, *24*(1), 26–31. doi:10.1057/ejdr.2011.49

Ndikumana, L., & Verick, S. (2008). The linkages between FDI and domestic investment: Unravelling the developmental impact of foreign investment in Sub-Saharan Africa. *Development Policy Review*, *26*(6), 713–726. doi:10.1111/j.1467-7679.2008.00430.x

Nunnenkamp, P. (2004). To what extent can foreign direct investment help achieve international development goals? *World Economy*, *27*(5), 657–677. doi:10.1111/j.0378-5920.2004.00620.x

Omisakin, O., Adeniyi, O., & Omojolaibi, A. (2009). Foreign direct investment, trade openness and growth in Nigeria. *Journal of Economic Theory*, *3*(2), 13–18.

Outreville, J. F. (2008). Foreign affiliates of the largest insurance groups: Location-specific advantages. *The Journal of Risk and Insurance*, *75*(2), 463–491. doi:10.1111/j.1539-6975.2008.00268.x

Piggott, J., & Cook, M. (2006). *International business economics: A European perspective*. Basingstoke, UK: Palgrave Macmillan. doi:10.1007/978-0-230-62776-5

Trakman, L. (2010). *Foreign direct investment: An Australian perspective*. UNSW Law Research Paper No. 2010-4. Retrieved from https://papers.ssrn.com/sol3/papers.cfm?abstract_id=1540289

UNCTAD. (2009). *World investment report*. Retrieved from www.unctad.org/wir

UNCTAD. (2014). *World investment report*. Retrieved from www.unctad.org/wir

Vernon, R. (1966). International investment and international trade in the product cycle. *The Quarterly Journal of Economics*, 190–207.

Vongpraseuth, T., & Choi, C. G. (2015). Globalization, foreign direct investment, and urban growth management: Policies and conflicts in Vientiane, Laos. *Land Use Policy*, *42*, 790–799. doi:10.1016/j.landusepol.2014.10.003

Wasaki, I., & Suganuma, K. (2015). Foreign direct investment and regional economic development in Russia: An econometric assessment. *Economic Change and Restructuring: Empirical and Policy Research on the Transitional and Emerging Economies*, *48*(3-4), 209–255. doi:10.100710644-015-9161-y

World Bank. (2016). *World development indicators. Data for various years*. Retrieved from www.worldbank.org

Xiaoying, L., & Xiaming, L. (2005). Foreign direct investment and economic growth: An increasingly endogenous relationship. *World Development*, *33*(3), 393–407. doi:10.1016/j.worlddev.2004.11.001

Zhao, H., & Zhu, G. (2000). Location factors and country-of-origin differences: An empirical analysis of FDI in China. *Multinational Business Review*, *8*(1), 60.

KEY TERMS AND DEFINITIONS

Corruption: It is dishonest or fraudulent conduct by those in power, typically involving bribery.

Developing Country: It is a nation or sovereign state with a less-developed industrial base and a low human development index relative to other countries.

Direct Investment: The term describes a category of international investment made by a resident entity in one economy with the objective of establishing a lasting interest in an enterprise resident in an economy other than that of the investor.

Emerging Market: A country that has some characteristics of a developed market but does not meet standards to be a developed market.

Export: An export is a function of international trade whereby goods produced in one country are shipped to another country for future sale or trade. The sale of such goods adds to the producing nation's gross output. If used for trade, exports are exchanged for other products or services in other countries.

Foreign Direct Investment: It is an investment in a business by an investor from another country for which the foreign investor has control over the company purchased.

Chapter 5
FDI as a Factor of Improving the Competitiveness of Developing Countries:
FDI and Competitiveness

Ivana S. Domazet
Institute of Economic Sciences, Serbia

Darko M. Marjanović
BB Trade, Serbia

ABSTRACT

In the process of globalization of the world economy, foreign direct investment has a significant impact on economic growth and development of the national economy. To adequately facilitate the development of competitiveness, these countries usually intervene through measures and instruments of tax policy. One of the main tasks of developing countries is to create a favorable environment for investors, considering that this is one of the methods to ensure greater capital inflows. The main objective of this chapter is to assess the role of tax policy in achieving the competitiveness of developing countries. For the creators of tax policy, it is very important to constantly review the tax rules to ensure that the country is attractive for foreign investments. The results that were obtained indicate that tax incentives significantly influence the improvement of competitiveness and the attraction of multinational companies as a key holder of foreign direct investment.

DOI: 10.4018/978-1-5225-3026-8.ch005

INTRODUCTION

The beginning of the XXI century is characterized by complex processes of world development, in which multinational corporations and modern technology dominate, both in economic, and other industries. The rapid development of the globalization of business, caused an increase of competition in the international market. In terms of globalization, when national borders are becoming less and less an obstacle to the movement of goods and capital, foreign investors are increasingly investing their capital internationally to ensure economic benefits and higher profits. The condition for this is, above all, economic and political stability of the country in which to invest the capital, with the presence of an appropriate economic system that will allow an adequate transfer of profits. By moving parts of the company to the countries with less expensive labor force, more responsive legislation and the dynamic expansion of the domestic market, multinational corporations retain acquired competitive advantage. With foreign direct investment (FDI) inflow and the arrival of the leading multinational companies, developing countries also achieve significant benefits, such as: reduction of the high unemployment rate, provision of the modern techniques and technology, improvement of organization and management, facilitating exports to third markets, etc.

Attention is directed on developing countries and their attraction of foreign direct investment, which represent a necessary condition for increasing production and exports to the level that will, in addition to other benefits, ensure a stable economic growth to the country. In order to create optimal conditions that will contribute to attracting FDI, it is extremely important to ensure a good investment climate for foreign investors. Most countries have liberalized regulations that define the framework of foreign investments, aiming their increased competitiveness, and therefore a greater inflow of foreign capital. Nowadays, investments are permitted in almost all sectors of the economy, and the movement of capital has almost no restrictions. Hence, the FDI are considered an effective means of raising the comparative advantages of a country.

Bearing in mind all the benefits to which the state comes through foreign direct investment, it is of utmost importance that tax policy makers focus their attention on the tax rules, as that is one of the ways to increase the attractiveness of the country as an investment destination. If this issue is not properly addressed, the state may have far-reaching consequences in terms of its competitiveness in attracting foreign capital. For this reason, the act of competition among countries is encouraging each of them to make their tax systems more attractive for investors.

In the process of attracting foreign direct investment, it is necessary to ensure greater competition in the capital market, which is achieved by implementing adequate tax policy measures. This is precisely the reason why the taxation systems introduced many changes, especially from the standpoint of tax incentives, exemptions and reliefs. For each country, it is necessary to determine the extent to which the above elements affect economic trends, and then execute performance analysis in relation to the achievement of fiscal, socio-economic, political and other effects. On the one hand, by using different measures of fiscal policy, the state seeks to ensure an optimal model of encouraging investments and, on the other hand, does not want to undermine the neutrality and consistency of the tax system.

Although today foreign investments in service industries present a major part of FDI in the world, and generally yield positive effects, it should be noted that these investments are in most cases oriented to servicing the domestic market. In addition to the necessary developmental effects, one of the most important objectives to ensure investments that will create new markets and thus ensure an increase in exports of goods and services, for each country it is necessary to ensure significantly greater inflow of investments that would be directed towards exports or b2b trade.

BACKGROUND

In the process of globalization, the capital – as a major factor in creating the global economy, can accelerate the economic development of a country in which the funds are invested. Principally, the countries that are offering the most favorable conditions attract more FDI. A part of the overall process of economic globalization is the financial globalization, which, due to the significance of financial economies, is becoming the most important segment of the current globalization process. Kose, Prasad, Rogoff and Wei (2009) suggest that measures of de facto integration show a large increase in financial globalization since the mid-80s of the last century, with the advanced economies significantly integrated into global financial markets. For emerging market economies, the average de jure openness has not changed much according to the measures of the IMF, but the de facto integration has increased over the past two decades. For other developing economies, de jure openness on average increased over the past decade to a level higher than that for emerging market economies, but the de facto rate for the period remained unchanged.

It is important to note that the process of globalization unfolds much easier if trade liberalization precedes financial integration. Thus, the interaction between financial globalization and this set of initial conditions determine the outcome of growth and volatility. Kose, Prasad, Rogoff and Wei (2009) came to the conclusion that financial globalization can represent a catalyst for a variety of other collateral benefits, but also can significantly worsen the balance of risks in relation to benefits if the initial conditions of these dimensions are inadequate. This does not mean that risks are completely eliminated over the threshold, or that the financial integration is doomed before reaching the threshold. However, the process of financial integration must be carefully managed, if the threshold requirements are not met.

Analyzing the processes of globalization, De Sousa (2002) shows the main features of the new world economy, such as the dominance of the financial system and investments on a global scale, flexible and multi-locational production processes, low transport costs, a revolution in information technology and communications, the deregulation of national economies, giving priority to the multilateral financial agencies and the creation of three major multinational economies: (a) American, supported by the United States and special relations this country maintains with Canada, Mexico and Latin America, (b) Japanese, based in Japan and other Asian countries and (c) European, supported by the European Union and its special relations with Eastern Europe and north Africa. Requirements and tendency of globalization, are reflected in the necessity of national economies of developing countries to open to the world market, with the alignment of domestic prices with international. In this case, preference is given to the export economy, where the efforts of fiscal and monetary policy should be directed at reducing inflation and the national debt, while maintaining the balance between export and import prices. It is also essential to improve mobility of resources, investments and profits by reducing government regulation to a minimum (Gurgul & Lach, 2014). When it comes to the benefits of financial globalization, supply and demand of financial instruments contact in a wider area - the international financial market, and there is increased competition in the financial sector at a lower cost of capital, while improving the allocation of financial resources and financial sector development. One of the advantages lies in the diversification of investors' portfolios in the international context, with the imposition of a solid framework for economic policy makers and the creation of new instruments in the international market. In contrast to the benefits offered by financial globalization, shortages are related to the currency crisis, the challenges regarding budget, uneven distribution of income, as well as increased risks for enterprises.

In terms of globalization, where there is a liberalized trade, competitiveness is constantly increasing, with companies forced to penetrate new markets by increasing their efficiency. At the beginning, the most attractive were those countries that had low costs within the business process. However, in the last ten years, there has been a division of the production processes which can be located in the best place in terms of cost and productivity, giving a strong impetus to the growth of FDI. With increasing competition, companies seek to invest their capital to other countries, where investments focused on efficiency. On this basis, the growth of FDI boosts competitiveness among businesses. (Adam & Kammas, 2007) Markets that are attractive and attracting the attention of companies are certainly those having macroeconomic stability, adequate legal framework, developed infrastructure and low costs in relation to labor productivity and market openness.

International movement of capital is one of the most attractive forms of international financing and mostly of autonomous nature, namely. It has his own motivation and is not caused by the condition of current transactions in the accounts of particular countries. If we look from the perspective of the provider of capital, particular attention should be focused on private equity (the capital which is granted by private companies, private banks and private individuals) and public capital (the capital granted by state-owned companies, state banks, state funds and other government and international financial institutions), which primarily occurs in the form of bilateral loans and credits, portfolio investments and in the form of economic aid and grants). International capital flow refers to the transfer of funds between the subjects from different countries with delayed counter-transfer for a certain period of time, with the aim of achieving certain economic and political interests of the participants in that transfer. The modern economy cannot be isolated from the need to perform export and import of capital. For this reason, the movement of capital between countries is bidirectional, where certain entities of the country in one case appear as donors, and in the second case as recipients of capital. Most of the international movement of capital takes place between developed countries or entities from these countries, as the main providers and users of capital on a world scale. Although developing countries most often appear as users of capital, it must be noted that lately, to some extent, among these countries there are those that appear as relatively important providers of capital.

International movement of loan capital according to Perović (2005) involves financial intermediation in the realization of the financial surpluses of one sector in financing the deficits of others. Until the late sixties, loan capital had a major share in international capital flows. During this period, developing countries have fell into serious roadblock, mainly due to inadequate servicing liabilities due to the countries of the creditors, which led them to become the main beneficiaries of loan capital. At the end of the eighties, there was an absolute stagnation in the volume of movement of classic loan capital, with a significant increase in portfolio investments and FDI. For portfolio investments, as a form of investment, attention is not focused on the management and control of the company, but to the safety of the investments themselves and gaining profit. The development of financial markets and financial instruments has enabled investors to get the opportunity to diversify their risk by investing in many different securities. Portfolio investment (OECD, 2002) increase the liquidity and efficiency of the domestic capital market, bring know-how, increase transparency and discipline in the capital markets, enabling higher quality information and more intelligent allocation of capital and resources in the local economy and increase the possibility of financing a variety of investments in the national economy due to the increased liquidity of capital markets. Foreign direct investment as a form of international capital flow, appear as long-term investments of private capital. The main goal of the investor is to acquire property in another country and to operate it. Unlike portfolio investments, representing investment in the short term and in which financial institutions or institutional investors are the most common investors, foreign direct investment is the investment in the long run, where companies engaged in the production of goods and services appear as investors.

The main cause of international financial flows lies in the imbalance between savings and investment, where the difference between savings and investment is equal to the net increase of international loans. In this situation, countries with greater investments from savings, borrow the savings of other countries to finance their investments. Countries that have higher savings compared to investments, may invest their surplus savings abroad. In the longer term, there is a higher profit rate in the countries emitting the capital, and then the inflow of foreign capital leads to a situation that the capital is cheaper in the countries where funds enter. The biggest benefit of investing in a particular country where there is a shortage of savings, and therefore the higher cost of capital, has a country that has a lack of investments compared to savings and for which the interest rate is low. Free international capital movement provides access to international capital markets, where the particular entities borrow funds from abroad, under unfavorable conditions for them, and invest resources abroad under good conditions. The increased mobility of capital allows the investment of funds in the countries where the return on investments is higher, thereby improving the allocation of resources, and thus economic development. If demand exceeds supply in a country that imports the capital, it can only benefit from it, since the import of capital will increase supply and reduce prices. This will result in higher profitability of investment projects, which automatically leads to increase of investments.

The motives for the movement of private the capital are primarily related to the achievement of a greater profit, by hiring cheap labor and low prices of raw materials and energy abroad, along with market expansion and quest for the completion of the production process. (Esqueda, Assefa & Mollick, 2012). The main motive for the export the capital is to achieve the largest possible profits or other income from invested capital (interest, dividends), while other motifs are usually indirect and in the function of the main one. Primarily, this refers to the motive of using richer and cheaper resources abroad, compared to those available to the country exporting the capital. In addition to the need for achieving the lowest cost of production, conquering the market is one of the key motives for the export of capital, mainly due to the size of that market and the possibilities for investments. For this reason, use of the local resources of supply, reduction of transport costs and benefits of protected status of domestic production in the context of the customs system of that country is a must. For this reason, use the local resources of supply, reduction of transport costs and benefits of protected status of domestic production in the context of the customs system of that country. The motive for the export of capital might be the intention to provide a certain political influence in a country, and is mainly present in the investment of capital from public sources (various programs of assistance, subsidies, etc.). Otherwise, the investment of public capital are largely aimed at facilitating the investment of private capital. One of the motives of international development institutions, in placement of capital, is the improvement of economic and social environment of the recipient country, in order to contribute to the harmonious development of the world economy.

Basic motive for the import of capital, whether it is a company or a state, is to provide resources, which, at a certain point, are missing for the needs of business and development, or implementation of specific projects and programs. This is happening at a time when there is no enough resources of its own, which means there is no local accumulation, or the conditions of their engagement are unfavorable. If we look at the macro plan, the import of capital covers the payments deficit and foreign trade balance, improves the supply of the domestic market, achieves rise in employment and production, as well as transfer of technology, which all have an impact on economic growth and development of the country.

MAIN FOCUS OF THE CHAPTER

Tax Competition: Fiscal Instrument in Creating an Investment Climate

In the modern global economic conditions in a number of countries the need for the implementation of business activity in the international market is becoming a key element of development. It is therefore necessary to develop competitive capacity to individual business entities and economic sectors, as well as the national economy as a whole. Essentially, what distinguishes the competitiveness of a country from the competitiveness of enterprises is the place that it occupies in the creation of economic value in society. The starting point is that the economic value is created by the companies only, while the state can establish an environment that supports or hinders the activities of the company. In modern conditions, special attention is given to international competitiveness, regardless of whether it comes to specific products, companies, industries or the overall national economy. According to the OECD, international competitiveness is a condition in which a country can, under free and fair market, produce goods and services that meet the demands of the world market, while maintaining or increasing the real income of its citizens.

Most developing countries have an interest in attracting foreign direct investments, which would in a certain time period should contribute to their development.

Therefore, it is necessary to create conditions that would be acceptable to foreign investors to invest the capital in a certain developing country. For this reason, it is very important that each country should adopt a strategy and determine the objectives to be achieved by attracting of FDI. It is essential that the strategy is effective and to properly make way for foreign investors to invest the capital in that country. In order to accomplish the set objectives in the best way, it is necessary to focus investments in those industries and areas where the effects will be the greatest.

Competitiveness arises in instances where individuals and companies get choices. The greatest satisfaction of individuals and companies, according to Keen and Conrad (2011), includes the tendency towards significantly smaller levies from the jurisdiction or the state in which individuals and companies performing the activity. Looking at the conditions where competition does not exist, we come to the market conditions where the supply is lacking of providers, but who therefore have the opportunity to determine market conditions, and define prices as well as other factors that only they are in favor.

Tax competition is a competition between states (jurisdictions) in attracting capital (investors) by tax instruments, in particular tax incentives. Tax competitiveness is most relevant to direct taxes - corporate income tax and tax on personal income. If for the same work there are other environments where it is possible to achieve the set goals, we come to the simplest consideration of the phenomenon of tax competition. To be able to talk about tax competition it is necessary to acquire certain conditions, namely to create a favorable environment for investors through the advantages over the competition, which should result in conditions for the inflow of foreign investment. Tax competition exists in situations where state, in the creation of its own fiscal policy, tries to reduce the tax burden (through lowering of tax rates, granting tax incentives or abolishing certain taxes), all with the aim to prevent the outflow of production resources while encouraging them to enter the market. For this reason tax competition involves a strategy that the government of a country uses to make the appropriate privileged tax measures to attract foreign investment. However, the tax factor is only one of many factors influencing the competitiveness of a country. (Domazet & Marjanovic, 2016) When choosing a potential country for investment of capital, investors take into account many macro indicators (political stability of the country, the national tax system, disposition of the banking system, infrastructure, rule of law, business law, conditions on the local capital market, the qualifications of the workforce, social organization, etc.).

The main reasons that explain the occurrence of tax competition, according to Davies and Voget (2008), are increasing flows of international trade and investments, increased labor mobility between countries, as well as faster technology transfer. In this economic environment it is very difficult to maintain high tax rates. Free movement of capital creates a kind of pressure on the government to reduce the rate of tax, primarily of income tax, in order to maintain its attractiveness. To the extent that the economic integration between countries grows, companies and individuals receive greater freedom to take advantage of various economic opportunities offered to them. Therefore, the tax factor significantly influence their decisions on capital investments. From the standpoint of economic competition participants themselves must take the initiative seeking to pursue their interests and take a more favorable position in the global market. In addition, the decisive role is played by market rules, which determine the movement of supply and demand. With the tax competition, the situation is, however, different. It is caused by pressure carried out by the countries with low tax burden, so other countries have to maintain their tax presses on an acceptable level, in order to avoid the situation that investors move their business in a more favorable tax environment. (Kalamov, 2013) If the tax systems between countries differ considerably, for investment of capital and operating a business, companies and individuals will choose the country in which the total effective tax burden is lower. The departure of tax payers to the countries where the tax burden is lower, automatically leads to a reduction in tax revenue in the countries with higher tax burden, causing difficulties in financing public expenditure.

In the process of attracting foreign direct investment, it is necessary to take measures of tax policy ensuring that greater competition in the capital market. This is precisely the reason why the taxation systems introduced many changes, especially from the standpoint of tax incentives, exemptions and deductions. For each country, it is necessary to determine the extent to which the above elements affect economic trends, and then execute performance analysis in relation to the achievement of fiscal, socio-economic, political and other effects. On the one hand, the state, by different measures of fiscal policy, seeks to ensure an optimal model of encouraging investment and, on the other hand, does not want to undermine the neutrality and consistency of the tax system.

Foreign direct investments are considered to be an effective means to raise comparative advantages of one country, where it requires the internationalization of business, in which the main actors are multinational companies. Foreign investors usually invest capital in developing countries on the principle of "cost savings". This "cost savings" refers to lower labor costs, conditional upon having approximate quality, compared to domicile country, as well as in lower cost of financing and lower fiscal obligations. Given that, in terms of open and globalized world market, the price of labor is lower in countries with larger population, countries with smaller population have fewer opportunities to compete to attract foreign direct investment. Tax competition between developing countries is very intense, so there are less differences in the structure of tax systems and growing demand to maintain full coverage of expenditure by income. Tax competition, which is reflected in the introduction of tax exemptions for foreign investors, reduces the tax base in the amount of exemption from payment of income tax. On the other hand, the above tax exemptions should encourage investors to invest capital that will contribute to the growth of employment. Employment growth allows for higher effective demand and increase of the tax base, due to greater purchasing power, as well as the increase of revenues from taxes collected on final consumption.

In recent decades one of the objectives of the European Union is to achieve harmonization of tax systems of member states, with the aim to provide the highest level of neutrality and fairness in the single internal market of the Union. However, the specificity of national tax systems, level of economic development of each country as well as political and budgetary reasons, make it difficult to establish a harmonized tax system, and lead to the tax competition between countries, especially in terms of the height of the effective tax burden. In the finance literature, it's widely accepted that high tax rates can contribute to economic growth and development of one country. Moving the factors of capital and labor from the countries with high tax burdens to the countries with low tax burdens allows them to carry out the necessary tax reform, which should provide faster and more efficient economic development and growth. (Heady, Johansso, Arnold, Brys & Vartia, 2009) Often, in terms of tax competition, some entrepreneurs do business with high productivity and therefore have an incentive to continue their activities in those countries that "reward" entrepreneurship and hard work by using lower taxes. It is this possibility, referring to the choice of location in which to perform business activity, which ultimately increases the total wealth, and favorable tax environment is the basis for it. In addition, tax competition promotes fiscal responsibility by limiting the increase in the state administration. Most of the budgetary expenditure is financed from the tax revenues, and therefore, the state that seeks to lower taxes, usually manages to control and reduce public spending in order to create a balance between revenue collected and expenditures to be financed. The objective of tax competition is not reducing the tax burden to the zero tax rate, but to provide a more efficient use of tax revenue. At the same time, it is also an attempt to attract, through more attractive tax regimes, mobile factors of production (capital, skilled and professional labor force). If the state provides better infrastructure and better provision of other public services, companies are willing to accept higher taxes.

Multi-National Companies: Holders of FDI Aimed at Improving the Competitiveness

Talking about FDI and their investment in a particular country, primarily refers to the multinational companies who have access to capital, technology and know-how and countries that do not have their own resources to finance development, but aim to attract foreign investments. As multinational companies invest their private capital in certain countries, hence the motive of these companies is economic. (Nishiyama & Yamaguchi, 2010). Principal motives of each multinational company to invest capital in foreign country, among others are: profit, new market, favorable conditions for the use of resources and benefits of the tax system. One of the important items when making a decision about investing capital is also cheap labor that is usually offered in the selected country. Thus, it can be seen that multinational companies have more incentive to invest their capital, but still, the greatest motif of all is the profit that the company will achieve within a certain period. In a situation where the domestic market has become too narrow for placement of goods and services, multinational companies seek to expand to new markets. To be able to attract foreign capital, developing country must first provide a favorable investment climate. This climate includes: stable economic conditions; political and social stability; favorable foreign trade, customs and foreign exchange treatment of joint ventures; viable, reliable and skilled labor force; and access to raw materials and other domestic sources of supply. (Marjanovic & Ahmetagic, 2013) Developing countries typically offer multinationals a variety of tax benefits in the form of low tax rates, tax reliefs and exemptions, and thus contribute to creating a favorable investment climate for foreign investments. The presence of multinational companies with modern infrastructure at any location in the world, speaks about the power of these companies and the importance for a country to have such a company under its tax jurisdiction. Multinational companies generate huge profits, which automatically enables a given country to collect a certain amount of public revenue, which it lacks. Large multinational companies for their investment choose the countries that, in a certain time period, offer the best conditions in terms of tax rates, exemptions and subsidies.

Multinational companies are the most important drivers of foreign direct investment. Investment arrangements require businesses to invest significant financial resources, while in return, they gain the greatest degree of control, reduced dependence on business and faster winning the local market. (Li, Wang & Liu, 2013) Due to the large expenditures, companies entering the international market, as a rule, initially opt for a particular form of partnership and cooperation with a local company or for knowledge and technology transfer. To protect themselves from the uncertainties related to the optimal allocation of resources, multinational companies globally implemented a variety of strategies, including: (a) the game of competitiveness, with the aim to be the leading company in the global market, (b) the ownership over a competitive company by merging or takeover and (c) the formation of strategic alliances with competitors, with the aim of strengthening the company. In the process of creating a global strategy, one of the major issues, according to Chun (2012), is to determine according to which markets a multinational company needs to shape its global strategy. When it is directed towards one big market, the company establishes the supremacy in this market, and then spreads to other national markets. If it is a larger number of markets, it primarily refers to the conditions when the preference of customers and the model of using the product in different countries is similar. However, if attention is directed towards segments on a number of markets, the company seeks to identify segments of the national market, which can be profitable, given that in some countries production costs cannot be justified, while the production for market segments in many countries justifies the cost of production.

Policy towards foreign investment consists of legal provisions and regulations affecting the entry of foreign investors and their operation in the country. These policies can range from a ban on entry of foreign investors to the policy of preferential treatment through a variety of benefits. Unstable economy, relatively high inflation, unstable exchange rates and other factors that make the investment climate uncertain force back foreign investors. The regulation of entry and functioning in it, refers to the legal provisions governing the legal position of foreign investors in the host country, or the process of entering the country and setting up the company. This is a very important determinant as it shows the risks that foreign investors can have in terms of treatment by the legislation of the host country.

For multinational companies it is not typical to have long negotiations with the country in which they want to invest, but very quickly seek to find a new location for placement of capital. Therefore, countries that intend to attract multinational companies do not have the ability to monitor, assess and control the investors. Dunning believes that foreign direct investment according to motives of investors can be divided into: (a) Investments motivated by the demand for resources, (b) Investments motivated by the demand for market and (c) Investments motivated by the demand for efficiency. Determinants of the host country relevant for foreign investors include the political and economic framework, and state measures to facilitate investment and business. The importance of individual determinants depends on the motives of the FDI implementation. Hence, the importance of individual economic determinants of the country varies depending on the motives for investing.

One of the most important motives for foreign investors when investing capital is certainly the expansion of the market. By entering a new market multinationals aim to become competitive in this environment, to avoid high transport costs and to adapt products to consumer preferences. For this reason, the task of multinational companies is to sell their products and services to foreign markets. To attract foreign investors, it is necessary for the state to adjust the system, and offer various incentives in the form of tax incentives, preferential customs duties and the like. Foreign direct investments that are motivated by market reasons appear also in a situation where the establishment of local production in a foreign country is cheaper than the total cost of production and transport if these products are exported from foreign country.

Figure 1. FDI determinants of the host country
Source: World investment report (1998)

Determinants of the host country
I Policy framework for FDI ➢ economic, political and social stability ➢ rules regarding entry and operations ➢ standards of treatment of foreign affiliates ➢ policies on functioning and structure of markets ➢ international agreements on FDI ➢ privatization policy ➢ trade policy and coherence of FDI and trade policies ➢ tax policy II Economic determinants III Business facilitation

FDI type according to Investor motives	**Principal economic determinants in host countries**
A. Market seeking	➢ market size and GDP per capita ➢ market growth ➢ access to regional and global markets ➢ country specific consumer preferences ➢ market structure
B. Resources seeking	➢ raw materials ➢ low-cost unskilled labor ➢ skilled labour ➢ technological, innovatory and other created assets ➢ physical infrastructure
C. Efficiency seeking	➢ cost of resources and assets ➢ other input costs, e.g. transport and communication costs to/from and within host economy and costs of other intermediate products ➢ membership of a regional integration agreement conducive to the establishment of regional corporate networks

This happens in a situation where the transport of certain products is very expensive, so it is more economical to produce in a foreign country.

Foreign party invests their own capital motivated by the demand for resources that are not available in their home country, or can be obtained at a much lower cost in a foreign country. These include, above all, natural resources (raw materials), semi-finished products and cheap labor, as well as investment in order to acquire the technological and innovative resources in a foreign country. Foreign investments directed to natural resources by the beginning of World War II amounted to about 60%, and after that their importance began to decline. Although the relative importance of such investments has declined in absolute terms the growth has continued, so that they are still an important form of investments in the countries that possess natural resources. Although the multinational companies will obtain the necessary resources within a certain period of time, they are trying to strengthen their competitive position in a given market while increasing profits.

Foreign investments by multinational companies is motivated by the efficient utilization of the comparative advantages of the economy of a particular country. The motive of multinational companies is the demand for greater efficiency in order to efficiently utilize the joint management with their affiliates, and in doing so to maximize the benefits deriving from it, as well as benefits offered by individual location. This especially applies to large multinationals with large plants that produce standardized products. All this contributes to the diversification of risk, increased economies of scale as well as greater efficiency in the use of price difference and availability of inputs at certain locations. The best conditions for such investments are offered by the countries with an open market.

Strategy of a developing country to attract foreign direct investment is part of the overall economic strategy of the country. In the last 20 years, the position of most countries regarding foreign capital and foreign investors are completely changed. Until the mid-80s of the last century, most countries observed relationship to foreign investors with caution. In the early 90s of the last century, there was a change in attitude toward foreign capital, so that today many countries have introduced various incentives to attract multinationals. Multinational companies are looking for the best investment opportunity around the world, entering and exiting certain markets in search for better conditions to invest, and thus bring these countries in a situation where they compete with each other to attract foreign capital. About the great importance of multinationals provide the following information: (a) Fortune 500 company achieves 1/3 of the global GDP and controls around 70% of world trade, (b) 1% 1% of the largest multinationals accounting for more than half of the world's FDI.

The positive effect for the FDI recipient country, is that import of capital represents import of additional accumulation from abroad, thus creating opportunities for new investments, which affects the growth of employment. Engagement of foreign capital enables the import and better supply of reproduction and raw materials, as well as the substitution of imported products. Capital imports can finance current account deficit and thus gain more time for the adjustment of the economy in order to ensure external balance. Increasing of competitiveness reduces costs and increases the chances for export, with a simultaneous increase in budget revenues through tax revenue growth.

The motive for the creation of new or expansion of existing markets is a logical response of multinational companies to a situation that their domestic market became too narrow for placement of goods and services. In the absence of raw materials in their own country or in the inability to secure them by imports, multinationals are motivated to get closer to sources of raw materials which are largely found in countries in transition, where one can provide cheaper labor, given that the level of wages is lower. (Dumludag, Saridogan, Kurt, 2007)

To be able to attract sufficient foreign investment, the country needs low costs, as a result of low wages and low tax rates compared to neighboring countries. Most multinational companies, finds this very reason as a key in choosing a location for their investment. In addition, of great importance for foreign investors is an institutional arrangement, considering that in a number of developing countries corruption is at a very high level. Exactly corruption may be one of the reasons why foreign investors refrain from investing in a particular country. As for the state, and for investors, of crucial importance is the macroeconomic stability of the country. Usually countries are burdened with barriers relating to operations within the country and between countries. It is therefore essential to establish macroeconomic stability, which should ensure the growth of the private sector.

SOLUTIONS AND RECOMMENDATIONS

One of the goals of tax policy of each developing country is the reduction of the tax burden, which should contribute to the entry of new investments, and prevention of their outflow. The result of all this should be an increase in the volume and quantity of capital inflows, the growth and development of the economy and increasing competitiveness. It is necessary to ensure a favorable environment for investors, which is reflected in the provision of better conditions compared to competitive country, which will create a benefit that will lead to new investments. In order to be attractive to foreign investors certain countries compete in lowering of tax rates, by creating an attractive tax environment.

Economic policy makers, who deal with the FDI issue, should give special attention on the development of policies and strategies for attracting foreign investment. One of the main objectives of developing countries should be to attract foreign capital in those projects that they cannot fund alone, and in technology and knowledge they need. In addition, it is necessary to make a contribution to an increase in employment, but also to the competitiveness of individual companies in the country, and the entire national economy. A precondition for increasing the inflow of foreign investments are a stable political situation, regulated legal and economic system as well as the total social environment that will be conducive to the inflow of foreign capital.

If developing countries are intended to attract foreign capital it is important that concrete projects that will stimulate investment, as well as industries or companies that they want to sell (especially state-owned companies) are transparent for foreign investors. If developing countries are intended to attract foreign capital it is important that foreign investors as transparent concrete projects that will stimulate investment, as well as industries or companies that want to sell (especially state-owned companies). In addition, it is necessary to pay attention to those investors whose previous investments were not large, but where potential exists that such investments will be repeated and increased, given that the current global economic crisis has greatly reduced the total foreign investment at the global level

FUTURE RESEARCH DIRECTIONS

Most developing countries supports the view that fiscal policy is a very powerful instrument for attracting investment, and that tax competition is one of the most important indicators of overall competitiveness. Based on the results that were obtained through this research, it can be concluded that using measures and instruments of tax policy, can to some extent influence the improvement of the business environment in developing countries.

In order to comprehend the issue in the more expedient way, in some future research attention should be directed to the empirical research, in order to identify factors that may affect the tax competitiveness, with a view to a deeper understanding of the problems and possible consideration of methods to overcome them by using examples of successful practice.

CONCLUSION

Global trends in the movement of capital, as well as the value of realized investments, indicate great importance of FDI, which is reflected in the development of national economy of each country. For this reason, the goal of every country is to attract more FDI, given that they are one of the factors of success of the national economy in the global market. Attracting FDI is a necessary condition for stable growth of most countries.

With the increase of opportunities for free movement of capital in the world market, all countries have come in the position to "compete" with each other for the favor of business entities, in order to attract more investments into its territory. If attention is directed to the movement in the capital and the labor force markets, looking from the standpoint of multinational companies, it may be noted that tax competition is becoming more crucial factor. Due to the impact of tax competition multinational companies have the opportunity to choose one region rather than another or one state rather than another, but it all contributes to the opening of new production facilities as well as employment of local labor. Developing countries support the position that fiscal policy is a very powerful instrument for attracting investment, and that the tax competitiveness is one of the most important indicators of overall competitiveness. For them it is very important to provide as much capital inflow, through favorable conditions for foreign investment, and favorable tax treatment. Special tax treatment involves the expansion of the tax base and / or a reduction in the tax rate of income tax.

The aim of foreign investors, in a situation where national borders are becoming less and less an obstacle to the movement of goods and capital is to invest their capital abroad and ensure a greater profit. The advantages that foreign direct investment offer to countries in which they invest the capital are reflected in the increase in production, improvement of technology and increase in the efficiency of domestic enterprises, human resource development, promotion of foreign trade and increasing revenue. It is important to point out that multinationals have the task to find a country that will offer the best conditions for investment, and thus have a direct impact on countries to compete among themselves and to attract foreign investors and their capital. Benefits provided to domestic investors are now available to foreign investors, but it often occurs that foreign investors enjoy additional incentives. In many countries, restrictions have been lifted, and the principle of national treatment and equal relationship of foreign and domestic investors is the most widely accepted. (Dunning, Zhang, 2007) Many countries now prepare strategies and programs to attract more FDI. Governments of countries seek to motivate companies to invest their capital in many ways, in particular when it comes to projects that will contribute to employment, introduction of new technologies as well as increasing exports.

ACKNOWLEDGMENT

This chapter is written as a part of the research projects III47009 (European Integrations and Social and Economic Changes in Serbian Economy on the Way to the EU) and OI179015 (Challenges and Prospects of Structural Changes in Serbia: Strategic Directions for Economic Development and Harmonization with EU Requirements), financed by the Ministry of Education, Science, and Technological Development of the Republic of Serbia.

REFERENCES

Adam, A., & Kammas, P. (2007). Tax policies in a globalized world: Is it politics after all? *Public Choice*, *133*(3-4), 321–341. doi:10.100711127-007-9190-9

Alguacil, M., Cuadros, O. A., & Orts, V. (2011). Inward FDI and growth: The role of macroeconomic and institutional environment. *Journal of Policy Modeling*, *33*(3), 481–496. doi:10.1016/j.jpolmod.2010.12.004

Anken, F., & Beasley, E. J. (2012). Corporate structure optimization for multinational companies. *Omega*, *40*(2), 230–243. doi:10.1016/j.omega.2011.06.003

Asano, T. (2010). Optimal tax policy and foreign direct investment under ambiguity. *Journal of Macroeconomics*, *32*(1), 185–200. doi:10.1016/j.jmacro.2009.12.006

Asteriou, D., & Stephen, G. (2011). *Applied Econometrics* (2nd ed.). London, UK: Palgrave MacMillan.

Bayraktar, N. (2013). Foreign Direct Investment and Investment Climate. *Procedia Economics and Finance*, *14*, 83–92. doi:10.1016/S2212-5671(13)00013-0

Becker, J., & Riedel, N. (2012). Cross-border tax effects on affiliate investment-Evidence from European Multinationals. *European Economic Review*, *56*, 1495–1511. doi:10.1016/j.euroecorev.2012.07.001

Benassy-Quere, A., Coupet, M., & Mayer, T. (2007). Institutional Determinants of Foreign Direct Investment. *World Economy*, *30*(5), 764–782. doi:10.1111/j.1467-9701.2007.01022.x

Blomstrom, M., & Kokko, A. (2003). *The economic of foreign direct investment incentives*. Retrieved November 20, 2016, from http://www.nber.org/papers/w9489

Brouthers, K., & Dikova, D. (2010). Acquisitions and Real Options: The Greenfield Alternative. *Journal of Management Studies*, *47*(6), 1048–1071. doi:10.1111/j.1467-6486.2009.00875.x

Buchanan, B., Lee, V. Q., & Rishi, M. (2012). Foreign direct investment and institutional quality: Some empirical evidence. *International Review of Financial Analysis*, *4*, 81–89. doi:10.1016/j.irfa.2011.10.001

Cazzavillan, G., & Olszewski, K. (2012). Interaction between foreign financial services and foreign direct investment in Transition Economies: An empirical analysis with focus on the manufacturing sector. *Research in Economics*, *66*(4), 305–319. doi:10.1016/j.rie.2012.08.001

Chun, B. G. (2012). Host country's strategic policies and multinational firm's choice of entry mode. *Economic Modelling*, *29*(2), 435–443. doi:10.1016/j.econmod.2011.11.014

Ćorić, B., & Pugh, G. (2013). Foreign direct investment and output growth volatility: A worldwide analysis. *International Review of Economics & Finance*, *25*, 260–271. doi:10.1016/j.iref.2012.07.011

Damijan, J., Rojec, M., Majcen, B., & Knell, M. (2013). Impact of firm heterogenity on direct and spillover effects of FDI: Micro-evidence from the transition countries. *Journal of Comparative Economics*, *41*(3), 895–922. doi:10.1016/j.jce.2012.12.001

Davies, R., & Voget, J. (2008). *Tax Competition in an Expanding European Union.* Retrieved December 5, 2016, from http://sbs.ox.ac.uk/sites/default/files/Business_Taxation/Docs/Publications/Working_Papers/Series_08/WP0830.pdf

De Simone, G., & Manchin, M. (2012). Outward Migration and Inward FDI: Factor Mobility between Eastern and Western Europe. *Review of International Economics*, *20*(3), 600–615. doi:10.1111/j.1467-9396.2012.01041.x

De Sousa, B. S. (2002). Procesi globalizacije. *Časopis za književnost i kulturu, i društvena pitanja*, *68*(14), 5–65.

Domazet, I., & Marjanović, D. (2016). *Improving the business environment in Serbia through tax incentives for foreign investors. Institute of Economics Sciences.*

Du, J., Lu, Y., & Tao, Z. (2012). Institutions and FDI location choice: The role of cultural distances. *Journal of Asian Economics*, *23*(3), 210–223. doi:10.1016/j.asieco.2010.11.008

Dumludag, D., Saridogan, E., & Kurt, S. (2007). *Determinants of Foreign Direct Investment: An Institutionalis Approach.* Retrieved November 27, 2016, from http://www.researchgate.net/publication/237732834

Dunning, J., & Zhang, F. (2007). *Foreign Direct Investment and the Locational Competitiveness of Countries.* Retrieved December 6, 2016, from http://www.researchgate.net/publication/255605733

Esqueda, O., Assefa, A. T., & Mollick, V. A. (2012). Financial globalization and stock market risk, *International Financial Markets. Institutions and Money*, *22*(1), 87–102. doi:10.1016/j.intfin.2011.07.006

Forssbaeck, J., & Oxelhelm, L. (2011). Corporate financial determinants of foreign direct investment. *The Quarterly Review of Economics and Finance*, *51*(3), 269–282. doi:10.1016/j.qref.2011.05.002

Globerman, S., Shapiro, D., & Tang, Y. (2004). *Foreign direct investment in emerging and transition European countries*. Retrieved December 10, 2016, from http://www.emeraldinsight.com/doi/abs/10.1016/S1569-3767%2805%2906017-6

Gondor, M., & Nistar, P. (2012). Fiscal Policy and Foreign Direct Investment: Evidence from some Emerging EU Countries. *Procedia: Social and Behavioral Sciences*, *58*, 1256–1266. doi:10.1016/j.sbspro.2012.09.1108

Gurgul, H., & Lach, L. (2014). Globalization and economic growth: Evidence from two decades of transition in CEE. *Economic Modelling*, *36*, 99–107. doi:10.1016/j.econmod.2013.09.022

Hanousek, J., Kočenda, E., & Maurel, M. (2011). Direct and indirect effects of FDI in emerging European markets: A survey and meta-analysis. *Economic Systems*, *35*(3), 301–322. doi:10.1016/j.ecosys.2010.11.006

Heady, C., Johansso, A., Arnold, J., Brys, B., & Vartia, L. (2009). *Tax Policy for Economic Recovery and Growth.* Retrieved December 21, 2016, from https://kent.ac.uk/economics/documents/research/papers/2009/0925.pdf

Herzer, D. (2012). How does Foreign Direct Investment Really Affect Developing Countries' Growth? *Review of International Economics*, *20*(2), 396–414. doi:10.1111/j.1467-9396.2012.01029.x

Hong, Q., & Smart, M. (2010). In praise of tax havens: International tax planning and foreign direct investment. *European Economic Review*, *54*(1), 82–95. doi:10.1016/j.euroecorev.2009.06.006

Hyndman, R., Koehler, B. A., Snyder, D. R., & Grose, S. (2002). A state space framework for automatic forecasting using exponential smoothing methods. *International Journal of Forecasting*, *18*(3), 439–454. doi:10.1016/S0169-2070(01)00110-8

Johnson, A. (2005). *Host country effects of foreign direct investment: The case of developing and transition economies.* Retrieved December 02, 2016, from http://hj.diva-portal.org/smash/get/diva2:4009/FULLTEXT01.pdf

Johnson, A. (2006). *FDI inflows to the Transition Economies in Eastern Europe: Magnitude and Determinants.* Retrieved December 15, 2016, from https://ideas.repec.org/p/hhs/cesisp/0059.html

Kalamov, Z. Y. (2013). Risk sharing and the efficiency of public good provision under tax competition. *Regional Science and Urban Economics*, *43*(4), 676–683. doi:10.1016/j.regsciurbeco.2013.03.002

Keen, M., & Konrad, A. K. (2011). *International Tax Competition*. Retrieved December 11, 2016, from http://eml.berkeley.edu/~burch/Keen-Konrad-handbook-11.pdf

Kose, M., Prasad, E., Rogoff, K., & Wei, J. S. (2009). Finansijska globalizacija: Ponovna procena. *Panoeconomicus*, *2*, 143–197. doi:10.2298/PAN0902143K

Lessmann, C. (2013). Foreign direct investment and regional inequality: A panel data analysis. *China Economic Review*, *24*, 129–149. doi:10.1016/j.chieco.2012.12.001

Li, X., Wang, J., & Liu, X. (2013). Can locally-recruited R&D personnel significantly contribute to multinational subsidiary innovation in an emerging economy? *International Business Review*, *22*(4), 639–651. doi:10.1016/j.ibusrev.2012.12.002

Marjanović, D., & Ahmetagić, D. (2013). Multinational Companies as Carriers of Foreign Direct Investment. In Tudomanyos Mozaik, 10 Kotet (pp. 265-274). Kalocsa, HU: Tomori Pal Foiskola.

Marjanović, D., & Radojević, P. (2013). Foreign Direct Investments As An Engine Of Economic Growth And Development of Serbia. In Post Crisis Recovery (pp.349-364). Belgrade: Belgrade Banking Academy.

Neto, D., & Veiga, J. F. (2013). Financial globalization, convergence and growth: The role of foreign direct investment. *Journal of International Money and Finance*, *37*, 161–186. doi:10.1016/j.jimonfin.2013.04.005

Nishiyama, H., & Yamaguchi, M. (2010). Foreign direct investment, international trade, and firm heterogeneity. *Economic Modelling*, *27*(1), 184–195. doi:10.1016/j.econmod.2009.08.005

OECD. (2002). *Global Forum on International Investment: Attracting Foreign Direct Investment for Development*. Retrieved December 12, 2016, from https://oecd.org/investment/investmentfordevelopment/2764407.pdf

Perović, J. (2005). Međunarodno kretanje kapitala kao generator i akcelerator globalizacije. *Ekonomija*, *12*(2), 369–383.

Reiter, S., & Steensma, K. H. (2010). Human Development and Foreign Direct Investment in Developing Countries: The influence of FDI Policy and Corruption. *World Development*, *38*(12), 1678–1691. doi:10.1016/j.worlddev.2010.04.005

Sanjo, Y. (2012). Country risk, country size, and tax competition for foreign direct investment. *International Review of Economics & Finance*, *21*(1), 292–301. doi:10.1016/j.iref.2011.08.002

Schwab, K., & Porter, M. (2008). *The Global Competitiveness Report 2008-2009*. Geneva, Switzerland: World Economic Forum.

Stock, J., & Watson, W. M. (2001). Vector auto regressions. *The Journal of Economic Perspectives*, *15*(4), 101–115. doi:10.1257/jep.15.4.101

Wamser, G. (2011). Foreign (in)direct investment and corporate taxation. *The Canadian Journal of Economics. Revue Canadienne d'Economique*, *44*(4), 1498–1524. doi:10.1111/j.1540-5982.2011.01682.x

World investment report. (1998). *Trends and Determinants*. Retrieved December 05, 2016, from http://unctad.org/en/Docs/wir1998_en.pdf

ADDITIONAL READING

Boubakri, N., Cosset, J. C., Debab, N., & Valéry, P. (2013). Privatization and globalization: An empirical analysis. *Journal of Banking & Finance*, *37*(6), 1898–1914. doi:10.1016/j.jbankfin.2012.12.014

Giofré, M. (2013). Investor protection rights and foreign investment. *Journal of Comparative Economics*, *41*(2), 506–526. doi:10.1016/j.jce.2012.07.002

Gordon, L. A., Loeb, M. P., & Zhu, W. (2012). The impact of IFRS adoption on foreign direct investment. *Journal of Accounting and Public Policy*, *31*(4), 374–398. doi:10.1016/j.jaccpubpol.2012.06.001

Josifidis, K., Allegret, J. P., Gimet, C., & Beker Pucar, E. (2013). Macroeconomic policy responses to financial crises in emerging European economies. *Economic Modelling*, *36*, 577–591. doi:10.1016/j.econmod.2013.09.035

Kim, Y. H. (2009). Cross-border M&A vs. Greenfield FDI: Economic integration and its welfare impact. *Journal of Policy Modeling*, *31*(1), 87–101. doi:10.1016/j.jpolmod.2008.08.005

Lee, I. H., & Rugman, A. M. (2012). Firm-specific advantages, inward FDI origins, and performance of multinational enterprises. *Journal of International Management*, *18*(2), 132–146. doi:10.1016/j.intman.2011.11.001

Marin, D., & Schnitzer, M. (2011). When is FDI a capital flow? *European Economic Review*, *55*(6), 845–861. doi:10.1016/j.euroecorev.2010.09.010

McGrattan, E. R. (2012). Transition to FDI openness: Reconciling theory and evidence. *Review of Economic Dynamics*, *15*(4), 437–458. doi:10.1016/j.red.2012.07.004

Perez, M. F., Brada, J. C., & Drabek, Z. (2012). Illicit money flows as motives for FDI. *Journal of Comparative Economics*, *40*(1), 108–126. doi:10.1016/j.jce.2011.03.007

Tagkalakis, A. (2011). Fiscal policy and financial market movements. *Journal of Banking & Finance*, *35*(1), 231–251. doi:10.1016/j.jbankfin.2010.08.006

KEY TERMS AND DEFINITIONS

Capital: Value (in the form of money, property, or human resources) that is invested in production or other economic activity with the main purpose to increase and yield the profit.

Foreign Direct Investment (FDI): Capital investment by the company or individual with the aim of performing profitable activities on the territory of one state.

Globalization: The process of economic, social, cultural, and political activity that goes beyond the boundaries of nation-states, is reflected in the transfer of knowledge and information, and increases the volume of world trade of goods, capital, and services.

International Movement of Capital: Transfer of financial resources between entities of different countries with delayed counter-transfer for a certain period of time, with the aim of achieving certain economic and political interests of the participants in this transfer.

Investment Climate: Framework that enables foreign and domestic companies to operate and make profit in a given country.

Multinational Company: The parent company based in one country and that is composed of a large number of companies (affiliates) that are located in a number of countries.

Tax Competition: One jurisdiction is trying to attract capital and investment by offering favorable tax treatment through tax exemptions and reliefs by lowering the tax base and/or tax rates.

Chapter 6
The Relative Importance of Trade vs. FDI-Led Economic Growth in Thailand

Sailesh Tanna
Coventry University, UK

Kitja Topaiboul
Payap University, Thailand

Chengchun Li
Changzhou University, China

ABSTRACT

This chapter investigates the relative strength of the contributions of trade openness and FDI inflows towards economic growth of Thailand, taking account of the importance of human capital and other conditioning factors as a source of technology transfer in facilitating growth. Using Granger causality tests conducted within a vector-error-correction framework, the authors find significant evidence of the complementarities between domestic investment and trade openness, providing support for import-led growth. In contrast, direct support for FDI-led growth is relatively weak, which implies that trade openness has played a more significant role than FDI in influencing Thai economic growth. However, the results reveal a subtle role for technology transfer through the complementary effect of trade on FDI, and FDI on government expenditure, which henceforth influences human capital development with spillovers into domestic investment and growth. This leads us to argue that there is a potential role for FDI interacting with human capital in influencing the future development of the Thai economy, given its active policy of FDI promotion over the past decade.

DOI: 10.4018/978-1-5225-3026-8.ch006

INTRODUCTION

The nature of causal mechanisms between openness and economic growth has been extensively studied in many developing countries that have adopted a policy of both trade and FDI-led liberalization. There are in effect two basic hypotheses linking this policy stance between outward orientation and economic growth.

The first is based on a model of endogenous growth in which foreign capital is treated as complementary to domestic capital formation in aiding economic growth, implying the importance of technology transfer or FDI spill overs in generating growth (Grossman & Helpman, 1991; Rodriguez-Clare, 1996). Technology transfer in this context occurs when the advanced technologies embodied in high technology imports or FDI inflows are transferred to domestic plants through the presence of superior technology of multinational firms. Such spill over effects of FDI affect the host economies through changes in industrial structure and transfer of technological, managerial and financial practices that multinational firms bring about. However, it is argued that for developing countries to benefit from such spill overs they need to nurture their own absorptive capacity, which depends on the human capital or skill labour content of their workforce (Nelson & Phelps, 1966; Borensztein, De Gregorio & Lee, 1998). These considerations suggest that, apart from domestic physical and human capital formation, promoting trade and attracting FDI inflows enhances economic growth.

The alternative, reverse linkage hypothesis relates to the importance of domestic economic growth in explaining the volume of trade and the existence of multinational firms, the latter implying that FDI is attracted to host countries because of the possibility of higher returns on investment. Viewed as a substitute for domestic investment, FDI inflows are a natural response to higher domestic demand for capital generated by economic growth in host countries. Expanding domestic markets also make it possible for multinational firms to exploit economies of scale (Markusen, 1995). Moreover, improvements in human capital, labour productivity and infrastructure through technological change and economic growth would increase the marginal returns to capital, thereby expanding the demand for investment including FDI (Zhang & Markusen, 1999). In short, better economic performance in host countries provides foreign investors with a better investment environment and greater opportunities for generating profits, which suggests the hypothesis of growth-driven FDI and import demand.

This paper seeks to investigate both these hypotheses by establishing the nature of the causal links between trade, FDI and economic growth using quarterly data for Thailand. In doing so, we account explicitly for the role of domestic economic factors, including human capital, following the approach of Borensztein et al. (1998) who carry out a cross-country empirical analysis and find that the positive growth-effect of FDI holds only when the host country has a highly educated workforce that allows it to exploit FDI spill overs.

However, in an open economy, technology and knowledge may also be transferred through exports and imports, and thus promote economic growth (Frankel & Romer, 1999; Grossman & Helpmann, 1991). Furthermore, growth also has positive effects on boosting trade (Rodriguez & Rodrik, 2000). Balasubramanyam, Salisu and Sapsford (1996) argue that many of the growth promoting factors identified by endogenous growth theory can be imitated and nurtured to promote economic growth through FDI, provided the domestic economic climate and the nature of the trade policy regime support the development of human capital, implying increasing returns to scale and spillover effects, as identified by new growth theory. Thus, as previously suggested in the development literature (Edwards, 1993), trade liberalization is an important channel for promoting growth, more fundamentally because it increases the size of the market and allows the country to use greater varieties of technologically advanced physical capital, which enhances the productivity of its own domestic resources (Grossman & Helpman, 1991).

The above considerations suggest that an appropriate investigation of the causal relation between outward orientation and economic growth should account for the relative importance of both trade and FDI flows as factors influencing economic growth. In testing this hypothesis for Thailand, we focus more specifically on the comparison between FDI-led growth and trade-led growth, as well as the reverse linkages from growth to FDI and trade. Our methodological framework for investigating these links is multivariate causality testing within a vector error correction model in which relevant control variables (e.g. domestic investment, human capital, government expenditure, etc.) are allowed to exert their influence on growth apart from FDI and trade. This allows us to investigate not only the direct but also the indirect causal linkages through which the control factors themselves may influence the association between trade/FDI and Thai economic growth.

From a historical perspective, the Thai economy experienced a transition from a trade regime of import substitution (IS) in the 1960s and 1970s to export promotion (EP) from late 1970s onwards, although the surge in FDI inflows is more recent (see Figure 1). In part, this reflects a shift in its policy of FDI promotion from import-substitution to more export-orientated industries (Kohpaiboon, 2003). Investigating the FDI effect on GDP using annual data for Thailand over the period 1970-1999, Kohpaiboon (2006) finds that FDI has a significant effect under the EP regime compared to the earlier IS regime, thus finding support for a positive growth impact of FDI associated with trade liberalisation. He conducts time-series regressions by incorporating an interaction term FDI*OPEN in a regression of the aggregate production function for Thailand, where OPEN is represented by a measure of trade openness. However, recent studies using Granger causality analysis

Figure 1. Thailand's key economic indicators (millions of Baht)
Source: World Bank (2016)

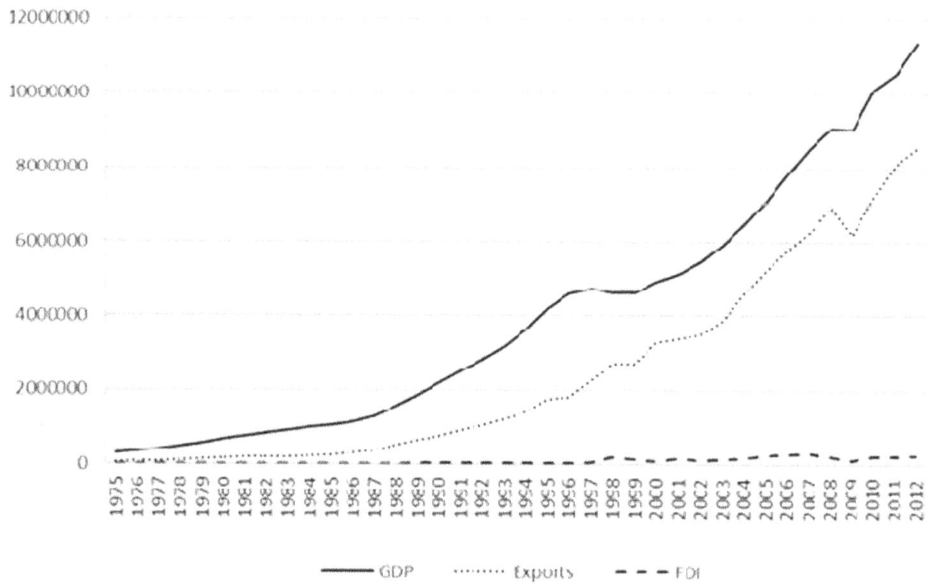

suggest somewhat mixed evidence for Thailand. For example, Chowdhury and Mavrotas (2006) employ the Toda and Yamamoto (1995) causality test for a set of developing countries and find evidence of bidirectional causality between GDP and FDI for Thailand and Malaysia using annual data for 1969-2000. In contrast, Herzer, Klasen and Nowak-Lehman (2008) conduct an investigation of the FDI-led growth hypothesis for 28 developing countries using cointegration-based causality testing on a country-by-country basis (mostly covering the period 1970-2003) and fail to find a positive unidirectional long-term effect from FDI to GDP for any of the countries, although they do find some evidence of short-run bivariate causality between FDI and GDP for Thailand.

The main contribution of this paper is to provide further and more recent evidence for Thailand by employing granger causality testing within a multivariate vector error correction (VECM) framework. In principle, we follow the methodological approach of Herzer et al (2008) but conduct causality testing using a higher order VECM model to account for the influence of both trade openness and FDI in GDP growth, conditional on a set of domestic economic factors. In addition, we use quarterly data for Thailand in contrast to the above studies which employed annual data. The evidence shows that trade openness (in particular import-led growth) has played a more significant role than FDI in Thai economic growth. However, our findings suggest a subtle role for technology transfer (or the transmission of causal links) through which openness via trade and FDI has influenced Thai growth through their effect on domestic economic factors. In this context we highlight the importance of causality testing within a multivariate framework, whereas most studies in the literature have employed bivariate causality tests.

The rest of this paper is set out as follows. Section 2 presents the methodological framework for testing granger causality within a multivariate framework. Section 3 presents the data and the empirical results. Section 4 concludes.

METHODOLOGY

Our methodological framework is based on a single equation model for unit root testing and a vector error correction model (VECM) for co-integration and causality testing, given the multitude of variables entertained. Although it is possible to test for causality among (nonstationary) time series data within the extended VAR framework proposed by Toda and Yamamoto (1995), this paper adopts the approach of using a vector error correction model as suggested by Toda and Phillips (1993). The latter entails that 'sufficient cointegration' exists among the relevant variables for causality inference to be asymptotically valid (Toda & Phillips, 1993; Caporale & Pittis, 1999). We attempt to address these issues by following the standard three-stage procedure: (i) unit root testing based on the Augmented Dickey-Fuller (ADF) test (Dickey & Fuller, 1981), (ii) testing for the number of cointegrating vectors using the Johansen reduced rank method (Johansen, 1992), and (iii) causality testing using the VECM model after determining the cointegration rank among the variables.

The existence of unit roots in a time series model is commonly tested using the Augmented Dickey-Fuller (ADF) test through a specification of the form:

$$\Delta y_t = \alpha + (\rho - 1) y_{t-1} + \sum_{i=1}^{p} \gamma_i \Delta y_{t-1} + \beta T + \varepsilon_t \qquad (1)$$

where $\Delta y_t = (y_t - y_{t-1})$ represents the first differences with p time lags, T being the time trend. The null hypothesis of unit root against the alternative of stationarity requires testing for $\rho = 0$. In the case where the inclusion of the time trend is not supported by the data, equation (1) is usually estimated with an intercept term.

To illustrate the procedure for cointegration and causality testing within a VECM framework, consider first the unrestricted VAR:

$$z_t = c + A_1 z_{t-1} + \ldots + A_k z_{t-k} + \varepsilon_t \qquad (2)$$

where z_t is (n × 1) vector and each of the A_i is an (n × n) matrix of parameters. A standard approach to testing for non-causality, assuming stationarity of the variables, is based on the partitioned VAR with $z_t^{'} = (y_t^{'}, x_t^{'})$, represented as

$$\begin{bmatrix} y_t \\ x_t \end{bmatrix} = \begin{bmatrix} c_1 \\ c_2 \end{bmatrix} + \begin{bmatrix} A_{11}^1 & A_{12}^1 \\ A_{21}^1 & A_{22}^1 \end{bmatrix} \begin{bmatrix} y_{t-1} \\ x_{t-1} \end{bmatrix} + \ldots + \begin{bmatrix} A_{11}^k & A_{12}^k \\ A_{21}^k & A_{22}^k \end{bmatrix} \begin{bmatrix} y_{t-k} \\ x_{t-k} \end{bmatrix} + \begin{bmatrix} \varepsilon_{1t} \\ \varepsilon_{2t} \end{bmatrix} \tag{3}$$

where y_t is (n_1 x 1) and x_t is (n_2 × 1) where $n_1 + n_2 = n$, and A_{ij}^h are the sub-matrices of parameters associated to the VAR, with superscripts denoting the order of the lags of the VAR, h = 1,…,k and c_1 and c_2 are the vectors of constants (with relevant time trend or dummies incorporated if necessary). In this representation, the absence of causality from y to x corresponds to jointly testing the null hypothesis $A_{21}^h = 0$ for h = 1,…k.

As argued by Granger (1988), standard Granger causality tests are invalid for non-stationary systems, although Toda and Yamamoto (1995) propose extending the lag length of the VAR by the maximal order of integration of the variables in the system and testing for causality as above. However, Toda and Phillips (1993) propose a testing procedure using the Johansen (1992) VECM-based method:

$$\Delta z_t = \Gamma_1 \Delta z_{t-1} + \ldots + \Gamma_{k-1} \Delta z_{t-k+1} + \Pi z_{t-k} + \varepsilon_t \tag{4}$$

where $\Gamma_i = -(I - A_i - \ldots - A_i), (i = 1, \ldots, k-1)$, and $\Pi = -(I - A_1 - \ldots - A_k)$. In this set-up, assuming that there are $r \leq (n-1)$ cointegrating vectors in the system, Π can be factorised as $\Pi = \alpha\beta'$, where β is a matrix of long run coefficients such that $\beta' z_t$-k represents the cointegrating vectors in the system. Thus, determining the number of cointegration vectors in the system amounts to checking the rank of Π (i.e. finding the number of r linearly independent columns in Π). Johansen (1992) proposes the use of likelihood ratio (LR) tests based on the trace and the maximum eigenvalue statistics for determining the reduced rank of Π.

For illustration of the procedures for testing causality in the Johansen based cointegrated framework, assume the VECM is partitioned as:

$$\begin{bmatrix} \Delta y_t \\ \Delta x_t \end{bmatrix} = \sum_{h=1}^{k} \begin{bmatrix} \varphi_{11}^h & \varphi_{12}^h \\ \varphi_{21}^h & \varphi_{22}^h \end{bmatrix} \begin{bmatrix} \Delta y_{t-h} \\ \Delta x_{t-h} \end{bmatrix} + \begin{bmatrix} \alpha_1 \\ \alpha_2 \end{bmatrix} \left(\beta_1^{'} y_{t-1} + \beta_2^{'} x_{t-1} \right) + \varepsilon_t \tag{5}$$

In this set-up, if $\alpha_2 = 0$ then the sub-system for Δxt contains no information about the long run and it is therefore valid to condition y_t on the 'weakly exogenous' x_t. If the null hypothesis $\alpha_2 = 0$ is accepted, then non-causality from y to x requires further joint testing of $\varphi_{21}^h = 0$ for h = 1,…,k. This amounts to a sequential procedure for testing non-causality, conditional on the acceptance of weak exogeneity (or the insignificance of the error correction term), using an asymptotic χ^2 test. This is a sufficient (but not necessary) condition for non-causality in VECM model (Toda & Phillips, 1993). On the other hand, if weak exogeneity is rejected, then an alternative procedure is to test $\varphi_{21}^h = 0$ for h = 1,…,k, conditional on acceptance of $\beta_1 = 0$. This amounts to the absence of long-run (or weak) causality, as suggested by Hall and Wickens (1993) and Hall and Milne (1994).

In general, an appropriate testing procedure for non-causality in the context of Johansen's (1992) VECM model requires determining the cointegration rank first, and establishing whether at least one of the relevant submatrices of α and β are of full rank. Then, if the rank restriction is valid, one can proceed to testing for the null hypothesis of non-causality by means of a Wald statistic, allowing valid inference based on an asymptotic χ^2 distribution (Caporale & Pittis, 1999). In contrast, Mosconni and Giannini (1992) propose the simultaneous testing of joint restrictions of non-causality using a likelihood ratio test, which avoids the inherent bias involved in the sequential two-step testing procedure. However, as argued by Caporale and Pittis (1999), this procedure is computationally burdensome, and we follow the sequential approach by first checking for cointegration and then conducting the testing procedure subject to the acceptance of weak exogeneity, as followed by Herzer et al (2008). This is equivalent to the two-step procedure for causality testing in the VECM model as suggested by Hall and Wickens (1993) and Hall and Milne (1994).

DATA AND EMPIRICAL RESULTS

Data

The empirical results reported in this section are based on quarterly data for Thailand collected for the following variables: GDP per capita (GDPPC), domestic investment (I), human capital (H), government expenditure (GX), exports (EX), imports (IM), and foreign direct investment (FDI). Additionally, we construct a measure of trade openness (OPEN = (EX+IM)/GDP) as a substitute for exports and imports. The data set covers the period 1973:2-2012:4. All data except human capital are extracted from International Financial Statistics published by the IMF, and expressed in real terms at 1995 Bhat prices. For human capital, we have used the index of educational attainment for Thailand taken from Barro and Lee (1993, 2013), extended and converted into quarterly by linear interpolation. This measures the average number of schooling years attended by population, both male and female, aged 25+. All variables are transformed into logs for empirical analysis and the component variables (I, GX, EX, IM and FDI) are entered as a proportion of GDP, in order to mitigate the degree of seasonal fluctuations associated with quarterly data.

Unit Root Tests

In order to test for non-stationarity of the time series, the order of integration of each variable is investigated using the ADF test. The selection of optimal lag is chosen by downward search from a pre-chosen lag length based on the Akaike criterion. Table 1 reports the results of ADF test on both level and first difference of the series, where we have chosen to include the trend in the former case as it was found to be mostly significant. The results show that the null hypothesis of unit root cannot be rejected for any of the level variables. However, when the logarithms of the time series are transformed into first differences, they satisfy the condition for stationary ($\rho = 0$) and consequently all variables are determined as integrated of order one, I(1). Moreover, all the variables in first differences showed no evidence of serial correlation or heteroskedasticity in the error term.

Table 1. ADF tests for unit root

Variables	Level (with trend)	1st Difference (without trend)
lnGDPPC	-1.98 (4)	-3.46* (3)
lnH	-2.23(4)	-3.18** (3)
ln(GX/GDP)	-2.06(4)	-3.68** (4)
ln(FDI/GDP)	-3.13 (0)	-6.67** (3)
ln(I/GDP)	-0.34(4)	-2.27* (4)
ln(EX/GDP)	-4.51(4)	-4.95** (4)
ln(IM/GDP)	-2.94(4)	-3.80** (3)
lnOPEN	-2.94(4)	-3.80** (3)

Notes: All variables are expressed in natural logarithms (denoted by prefix ln). Null hypothesis is that each time series has a unit root. ** and * denote significance at the 1% and 5% levels, respectively, based on MacKinnon (1991) critical values. Figures in parentheses show the minimum lag order used based on the AIC criterion (with maximum lag 4).

Cointegration Tests

Since all series are I(1), the Johansen procedure is used to establish the order of cointegration among the variables before causality testing using the VECM model. We consider three alternative specifications to encompass different measures of trade openness and FDI, along with GDP per capita and the conditioning variables: I, H, GX. The first specification includes imports and exports as separate components and excludes FDI in order to focus solely on the influence of trade. The second specification excludes imports but includes exports (EX) and FDI in order to explore causality issues in the triangular FDI-exports-GDP nexus as examined in other studies (Hsiao & Hsiao, 2006). Finally, the third specification includes FDI and OPEN as a measure of trade (thus reflecting the influence of both exports and imports) in order to account for the role of both trade and FDI in causality tests. In each case, the lag length in VAR/VECM model is set to a maximum of 4 by the AIC criterion, which turns out to be optimal given a sufficiently long time series. In the estimation process, we also included a time trend where significant and experimented further by including a dummy variable in addition to the constant term to take account of the effects of the 1997 East Asian and 2007-08 global financial crises, although these did not make any difference to the cointegration results.

Table 2 summarises the results of the Johansen cointegration tests. Both the trace and the maximum eigenvalue tests indicate that the corresponding variables are cointegrated. Although the number of cointegrating vectors differs according to the test statistics, the inclusion of imports in the VAR specification clearly increases the cointegration rank. The final column of Table 2 states the number of cointegrating vectors chosen for causality testing in the VECM model, based on the outcome of both tests which represents the best compromise given the slightly differing outcomes of the two test results.

Table 2. Johansen cointegration tests

VAR Specification (Lag Length=4)	**No. of cointegrating vectors significant at 5% level (1% level)**		
VAR Model	**Trace**	λ_{Max}	**Used in VECM**
1: lnGDPPC, lnH, ln(I/GDP), ln(GX/GDP), ln(IM/GDP), ln(EX/GDP)	3(3)	3(0)	3
2: lnGDPPC, lnH, ln(I/GDP), ln(GX/GDP), ln(EX/GDP), ln(FDI/GDP)	2(1)	0(0)	1
3: lnGDPPC, lnH, ln(I/GDP), ln(GX/GDP), ln(OPEN), ln(FDI/GDP)	2(1)	1(1)	1

Notes: All variables are expressed in natural logarithms (denoted by prefix ln). Null hypothesis is that there is no cointegration among the set of variables in the VAR model.

Bivariate Granger Causality Tests

To establish causal links between pairs of variables prior to the multivariate causality analysis based on the VECM model, we present in Table 3 the results of Wald Tests for varying bivariate VAR lag lengths (i.e. 2,3,4 and 5). Before testing for bivariate causality, we checked for the absence of cointegration between pairs of variables considered. Hence the bivariate VAR is specified in first differenced form, which effectively tests for short-run causality. With log-differences, the causality evidence in this context may be interpreted as occurring between the growth rates of variables. The results indicate bi-directional causality between per capita GDP growth and investment growth, which is significant across all lag lengths. There is also evidence of causality from GDP growth to export and import growth (and also trade openness), and some evidence of short-run causal link in the opposite direction, although not significant at all lag lengths. Most notable is the absence of any causal links between growth of FDI and GDP growth.

Weak Exogeneity Tests

Table 4 reports the outcome of weak exogeneity tests, conducted using a multivariate VECM model, for the specifications listed in Table 4. As noted earlier, the absence of long-run causality implies that the behaviour of the dependent variable in question is not affected by co-movement of other variables in the VECM model, as reflected in the error correction term. Failure to reject long-run causality implies, in turn, that there is evidence of bi-directional causality between the cointegrating variables.

As shown in Table 4, the null hypothesis of long-run non-causality (implied by weak exogeneity of the conditioning variables) cannot be rejected for most of the variables. The only variable for which the null is rejected (at 1% significance level) is government expenditure (GX) in models 2 and 3. Additionally, non-causality is also rejected for OPEN in model 3, albeit at the 5% level. Overall, based on these results, it would be appropriate to base further inferences about non-causality based on the VECM model.

Multivariate Granger Causality Tests

The results of Wald tests, reported in Table 5, are for the null hypothesis that all lagged coefficients of the relevant conditioning variable in the VECM model are jointly zero. These comprise the second set of restrictions implied by Granger non-causality. They are conducted and presented pairwise, so that for each dependent variable the reported values in Table 5 are the Chi-square statistics of the relevant causality test for each causal variable taken in succession. Thus, the values down the

Table 3. Granger causality tests based on Bivariate VAR

VAR Lag Length	2	3	4	5	Summary
Dependent variable: Δ (lnGDPPC)					
Causal variable	X^2	X^2	X^2	X^2	
Δ (lnI/GDP)	21.16***	63.64***	27.73***	24.84***	
Dependent variable: Δ (lnI/GDP)					Bi-directional causality
Causal variable	X^2	X^2	X^2	X^2	ΔlnGDPPC ⇔ ΔlnI
Δ (lnGDPPC)	46.12***	49.67***	23.44***	14.40***	
Dependent variable: Δ (lnGDPPC)					
Causal variable	X^2	X^2	X^2	X^2	
Δ (lnEX/GDP)	3.44	3.22	7.20*	11.87*	ΔlnEX ⇒ ΔlnGDPPC
Dependent variable: Δ (lnEX/GDP)					At lag length 4 and 5
Causal variable	X^2	X^2	X^2	X^2	
Δ (lnGDPPC)	3.53	4.29	2.11	2.30	No causal link
Dependent variable: Δ (lnGDPPC)					
Causal variable	X^2	X^2	X^2	X^2	
Δ (lnIM/GDP)	0.88	8.57**	4.95	6.52	ΔlnEX ⇒ ΔlnGDPPC
Dependent variable: Δ (lnIM/GDP)					At lag length 3 only
Causal variable	X^2	X^2	X^2	X^2	
Δ (lnGDPPC)	0.89	11.94***	4.79	3.90	ΔlnGDPPC ⇔ ΔlnIM
					At lag length 3 only
Dependent variable: Δ (lnGDPPC)					
Causal variable	X^2	X^2	X^2	X^2	ΔlnGDPPC ⇔ ΔlnOPEN
Δ (lnOPEN/GDP)	0.89	8.57**	4.95	6.51	At lag length 3 only
Dependent variable: Δ (lnOPEN/GDP)					
Causal variable	X^2	X^2	X^2	X^2	
Δ (lnGDPPC)	16.19***	11.94***	4.79	3.90	ΔlnGDPPC ⇒ ΔlnOPEN
					At lag length 2 and 3
Dependent variable: Δ (lnGDPPC)					
Causal variable	X^2	X^2	X^2	X^2	
Δ (lnFDI/GDP)	1.21	1.58	2.17	3.38	No causal link
Dependent variable: Δ (lnFDI/GDP)					
Causal variable	X^2	X^2	X^2	X^2	
Δ (lnGDPPC)	0.50	0.42	2.47	2.90	No causal link

Note: All variables are expressed in natural logarithms (denoted by prefix ln). Δ denotes log-difference between present and previous quarter value. *, ** and *** denote significance at the 10%, 5% and 1% levels, respectively.

Table 4. Weak exogeneity tests (H0: the appropriate row of matrix α is zero)

VECM Model 1			
Lag length (4)	**LR Test**	**p-value**	
lnGDPPC	0.83	0.36	A
lnH	0.78	0.38	A
ln(I/GDP)	0.16	0.69	A
ln(GX/GDP)	2.29	0.13	A
ln(IM/GDP)	2.03	0.15	A
ln(EX/GDP)	0.31	0.58	A
VECM Model 2			
Lag length (4)	**LR Test**	**p-value**	
lnGDPPC	0.08	0.78	A
lnH	0.03	0.87	A
ln(I/GDP)	0.71	0.40	A
ln(GX/GDP)	8.22	0.00	R
ln(EX/GDP)	2.32	0.13	A
ln(FDI/GDP)	0.00	0.98	A
VECM Model 3			
Lag length (4)	**LR Test**	**p-value**	
lnGDPPC	0.17	0.68	A
lnH	0.17	0.68	A
ln(I/GDP)	0.65	0.42	A
ln(GX/GDP)	19.24	0.00	R
lnOPEN	4.55	0.03	R
ln(FDI/GDP)	1.30	0.25	A

Note: R denotes rejection, A denotes acceptance, of the null H_0.

columns, as presented in Table 5, are the results of all Wald tests for specified VECM model, while the corresponding values along the rows are the results of the causality test for each causal variable conducted across all three model specifications. This way of presenting the test results makes comparisons across the three models easier.

Evidence of bi-directional causality between investment growth and per capita GDP growth, shown in Table 3, is confirmed in the multivariate case too, as the causality tests reveal significant Chi-square statistics in Table 5. Of particular interest are the results of the causality tests on GDP growth, which reveal that investment (I) and exports (EX) are the main causal factors influencing GDP growth. Furthermore, the results reveal that imports (IM) do not affect GDP growth directly, and therefore

Table 5. Multivariate Granger causality tests

Dependent variable: ΔlnGDPPC			
VAR lag length = 4			
Model	**1**	**2**	**3**
ΔlnH	3.02	1.50	1.21
ΔlnI/GDP	19.30***	16.54***	22.86***
ΔlnGX/GDP	3.59	3.74	3.73
ΔlnIM/GDP	1.79		
ΔlnEX/GDP	6.74	8.62*	
ΔlnOPEN			7.14
ΔlnFDI/GDP		0.70	1.69
Dependent variable: ΔlnH			
VAR lag length = 4			
Model	**1**	**2**	**3**
ΔlnGDPPC	4.80	1.69	5.05
ΔlnI/GDP	12.66***	3.30	8.36*
ΔlnGX/GDP	13.87***	14.55***	11.23**
ΔlnIM/GDP	6.91		
ΔlnEX/GDP	1.13	2.01	
ΔlnOPEN			7.33
ΔlnFDI/GDP		10.22**	12.23**
Dependent variable: ΔlnI/GDP			
VAR lag length = 4			
Model	**1**	**2**	**3**
ΔlnGDPPC	8.28*	4.62	5.20
ΔlnH	10.10**	7.31	11.01**
ΔlnGX/GDP	1.09	1.53	0.97
ΔlnIM/GDP	13.86***		
ΔlnEX/GDP	5.80	5.14	
ΔlnOPEN			10.12**
ΔlnFDI/GDP		3.14	`1.62
Dependent variable: ΔlnGX/GDP			
VAR lag length = 4			
Model	**1**	**2**	**3**
ΔlnGDPPC	12.79***	14.98***	20.65***
ΔlnH	3.44	5.52	5.05

continued on following page

Table 5. Continued

ΔlnI/GDP	0.94	8.94*	2.06
ΔlnIM/GDP	7.35		
ΔlnEX/GDP	8.99*	6.58	
ΔlnOPEN			11.14**
ΔlnFDI/GDP		4.08	9.06*
Dependent variable ΔlnIM/GDP			
VAR lag length = 4			
Model	**1**	**2**	**3**
ΔlnGDPPC	5.71		
ΔlnH	12.74***		
ΔlnI/GDP	22.79***		
ΔlnGX/GDP	4.14		
ΔlnEX/GDP	4.37		
ΔlnOPEN			
ΔlnFDI/GDP			
Dependent variable ΔlnEX/GDP			
VAR lag length = 4			
Model	**1**	**2**	**3**
ΔlnGDPPC		2.68	7.66*
ΔlnH		1.80	7.47
ΔlnI/GDP		7.07	6.08
ΔlnGX/GDP		5.43	10.60**
ΔlnIM/GDP		3.06	
ΔlnOPEN			
ΔlnFDI/GDP			8.05*
Dependent variable ΔlnOPEN			
VAR lag length = 4			
Model	**1**	**2**	**3**
ΔlnGDPPC			6.11
ΔlnH			15.53***
ΔlnI/GDP			23.79***
ΔlnGX/GDP			
ΔlnIM/GDP			
ΔlnEX/GDP			
ΔlnFDI/GDP			6.44

continued on following page

Table 5. Continued

Dependent variable ΔlnFDI/GDP			
VAR lag length = 4			
Model	**1**	**2**	**3**
ΔlnGDPPC		0.74	0.38
ΔlnH		3.60	2.68
ΔlnI/GDP		10.26**	8.61*
ΔlnGX/GDP		7.53	1.81
ΔlnIM/GDP			
ΔlnEX/GDP		14.84***	
ΔlnOPEN			1.97

Note: All variables are expressed in natural logarithms (ln) and Δ denotes log-difference. *, ** and *** denote significance at the 10%, 5% and 1% levels, respectively.

the significance of trade openness (OPEN) on growth comes mainly through exports. This may lend credence to the export-led growth hypothesis for Thailand, although the causality tests for investment growth reveal that imports might have an indirect effect on growth through its impact on domestic investment. The same goes for human capital, which does not directly affect growth but may be having an indirect effect given evidence of its bi-directional causality with domestic investment. Most noteworthy is the lack of any significant effect of causality from FDI to GDP growth, directly or indirectly (via domestic investment). Whatever impact FDI has on GDP growth appears to be indirect through its impact on human capital and government consumption.

Direct support for growth led-FDI hypothesis is also weak, although an indirect effect from GDP growth to FDI may be coming through the causal links from investment and exports to FDI. However, there is significant impact of GDP growth and FDI on government expenditure, a finding possibly explained by Thailand's investment in public infrastructure (including education) fuelled by the availability of foreign capital and joint ventures with foreign multinationals. But there is little evidence to suggest that this has affected economic growth directly, although the causality tests show that government expenditure has significantly influenced the development of human capital in Thailand.

One possible explanation for the lack of causal FDI effect on GDP growth is that there is hardly any upsurge in FDI inflows to Thailand for the effect to be significant over the period of investigation (see Figure 1). By contrast, exports have seen steady growth since the 1990s. Thus, in the case of Thailand, which has pursued a deliberate policy of the export promotion (EP) since 1972 and FDI promotion since 1997, it is perhaps not surprising to find that evidence for export-led growth is strong while that for FDI-led growth is relatively weak.

CONCLUSION

This paper has investigated the relative importance of trade and FDI led economic growth for Thailand, using multivariate Granger causality tests conducted within a VECM framework. The main contribution of the paper has been identified the causal links between exports, imports, FDI and GDP growth, ensuring that causality inferences drawn for the empirical analysis were robust with respect to changes in the VAR/VECM specifications. In the process, the importance of human capital is highlighted as complementary to trade and FDI inflows, underlying the importance of technology adoption. We find that, after controlling for domestic investment and government expenditure, support for FDI-led growth is not as strong as trade-led growth.

Taken together, the results reveal that economic growth in Thailand has been driven largely by domestic investment, as would be expected, but also that domestic investment has been fuelled by higher economic growth. Controlling for domestic investment growth as well as other factors, causality tests also show support for the export-led growth hypothesis, but not for FDI-led growth in Thailand. Support for this is also revealed in bivariate granger causality tests, although in a multivariate context it has been possible to identify other possible channels through which imports and FDI may have influenced economic growth. For example, multivariate causality test results have shown that imports have not contributed to GDP growth directly, although its effect has been indirect through domestic investment. Similarly, the causal effect FDI on GDP growth is also indirect through its impact on human capital and government consumption.

REFERENCES

Balasubramanyam, V. N., Salisu, M., & Sapsford, D. (1996). Foreign direct investment and growth in EP and IS countries. *Economic Journal (London)*, *106*(434), 92–105. doi:10.2307/2234933

Barro, R. J., & Lee, J. W. (1993). International comparisons of educational attainment. *Journal of Monetary Economics*, *32*(3), 363–394. doi:10.1016/0304-3932(93)90023-9

Barro, R. J., & Lee, J. W. (2013). A new data set of educational attainment in the world, 1950–2010. *Journal of Development Economics*, *104*, 184–198. doi:10.1016/j.jdeveco.2012.10.001

Borensztein, E., De Gregorio, J., & Lee, J. W. (1998). How does foreign direct investment affect growth? *Journal of International Economics*, *45*(1), 115–135. doi:10.1016/S0022-1996(97)00033-0

Caporale, G. M., & Pittis, N. (1999). Efficient estimation of cointegration vectors and testing for causality in vector autoregressions. *Journal of Economic Surveys*, *13*(1), 1–35. doi:10.1111/1467-6419.00073

Chowdhury, A., & Mavrotas, G. (2006). FDI and growth: What causes what? *World Economy*, *29*(1), 9–19. doi:10.1111/j.1467-9701.2006.00755.x

Dickey, D. A., & Fuller, W. A. (1981). Likelihood ratio statistics for autoregressive time series with a unit root. *Econometrica*, *49*(4), 1057–1072. doi:10.2307/1912517

Edwards, S. (1993). Openness, trade liberalisation and growth in developing countries. *Journal of Economic Literature*, *31*(3), 1358–1393.

Frankel, J., & Romer, D. (1999). Does trade cause growth? *The American Economic Review*, *89*(3), 379–399. doi:10.1257/aer.89.3.379

Granger, C. W. J. (1988). Some recent developments in the concept of causality. *Journal of Econometrics*, *39*(1-2), 199–211. doi:10.1016/0304-4076(88)90045-0

Grossman, J., & Helpman, E. (1991). *Innovation and Growth in the Global Economy*. Cambridge, MA: MIT Press.

Hall, S. G., & Milne, A. (1994). The relevance of P-star analysis to UK monetary policy. *Economic Journal (London)*, *104*(424), 597–604. doi:10.2307/2234634

Hall, S. G., & Wickens, M. R. (1993). *Causality in integrated systems.* Centre for Economic Forecasting Discussion Paper No. 7-93, London Business School.

Herzer, D., Klasen, S., & Nowak-Lehmann, D. F. (2008). In search of FDI-led growth in developing countries: The way forward. *Economic Modelling*, *25*(5), 793–810. doi:10.1016/j.econmod.2007.11.005

Hsiao, F. T., & Hsiao, M. W. (2006). FDI, exports, and GDP in East and Southeast Asia: Panel data versus time-series causality analyses. *Journal of Asian Economics*, *17*(6), 1082–1106. doi:10.1016/j.asieco.2006.09.011

Johansen, S. (1991). Estimation and hypothesis testing of cointegration vectors in Gaussian vector autoregressive model. *Econometrica*, *59*(6), 1551–1580. doi:10.2307/2938278

Kophaiboon, A. (2003). Foreign trade regimes and the FDI-Growth nexus: A case study of Thailand. *The Journal of Development Studies*, *40*(2), 55–69. doi:10.1080/00220380412331293767

Kophaiboon, A. (2006). Foreign direct investment and technology spillover: A cross-industry analysis of Thai manufacturing. *World Development*, *34*(3), 541–556. doi:10.1016/j.worlddev.2005.08.006

Markusen, J. (1995). The boundaries of multinational enterprises and the theory of international trade. *The Journal of Economic Perspectives*, *9*(2), 169–189. doi:10.1257/jep.9.2.169

Mosconi, R., & Giannini, C. (1992). Noncausality in cointegrated systems: Representation, estimation and testing. *Oxford Bulletin of Economics and Statistics*, *54*(3), 399–417. doi:10.1111/j.1468-0084.1992.tb00009.x

Nelson, R., & Phelps, E. (1966). Investment in humans, technological diffusion and economic growth. *The American Economic Review*, *51*, 69–75.

Rodriguez, F., & Rodrik, D. (2000). Trade policy and economic growth: A sceptic's guide to the cross-country evidence. In B. Bernanke & K. Rogoff (Eds.), *NBER Macroeconomics Annual 2000, 15*. Cambridge, MA: MIT Press.

Rodriguez-Clare, A. (1996). Multinationals, linkages and economic development. *The American Economic Review*, *86*(4), 852–873.

Toda, H. Y., & Phillips, P. C. B. (1993). Vector autoregressions and causality. *Econometrica*, *61*(6), 1367–1393. doi:10.2307/2951647

Toda, H. Y., & Yamamoto, T. (1995). Statistical inference in vector autoregressions with possibly integrated processes. *Journal of Econometrics*, *66*(1-2), 225–250. doi:10.1016/0304-4076(94)01616-8

Zhang, K. H., & Markusen, J. R. (1999). Vertical multinational and host country characteristics. *Journal of Development Economics*, *59*(2), 233–252. doi:10.1016/S0304-3878(99)00011-5

Chapter 7
FDI Inflows and Current Account Evidence From BIMSTEC

Nida Rahman
Aligarh Muslim University, India

Shehroz Alam Rizvi
Aligarh Muslim University, India

ABSTRACT

The liberalisation drive that swept across the globe post-1990s gave way to FDI in emerging as a catalyst of economic development for a majority of economic groups and nations. With the objective of realising economic development by transiting from debt flows to FDI flows, several economies tied up in regional groups in the Asian region to foster trade and investment sectors and other areas as well. In this regard, the BIMSTEC group came forth in 1997 as an initiative on the part of selected South Asian and South East Asian countries to collaborate and work together for the economic wellbeing of the member countries. The current account balance of the member nations and its nexus with inward FDI needs to be counted while forging over economic soundness of the participating nations. In this respect, the chapter attempts to search for evidences of causality among FDI inflows and current account balance across member countries of BIMSTEC group. The chapter utilises annual data for the member countries for a time frame ranging 1991-2014 from UNCTAD STATISTICS Database.

DOI: 10.4018/978-1-5225-3026-8.ch007

INTRODUCTION

Foreign Direct Investment, since times immemorial has been counted upon as an instant means to accentuate economic growth by nations. However, it was after some crises in the financial scenario of world economy as a whole and individual nations in specific that Foreign Direct Investment Inflows appeared as a counteractive force to economies in regard to debugging the inappropriate repercussions of financial crises on the economic position of nations. Globalisation has added much to imparting Foreign Direct Investment Inflows this prominent status of acting as an agent of growth and economic fortune though the aftereffects showed a variation as per the nature of economies that became home to these flows. It was majorly the period post liberalisation that witnessed a boom in Foreign Direct Investment flows. In 1997, Direct Foreign Investment accounted for about half of all private capital (Aitken & Harrison, 1999). The underlying reason for this upturn was the extensive liberal reforms and incentives adopted by countries in order to let loose their economy in hands of foreign players to invest. For many South Asian countries, the liberalisation process arrived sooner than other economies of the region. For instance, Sri Lanka liberalised its economic reforms way back in 1977 when many other developing countries were strongly enclosed in narrow minded and conservative reforms.

With growing need to integrate to a wider extent into the world economy, countries chiefly the developing ones engaged in liberalising FDI regimes to an ever-increasing degree. However, little was thought about its spill over effects on the macro-economic indicators. Foreign Direct Investment is not always about good fortune and miracles when it comes to macro-economic condition of the host nations. Being a mixed blessing, Foreign Direct Investment flows many a times debilitate the economy hosting these by splashing out even the good prospects the economy is endowed with. One such problem is that of Current Account Deficits that appears to be a critical issue in the present-day world order especially in context of Developing countries. Developing countries normally ran current account deficit problems and the surge in international capital flows to developing countries have coincided with widening current account deficits in many of these countries (Calvo et al., 1996). In 1997, the FDI figures counted for 40 per cent of total capital flows to developing countries (Aitken & Harrison, 1999). With huge figures of Foreign Direct Investment Inflows pooling in host economies especially the developing world economies, the negating effects are acknowledged to be widening as against the positive effects. Foreign Direct Investment, being a component of Capital Account of the Balance of Payments has an effect on overall Balance of Payments as also specifically on Current Account of the BOP.

Asian Continent, well acknowledged as a hub of trade activities and foreign exchange in todays full-fledged globalized world has an endless listicle of economies under its umbrella that have acclimatized way too well with the globalisation drive and has stepped ahead in luring investors to pour in funds in their economies. This attitude of Asian economies is apparent in the liberal trade and investment policies forged ahead by them. Not only individual economies, but in the backdrop of Asian financial crisis of 90s a multitude of regional groups emerged coalescing in order to achieve collective goals. Many such regional groups and sub- regional groups have appeared as an avenue to ameliorate economic cooperation and work as a single entity to enrich the member nations by mutually assisting in meeting objectives. In line with this object of Asian economies to do away with policies that are suspicious of leading them to yet another market and financial failure such as that of the financial crisis of 1997, economies have started tying up with other nations in the continent to mutually succeed in trade and foreign investment activities. Expansion of foreign trade, direct investment and financial flows has created a naturally integrated economic zone in East Asia (Kawai, 2005).

One such attempt is the Bay of Bengal Initiative for Multi sectoral Technical and Economic Cooperation (BIMSTEC) brought into reality in the year 1997 with a coalition of four-member nation's viz. Bangladesh, India, Sri Lanka and Thailand. Later, Myanmar and Bhutan also joined the regional bloc in 2004. BIMSTEC, an assemblage of seven south Asian and South East Asian countries has an aim to integrate its member nations on not only economic fronts and activities but also on cultural and natural endowment activities. Each of the member nations has got a discretion over its policy regarding capital transfers and also overall economic policies. With a variation in policies governing economic activities across member nations, the Foreign Investment trend is also vivid and distinct. India and Thailand stand a prominent place in extracting huge amounts of capital inflows from developed nations. However, other member nations like Bhutan have joined in the process of capital transfers lately in comparison to countries like India, Bangladesh, and Thailand etc. For many member nations, Foreign Direct Investment Inflows has had either a salutary effect on Current Account Deficits or an un-advantageous one. The upturn felt in Foreign Investment activities in the region has a lot to owe to the market and investment credentials and low-cost labour advantages offered to foreign investors and another thing that attracts investors' attention is the vast natural endowment reserves owned by the south Asian and south east Asian nations. Several countries consider inviting and attracting FDI Inflows as a directional strategy towards achieving economic development (Rahman, 2016). What is of paramount importance, apart from attracting more FDI, is having a check on the impact it has on the Balance of Payments position (Rahman, 2015).

As a result of the ongoing transition in the BIMSTEC region regarding the growth in Foreign Investment activities, it is necessary to gauge how beneficial this transition is for the Balance of Payments. Current Account, being an indispensable constituent of BOP in portraying the economic condition of the country needs to be considered for assessing its relationship with FDI Inflows.

CONCEPTUAL FRAMEWORK

OECD in 2008 and IMF in 2009 defines Foreign direct investment (FDI) as an investment involving a long-term relationship and reflecting a lasting interest and control by a resident entity in one economy (foreign direct investor or parent enterprise) in an enterprise resident in an economy other than that of the foreign direct investor (FDI enterprise or affiliate enterprise or foreign affiliate). This lasting interest of foreign direct investor in the affairs of foreign nations entity means that the foreign direct investor have an effective stand in the management affairs of the entity in which the investment is pooled. Foreign Direct Investment is generally a form of long term international capital movement, made for the purpose of productive activity and accompanied by the intention of managerial control or participation in the management of a foreign firm (Bhasin, 2012). This kind of capital movement entails that the investor sustains the investment poured in the host country. The foreign investor can be both an individual or an entity and the investments injected in the host nation can take the form of one of the three cases; establishing an equity underpinning in a pre-established foreign entity, forming a subsidiary, or establishing a joint venture entity in the host nation.

Current Account is a key component of Balance of Payments Account of a nation; the other two necessitous elements being the Capital Account and the Financial Account. Current Account is a statement that records a country's earnings and payments through transactions relating to trade in goods and services with the rest of the world. This trade in goods and services explains the base of two elements of Current Account i.e. the Merchandise trade activities and the invisible trade activities. Thus, Current Account is that constituent of International payments account which deals in transactions pertaining to sale and purchase of goods and services with the foreign countries of the world. The Current Account pertains to goods and services, incomes and current transfers (BOP Manual). Also, Current Account displays a clear picture of the financial health of a nation by keeping a record of the extent to which a particular transaction accentuates the foreign exchange resources or reduces the reserves.

REVIEW OF LITERATURE

Foreign Direct Investment has always been a topic of great relevance and an extensive literature exist of its preponderance in the developing world. Furthermore, a lot has been investigated and enquired on its supremacy over other capital flows by its nature of not adding up to debt. FDI is assumed to accrue more benefits than other types of financial flows (Rahman & Bristy, 2015). Though substantial literature has addressed the issue of enormous flow in of Foreign Direct Investment into the developing economies, it still lags behind in capturing the causal connection among Foreign Direct Investment Inflows and macro-economic pointers of the economies across regional groups.

There are evidences of mixed effects of FDI on host nations. FDI brings benefits and costs to both home and host countries (Accolley, 2003). There is little reason to expect that the effects of inward investment should be the same for all host countries (Lipsey, 2006). Economies accommodated with sound financial as well as legal environments tend to attract much FDI and benefit more from it as against economies that reflect a poor political climate. On the other hand, Bacchetta and Wincoop (2000) are of the opinion that in the absence of a sound financial system, developing economies may experience a tide in improficient domestic investment and thus can eventually deteriorate the Current Account position of these economies. In varied cases, the existence of an adequate level of human capital, technological strides and educational attainment were seen as prerequisites for creating a positive spill over of FDI on Economic Growth. A strata of developing countries well equipped in certain parameters such as human capital, income, parallel market premium for foreign exchange and government consumption were found to be positively related with Foreign Direct Investment Inflows (Borensztein et al., 1998). Also, a view is that Foreign Direct Investment adds more to the host economy than domestic investment does. FDI aids in boosting up domestic investment provided the FDI flow brood over sectors where domestic competition does not prevail (Agosin & Mayer, 2000). Asian economies tend to have a soothing effect of FDI on domestic investment (Agosin & Mayer, 2000). Jones, 1996 held the view that an inflow of Foreign Direct Investment builds up domestic saving of the recipient nation. However, FDI has an antagonistic effect on local firms as the foreign firms well adorned with technological expertise and higher competitiveness impedes the growth prospects of local firms (Jones, 1996). In terms of Causality, there are evidences of a bi-directional causality among FDI and economic growth for Pakistan economy (Iqbal et al., 2010). On the Contrary, Wang in 2010 concluded Foreign Direct Investment to be debilitating domestic investment of developing countries while influencing domestic investment of less developed countries affirmatively. The positive effects of FDI on economic growth felt in the short run dilapidates in the long run as a consequence of repatriation activity. (Jurcic et al., 2011). For SAARC countries, the effect of FDI Inflow on GDP is found to be positive and overwhelming. A strong and positive correlation among Foreign Direct Investment and GDP is carved out for countries like Bangladesh, Maldives, Nepal, India, Sri Lanka whereas a contrary effect is found on GDP of Bhutan and Pakistan (Rahman & Bristy, 2015). Foreign Direct Investment has positive effect on economic growth on all South East Asian countries except Sri Lanka (Javed et al., 2012). Foreign Direct Investment, having a pivotal role in augmenting or corroding domestic investment of the recipient economies can have a chain effect on the international accounts of these economies.

A gob of literature works have dealt in enquiring the repercussions of FDI Inflows on the Balance of Payments of recipient nations in general and also on the components of Balance of Payments in specific. FDI may cause current account balances at the hand of a fallout on imports, exports, activities of MNCs regarding profit repatriation and transfers to parent company (World Bank, 2009). Some studies are of the view that FDI acts as a pivot in financing the Balance of payments disequilibria of developing countries while some state otherwise. An inflow of FDI with 0.76 br. proves advantageous in financing Current Account Imbalances (Zafir et al. 2012). According to Sen (1995), Foreign Direct Investment should not be considered as a financing tool for the Balance of Payments imbalances. FDI, by impacting the import and exports of Thailand positively enriches the Balance of Payments Account in whole and its components in particular (Hossain, 2008). However, Foreign Direct Investment taking the form of selling down of Assets splashes out the positive externality of FDI flows in the long run and thus paralysing the Current Account position of economies in the NMS of EU (Mencinger, 2008). The long run effects of FDI Inflow may deviate from what is derived in the short run. With enormous forces into play that alters the after effects of FDI, the causal association among FDI and Current Account may vary across host economies. According to Yan (2007), capital mobility in emerging economies leads to devastation in Current Accout Balances. Surfacing this issue, studies have concluded a bi-directional causality among FDI and Current Account (Forogue & Veloce, 1990; Kim & Kim, 2010; Mastroyiannis, 2012; Saglam & Yalta, 2015). Also, a bi-directional causality was devised among FDI and Exports and Imports (Iqbal et al. 2010; Kaur et al., 2012; Topalli, 2015). There runs a one-way causality from Foreign Direct Investment to Current Account or the causality is uni-directional amid the two (Ersoy, 2011; Akkaya & Akcaci, 2012; Kaur et al., 2012; Siddiqui et al., 2012; Akbas, 2013). There are even evidences of no causal connection among FDI and Exports and eventually among FDI and Current Account (Manda, 2014; Stamatiou & Dritsakis, 2014). Nguku in 2013 concluded that Foreign Direct Investment does not pose a convincing influence on Exports, Imports, and Current Account and on the overall Balance of Payments Account of the economy of Kenya. For a majority of SAARC nations (India, Maldives Pakistan and Sri Lanka), a negative and critical relationship among FDI and Current Account is found excluding Bangladesh and Bhutan that have displayed a positive alliance among FDI and Current Account (Rahman & Bristy, 2015). For developed countries, the Current Account impositions forged by capital flows are not prominent (Yan & Yang, 2008).

Despite the quantum of studies supporting the stance that foreign capital flows impede the Current Account of developing economies, several studies have inclined over an opposite stance. Maxwell in 1996 discussed how FDI Inflows have contributed affirmatively to the Current Account of a group of developing economies from Pacific Asia. In line with this positive impact on Current Account, the foreign capital movement has also added to domestic investment, exports and economic growth of these developing economies. However, Saluja et al. in 2013 concluded that FDI flows are inversely related with Current Account of India. In similar context, Jansen (1995), Campbell (2001), Saluja et al. (2013) asserts that FDI Inflows into host countries leads to a widening in Current Account Deficits. Foreign Direct Investment impacts both the Current Account and the Capital Account (Accolley, 2003). Adding consensus to the existing literature on a negative association of FDI and Current Account, Sarode (2012) conclude that FDI Inflows into the Indian economy for a time frame 1997-2011 has gloomy effect on Current Account while the effect on Capital Account is encouraging and positive. This positive impact of Foreign Direct Investment on Capital Account is also proved by a study conducted by Saluja, Bhatia and Patel (2013). There is a bi-directional causality between Capital Account Balance and Foreign Direct Investment Inflows (Rahman, 2016).

The present study is a workout to cover up the cavities perceived in the existing literature reservoir regarding Foreign Direct Investment and Current Account across regional groups. To the best of the author's knowledge, no study has delved into investigating causality dynamics between FDI and Current Account for the BIMSTEC region.

FOREIGN DIRECT INVESTMENT FLOWS IN BIMSTEC REGION

The BIMSTEC regional group, with its objective to achieve cooperation among member nations in terms of economic, cultural as well as societal activities has collaborated with major foreign players in order to flourish from their expertise and managerial decorum. Southeast Asian nations has a history of gaining enormously from Foreign Direct Investment Inflows and much of the development and progress acknowledged by countries in this region is credited to the liberalisation in regimes that accentuated the transfer of capital in the form of FDI. Among the South Asian countries, Sri Lanka was the one to initiate the process of relaxations in terms of FDI and other flows. Member countries like Thailand, India, and Sri Lanka at present are host to massive foreign investments from major investors of the world. India saw its liberalisation in the investment regimes in four phases and thus the development in foreign participation was not instantaneous. Nevertheless, India has attracted the attention of foreign investors heavily by forging ahead variety of incentives and benefits to the investors. Thailand has also gained extensive foreign investments from some top foreign investors of the world. The participation of each member nation of BIMSTEC region in reference to FDI inflows is depicted in Figure 1.

The gush in liberalism and gratification offered by host countries post 1991 to lure foreign investors to pour in FDI into their entities became a landmark as it was after this unleashing of economies that resulted in FDI Inflows surge. It is identifiable from Figure 1 that two economies i.e. Thailand and India are overpowering other member nations in annexing huge capital inflows, particularly FDI. Post 1991, even India's share is lesser in numbers than Thailand but as liberalisation process gained momentum, India outshined Thailand and this acceleration in pace was witnessed in 2000 decade. However, other member nations of the BIMSTEC region hold a minimal share of total pie. Bangladesh adapted to the liberalisation process in full swing in the later years of 90s and still lags behind in attracting FDI Inflows in comparison to India and Thailand. Myanmar started satisfactorily but its position in capturing FDI inflows has joined the pace witnessed by Sri Lanka. Nepal and Bhutan remains sluggish in its pace of adapting to increased penetration of FDI flows

Figure 1. FDI inflows in BIMSTEC group

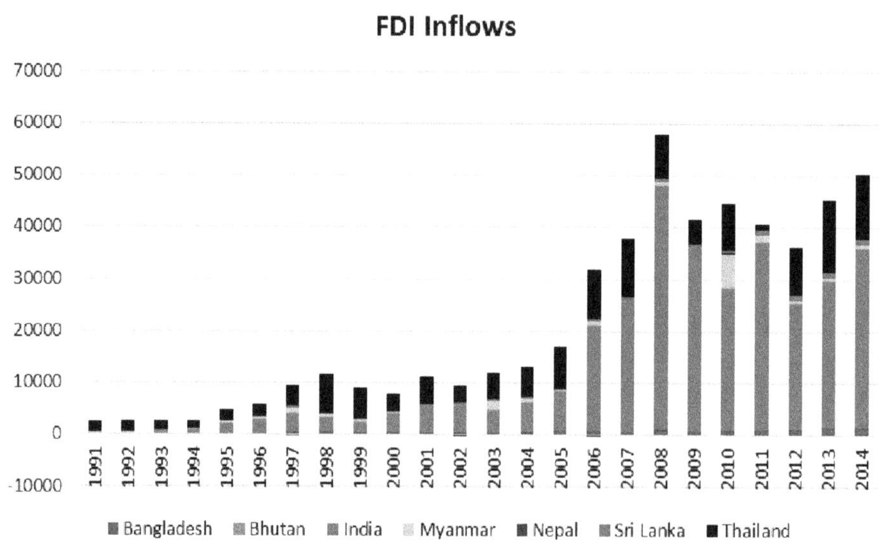

to member nations. A major reason to be considered in the sluggish performance of these member countries is the policy framework they reckon on and their heavy concentration towards agricultural and cultural sectors than towards economic activities. Nevertheless, Bhutan has started flourishing in hydroelectric projects in recent years.

A main reason that has added to the prosperous count of FDI Inflows in Thailand and India is the policy alterations that has made foreign investment climate conducive as per the interest of foreign multinationals and investors.

CURRENT ACCOUNT BALANCE IN BIMSTEC REGION

The Asian Region has a long story of imbalances in its Balance of International Payments as well as in its Current Account. Owing to the turmoil experienced by the Asian economies in 1997 and 1998 that seeped into the nations and created a fuss in the economic environment, the low economic activity further encroached upon and persisted for over a decade. Even before the Asian Financial Crises set in, a great number of Asian countries were into deep structural asymmetry. The reasons for this asymmetry in structural framework can be accounted to the deformities in policies and rules regarding private and corporate dynamics, macro-economic failures like persistent Current Account imbalances, foreign indebtedness, composition of capital inflows, political unrest, banking crises and financial vulnerabilities etc. It was majorly the tenacity in Current Account imbalances that aggravated the financial turmoil of 97 and 98. Current Account Deficits were swaying over the region even before the financial crises set its foot forth. The potential role of Current Account Deficits as a source of disruptive tensions in the financial markets has been repeatedly emphasized in the literature (Corsetti, Pesenti & Roubini, 1998). Almost all member states of BIMSTEC region have a record of persistent and wieldy Current Account deficits since the 90s. The regions Current Account dynamics is presented in Figure 2.

It is apparent in Figure 2 that the two prominent members of BIMSTEC in terms of capturing FDI flows have shown a deficit in Current Account since 1991 upto 1998. Though, the next few years were fruitful for Thailand as it sighted a surplus in Current Account consistently for seven years from 1998 to 2004, the surplus downsized from 12.55% of GDP in 1998 to a scant of 1.60% of GDP in 2004. This surplus in Current Account was aggregated on account of a revival in the export numbers and thereby a surplus in Balance of Trade of Thailand post the financial crisis of 97. For India, the Current Account stir has seen downturns as a consequence of an ever-increasing imports of oil and petroleum products. Also, the situation is a lot credited to the excessive gold imports and an expansion of trade

Figure 2. Current account balance in BIMSTEC

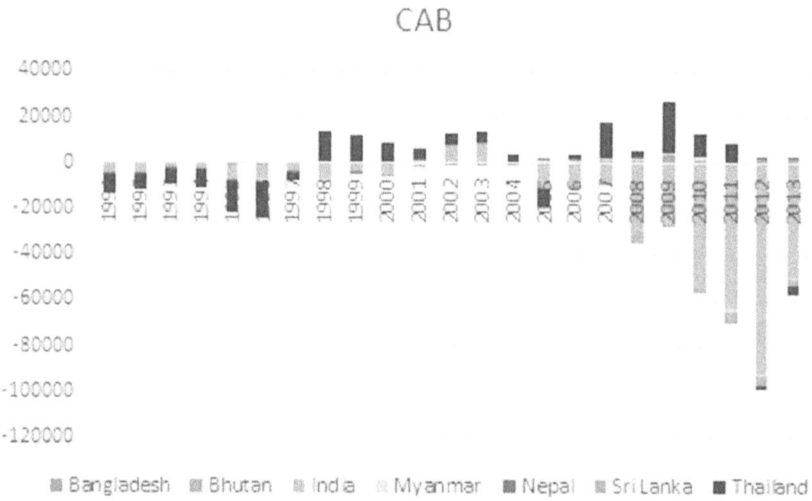

deficit. Leaving a few years i.e. 2002, 2003 and 2004; the whole era since 1991 has witnessed deficits in Current Account.

Bhutan experienced a surplus in Current Account for five consecutive years from 1995 to 1999. However, the situation declined and reached on a position of 9% of GDP. This position further aggravated till 2005. The rising imports and accentuation in payments to foreign human capital added up with a reduction in foreign grants to Bhutan emerged out as a cause of this undermining performance of Current Account in Bhutan. Nepal, which mainly relies on remittances from its labour employed in foreign nations to finance its import needs which has taken a toll because of heavy imports of petroleum and agricultural products has seen Current Account Deficits since 1991 upto 2001. From 2002 onwards Nepal didn't revert back to the previous downturn in Current Account and continuously ran a surplus till 2014. However, in recent years the situation may dampen because of a loss in remittances from foreign employment of human capital for Nepal. Also, the trade deficit is on a verge of expanding in coming years. In similar context, the Sri Lankan economy which is believed to sustain its imports through remittances from foreign nations in employing Sri Lankan labours, exports in specific agricultural items and through tourism industry has sighted a lessening in Current Account Deficit since 1994. However, as an aftereffect of global financial crisis of 2008, the remittances from tourism industry suffered severely and thus the Current Account Deficit widened to 9.54% of GDP which is enormously devastating. For Myanmar, the Current Account Deficit has acknowledged an upturn since 2012 and it is on a rise. However, Bangladesh in the recent years is flourishing with a positive trend in its Current Account position as against the BOP turmoil it once experienced post 2008 global financial crisis. However, the crisis in Bangladesh was not because of the only impeding leverage of global financial crisis but a mixture of excessive imports, declining exports, political uncertainties, currency depreciation, reduced remittances and high inflation.

EMPIRICAL SPECIFICATION AND DATA

The Data

The Panel Data for the seven-member nations constituting BIMSTEC region is taken from UNCTAD STATS Database. The data covers the period 1991-2014; which accounts as a crucial time frame because of the liberalisation and globalisation drive marking the period as a landmark in the history of major upheavals in economic activities across the world.

Empirical Analysis and Interpretation

The present research note utilises the Panel Granger Causality Test to determine the causality flow among Foreign Direct Investment and Current Account for the member nations of BIMSTEC group as a whole. The analysis moves in a series of steps. As against the case of Time Series Data wherein it is necessary to check for stationarity of data in order to avoid discrepancies and spurious results, the Panel Data is an advantage in this respect as it is no pre-requisite for Panel Data to ascertain its stationarity. Thus, we move forward with setting up a VAR model with an initial lag of 1. However, the residual statistics are non-supportive of VAR(1, 1). Therefore, we set up a VAR (1, 2). The output of VAR (1, 2) is presented in Table 1.

Before pondering ahead, the stability of the present VAR (1, 2) model is checked. For this purpose, the AR Roots Graph is first used. From the AR Roots Graph, it is evident that the all the unit points within the circle which is a requirement for the VAR (1, 2) to be stable. Thus, the AR Roots Graph criteria validates the VAR (1, 2) model to be stable.

The next step is the check on whether the lag selected for the VAR model is appropriate. This objective is dispensed by acting into play the Lag Selection Criteria. The results of Lag Order Selection Criteria is displayed in Table 2.

Since at lag 2, the AIC has its minimum value therefore lag 2 is appropriate for the VAR modelling. The Third and the final step to check the stability of VAR model is the LM Autocorrelation Tests. Table 3 displays the output of LM Autocorrelation Test.

Table 1. VAR (1, 2) output

Vector Autoregression Estimates		
Standard errors in () & t-statistics in [ ]		
	CAB	FDII
CAB(-1)	0.645284	0.033775
	(0.08679)	(0.04413)
	[7.43539]	[0.76538]
CAB(-2)	-0.013985	-0.055098
	(0.08241)	(0.04190)
	[-0.16970]	[-1.31495]
FDII(-1)	-0.167460	0.797796
	(0.16028)	(0.08150)
	[-1.04481]	[9.78930]
FDII(-2)	-0.389052	0.187645
	(0.18087)	(0.09197)
	[-2.15103]	[2.04037]
C	656.3512	374.7667
	(528.839)	(268.899)
	[1.24112]	[1.39371]
R-squared	0.761044	0.845305
Adj. R-squared	0.754629	0.841152
Sum sq. resids	5.36E+09	1.39E+09
S.E. equation	5997.074	3049.336
F-statistic	118.6362	203.5469
Log likelihood	-1555.625	-1451.468
Akaike AIC	20.26786	18.91516
Schwarz SC	20.36646	19.01377
Mean dependent	-2232.727	3269.727
S.D. dependent	12106.75	7650.945
Determinant resid covariance (dof adj.)		3.34E+14
Determinant resid covariance		3.13E+14
Log likelihood		-3006.997
Akaike information criterion		39.18178
Schwarz criterion		39.37898

Source: Prepared by the author through Eviews output

Table 2. Lag order selection criteria

Lag	LogL	LR	FPE	AIC	SC
0	-3214.954	NA	4.78e+15	41.77862	41.81806
1	-3012.505	397.0087	3.63e+14	39.20137	39.31969*
2	-3006.997	10.65930*	3.56e+14*	39.18178*	39.37898
* indicates lag order selected by the criterion					
LR: sequential modified LR test statistic (each test at 5% level)					
FPE: Final prediction error					
AIC: Akaike information criterion					
SC: Schwarz information criterion					

Source: Prepared by the author through Eviews output

Table 3. LM autocorrelation test. Null Hypothesis: no serial correlation at lag order h

Lags	LM-Stat	Prob.
1	9.876845	0.0426
2	13.86035	0.0078
3	9.096750	**0.0587**
4	116.9443	0.0000
5	6.681863	**0.1537**
6	3.974915	**0.4094**
7	9.557840	0.0486
8	5.873425	**0.2088**
9	1.029145	**0.9053**
10	1.799008	**0.7727**
Probs from chi-square with 4 df.		

Source: Prepared by the author through Eviews output

From the output table of Autocorrelation test, it is apparent that out of 10 lags, 6 lags carry a probability value greater than 0.05 which is a clear indication of the acceptance of null hypothesis of no serial correlation at lag order h. Thus, the model is free of any problem of autocorrelation. Once this is clear, the final step of ascertaining the causal connection is acted upon.

The null hypothesis for gauging the causality among CAB and FDII are:

H01: FDII does not Granger cause CAB for the panel of BIMSTEC

The results of Granger Causality for hypothesis 01 when CAB is the dependant variable are presented in Table 4.

As is evident from Table 4, the probability value is less than 0.05 that leads to reject the null hypothesis of FDII does not Granger cause CAB for the panel of BIMSTEC.

- **H02:** CAB does not Granger cause FDII for the panel of BIMSTEC

The results of Granger Causality when FDII is the dependent variable are presented in Table 5.

Table 4 justifies the acceptance of null hypothesis of CAB does not Granger cause FDII for the panel of BIMSTEC as the probability value as ascertained by granger causality test comes out to be 0.4055 which is greater than 0.05.

RESULTS

The study proposed to cater to the increasing need of searching for causal connection among Foreign Direct Investment Inflows and Current Account for a panel of BIMSTEC. The Panel Granger Causality Test is used in the study to reach onto results. The test of Panel Granger Causality identifies the presence of a causality running from Foreign Direct Investment Inflows to Current Account Balance of BIMSTEC group. This result is deduced from the rejection of the foremost null hypothesis of "FDII does not Granger cause CAB for the panel of BIMSTEC." Though, the Panel Granger Causality Test proves a causality among FDII and CAB for BIMSTEC,

Table 4. VAR granger causality for CAB

Excluded	Chi-sq.	Df	Prob.
FDII	28.91814	2	**0.0000**

Source: Prepared by the author through Eviews output

Table 5. VAR Granger causality for FDII

Excluded	Chi-sq.	Df	Prob.
CAB	1.805165	**2**	0.4055

Source: Prepared by the author through Eviews output

we cannot say that the causality runs the other way round also i.e. from CAB to Foreign Direct Investment Inflows. This is evident from the acceptance of the latter null hypothesis of "CAB does not granger cause FDII for the panel of BIMSTEC." Thus, the results of analysis dictate the presence of a causality among Foreign Direct Investment and Current Account for the countries constituting BIMSTEC; however, this causality is found to be one-directional only.

CONCLUSION AND FURTHER CONSIDERATIONS

Foreign Direct Investment flows have overpowered other capital flows since the decade that marked notable liberalisation and heavy relaxations in foreign investments and trade regimes. Though the liberal attitude in foreign investment policies was not adopted unanimously by developing nations of the world altogether; it still slowly and gradually took over the stage. History is witness to the massive transformation in the economic perceptions of host nations that reflect the overwhelming response Foreign Direct Investments captured from developing nations on the count. Even after emerging out as the forerunner in the capital environment, Foreign Direct Investments failed tremendously in financing the Current Account Deficits that seemed to seep into developing economies. The literature suggests how Current Account Deficits have been prolonged and propagated by increasing Foreign Direct Investment. The study excavates the same notion and reach onto a similar stance for the BIMSTEC regional group. With seven member countries of both South and Southeast Asia, the BIMSTEC is a strong regional bloc in terms of the challenging prospects it has for economic and cultural integration of member countries. The study concludes that Foreign Direct Investment Inflows pouring into the host economies of BIMSTEC causes Current Account Balance in the region. This outcome is in perfect conformity with the existing empirical works that reckons that Foreign Direct Investment causes Current Account. However, the causality is deduced to be uni-directional. No causality was devised running from Current Account Balance to Foreign Direct Investment Inflows. Therefore, it can be said that Current Account Balances in member nations of BIMSTEC group do not cause Foreign Direct Investments to pool in. May be there are other factors that cause an inflow of Foreign Direct Investment into the region such as market prospects, low cost labour, symmetry in FDI policy, liberal trade regime, Infrastructural capacities, sound political and institutional set up etc.

It will be beneficial for the countries conglomerated in BIMSTEC to attend to the empirical findings of the existing literature on causality between Foreign Direct Investment and Current Account. BIMSTEC, a host to gigantic Foreign Direct Investment Inflows requires to take heed of the consequences it poses on broad economic pointers such as Balance of Payments in general and its components in specific. Since the present study sights Foreign Direct Investment Inflows to be causing Current Account Balance for a time frame 1991-2014 which accounts for a crucial period, intensive policy adjustments need to be considered before losing it all to foreign interventions. Thorough indulgence is required in the policy framework of BIMSTEC in order to grasp more from FDI flows and the local industries need to be super absorptive of FDI Inflows to benefit more from the spillovers it proliferates.

ACKNOWLEDGMENT

The present research piece is an original work disseminated to add to the existing body of knowledge on the issue. Any work reproduced in part or in whole is genuinely stated and referred thereof. All errors and omissions are the author's own.

REFERENCES

Accolley, D. (2003). *The Determinants and Impact of Foreign Direct Investment* (Master's Dissertation). Retrieved from: http://mpra.ub.uni-muenchen.de/3084/

Agosin, M., & Mayer, R. (2000). *Foreign investment in developing countries: Does it crowd in Domestic investment.* UNCTAD Discussion Paper No. 146.

Aitken, B. J., & Harrison, A. E. (1999). Do Domestic firms benefit from Direct Foreign Investment? Evidence from Venezuela. *The American Economic Review, 89*(3), 605–618. doi:10.1257/aer.89.3.605

Akbas, Y. E., Senturk, M., & Sancar, C. (2013). Testing for causality between the Foreign Direct Investment, Current Account Deficit, GDP and Total Credit: Evidence from G7. *Panoeconomicus, 6*(6), 791–812. doi:10.2298/PAN1306791A

Akcaci, T., & Akkaya, O. (2012). How have FDI flows effected to Current Account Balance: In Turkey Case. China-USA Business Review, 11(12), 1565-1571.

Bacchetta, P., & Wincoop, E. V. (2000). Does Exchange Rate Stability increase Trade and Capital Flows? *The American Economic Review, 90*(5), 1093–1109. doi:10.1257/aer.90.5.1093

Bhasin, N. (2012). *Foreign Direct Investment (FDI) in India: Policies, Conditions and Procedures.* New Delhi: New Century Publications.

Borensztein, E., Gregorio, J. D., & Lee, J. W. (1998). How does Foreign Direct Investment affect Economic Growth? *Journal of International Economics*, *45*(1), 115–135. doi:10.1016/S0022-1996(97)00033-0

Calvo, G. A., Leiderman, L., & Reinhart, C. M. (1996). Inflows of Capital to Developing Countries in the 1990s. *The Journal of Economic Perspectives*, *10*(2), 123–139. doi:10.1257/jep.10.2.123

Campbell, T. (2001). Foreign Direct Investment Inflows and their Impact on Barbados' Current Account: Implications for Policy. In *Canadian Economic Association (2001) annual meeting*. McGill University.

Ersoy, I. (2011). The Causal Relationship between the Financial Account and the Current Account: The Case of Turkey. *International Research Journal of Finance and Economics*, *75*, 187–193.

Forogue, A., & Veloce, W. (1990). Causality and Structure of Canada's Balance of Payments. *Empirical Economics*, *15*(3), 267–283. doi:10.1007/BF02426969

Fry, M. J. (1996). How Foreign Direct Investment in Pacific Asia improves the Current Account. *Birmingham Journal of Asian Economics*, *7*(3), 459–486. doi:10.1016/S1049-0078(96)90021-4

Hossain, M. A. (2008). *Impact of Foreign Direct Investment on Bangladesh's Balance of Payments: Some Policy Implication. Policy Note No. 08005*. Dhaka: Bangladesh Bank.

Iqbal, S. M., Shaikh, F. M., & Shar, A. H. (2010). Causality Relationship between Foreign Direct Investment, Trade and Economic Growth in Pakistan. *Asian Social Science*, *6*(9). doi:10.5539/ass.v6n9p82

Jansen, K. (1995). The macroeconomic effects of Foreign Direct Investment: The Case of Thailand. *World Development*, *23*(2), 193–210. doi:10.1016/0305-750X(94)00125-I

Javed, K., Sher, F., Awan, R. U., & Ashfaq, M. (2012). Foreign Direct Investment, Trade and Economic Growth: A Comparison of selected South Asian Countries. *International Journal of Humanities and Social Science*, *2*(5).

Jones, G. (1996). The Evolution of International Business: An Introduction. Routledge.

Jurcic, L., Bilas, V., & Franc, S. (2011). *The effects of FDI on the Recipient Country*. Academic Press.

Kaur, M., Yadav, S. S., & Gautam, V. (2012). Foreign Direct Investment and Current Account Deficit- A Causality Analysis in context of India. *Journal of International Business and Economy*, *13*(2), 85–106.

Kawai, M. (2005). East Asian Economic Regionalism: Progress and Challenges. *Journal of Asian Economics*, *16*(1), 29–55. doi:10.1016/j.asieco.2005.01.001

Kim, C. H., & Kim, D. (2010). Do Capital Inflows Cause Current Account Deficits? *Applied Economics Letters*, *18*(5), 497–499. doi:10.1080/13504851003724267

Manda, S. (2014). Capital flows and Current Account Dynamics in Zimbabwe. *Journal of Economics and International Business Management*, *2*(4), 82–99.

Mastroyiannis, A. (2012). Causality Relationships in the Structure of Portugal's Balance of International Payments. *International Journal of Business and Social Science*, *3*(15), 54–61.

Mencinger, J. (2008). *Direct and Indirect effects of Foreign Direct Investment on Current Account*. Academic Press.

Nguku, E. K. (2013). *Relationship between Foreign Direct Investment and Balance of Payments in Kenya*. Academic Press.

Organisation for Economic Cooperation and Development. (2008). *OECD Benchmark Definition of Foreign Direct Investment* (4th ed.). OECD.

Rahman, M. N. (2016). Impact of Foreign Direct Investment Inflows on Capital Account of India's Balance of Payments. *Business and Economic Review*, *6*(1), 111–128. doi:10.5296/ber.v6i1.8965

Rahman, N. (2015). Trends in FDI Inflows and Current Account of India's BOP Since 1991. *International Journal of Economics. Commerce and Research*, *5*(5), 1–12.

Rahman, S. M. Z., & Bristy, J. F. (2015). Macroeconomic Impact of Foreign Direct Investment: A Study on SAARC Countries. *European Journal of Business and Management*, *7*(34), 2222–2839.

Saglam, B. B., & Yalta, A. Y. (2015). Current Account Imbalances and Capital flows: Further Evidence from Emerging Markets. *Global Journal of Emerging Market Economies*, *7*(2), 201–213. doi:10.1177/0974910115574170

Saluja, M. S., Bhatia, N. K., & Patel, N. (2013). A Cointegration and VECM approach in explaining relationship of FDI with Current and Capital Account of India. *International Journal of Advanced Research in Computer Science and Management Studies*, *1*(6).

Sarode, S. (2012). Effects of FDI on Capital Account and GDP: Empirical Evidence from India. *International Journal of Business and Management*, *7*(8), 102–107. doi:10.5539/ijbm.v7n8p102

Sen, P. (1995). Foreign Direct Investment: A Solution to Balance Of Payments Problems? *Economic and Political Weekly*, *30*(30), 1921–1927.

Siddiqui, D. A., & Ahmad, M. H. (2012). The Causal Relationship between Foreign Direct Investment and Current Account: An Empirical investigation for Pakistan Economy. *European Journal of Economics, Finance and Administrative Sciences*, *44*.

Stamatiou, P., & Dritsakis, N. (2014). Exports, Foreign Direct Investment and Economic Growth for Five European Countries: Granger Causality Tests in Panel Data. *Applied Economics*. doi:10.3790/aeq.60.4.253

Topalli, N. (2015). A Causal Relationship between Foreign Direct Investment, Economic Growth and High Technology Exports. *International Journal of Social Sciences and Education Research*, *1*(1).

Wang, M. (2010). Foreign Direct Investment and Domestic Investment in the host country: Evidence from Panel Study. *Applied Economics*, *42*(29), 3711–3721. doi:10.1080/00036840802314580

Yan, H. (2007). Does capital mobility finance or cause a Current Account imbalance? *The Quarterly Review of Economics and Finance*, *47*(1), 1–25. doi:10.1016/j.qref.2005.08.001

Zafir, C. Z., & Funda, H. S. (2012). Analysis of the effects of Foreign Direct Investment on the financing of Current Account Deficits in Turkey. *International Journal of Business and Social Science*, *3*(10), 68–78.

Chapter 8
The Comparative Study of the FDI in India and China in Retail Sector

Rita Naraindas Khatri
H. R. College of Commerce and Economics, India

ABSTRACT

Every economy across the globe is developing at a rapid pace. Offshore investment opportunities have not only transformed some of the business sectors like infrastructure, technology, media, and telecommunication, but it has also brought some dynamic changes in the life style and shopping preference of the consumers. One such sector that has diverted the attention of the mass is the retail sector. Over the last few years, retail sector has experienced drastic transformation. Some countries are well developed while others are emerging in the retail sector. India and China are among the top developing countries attracting huge foreign direct investment. China follows open investment policy and has liberalized the investment for foreign players while India adopted conservative investment policy with strong government involvement. Retail growth in India is very slow as compared to China. Therefore, this chapter attempts to highlight the economy of India and China and has compared some of the parameters of the economy to reflect the difference in the growth in India and China.

DOI: 10.4018/978-1-5225-3026-8.ch008

INTRODUCTION

In the era of globalization and liberalization every economy across the world is developing at the rapid pace. These developments have not only changed some of the business sectors like infrastructure, technology, media, telecommunication but it has also brought some dynamic changes in the life style of the consumers and in their preferences for shopping. All these changing trends have brought greater impact on the retail business across the globe. Ample opportunities are available in retail sector and immense changes are noticed in world retail market. It has not only emerged as the profitable sector but is also dominating the economies of many countries to become the next booming sectors across the world. Today's retail sector is largely fragmented into organized and unorganized retail sector but the proportion of this fragmentation is not same worldwide the percentage of organized retail development is more in developed countries and it is growing in developing countries. Two such countries that has attracted world foreign direct investment and large opportunities for employment is India and China.

Over the last few years due to change in consumer preference retail sector has shown enormous progress in India and China. In India the retail sector is bound to come across opportunities like never before. The retail sector in India was more of an unorganized one with petty vendors dominating the chunk of the industry but now the scenario has fast been changing. Finally, the sector is converting into what we call as organized retailing. Not only Indian corporate majors like Reliance, ITC and Pantaloon have entered into the segment but more and more foreign players are also showing interest in USD 600 billion Indian retail markets. Hence both the economies have shown a different phase of growth in organized retail business This has been due to foreign direct investment policies of India and China. China follows open investment policy and have liberalize the investment for foreign players while India adopted conservative investment policy where there is government involvement in most of the foreign investment projects. Because of strict FDI regulation the growth of organized retail is slow as compared to China. Hence the need was felt to study the growth and development of retail business and do a comparative analysis between two powerful economies.

OBJECTIVES OF THE STUDY

- To study the economy of India and China.
- To analyze the foreign direct investment in India and China.
- To understand the FDI policy in retail sector in India and China.

- To identify the factor responsible for the difference in the growth of the retail trade and compare the difference in the growth of retail business in India and China.

Research Methodology

The study is based on secondary data analysis only. In order to collect the data, the researcher has referred various reports on India- China retail developments like China retail report, India retail report, Ernst and young report, and Deloitte report on India China retail. Past research has also been reviewed by referring the article and research paper published by the research organization in order to find the strength and weakness of the economy. Data has also been collected from case studies, books, journals, newspapers and online databases and websites of DIPP (Department of Industrial Policy and Promotion), RBI (Reserve Bank of India) and FICCI (Federation of Indian Chambers of Commerce and Industry), Ministry of commerce of India and Ministry of Commerce of China.

Key Terms

Cash and Carry Wholesale Trading/Wholesale Trading

This would mean sale of goods/merchandise to retailers, industrial, commercial, institutional or other professional business users or to other wholesalers and related subordinated service providers. Wholesale trading would, accordingly, imply sales for the purpose of trade, business and profession, as opposed to sales for the purpose of personal consumption. The yardstick to determine whether the sale is wholesale or not would be the type of customers to whom the sale is made and not the size and volume of sales. Wholesale trading would include resale, processing and thereafter sale, bulk imports with ex-port/ex-bonded warehouse business sales and B2B e-Commerce.

E-Commerce

E-commerce means buying and selling of goods and services including digital products over digital and electronic network. ii)E-commerce entity- E-commerce entity means a company incorporated under the Companies Act 1956 or the Companies Act 2013 or a foreign company covered under section 2 (42) of the Companies Act, 2013 or an office, branch or agency in India as provided in section 2 (v) (iii) of FEMA 1999, owned or controlled by a person resident outside India and conducting the e-commerce business.

Multibrand Retail

It means retail store with foreign investment can sell multibrand under one roof.

Haats, Mandis, and Melas

Haats are the market especially held on regular basis in a rural area. While mandis are market set up by the state government for the sale of agricultural produce directly from farmers. Melas are the fair which exhibit all products. It may range from commodity fairs to religious fairs.

REVIEW OF LITERATURE

A study "Retail sector in India: Is it necessary to invite FDI" (2012) by Goyal, Kumar and Roy in their paper supports the FDI in retail sector. The study evaluates various positive effects of promoting FDI in Indian retail. Taking an example from various developed nations, the study discusses the retail growth as one of the major reasons for the success of their economies. Allowing FDI in retail may offer consumers good quality products at lower prices. Also, the paper points that presence of foreign retailers will help in increasing the Indian exports which will also improve our balance of payment.

On the other hand, Ravindra, Murthy and Rao in their study "Will Foreign Direct Investment in retail sector is viable for Indian economy?" (2013) attempts to view the viability of allowing FDI in Indian retail. The main objective of the study was to observe the growth and evolution of retail sector in India. The study is based on secondary data. The study further enumerates that FDI will have a spillover effect for Indian economy by integrating the Indian economy around the global. However, the FDI should be allowed with precautions but it should not be discouraged.

Uppal and Juneja in their study "Emerging trends of FDI inflows in India: responses and challenges" (2013), highlights that FDI is the most essential instrument needed for economic development of nation. The study is focused on analysing FDI inflows from different nations in India.

Chopra and Sachdeva conducted a study on "Analysis of FDI inflows and outflows in India" (2014) have concluded the role of foreign direct investment and trade in promoting economic growth across selected budding country i.e. India and the interface among FDI, trade, and economic growth. They evaluated a strong positive interface between FDI and trade in advancing economic growth.

Nandal in his study "Impact analysis of FDI in retail industry in India" (2013) has supported the inflow of FDI in India. Huge investments in infrastructure would lead to augment in farm productivity, manufacturing and food processing as well as cold storage facilities.

China today is one of the biggest superpower country of the world. While analyzing previous literature the FDI inflows in China and growth of retail sector. Xiaowen Tian book on "Managing International Business in China" (2007) provides a general picture of China economy. Where he focused on China's foreign trade and foreign direct investment. He also focused on the market entry strategy and key issues with relation to the topic. Thus, this book provides comprehensive overview of Chinese business environment up to recent years and covers important managerial issues that the foreign companies encounter in China, and also the product differentiation versus standardization in China. Therefore, the author overviews the present China marketing environment and utilizes number of China based cases to explain how foreign companies make relevant business decisions.

Another article by Konana, Dogget et al (2004) "Comparing India and China growth strategies- chaotic or planned" compares the growth strategies in India and China which influence worldwide job migration and provides valuable lesson for other developing countries. China's strategy is methodical and deliberate and while of India is chaotic and opportunistic. While China has followed a conventional path in transiting from an agricultural economy to a robust industrial economy. India is attempting to leapfrog from a predominantly agricultural economy to a knowledge based service economy. Further China is building vital linkages among its agricultural, industrial and service sector and systematically encouraging domestic consumption in parallel with sharp focus on exports while India ignore the lack of linkages. Thus this article focuses that if the economy wants to pursue politically and economically it must focus on linkages.

The next article on Foreign Direct Investment in India and China: A comparative study by Leena Mary Eapen (2006) covers the aspects and explain why China is ahead of India in attracting FDI. According to the author India has been the underachiever in securing FDI as compared to China. In this regard the FDI policy need to be constantly reviewed and more importantly the institutional environment in India must be reformed to attract FDI from the multinational companies. India must adopt policies to target the right type of FDI for enhancement of export.

Also, the Chung Ming Lau and Garry Bruton (2008) in one of the article on FDI in China: What we know and what we need to study next" has explored the reasons for China to become the powerhouse of the world. According to the author FDI into China is more than $80 billion per year. In comparison FDI represents just $2 bn to $3 bn per year in India. The author also highlights that the Chinese for economic development with its heavy reliance on FDI id increasingly copied by other developing economies. China has concentrated its FDI in three major locations: Jiangsu, Guangdong, and shanghai. It is also found that in China role of the government is the central factor in the institutional environment.

INDIAN ECONOMY AND GROWTH OF RETAIL SECTOR

The economy of India is the seventh largest economy of the world by nominal GDP and fourth largest in term of purchase power parity in the world. Since independence it is gradually growing and today India is one of the fastest growing nations in the world. Due to economic liberalization of the policy in 1990 by Dr. Manmohan Singh the country steadily climbed up the economic ladder and by the year 2008 it became the second fastest growing economy. Today the share of service sector account around 54% of the annual Gross Domestic product. The growth rate of the decades is around 6%. Table 1 highlights the annual growth rate of India's GDP since 2013. India's gross domestic product advanced 7.1 percent year-on-year in the second quarter of 2016, slowing from a 7.9 percent expansion in the previous period and missing market expectations of 7.6 percent growth. It was the lowest reading since the fourth quarter of 2014, as private consumption expanded at a slower pace while fixed investment dropped further. GDP Annual Growth Rate in India averaged 6.08 percent from 1951 until 2016, reaching an all-time high of 11.40 percent in the first quarter of 2010 and a record low of -5.20 percent in the fourth quarter of 1979. GDP Annual Growth Rate in India is reported by the Ministry of Statistics and Programme Implementation (MOSPI).

Table 1. Annual GDP growth rate in India

Sr no	Month and year	Growth rate(%)
1.	July 2013	7.5
2	Jan 2014	6.3
3	July 2014	6.7
4	Jan 2015	7.1
5	July 2015	7.5
6	Jan 2016	7.2
7	June 2016	7.1

Source: Adapted from www.tradingeconomics.com

Retail Sector in India

The word retail is derived from the French word "retailer", meaning to cut a piece off or "to break bulk". In simple terms it is the first-hand transaction undertaken by the retailer with the customer. A retailer is a company, organization or individual that purchases the product from individual intermediaries or companies with the intention to resell the goods and services to the final customers. The Indian retail landscape is evolved from the bricks and mortar model to adopt technology for connecting consumers. Since ages the Indian retail sector has been dominated by traditional retailers which are also called as unorganized retailers. These are the unorganized low structure usually administered by owner with little or no tax to pay. They predominantly consist of small, independent, owners, managed shops. There are around 14 million retail outlets in unorganized sector that comprised of small vendors like cloth stores, grocery stores, snacks center etc. consumer familiarity that runs from generation to generation is one big advantage enjoyed by traditional retail sector.

The evolution of retail started with barter trade which is considered as the oldest form of retail trade since independence. Haats, mandis and melas have always been a part of Indian landscape. Later public distribution system emerged as the single largest retail chain in the country. The system however continued to remain as essentially urban oriented activity. In fact, towards the end of first five years plan the system started losing its relevance due to comfortable grain availability. The cooperative movement was again championed by the government that encouraged to set up more kendraiya bhandar in 1963. In maharashtra bombay bazaar which runs stores under the label of sahakari bhandar and apna bazaar.

In the past decades, Indian market place has been transformed dramatically. Globalization, Privatization and Liberalization paved the way encouraging private companies to invest money in retail sector and many individual business houses started establishing independent stores. Stores like Akbarallys, Nallis, Raymond were the one to establish the concept of organized retailing in India. Later Bombay dyeing, Vimal showroom and many others were encouraged to set up independent retail show room in India. Therefore, the chain stores were a successful beginning toward the new concept of retailing.

The concept of retail as the entertainment came in 2000 with the advent of malls. The concept of mall fragmented the market and brought the new concept of retail called as organized retailing. Organized retailing are the compact structures managed by professional with greater efficiency and commitment These forms of retail started growing in India by various format like super market, hypermarket, department stores discount stores and so on.

The India retail accounts over 10% of the country's GDP and contribute towards 10% of the total employment. The current estimated value of the India retail sector is about 600 billion USD and is pegged to reach to 1.3 trillion USD by 2020.The industry has long way to go as there is huge opportunity in streamlining the sectors. Currently India constitutes only 8% of organized retail and remaining 92% is left unorganized which may grow much faster than traditional retail. Various estimates highlights that Indian organized retail will increase to 20% by 2020. This could be due to the foreign direct investment that is paving its way in India retail sector.

Foreign Direct Investment in India

Foreign direct investment implies allowing external financial investment in the economy. It basically covers cross border investment made by investor with a view to establish lasting financial interest and thereby exercising a significant management influence. FDI is a key component of natural development for almost all countries and especially developing economies. With good economic growth and rising GDP India has been the attractive destination for FDI. It influences the economy of the host country in numerous ways and provides the opportunity to cater complex geographical region of the world.

With the advent of the new economic policies, the FDI policies are simplified and have encouraged larger inflows into the nation.

Foreign direct investment implies allowing external financial investment in the economy. It basically covers cross border investment made by investor with a view to establish lasting financial interest and thereby exercising a significant management influence. FDI is a key component of natural development for almost all countries and especially developing economies. With good economic growth and rising GDP India has been the attractive destination for FDI. It influences the economy of the host country in numerous ways and provides the opportunity to cater complex geographical region of the world.

With the advent of the new economic policies, the FDI policies are simplified and have encouraged larger inflows into the nation. Table 2 represent FDI inflows in($billion)

As per table 2 India continues to be among the top ten countries in terms of foreign investment inflows globally and fourth in developing Asia as per the world investment report 2016 by united nation conference for Trade and development. India's FDI inflows have increased to $44 billion in 2015 as compared to $35 billion in 2014, while China occupies third postion in terms of Foreign direct investment and total FDI inflows have increased to $136 billion in 2015 as compared to $129billion.

An international retailer can enter the Indian retail market through any one of the following methods.

Table 2. FDI inflows in $ billion

Countries	2014	2015
US	107	380
Hongkong	114	175
Ireland	31	101
Netherland	52	73
Singapore	68	65
China	**129**	**136**
India	**35**	**44**
Brazil	73	65
Switzerland	7	69
Canada	59	49

Source: modified from world investment report 2016

1. Acquiring stock of the existing foreign enterprise to participate in the management of the concern enterprise.
2. Establishing abroad new subsidiaries with 100% ownership.
3. Participating in joint ventures through stock holdings.
4. Establishing new branches or expanding the existing FDI in Retail Sector

Indian government policy with regard to development of retail industry has been liberal and motivating. The government is now set to initiate second wave of reform in the segment by liberalizing investment norms. This will not only favor the retail sector to develop in terms of design, construction quality but also help in creating customer friendly environment. Over the years it has been the trend that Indian retailers can register their outlets with concern authorities in various states and can run their retail business. As such there are no constraints on the entry of any domestic business house into retail sector. Therefore, today India has more than 15 million kiryana stores making India a hub of retail shops. With rising disposable income of Indian middle class and 10% of GDP growth Indian retail market has attracted global players to enter and explore the opportunities in untapped retail market. Considering the future of these shop keepers policy makers and even some state government have been planning to restrict foreign investment. As the allotment of land is subject matter, central government is concerned with FDI approvals. FDI in retail was first permitted in 1993 but due to political compulsion and opposition the government has restricted FDI since 1997.

The government has recently made changes in the foreign direct investment policy regime by enhancing FDI limits in various sectors like Defense, Civil Aviation etc.

The FDI limit in various sector is not uniform. Further FDI is also allowed through two different routes namely, Automatic route, Foreign entities do not need the prior approval of the government to invest. However, they have to inform RBI about the amount of investment within a stipulated time period. In specific sectors, FDI is through FIPB (Foreign Investment promotion board) or the government route where the FIPB has to approve each investment. Table 3 highlight the legal provision of FDI in retail sector. Foreign players were allowed to enter Indian market only if they manufacture or source locally, enter into franchising agreement, if they are cash and carry operators (Mukhrjee & Patel, 2005).

Policy for FDI in Multi Brand Retail Trading

- At least US$ 100 million as equity into Indian company.
- At least 50 percent of the total FDI to be invested in Back end infrastructure within 3 yrs.
- At least 30% of the value of procurement of processed product shall be sources from small industries.
- Fresh agricultural product is permitted to be sold unbranded.
- Indian states have been given discretion to accept or refuse to implement FDI.
- Retail outlets can be set up in cities having a population of at least one million.

Table 4 depicts about some of the companies that have entered in India through Foreign Direct Investment

Table 3. FDI provision in retail sector

Sector	FDI Limit	Entry Route & Remarks
Cash & Carry Wholesale Trading	**100%**	**Automatic**
E-commerce activities (e-commerce entities would engage only in Business to Business (B2B) e-commerce and not in Business to Consumer (B2C) e-commerce.)	**100%**	**Automatic**
Single Brand retail trading Local sourcing norms will be relaxed up to three years and a relaxed sourcing regime for another five years for entities undertaking Single Brand Retail Trading of products having 'state-of-art' and 'cutting edge' technology.	**100%**	**Automatic up to 49%** **Above 49% under Government route**
Multi Brand Retail Trading	**51%**	**Government**
Duty Free Shops	**100%**	**Automatic**

Source: https://factly.in/sectors-fdi-allowed-india/ and http://dipp.nic.in/English/Policies/FDI_Circular_2016.pdf

Table 4. Entry route for Foreign Direct Investment

Entry Route	Players
Franchisee	Pizza Hut Marks/Spencers Nike Tommy Hilfiger Subway
Cash/Carry Wholesale	Metro
Distribution	Hugo Boss Mango Swarovski
Joint Venture	Reebok Mc Donalds
Manufacturing Facility	Benetton Bata

Source www.Ibef.org

Table 5. Top ten global retailers operating in India

Sr No	Name of the Country
1	Walmart
2	Amazon
3	McDonalds
4	Apple stores
5	Yums Brand
6	Star bucks
7	Subway
8	Gap
9	Burger King worldwide
10	Wendy's

Source:http://www.indiaretailing.com/2016/07/11/retail/top-10-global-retailers-operating-in-india/

Therefore, FDI in retail would bring in millions of dollars of investment, technology, Inventory management and IT in retailing. The economies of scale would reduce the cost, increase the efficiency and stimulate the production of quality agriculture and Industrial output. This would facilitate a higher growth. So FDI through multiplier would have an impact on the entire economy. The retail sector would not only stimulate but many other activities such as manufacturing, food processing and packaging would generate large employment opportunities. The benefits of FDI do

Table 6. Sector specific FDI inflows in retail sector in India

Years	FDI in flows in US $million
2006-2007	47
2007-2008	200
2008-2009	294
2009-2010	536
2010-2011	391
2011-2012	567
2013-2013	551
2013-2014	1139
% increase	23.33
CAGR	309.4

Source: compiled from RBI website

not accrue automatically. In order to reap maximum benefit from FDI there is a need to establish a transparent broad and effective policy environment for investment and to put in place the effective frame work for their implementation.

DRIVERS RESPONSIBLE FOR FDI IN RETAIL SECTOR IN INDIA

Economic Development

FDI in retail sector will result in expansion of market and will bring change in the consumers spending pattern which will eventually increase the GDP of the economy. It will also be the source of revenue generation for the government in the form of regular tax collection from the organized retailers and even today there are leakages in the unorganized sector toward tax collections.

Support to the Allied and Small Industries

The inflow of FDI in retail sector will be important driver for developing allied industries. As retail industry grows it will simultaneously develop food processing sector, textile sector and suppliers who are product goods and services to retail sector. Also, due to FDI policy of 30% procurement from small scale industries will boost the development of small scale industries and revive them to support the economy.

Improvement in Supply Chain Systems

Logistic and supply chain system is very inefficient in India. According to the government policy on FDI the inflow of foreign currency would improve the inefficient supply chain systems. The belief rest on the premise that a component of the capital inflow into the retail sector will go into developing an extremely efficient and organized supply and logistic system that will take care of collection, storage and transportation of food product seamlessly. Globally logistics accounts for around 5% of the total cost to the retail player while in India it is as high as 10% thus making dent in its attractiveness.

The Young India

Against the backdrop of an ageing world, India possesses the advantage of having a largely young population. 35 percent of India's population is under 14 years of age and more than 60 per cent of the population is estimated to constitute the working age group (15-60) till 2050. Two-thirds of Indian population is under 35, with the median age of 23 years, as opposed to the world median age of 33. India is home to 20 per cent of the global population under 25 years of age. This trend is projected to continue for the next decade, with the share set to reach its maximum in 2010. The large proportion of the working-age population translates to a lucrative consumer base vis-à-vis other economies of the world, placing India on the radar as one of the most promising retail destinations of the world.

Employment Generation

It is being estimated that there will large scale job creation in the economy. Union minister of Commerce and Industry Anand Sharma went up one step further by quoting a figure of 10 million new jobs to be created with bulk of that supposedly coming from the logistics sector.

ECONOMY OF CHINA

During the last decades China's economy has witnessed a remarkable transition. Chinese economy a home for more than 1.3 billion population has been expanding at the rate of more than 8% annually since 1980. The workshop of the world has conquered a global manufacturing turf by churning out low cost quality goods across the globe.

Over the quarter century China was largely an agricultural nation but today it is rapidly transformed itself into an industrial nation and thereby raising its living standards. This robust growth is attributed by the interrelated drivers that include a more to the market economy, rapid urbanization, rapid progress of privatization, the application of new technology and massive foreign capital inflows. One the other the important things about the Chinese economy is that it is the economy built around small and medium enterprise like Korea and Japan.

China has a history that covers over four thousand years. Education and R& D have become priority in China. China is no longer the country which produces merely cheap and therefore cheap quality products but more and more high-quality products have entered international markets. China is today biggest representative of Asian nations. China has four distinct periods in its 4000 year history. Until 16th century China's economy performed on par with countries elsewhere in the world.

China Economy outperformed that of western Europe for more than 1000 yrs. Towards the end of Ming dynasty (1368-1644) however and throughout the Ching dynasty (1644-1912) China stagnated its GDP rising virtually Zero for more than 300 years. During the same period Western Europe enjoyed rapid economic development riding scientific revolution that begins in 11th century. After the 18th century growth in the Western Europe skyrocketed while China slipped into decline as it shunned progress and close its doors to the outside world. China's Isolationism eventually led to invasion from western and Japanese forces driving nation's GDP per capital back down to level seen in 2000 year. Just a quarter century ago China awakens from its 500 years sleep and today it is rapidly catching up with the world. The year 1978 marks the turning point into China's modern history that's when Deng Xiaoping began to remake the economy round most market principles. In 1978, China has the world's ninth largest economy with GDP just 1/8 that of the United states and third that of Japan. But by 2001 China had grown to the world's second largest economy with the national output over half of the United States and 60% larger than Japan. Thus, with its large population which is 4.5 times of US and labor force six times more than US it is truly a giant country. Table 7 represent GDP growth rate in China

According to Table 7, the Chinese economy expanded an annual 6.7 percent in the September quarter of 2016, the same pace as in the previous two quarters. The figure was in line with market expectations, supported by an increase in government spending, fixed asset investment and retail sales while industrial output eased. For 2016, the Chinese government is targeting the economy to grow between 6.5 to 7.0 percent. A year earlier, the economy expanded by 6.9 percent, while in 2014 the GDP growth rate was 7.6%. On a quarterly basis, the GDP advanced 1.8 percent, the same as in the June quarter and matching consensus. GDP Annual Growth Rate in China averaged 9.79 percent from 1989 until 2016, reaching an all-time high

Table 7. The GDP growth rate in China

Sr no	Month and year	Growth rate (%)
1.	Jan 2014	7.6
2	March 2014	7.3
3	Sept 2014	7.1
4	Jan 2015	7.2
5	Jul 2015	7.0
6	Sept 2015	6.9
7	Jan 2016	6.8
8	March 2016	6.7
9	July 2016	6.7
10	Sept	6.7

Source: www.tradingeconomics.com: National Bureau of Statistics of China.

of 15.40 percent in the first quarter of 1993 and a record low of 3.80 percent in the fourth quarter of 1990. GDP Annual Growth Rate in China is reported by the National Bureau of Statistics of China.

Foreign Direct Investment in China

Foreign Direct Investment represents capital invested in a country that provide manufacturing and service capabilities for both native consumers and world market. FDI is instrumental in bringing goods and services to the global market place. The benefits of FDI flow to both the supplier of capital as well as to the host region. China is one country that has stepped up to capitalize on these benefits.

During the Mao period (1949-1976), China spurned foreign investment and paid back all its foreign loan (mostly to the Soviet Union) by 1965. Fu (2000) and Zhang (1999) identified three periods of reform of foreign investment policy after 1979: the initial phase (1979-85); the continuous development stage (1986-91); and the high-growth period (1992 onwards). In the initial phase, a number of laws and regulations were released to attract foreign investors into China. A noticeable inflow of foreign capital surged into China in the period of high growth. The central government started lifting its ban on foreigners for having joint ventures.

After five decades of state controlled economy the end of the 20th century sees China making important steps towards the open economy market giving special emphasis on the production and export of consumer goods. After taking over economic policy by the end of 1978, Deng Xioping opened up China to foreign trade and investment and in the early 1980 the first special Economic Zone were set up to absorb direct investment from Hong Kong and elsewhere Deng Xiaoping toured Guanddong and Shanghai in early 1992, encouraging a further and much more massive wave of foreign direct investment increasing in the form of wholly-owned subsidiaries of foreign companies which contributed toward an acceleration in GDP growth and inflation. FDI inflows peaked at over US$ 45 bn a year in 1997-98. A further surge in FDI preceded and accompanied China's accession to the World Trade Organization in December 2001, promoting China to top position as an FDI destination.

By the end of 1996, China had approved 283,575 foreign invested projects. These projects had a contract value of US$488.1 billion and the total amount of foreign capital actually used reached US$52.743 billion in 2002.

China has generally implemented reforms in the gradual and piecemeal fashion including sale of the minority shares in four of China's largest states. By the end of 2007, more than 5,000 domestic Chinese enterprises had established direct investments in 172 countries and regions around the world. Economic development has been more rapid in coastal provinces than in the interior, and approximately 200 million rural laborers have relocated to urban areas to find work. According to China's commerce ministry, FDI in 2010 surpassed $100 billion for the first time. Over the entire year ending December 2010 inbound FDI increased 17.4% to $105.74 billion. As per ministry of commerce of the People's Republic of China FDI in 2016 is 95.09 billion dollars

Factors Responsible for FDI That Pours in China

Several factors affect the amount of FDI that pours into China:

- **Competitiveness:** China attractiveness as the destination for investment depends on the development of infrastructure, resource availability and workforce skills. The level of maturation of these elements makes china more attractive for FDI relatives to other nations. A growing and developing economy requires infrastructure and resources in order to facilitate the sale of goods and services. Lower Transaction costs due to the maturation of these elements enables investor to earn returns on their investment as their enterprise are able to generate profits.
- **Regulatory Environment:** The regulatory environment towards foreign investment in China is largely favorable as compared to India. Excessive regulations tend to hinter entrepreneurial and commercial activities as managers and employees must spend more time and money to comply with

rules and regulations. The start-up cost, legal procedure and other compliances are encouraging in China. This conducive business climate encourage more foreign investment in China.

- **Stability:** Political and economic stability can facilitate an influx of FDI. Stability represents predictability and the opportunity for enterprise to gain better foresight for future alternatively constant unrest, rioting, rebellions and social turmoil are setting not conducive to business. Over the years China has been providing a stable environment to the business community. To encourage foreign investment the law and order mechanism should be vigilant for the safety of the foreign investment.
- **Local Chinese Market:** The most glaring aspects of China is the sheer size of its population and market and the prospects for growth that results from its size. The ability of enterprises backed by foreign capital to sell to a sizable local market makes China an attractive destination for FDI.As the Chinese economy continues to prosper, evolve and mature higher-end industries such as Health care, information technology, engineering, robotics and luxury goods, among others can gain a bigger footprint in China as its local conditions, resources and other FDI determinants are enhanced. The more the region attracts FDI, the more it grows. The more it grows, the more investors are willing to provide FDI.
- **Openness to Regional and International Trade:** Market openness serves important role in attracting FDI. China's market has always been favorable for regional and international trade. Trade barriers such as tariffs are typically viewed as disincentives by other nations.

FDI Investment in Retail Sector in China

China has 31 provinces the largest being Henan, followed by Shandong and Sichuan. There are 666 cities in China with most major cities located within China's eastern and southern regions. Of the major cities 11 cities have a population of more than two million and 23 cities have a population between one and two million. Urban migration continues to expand in China. Half of China's population resided in urban areas such as Beijing, shanghai, Guangzhou, Tianjin and Chongqing in 2011. This growing urbanization is leading to a greater concentration of urban consumers who live busier lifestyle and earn high incomes. These urban consumers are increasing demand for imported food products that are convenient and quick such as ready meals and are key target market for imports. This has also led to strong growth in China's second tier, smaller cities, boosting demand and retail development in these regions (IGD, 2010).

In the overall scheme of China's economic reforms, the retail and distribution sectors have been amongst the last to be deregulated. The broad thrust of China's economic policy over 20 years has been to develop manufacturing, particularly export oriented manufacturing. The modern retail trade did not emerge from the central planning system until the mid-1990s and so to allow local firms to develop sufficiently to be able to meet foreign competition, foreign access to domestic retail and distribution market was only gradually permitted.

The first time that FDI was allowed in retail was in 1992 at 26 percent. Global retailers like Walmart, Carrefour and Tesco among other eagerly entered the market. In the initial years foreign retailers were allowed to open in selected metropolises and even within metropolises like Beijing and shanghai, foreign retailers were allowed to operate only in districts where there were no local competitors. Through these measures, protection was provided to local retailers. Ten years later, in 2002, FDI in retail was raise to 49%. It was only in year 2004 that 100 percent FDI in retail sector was allowed. By this time made in China has already taken a concrete shape. Even today the top five local retail chains in the country are dominated all of Chinese origin. The success of local retailers was enabled by the government which controlled the speed of the process of opening up which provided local retailers with enough time to adapt. The real benefit of FDI in China was it led to a rapid increase in the small outlets from 1.9 million to over 2.5 million since liberalization of the sector in 1992 and this doubled the employment in both retail and wholesale. As the manufacturing sector took off in the country because of special economic zone, tax incentives for foreigner and subsidies, suppliers began serving retailers such as Walmart. In fact, in 2010 as many as 15000 Chinese suppliers were serving the Walmart and company expanded its presence to 352 markets in 130 cities across China. The most important advantage of allowing FDI in multibrand retailing would be the elimination of intermediaries between the farmers and consumers in the form of retailers and sub retailers. In prevailing circumstances, the farmers sells their product to the first intermediary and receive only 1/3 or 1/4 of the price paid by the consumers. The intermediaries add up their profit margin hiking the prices for the consumers who have almost no choice but to buy at stated price.

During these 20yrs China's astonishing economic growth and increasing openness to the outside world have led to the rapid emergence of an urban middle class of increasingly sophisticated consumers who are demanding higher quality variety and innovations from their retailers. However, China's retail revolution is not limited to major urban centers. The unprecedented migration from the country side to the cities has boosted the size of second and third tier urban market, rural market remains significant. The complexity of this unevenly developed market and sheer size of the country make China both an attractive and daunting market to understand and approach. Prior to the China's accession to the WTO, foreign retailers had to accept a host of restriction on their operation designed to slow their rate of growth. However, since 2002 most restrictions have been eased and multinational retailers enjoyed unprecedented freedom including the options to establish wholly-owned foreign enterprise rather than operate through joint venture. As a result foreign retailers are growing both organically, by opening new stores and also through merger and acquisition by buying existing chain. A decision of the Ministry of Commerce (Mofcom), the industry regulator, to devolve responsibility for approving small-and medium-sized foreign-invested retail operations from Beijing to local provincial Mofcom entities from 1 March 2006 further eases the process for multinational retailers. In 2013 China's National Bureau of Statistics reported nominal sales growth of 13.1% led by sales of communication appliances and furniture, both of which rose by more than 20%. Over the next five years sale volumes in China are expected to rise by an annual average of 8.4% significantly higher than any other global market. In fact, this year in volume terms, China will be the second fastest growing retail market of the 60 countries covered by The Economist Intelligence Unit.

Table 8 highlights the retail opportunity in China. It represents three-year estimated sales, growth rate, consumption expenditure and household earning over $25000.As per table 8 there can be slight drop down in the growth rate of retail sales. But it is also predicted that the consumption expenditure will show a growth of US$4478 in 2018 which can boost the sales of retail sector in China. House hold consumption has begun to climb even as the pace of investment has fallen. It has also been predicted that the percentage of household earning over $25000 will increase to 14.7 percent in 2018. By 2018 retail sales in China will be valued at almost UD$ 5 trillion overtaking US as the world's largest retail market in the process.

China has always remained a strategic priority for many firms looking to expand. British retailer M&S has put China at the head of a new 250 international store expansion strategy. Fast fashion retailers have taken a particular interest. H&M has announced plans for 80-90 Chinese stores this year, while Gap is looking at adding a further 35 stores. Uniqlo has unveiled an ambitious store opening program that

Table 8. Retail opportunity in China

Particulars	2016	2017	2018
Retails sales	380 7731	4281417	4758564
Retail sales growth(%)	8.6	7.9	7.8
Consumption expenditure(US$ per head	3643	4063	4478
Percentage of household earning over $25000	10.1	12.4	14.7

Source: compiled from Economic Intelligence unit 2014

specifically targets smaller interior cities. Wal-Mart has a fairly broad spread of around 400 stores in about 140 Chinese cities, and is possibly the best example of the strategic indecision over whether to open or close stores. The world's largest retailer has repeatedly announced plans to embark on an ambitious store-opening program of 110-130 stores over a three-year period, employing nearly 20,000 staff in the process. Table 9 will highlight top ten retailers in China.

According to the Table 9 the opportunity in China is already well established and retail chains are looking beyond coastal strongholds into interior cities, towns and villages. However, the market remains incredibly fragmented and one that is still largely a regional affair as most of the retail chain in top ten retail are the local giants. Of China's domestic retailers, only Suning, Balian and Gome achieved revenue exceeding Rmb100 m in 2012-13, with China Resources Vanguard close behind. The global retailers like Walmart and carrefour are way behind the local giant. For international retailers looking to break into China, fragmentation is

Table 9. Top ten retailers in China

Sr no	Name of the retailers	Amount in RMB Billion
1	Suning commerce group	20.0
2	Bailan group	19.7
3	Gome Electrical appliances	18.9
4	China Resource Vanguard	15.2
5	RT Mart International	11.7
6	Walmart China	9.4
7	Chongqing General trading group	8.8
8	Yum restaurant china Investment	8.4
9	Shandong Commercial group	8.0
10	Carrefour China	7.5

Source: Compiled from China chain stores and Franchise association and Economic intelligence unit 2014

Table 10. Retail sales volume growth in China and India (% pa)

Territory	2011	2012	2013	2014	2015	2016	2017	2018
China	9.1	8.7	9.3	8.8	8.7	8.6	8	7.9
India	5.7	2.7	1.7	4.0	5.2	6.2	6.2	6.6

Source: adapted from economic intelligence unit.

2014 onwards sales are the forecast and others are actuals

considered an opportunity. Those who recruit a local partner will inevitably be better placed for tapping into the faster growing interior cities more quickly. The local expertise provided by the domestic partner can prevent logistical pitfalls and supply an established retail presence or market share to leverage.

Table 10 highlights percentagewise retail sales volume growth in China and India. According to Table 10 due to liberal policies in China the retail sales volume growth has shown increasing trend in 2013 which is estimated to drop down in the years to come but when we analyze the sales volume growth of India it can be seen that retail sales volume growth has dropped down from 2012 and it has been to 1.7 percent in 2013 which could be due to change in the FDI policy in multibrand retailing from 100 percent to 51 percent and also due to the huge protest by opposition parties. This has made many retail giants to take back their retail investment proposal from Indian retail market. But it has been estimated to increase to 6.6% in 2018.

Further if Asia 's clothing market is analyzed it can been seen that it is growing rapidly. As more household will move towards middle class income bracket consumer complexity will increase and consumer fashion will form a part of their identity. India and China today are the largest market for clothing in the Asia region as shown in table 11. Comparing to India China gravitational pull towards the demand of clothing cannot be ignored. Seeing this rising demand leading brand like Zara, Gap, Inditex, Uniqlo are planning to establish more retail stores in China. Total retail sales in China will reach 4.886 trillion in 2015 bypassing the U.S to be the largest retail market in the world.

The Chinese experience shows that consumers actually benefit when options in the form of carrefour for that matter was introduced in the market. But it was not easy to introduce foreign giants in China. According to several Chinese activist and academics, problem exist in the form of low wages, gender based discrimination, worker intimidation, unpaid overtime etc. Several workers from across the country have filed cases in local court against several of these foreign retail giants. Over all there is great opportunity sector in India and China and that is driving foreign investment in these countries.

Table 11. Clothing retail Market demand in China and India

Teriroty	2011	2012	2013	2014	2015	2016
China	50918	58054	64368	71248	79542	88218
India	7182	7025	7220	7873	9217	10932

Source: adapted from economic intelligence unit.
2014 onwards sales are the forecast and others are actuals

FINDINGS OF THE STUDY

1. India and China have been described as "non-identical twins." The two countries have much in common: a proud, ancient culture with a central global role in the pre-colonial era, intellectual sophistication, and recently, poverty, and a large, young, hard-working population, which is nationalistic and has high aspirations. Both nations want to reassert their historical roles, but have chosen different paths to achieve their goals. India's path has been democratic, China's authoritarian.
2. China and India together account for nearly 40% of the world's population. The combined output of China and India accounts for almost 25% of global GDP when measured appropriately. Specifically, when GDP is measured using PPP (purchasing power parity) exchange rates which reflect the actual purchasing power of a country's currency, China has the world's second largest economy after the US. India is fourth after the US, China, and Japan. Moreover, China and India together accounted for roughly half of global GDP growth. In addition, China's economy has grown faster than that of India throughout the period of economic revival.
3. More than 50%of the population in India as seen in is under the age of 25-30 years and has grown up in post liberalization era. Urban population is projected to increase from the current 28%to 40%of the total population by 2020. While China has a population age between 40-44 years. Thus here India stands in a better position in terms of young potential manpower which can drive India toward achieving number one position as compared to China.
4. Looking at the Similarities between the Economies of India and China, both are conscious of their role in the world economy. Both seek to play a bigger political role on the world stage. Now observing the differences between the economies of India and China one can see that China is taking tangible but slow steps towards embracing private entrepreneurship. India on the other hand is continuing to struggle with making things easier for multinationals. Although the differences are arguably narrowing, but the first-order effect of all this is still "a big difference". The robust growth in china is attributed by the interrelated drivers that include a move to a market economy, rapid penetration into global exports, rapid progress of privatization, labor market regulation, rapid urbanization, the application of new technology and massive foreign capital inflows.
5. The other factor which was observed was the slow penetration of foreign direct investment. This also indicates that in last 20 years of liberalization, globalization and privatization. The government has focused much on privatization forgetting the fruits of foreign investment which the country can

get due to liberal policies in some of the priority sectors of India. On the other hand, Chinese main strength was liberalization foreign inflow and exports due to which it was able to grow much faster than any Asian countries and its FDI inflow has been multiple times more than India.

6. FDI in retail sector is growing at a rapid speed in China as compared to Indian retail market. This can be proved from the fact that China's retail markets reached 30 trillion yuan ($4.6 trillion) in 2015, after more than a decade of double-digit growth. Household consumption has begun to climb, even as the pace of investment has fallen, and now exceeds 6 percent of GDP. While size of Indian retail market has been US$ 600 billion which depict very clearly that China is way ahead of India in retail development.
7. The study also observed that local retail giants play a dominant role toward the development of china retail market. It has been observed the international giant have to partner with local giant to stay in the retail market.

RECOMMENDATIONS

1. The Indian government need to give immediate attention toward the growth of foreign investment in various sector. Fiscal policies, FDI policies need to be redefined so that it can bring economic development in needed sector as India is no more a closed economy but going to become the next superpower country after China.
2. Implementation of the policy at right point is very important for any country to succeed. Indian bureaucratic system, political interference, tedious procedures often delays the decision making of most of the policies in India. So, it is essential for the policy maker to note that just fixation of the policy is not going to invite economic development but it effective and timely implementation is essential for evenly progress of country like India which China is really following in practice and this should be adopted by India as well.
3. If we compare China with India in term of foreign direct investment it was found that government of China has been really supportive to invite foreign investment as they understood and if a China want to progress and move ahead, then the only solution is to liberalize the economy and invite more and more foreign participation which they followed and today they are in top five nation of the world in term of export, manufacturing, foreign exchange and so every country is trying to understand China economy. On the other hand, Indian government should not fall in the controversy create by oppositions. So the suggestion is taking into account the demand of the rising expectation of the consumers, strong market condition and rising disposable income, the

government should liberalize the foreign investment in retail sector from 51% in multibrand retailing around 100% due to which India economy will find a sea change in retail sector in future.

4. To develop organized retail in India two parameters are very important one is infrastructure and other is technology and this hampers the acceptance of new concept in India so foreign investment should be first invited in development of infrastructure and new technology which will automatically pool may new concept of retail in India. For ex Wal-Mart has maintained a presence in China for about 20 years now, opening its first stores in 1996 But till 2006 Wal-Mart in China opened only 56 stores, including 51 Wal-Mart Supercenters, three Sam's Clubs and two community stores but Wal-Mart faces different challenges in the smaller cities of China. Firstly, the distribution and supply chain networks (logistics, etc) are still under-developed as Wal-Mart is not properly accessible in small town as the infrastructure of China is not well developed, so government took effective step to create adequate infrastructure for the foreign player to penetrate. Today there are more than 350 Walmart stores in China. Technology usage is low in India today, compared to levels achieved in advanced economies. Retailers like Wal-Mart and Metro have started experimenting with Radio Frequency Identification (RFID) technology which is expected to provide much better inventory visibility and hence facilitate efficient management of much better inventory visibility

CONCLUSION

In rapidly growing yet still underdeveloped retail market of India and China has witnessed growth over the years. These markets have been taken by the retailers as the function of experimentation. Both will grow rapidly taking a much large share of GDP. Yet for the foreseeable future it is likely that China will continue to grow more rapidly than India. In both countries domestic market will become increasingly attractive to global companies. Both countries will create new world class companies that will be competitive with companies based in the west. Retailers need to understand the shopping occasion that are unique to the shopper they are trying to serve. They must recognize that inherent strength of the formats they have and develop value proposition. so foreign direct investment should be investment in the areas that create customer satisfaction. China has been marching ahead and have created various format that gives intrinsic value to the customer. But in India the intention of investment is to provide modern format. Thus, the holistic approach to understanding both shoppers need and the business environment is imperative for devising a retail format strategy and implementing it successfully.

REFERENCES

Ahya, C., & Xie, A. (2004). India and China: A Special Economic Analysis. Morgan Stanley Equity Research.

Bajal, Tuli, &Srivastava. (2009). *Retail management*. Oxford University Press.

Berman & Evans. (2010). *Retail management a strategic approach* (8th ed.). Prentice Hall of India Publication.

Chopra, S., & Kaur, S. (2014). Analysis of FDI Inflows and Outflows in India. *Journal of Advanced Management Science*, *2*(4), 326–332. doi:10.12720/joams.2.4.326-332

Dangi. (2013). fdi in retail sector opportunities and challenges. *Innovative Journal of Business and Management, 2*, 103 - 108.

Eapen. (2006). *Economic Growth in India and china-a comparative study* (vols. 1-2). ICFAI University Press.

Goyal, S., Kumar, K.P., & Rao, K.S. (2012). Retail Sector in India – Is it Necessary for Inviting FDI? *Indian Journals.com, 12*(4), 286-295.

Goyal & Bansal. (2016). Trends of FDI inflows in retail sector. International Journal of Innovative Research and Development, 5(2).

Hundt, R. (2006). *In China's Shadow: The Crisis of American Entrepreneurship*. Yale University Press.

Jhamb, S., & Bhardwaj, A. (2006). The Case of FDI in Retail Sector in India. *Asia Pacific Business Review*, *2*(2), 55–60. doi:10.1177/097324700600200207

Johnson & Tellis. (2008). Drivers of success for market entry into India and china. *Journal of Marketing*, *72*.

Joseph, M., & Soundarajan. (2009). *Retail in India: A critical assessment*. New Delhi: Academic Foundation, in association with Indian Council for Research on International Economic Relations.

Joseph, M., Soundararajan, N., Gupta, M., & Sahu, S. (2008). *Impact of Organized Retail on Unorganized Retail*. Indian Council for Research on International Economic Relations.

Konana & Doggnet. (2004). *Comparing India and China Growth Strategies: Chaotic Or Planned?* Retrieved from faculty.mccombs.utexas.edu/prabudeva.konana/indiachina.pdf

Madaan. (2009). *Fundamentals of Retailing*. Tata McGraw Hill Education Private Ltd.

Mukherjee & Patel. (2005). *FDI in Retail sector India.* Academic Foundation in Association with ICRIER and Ministry of Consumer Affairs, Food and Public Distribution (Govt. of India).

Mukhrjee, P., & Patel, N. (2005). *FDI in Retail Sector in India.* Academic Foundation.

Nandal, S. (2013). Impact Analysis of FDI on Retail Industry in India. *International Journal of Marketing, Financial Services & Management Research, 2*(1), 12–20.

Pal. (2013). FDI in multi-brand retailing: opportunities and threats for rural India. *Innovative Journal of Business and Management, 2*(6), 131 - 136.

Pandit, Levy, & Weitz. (2009). *Retailing management.* Tata McGraw Hill Companies.

Penelope & Kulkarni. (2007). *Economic Development in India and China.* Serial Publication.

Ramkishen, Rongala, & Ghost. (2008). *Attracting Foreign Direct Investment (FDI) to India.* International Professional Services Organization.

Rao. (2004). *Chinese economy- Issues and perspectives.* ICFAI Publishing House.

Ravindra, P. S., Murthy, O. N., & Rao, C. T. (2013). Will FDI in Retail Sector is Viable for Indian economy. *Asian Journal of Research in Economics and Business Management, 3*(2), 110–123.

Renuka, R., Ganesan, M., & Durgamani, M. K., (2013). Impact of FDI in Indian Economy with special reference to Retail sector in India. *Global Research Analysis, 2*(1), 22-24.

Roy, S. K., & Pandit, S. K., (2012). FDI in Multi Brand Retailing: What are they fighting about in India. *The Management Accountant, 47*(6), 652–658.

Singh. (2009). *Retail management- A global perspective text and cases.* S. Chand & Company Ltd Edition.

Srinivasan & Tendulkar. (2003). *Reintegrating India with the World Economy.* Washington, DC: Institute for International Economics.

Srivastava. (2007, September). India retail new face of India. *Marketing Mastermind,* 59-61.

Tian, X. (2007). *Managing International Business in China.* Cambridge University Press. doi:10.1017/CBO9780511810558

Uppal, R., And, K., & Juneja, A. (2013). Emerging Trends of FDI inflows in India: Responses and Challenges. *Asian Journal of Research in Business Economics and Management*, *3*(9), 218–222.

Wang & Li. (2005). The Development of the Retailing Industry in China: 1981-2005. School of Economics and Management Tsinghua University (China).

Zhang, K. H. (2001). China's inward FDI boom and the greater Chinese economy. *Chinese Economy*, *34*(1), 74–88. doi:10.2753/CES1097-1475340174

Zhang, K. H., & Song, S. (2000). Promoting exports: The role of inward FDI in China. *China Economic Review*, *11*(4), 385–396. doi:10.1016/S1043-951X(01)00033-5

Zhang, X. (1999). Foreign investment polic, contribution and performance. In *Foreign direct investment and economic growth in China.* University of Michigan Press.

Chapter 9
M&A vs. Greenfield:
FDI for Economic Growth in Emerging Economies

Sana Moid
Amity University, India

ABSTRACT

The chapter has raised two critically important questions. First, is the M&A boom a one-time effect of privatization, or is it likely to be followed by a rise in Greenfield investment? Second, do these two types of FDI mode have different macroeconomic consequences in terms of aggregate investment and growth? The main purpose of this chapter is to analyze the two entry modes, mergers and acquisitions and Greenfield investment, specifically, and to present a comparative view of the same and how it leads to the economic growth of a nation. It is concluded that one should choose the right mode according to the different situation about the firms in the international market. The present chapter also concludes that Greenfields and M&As do have a positive homogenous effect on growth. Additionally, the enhancement of human capital is an important condition for the host countries to derive the maximum benefits from Greenfields and M&As. Also, there is empirical evidence of a two-way linkage between FDI and growth. However, the bidirectional relationship exists only for the M&A's growth nexus.

DOI: 10.4018/978-1-5225-3026-8.ch009

INTRODUCTION

The multinational enterprises (MNEs) and foreign direct investment (FDI) have always played a pivotal role in spurring economic growth and jobs by integrating the economy to the world market, transferring new technology and innovation, and developing human resources. FDI has grown rapidly since 1990 far exceeding the volume of world trade. The positive contribution of MNEs and FDI in economic development and growth is recognized and supported by economic literature, MNEs' FDI decisions are little understood and until recently why they choose certain entry mode versus another has not been adequately explained in both theoretical and empirical sense.

The official definition of foreign direct investment specifies that a financial-account transaction is considered as FDI if a company's stake in a subsidiary exceeds ten percent (OECD, 2008a). However, this definition brings together two different forms of foreign investment: Greenfield investment, whereby foreign investors build a new productive unit from scratch, and mergers and acquisitions (M&As), whereby foreign investors acquire existing assets. While the former implies an accumulation of capital, latter is essentially a transfer of ownership.

Within the neo-classical model, FDI is expected to promote growth through its contribution to capital formation (Solow, 1975). In latter study, Herzer *el al.* (2008) claim that supplementary capital brought about by FDI under the Solow-type standard framework does not have long-term effect on growth. The new endogenous growth model on the other hand reflected the importance of human capital and technology in the production function of the recipient economies. According to De Mello (1997), FDI might have encouraged the incorporation of new technologies and knowledge transfer from more developed nations to less developed ones. A number of studies have suggested that the positive technological and knowledge spillovers proposed by endogenous growth theories may not exist in less-developed nations. According to Kokko *et al.* (1996), domestic firms in less-developed countries, with backward production technologies and a low-skilled labour, may not be able to learn and benefit from multinational enterprises if the technology and knowledge gap is too wide. Aitken and Harrison (1999) eventually found that the increasing existence of foreign enterprises could have negative impacts on the host country's economy. This could be problematic if investment inflows into a less-developed country are primarily in the form of resource-seeking FDI – a situation in which foreign investors invest abroad to obtain resources and other input supplies that are either too costly to obtain or unavailable in the home market (Brouthers *et al.*, 2008). Thus, if FDI draws away a country's scarce-resources, while labour skill and technological level is not insufficient to absorb advancements and other benefits from FDI, then such investments could discourage the positive spillovers.

The distinction between the two modes is that Green Field investment relies on the internal capabilities of the multinational enterprise (MNE), as is most clearly embodied in the notion of building a new subsidiary from the ground; MA involves transfer of ownership of an existing asset. Further, what does exist almost exclusively relies on data for a single developed country. However, similarities exist as well. For example, both tend to come from the developed countries and are affected by variables like GDP and distance. Similarly, both are dominated by manufacturing, although services form a significant share of overall FDI flows. Nevertheless, there are key differences across modes. While the developed countries receive the majority of MAs, developing countries receives the bulk of GF FDI. MA investment is more responsive to barriers of the origin and destination countries, including investment cost and geographical and cultural barriers. MA involves transfer of ownership (arising from a desire to integrate or exploit arbitrage opportunities) whereas GF relies more on a firm's own capacities (which are intrinsically linked to the origin country's attributes).

LITERATURE REVIEW

Existing literature on the economic consequences of Greenfields and M&As has pointed out the fact that Greenfields contribute towards increasing the recipient's capital formation and productivity, while M&As may not (Kim, 2009). This is because, Greenfields involve the direct investment and construction of new facilities and cross-border M&As involves transfer of the recipient country's income to the home market. As a result, M&As might not lead to any capital formation and/or productivity enhancement of the host country. Under these circumstances, although some studies (i.e. Blonigen and Slaughter, 2001) suggested that Greenfields do not contribute much to skill-upgrading – an important driver of growth.

In addition, according to Agosin and Machado (2005), FDI in the form of cross-border M&As may not actually lead to any increase in the physical capital of a capital-scarce country and merely represents the ownership transfer of existing assets from domestic to foreign entities. Thus, if the proceeds from the selling of these assets are spent on consumption and imports, FDI would not directly promote the growth of productive capacities, and therefore economic growth (Mencinger, 2003). However, some other studies (see, i.e. Barrell and Pain (1997); and Conyon et al. (2002)) claim the contrary, that cross-border M&As could actually improve the rate of technical progress and productivity in the recipient country therefore promoting the long-run rate of economic growth.

The theory on mode choice starts at the firm level, where an individual firm chooses its entry mode analyzing the costs and benefits of each, a decision which can then be included in a general equilibrium model. Nocke and Yeaple (2008) provided a model in which MNE establishes a subsidiary for two reasons: for reducing production costs and for hiring new entrepreneurs who provide headquarter services. While both modes seek lower production costs, only MA acquire new entrepreneurs by purchasing an acquisition target. The tradeoff between the two modes depends on their relative costs. When targets in the destination are scarce, making MA costly, GF will automatically dominate. Conversely, if the establishment of a GF subsidiary is more difficult, MA will dominate. As per different theories price of MA is a crucial component in deciding whether to choose GF or MA. For example, Raff et al. (2009) provide a model where the acquisition price is forward looking and can lead to GF investment which increases the number of firms and has consequences for their profits. Muller (2007) provides a model in which changes in competition feed into the acquisition price and shows that it depends on the extent of existing competition in the country.

Globerman and Shapiro (2004) compare how FDI inflows and outflows vary with gravity variables like measures of market size and trade and investment costs for both full and MA only samples. It was found that all FDI is attracted to larger economies, with MA particularly so. Neto et al. (2009) extend this analysis to a panel and include cultural variables, finding that they appear to be more important for GF than MA. Hebous et al. (2011) have bilateral data dividing FDI into GF and MA for outbound German investments. In this comparison of GF and MA FDI across US states, Swenson (2001) finds a similar difference in tax sensitivities. These results are consistent with the model of Becker and Fuest (2010), who reflects that tax advantages of a particular destination are likely to be capitalized into the acquisition price, something which would not happen with GF. Outside of these tax-oriented studies, in a comparison between MA flows and total FDI flows, Klein and Rosengren (1994) find that inbound US MA investments are more sensitive to exchange rate variation than are aggregate flows. This lends support to the notion of "fire sale" FDI, that is, investments which are spurred by a decline in the cost of establishing/acquiring the affiliate due to exchange rate movements (Froot and Stein, 1991).

Combining the above results, several predictions emerge. First, it is expected that both the levels of GF and MA respond in different ways to the traditional gravity variables, i.e. levels of FDI are greater between large, wealthy countries with small barriers between them. Second, it is anticipated that MA (which generally originates in high-income countries) is particularly drawn to high income countries, both due to the availability of potential targets as well as the assignment predictions of their model. Third, it is anticipated that MA is relatively more sensitive to destination financial depth and institutional quality. Finally, it is expected that GF is more sensitive to destination taxes whereas MA is more responsive to exchange rate fluctuations.

OBJECTIVES

1. To understand and analyze the two entry modes: Mergers & Acquisitions and Greenfield investment
2. To compare the two modes M&A and Greenfield investment from external and internal impact.
3. To present the current status of M&A and Greenfield investment in Emerging Economies.
4. To make suggestions and recommendations for implementation.

GLOBAL INVESTMENT TREND

Global FDI flows increased by 38 per cent to $1.76 trillion in 2015, their highest level since the global economic and financial crisis of 2008–2009. However, they still remain 10 per cent short of the 2007 peak. A surge in cross-border mergers and acquisitions (M&As) to $721 billion, from $432 billion in 2014, was the main factor behind the global rebound. Discounting these large-scale corporate reconfigurations implies a more moderate increase of about 15 per cent in global FDI flows. The value of announced Greenfield investment projects remained at $766 billion. FDI flows are likely to decline in both developed and developing economies, barring another wave of cross-border M&A deals and corporate reconfigurations. Over the medium term, global FDI flows are projected to resume growth in 2017 and to surpass $1.8 trillion in 2018.

The services sector accounts for almost two thirds of global FDI stock. In 2014, services accounted for 64 per cent of global FDI stock, followed by manufacturing (27 per cent) and the primary sector (7 percent), with 2 per cent unspecified.

In 2015, cross-border M&As in manufacturing soared, with developed and developing economies presenting different industrial patterns. The total value of cross-border M&As, as well as their sectoral breakdown, has changed significantly over the past few years. Although the combined amount of cross-border M&As in services increased by $95 billion in 2015, the balance tilted in favor of manufacturing, which accounted for 54 per cent of all cross-border M&As, compared with 41 per cent in 2012, and 28 per cent in 2009.

UNCTAD's preliminary estimates indicate that FDI flows to developed countries increased sharply in 2015, reaching their second highest level ever at US$936 billion, and accounting for the majority of the increase in global flows. Cross-border M&A activities, most notably acquisitions of assets in the United States by foreign MNEs, boosted FDI flows. MNEs seeking growth, rushed to make acquisitions. The low interest environment and strong balance sheets facilitated such movement.

Therefore, the growth of FDI inflows did not resulted into an equivalent expansion of productive capacity, as it was due in large part to cross-border M&As and with only a limited contribution from Greenfield investment projects in productive assets.

In Focus: India Overtakes China

In 2015, India replaced China as the leading destination for FDI projects in the Asia-Pacific region with $63bn of inward capital investment across the year, accounting for 53% of FDI into China and India collectively. India, unlike China, has experienced growth in both project numbers and capital investment for the past two years. In 2015, a 23% decline in capital investment has mirrored the 16% decline in projects destined for the country. India, on the other hand, had a turbulent five years but achieved growth in both 2014 and 2015 for capital investment and project numbers, bolstering its position and allowing it to overtake China. Of the top 10 destination states for FDI in 2015, India claims five places, with the top place going to Gujarat, which attracted $12.4bn and claimed 10% of all capital investment into both countries. In 2011, Gujarat was ranked the 14th most popular state for FDI within the two countries. Maharashtra in western India has been one of the strongest performers across the years and it has continued to close the gap on the top Chinese destination, Shanghai Municipality, with the locations attracting $8.3bn and $10.6bn, respectively, in 2015. According to FDI Markets, the motives cited by companies investing in the two countries are quite similar in nature. For both countries, companies identify domestic market growth potential and proximity to markets as the main two reasons for investing.

Key trends of 2015 could be summarized as:

- While the number of FDI projects in Asia-Pacific decreased by 7%, the total capital investment increased by 29% to $320.5bn.
- China suffered a 23% decline in capital investment and a 16% reduction in FDI projects. Pakistan increased its capital investment figure by 147% to $18.9bn backed by energy-related major investments.
- The top three countries for capital investment, India, China and Indonesia, accounted for almost half (49%) of FDI in the region
- The total number of FDI projects out of Asia-Pacific decreased by 1% to 2802, which was offset by a 13% increase in capital investment
- Outward capital investment from China decreased by 10%, while project numbers increased by 7%.
- Capital investment globally, with $113.5bn of announced FDI recorded in 2015

- The top three sectors by project numbers – software and IT services, business services and financial services – contribute more than one-third (35%) of all FDI globally by project numbers
- Real estate continues to recover in 2015, with FDI project numbers up 6% and capital investment up 17% to $96.6bn
- Within top five sectors by project numbers, business services was the only sector to witness growth, with 1413 projects recorded in 2015
- FDI into aerospace rose marginally, with 154 projects recorded at a value of $5.8bn
- Investment into the software and IT services and communications sectors dropped in 2015, with capital investment figures falling to $22bn and $46.2bn, respectively, reflecting the decline in project numbers

FDI and Economic Growth

Adam Smith (1976) in his book *The Wealth of Nations* wrote, that the average level of country prosperity can be measured by country's income per person: "The annual labour produce of every nation is the fund which originally supplies it with all the necessities and conveniences of life…to the number of those who have to consume it…" Hence the annual level of real GPD per person should be of high importance considering the welfare. Consequently, GDP growth, is one of the most important economic variables. The process of growth is seen as the way country can reach higher level of income. Moreover, GDP per capita indicates average standard of living of country and GDP per worker shows average productivity of labor in the country. In most of recent growth models the technological progress is an ultimate source of GDP growth. The economic growth under the diminishing returns to scale is explained by external technological progress, which could be affected by the capital and labor accumulation, as well as their efficiency. In addition to this, the increase in total factor productivity, which is intangible factor, ranging from technology to knowledge may contribute to the progress in productivity too. In more modern endogenous growth theories, increasing returns to scale are also explained through the technology prism, but the action is different. Here the increase in GDP per capita is affected by endogenous forces rather than exogenous. As a result the investments in human capital, innovation and knowledge are held significant determinants of the economic growth. The externalities occur, for example, when workers face new, often more modern and therefore obtain better and more sophisticated skills. In R&D-backed growth models, the main interest is put on understanding how R&D contributes to the economic growth.

FDI is much related to cross-border technology transfer and R&D. Therefore it is rational to assume comprehensive effect of FDI on economic growth in cases, M&A and Greenfield investment, before making a decision to enter a foreign market. Moreover, R&D internationalization by MNE is quite a recent phenomenon. Until mid of 2000's knowledge-intensive corporate functions almost exclusively were kept in developed countries, but in the last decade industries such as automobile, pharmacy, electronics established R&D in developing countries in order to reach engineers, scientists and meet the demands of expanding sophisticated markets (UNCTAD WIR, 2005). Lipsey (2002) argues that results of positive spillovers on total factor productivity from foreign enterprises to local firms are mixed .He also admits that overall productivity should improve because of the presence of foreign-owned operations. It is also stated that when a host economy is introduced with new products or new international industries due to presence of MNE, it benefits from being linked to world trading system. Therefore, productivity effects and development of new products should contribute to faster economic growth.

MAIN METHODS OF FOREIGN MARKET ENTRY

With two main methods to enter a foreign market, the choice between M&A and Greenfield FDI is influenced by industry-specific factors. Technology and production are more relevant for those implementing a Greenfield investment, while culture, transactions costs, attitude towards acquisitions by foreigners, conditions in capital markets, and importance of future intermediary are more important for M&A deals. Before 1980's, Greenfield investment was a dominant market entry mode of FDI. Afterwards, the value of acquisitions in host countries exceeded the value of building new plants or opening new subsidiaries by foreign enterprises and hence M&A became a trend for 15 years. History and statistical data show that cross-border M&A were more often executed between developed countries in terms of number of projects and value, whereas Greenfield investments were done by multinationals from developed countries into emerging or transition economies. A rise of emerging markets in the last decade increased the number of Greenfield investments and the importance of collecting data for it that was not the case before beginning of 2000.

Mergers and Acquisitions

Even though M&A is normally used as a single word, these two are not the same and the distinction between these two could be depending on each special case. Merger happens when two or more companies join and become one company. Then stocks are surrendered by shareholders in exchange of stocks of a new company that has just merged. Firms combine resources in order to accomplish common targets. Accordingly, acquisition is when one firm purchases stocks of other enterprise in order to have control over the company (10 to 50 percent of total shares) or to increase the ownership significantly (more than 50 percent).

Statutory merger means that one targeted company after the agglomeration cease to exist and the acquiring firm takes over assets and liabilities of the merged firm. The shareholders of the targeted firm usually become joint owners of new combined company. The other type - consolidation - reflects establishment of completely new firm from two or more consolidating firms. The entities after the merger do not exist anymore and shareholders of former firms become owners of the new firm. The third type of merger subsidiary means that the acquired firm will be transformed to a subsidiary of the mother-company. Reverse merges represent a situation when the acquiring firm merges with the targeted company and afterwards acquirer ceases it existence. After the merger, the acquirer launches external funds through the stock exchange channels or gets an access to a bigger market-share using its new brand. The last type merger of equals happens when two firms, often of equal size, decide to form a new firm and continue to operate under the new established firm. Old stocks are surrendered and new ones are issued.

There are four main types of acquisitions. Friendly takeover is done between two companies which have common interests and no rejections from the target firm management (board of directors). Additionally, an agreement to be acquired could be issued. If the board is of the opinion that the acquisition will benefit shareholders, they usually recommend to owners to accept the offer. Conversely, hostile acquisition occurs when target company management is unwilling to accept the deal, but the bidder continued offering and making official announcement of its intentions. Reverse takeover refers to a sales transaction when the purchaser is smaller than the target firm or when a private firm purchases a publicly listed company with an aim to launch public share market in efficient way. Backflip takeover is the type of acquisition when the purchaser becomes a subsidiary of the target firm after the execution of the deal. It is a very convenient way for a larger but less-known firm to use the well-known name of the purchased company, which currently might be not at the best business condition.

Greenfield Investment

Greenfield investment is a method of foreign market entry, which includes 100 percent offshore ownership and requires setting up all necessary infrastructures starting from zero to operate the business. As a matter of fact, Greenfield projects are a popular sort of investment in less competitive markets, emerging markets or developing markets because of expected economic growth and higher returns. However, because of uncertainty in those markets, credit ratings, political instability's potential or military intervention, it is also considered to be a risky investment. Currency risk, difficulty raising capital, poor corporate governance system, and liquidity constrains could even provoke additional risks. Contrarily, a newly established company in a host country may be in danger if its parent firm faces financial burden. Analyzing motives of choosing Greenfield investment to enter a foreign market, one can think of relatively low transaction costs, greater project coordination and efficiency in comparison to M&A. As there is no target company, there is no need for additional investigation on proper integration and evaluation. Avoidance of external market deals may protect from usual time lags managing international cooperation.

The Comparison Between M&A and Greenfield Investment

It is assumed that M&A bring fewer benefits to host economy at the time of market entry than greenfield investment because M&A do not add productive capacity and only transfer ownership from domestic to foreign and close some of target firm activities. Whereas, greenfield venture provides fresh capital and new jobs. If the acquiring firm is a global oligopolist, this could disturb competitive market development by its dominance. As enterprise purchases a foreign firm it immediately gets competitive advantage in form of local market share, brand name, technology and other specific assets and in doing so brings needed competition and fosters host market development. Therefore, the impact can be ambiguous - the future of local market conditions depends on investors' characteristics, target company stance and local participants' business health. Such foreign control may also hurt local entrepreneurship and technology and capacity building. M&A can result in economic, social and cultural concerns. For example, in such industries as entertainment and media, purchases of local firms could threaten national identity. Also big transnational corporations are usually associated with globalization, thus their presence may adversely affect local small and medium-size enterprises (SME). Thus, in such context, M&A are seen from negative point of view, whereas greenfield investment from the opposite. The other interesting thing is that the host country's media tend to advertise more takeovers made by national companies rather than foreign ones or even describe with indignity M&A made by foreigners.

Greenfield investment and M&A differ in characteristics and impact of entering. In developed markets, Greenfield investment and M&A can be seen as alternatives, but in developing or in transition markets - they are not. There might be potential to invest but only few firms to acquire. Looking from the government policy perspective, it is still often the case that M&A are allowed. Moreover, corporate governance is different among developed and developing countries, and consequently can influence the mode of FDI. In the times of large privatization programme, as happened in

CEE during the 1990's, government welcomes both greenfield investment and M&A. Considering the financial matters of these two methods and their impact on local currency, there are important differences. In the case of M&A, the funds are transferred immediately, whereas in Greenfield investment this transfer is done gradually. If M&A deal value is overwhelmingly high, the local currency might be affected and, hence without a central bank intervention through open market operation and sterilization – it will appreciate. The stock market soundness has its own role on M&A. Usually M&A is more sensitive to financing conditions due to turmoil in stock market than Greenfield investment. Accordingly, the depressed stock prices reduce value of M&A deals. Giovanni (2005) also finds that home country's total market capitalization has a positive impact on domestic firms investing abroad.

Comparison From Implementations

A firm can establish a wholly owned subsidiary in a country by building a subsidiary from the ground level, called green-field strategy, or by acquiring an enterprise in the target market known as M&A. From their definitions we can see that Green field investment is a way of internal growth and M&A is of external growth.

The basic difference between M&A and Greenfield Investment lies in implementation. M & A is an investment model implemented by expanding the internal organization of firms through the external market trading, with regards to enterprise as a special commodity. At first the acquiring firms often overpay for the assets of the acquired firm. In the beginning, it will not increase host country's production capacity. This point may lead the host country worry about their industry market's structure and competition. Especially to developing countries, it may cause the adverse concern whether this mode of investment can influence the host country's economic sovereignty. Greenfield investment attaches importance to make good use of the capacity of the enterprises' internal organization and resources, then in order to establish the new production capacity and obtain the scale, purchasing land, machinery and means of production from the market. In the model of Greenfield, the behavior of market transactions have been replaced by the behavior of trading in the enterprises' internal organization, although eliminating some cost caused by market transactions, the internal management also exists cost of the same page.

In addition to cost, M&A and Greenfield Investment also show some differences in the effects of external factors and internal configuration. With the development of the strategic theory, enterprises are not only pursuing short-term interest but also pursuing long-term strategic objectives; by considering the effective and efficient investment behavior from comprehensive sides. They aim to achieve a strategic business activities and access to sustainably competitive advantage at the core.

Comparison From the External Impacts

Intensity of Market Competition

With reference to this, difference is that M&A is an adjustment to the market's present firms in an industry, while Greenfield Investment adds the new supply to the market. In the market-oriented environment, weak competition often accompanied with high profits of the industry. At this time, FDI is inclined to Greenfield Investment to enter in the market. When the effective supply on the market is far from meeting the demand; then Greenfield Investment may be able to find a place in such a situation, which can gain its competitive advantages. Due to the promising market prospects, it will attract a large number of investors, but the appropriate acquired firms will be very scarce and at the same time the cost will be very high. As a result, wise investors would prefer Greenfield Investment rather than M&A.

The degree of competition in the market is often accompanied by the development of the industry cycle. Most of the development of the industry experienced the four processes of start-up, development, maturity and the decline. With the appearance of new products and new technologies, the industry began to experience a new developing cycle. In the initial stage of the development, because of less competition, Greenfield Investment is the mainstream during this period. As the industry maturing and competition increasing step by step, enterprise started to pursue economies of scale and excess production capacity. Greenfield investment model should be replaced by M&A. Under the influence of competition, M&A will become the mainstream of the FDI.

Resource Constraints

Company's core competitiveness lies in its main product and the form of the product depends on a specific resource. Different enterprises have different investment performances according to the characteristics of the resources. From another perspective, the choice of investment models is constrained by the objective conditions which are caused by specific resources. Sometimes, good resources bring competitive advantage to the enterprise. However, some resources are limited to the number or location of the binding nature. In this case, in order to obtain advantages of resources, M&A may be the only way.

Transferability of Resources

M&A and Greenfield Investment is essentially expanding own companies' ability and resources. Companies expand the core competencies within the enterprise through the way of Greenfield Investment. The way through M&A is a part of the strategies that the enterprise transplants other companies' core competencies or core resources as a whole. Therefore, M&A or Greenfield Investment is determined by whether the resources and capabilities own the ability of transferability. If it is the capital centralized then the investment tends to Greenfield Investment. If it is the human capital centralized then the investment tends to M&A.

Comparison From Internal Impacts

Quick Execution

By acquiring an established enterprise, a firm can rapidly build its presence in the target foreign market as compared to Greenfield Investment. For business expansion, majority of enterprises would regard M&A as a short cut. In terms of economic globalization, the pace of corporate is not only the key to access the relevant market, but also has a bearing on the survival and development of enterprises. Keeping pace in mind, M&A is often the first choice for decision-makers. Through M&A, the company can significantly reduce the project's construction period. Acquiring firm result in accessing the local market with a high speed; and gain a head start in the market among the fierce competition. If we choose Greenfield Investment, we have to prepare enough time to face the complicated procedure. It is related to the general argument, the examination and the official approval, infrastructure, equipment installation and so on.

Corporate Culture

When a company acquired another company, it is a long way to go due to their culture difference because of different countries or different industries. From the perspective of corporate culture, Greenfield Investment is much better than M&A because enterprises can build a new one and implant new culture into the new body enabling investors to maintain a high degree of consistency. However, the company whose culture is less distinct and more likely to achieve diversity, M&A does matter under this culture.

Management

Organizations operate with lesser efficiency not because of low resources but due to inefficient management. Therefore, one of the intrinsic motivations for M&A is the different level of management. For illustration, there are two companies A and B, when A's management is more efficient than B's, A can gain more if he implant his management to B. Then A has the motivation to acquire B. Through M&A, the Company A's management resources can make maximal return. However, to some extent, enterprises with low management level had better choose Greenfield Investment to circumvent the high level of risk of management.

CONCLUSION

The choice between M&A and Greenfield Investment is not easy to make. Both modes have their advantages and disadvantages. In general, the choice depends on the circumstances faced by the firm. If the firm is seeking to enter a market where there are already well-established incumbent enterprises, and where global competitors are also interested in establishing a presence, it may pay the firm to enter via an acquisition. In such circumstances, Greenfield Investment may be too slow to establish a sizeable presence. However, if the firm is going to make an acquisition, its management should be aware of the risks associated with acquisitions that were discussed earlier and consider these when determining which firms to purchase. It may be better to enter by the slower route of a Greenfield Investment than to make a bad acquisition. If a firm is considering entering a country where there are no incumbent competitors to be acquired, then a Greenfield Investment may be the only mode. Even when incumbents exist, if the competitive advantage of the firm is based on the transfer of organizationally embedded competencies, skills, routines and culture, it may still be preferable to enter via a Greenfield Investment. Things like skills and organizational culture based on significant knowledge that is difficult to articulate and codify, are much easier to embed in a new venture than they are in an acquired entity, where the firm may have to overcome the established routines and culture of the acquired firm. Greenfields and M&As do have a positive homogenous effect on growth. Additionally, the enhancement of human capital is an important prerequisite for the host countries to derive the best benefits from Greenfields and M&As.

Foreign direct investment (FDI) comes in different forms: its Greenfield variant implies the creation of *new* productive units, while M&A variant reflects a change of ownership of already *existing* firms. The volume of Greenfield FDI reflects the expansion of the host country's capital stock, some of the proceeds from M&A sales just represent rents for the domestic firms' previous owners. Despite the productivity gain that is associated with foreign ownership, any dollar of M&A sales therefore has a weaker effect on growth than a dollar of Greenfield FDI.

REFERENCES

Agosin, M., & Machado, D. (2005). Foreign Investment in Developing Countries: Does it Crowd in Domestic Investment? *Oxford Development Studies*, *33*(2), 149–162. doi:10.1080/13600810500137749

Aitken, B. J., & Harrison, A. E. (1999). Do domestic firms benefit from direct foreign investment? Evidence from Venezuela. *The American Economic Review*, *89*(3), 605–618. doi:10.1257/aer.89.3.605

Alfaro, Chanda, Kalemli-Ozcan, & Sayek. (2002). *FDI and Economic Growth: The Role of Local Finance Markets*. Harvard Business School.

Barrell, R., & Pain, N. (1997). Foreign Direct Investment, Technological Change, and Economic Growth Within Europe. *Economic Journal (London)*, *107*(445), 1770–1786. doi:10.1111/j.1468-0297.1997.tb00081.x

Becker, J., & Fuest, C. (2010). Taxing Foreign Profits with International Mergers and Acquisitions. *International Economic Review*, *51*(1), 171–186. doi:10.1111/j.1468-2354.2009.00575.x

Broner, F. A., & Rigobon, R. (2006). Why are Capital Flows so Much More Volatile in Emerging than in Developed Countries? In R. J. Caballero, C. Calderon, & L. F. Cespedes (Eds.), *External Vulnerability and Preventive Policies*. Santiago: Central Bank of Chile.

Conyon, M., Girma, S., Thompson, S., & Wright, P. (2002). The Productivity and Wage Effect of Foreign Acquisition in the United Kingdom. *The Journal of Industrial Economics*, *50*(1), 85–102. doi:10.1111/1467-6451.00169

Davies, R. B., & Desbordes, R. (forthcoming). Greenfield FDI and Skill Upgrading: A Polarised Issue. *The Canadian Journal of Economics. Revue Canadienne d'Economique*.

De Mello, L. R. (1999). Foreign direct investment-led growth: Evidence from time series and panel data. *Oxford Economic Papers*, *51*(1), 133–151. doi:10.1093/oep/51.1.133

Drogendijk, R., & Slangen, A. (2006). Hofstede, Schwartz, or Managerial Perceptions? The Effects of Different Cultural Distance Measures on Establishment Mode Choices by Multinational Enterprises. *International Business Review*, *15*(4), 361–380. doi:10.1016/j.ibusrev.2006.05.003

Eicher & Kang. (2005). Trade, foreign direct investment or acquisition: Optimal entry modes for multinationals. *Journal of Development Economics, 77*, 207–228.

Froot, K. A., & Stein, J. C. (1991). Exchange Rates and Foreign Direct Investment: An Imperfect Capital Markets Approach. *The Quarterly Journal of Economics, 106*(4), 1191–1217. doi:10.2307/2937961

Gassebner, M., & Méon, P.-G. (2010). *Where do Creditor Rights Matter? Creditor Rights, Political Constraints and Cross-border M&A Activity*. CEB Working Paper No. 10-019.

Globerman, S., & Shapiro, D. (2004). *Assessing International Mergers And Acquisitions As A Mode Of Foreign Direct Investment*. International Finance 0404009, EconWPA.

Hebous, S., Ruf, M., & Weichenrieder, A. J. (2011). The Effects Of Taxation On The Location Decision Of Multinational Firms: M&A Versus Greenfield Investments. *National Tax Journal, 64*(3), 817–838. doi:10.17310/ntj.2011.3.03

Kim, Y. (2007). Impacts of regional economic integration on industrial relocation through FDI in East Asia. *Journal of Policy Modeling, 29*(1), 165–180. doi:10.1016/j.jpolmod.2006.04.008

Kim, Y. H. (2009). Cross-border M&A vs. greenfield FDI: Economic integration and its welfare impact. *Journal of Policy Modeling, 31*(1), 87–101. doi:10.1016/j.jpolmod.2008.08.005

Klein, M. W., & Rosengren, E. S. (1994). The Real Exchange Rate and Foreign Direct Investment in the United States: Relative Wealth vs. Relative Wage Effects. *Journal of International Economics, 36*(3-4), 373–389. doi:10.1016/0022-1996(94)90009-4

Kokko, A., Tansini, R., & Zejan, M. C. (1996). Local technological capability and productivity spillovers from FDI in the Uruguayan manufacturing sector. *The Journal of Development Studies, 32*(4), 602–611. doi:10.1080/00220389608422430

Mercado, R. Jr, & Park, C.-Y. (2011). What Drives Different Types of Capital Flow and their Volatilities in Developing Asia? *International Economic Journal, 25*(4), 655–680. doi:10.1080/10168737.2011.636628

Muller, T. (2007). Analyzing Modes of Foreign Entry: Greenfield Investment versus Acquisition. *Review of International Economics, 15*(1), 93–111. doi:10.1111/j.1467-9396.2006.00634.x

Neto, P., Brando, A., & Cerqueira, A. (2009). *The Macroeconomic Determinants of Cross Border Mergers and Acquisitions and Greenfield Investments. GEE Papers 0017*. Gabinete de Estratgia e Estudos, Ministrio da Economia e da Inovao.

Nocke, V., & Yeaple, S. (2008). An Assignment Theory of Foreign Direct Investment. *The Review of Economic Studies*, *75*(2), 529–557. doi:10.1111/j.1467-937X.2008.00480.x

Park, C.-Y., Byun, H.-S., & Lee, H.-H. (2012). *Assessing Factors Affecting M&As versus Greenfield FDI in Emerging Countries*. Papers and Briefs, Economics Working Papers 18414, National Bureau of Economic Research, Inc.

Raff, H. (2004). Preferential Trade Agreements and Tax Competition for Foreign Direct Investment. *Journal of Public Economics*, *88*(12), 2745–2763. doi:10.1016/j.jpubeco.2004.03.002

Raff, H., Ryan, M., & Sthler, F. (2009). The Choice of Market Entry Mode: Greenfield investment, M&A and Joint Venture. *International Review of Economics & Finance*, *18*(1), 3–10. doi:10.1016/j.iref.2008.02.006

Slangen, A., & Hennart, J.-F. (2007). Greenfield or Acquisition Entry: A review of the Empirical Foreign Establishment Mode Literature. *Journal of International Management*, *13*(4), 403–429. doi:10.1016/j.intman.2007.08.001

Solow, R. M. (1957). Technical Change and the Aggregate Production Function. *The Review of Economics and Statistics*, *39*(3), 312–320. doi:10.2307/1926047

Swenson, D. L. (2001). Transaction Type and the Effect of Taxes on the Distribution of Foreign Direct Investment in the United States. In J. J. Hines (Ed.), *International Taxation and Multinational Activity* (pp. 89–112). University of Chicago Press. doi:10.7208/chicago/9780226341750.003.0005

UNCTAD. (2007). *World Investment Report 2007: Cross-border Mergers and Acquisitions and Development*. Geneva: United Nations.

UNCTAD. (2014). *World Investment Report 2014*. New York: United Nations.

Wang, M., & Wong, M. C. S. (2009). What Drives Economic Growth? The Case of Crossborder M&A and Greenfield FDI Activities. *Kyklos*, *62*(2), 316–330. doi:10.1111/j.1467-6435.2009.00438.x

Chapter 10
Patterns of Technology Acquisition:
Upstream Linkages Between MNEs and Local Suppliers

António Carrizo Moreira
University of Aveiro, Portugal

ABSTRACT

Although MNEs are important players in the present global world, there has been a debate regarding, on one hand, how MNEs contribute to the development of indigenous firms in host countries, and on the other hand, how indigenous suppliers are able to cope with their international technology demanding clients. This chapter analyzes the patterns of technology acquisition of 40 firms that supply eight multinational firms that belong to four different industries. It is possible to conclude that there are certain differences among foreign and indigenous suppliers as well across the industries they belong to. These differences are the result of a cumulative process over time, which reflect the different performances of the companies and their relationships with the environment.

INTRODUCTION

The erosion of barriers to international flows of goods, knowledge and products brought about new challenges for all firms and for policy makers agendas, namely in developing and sustaining competitive advantages in the international arena.

Studies analyzing foreign direct investment (FDI) and multinational enterprises (MNEs) proliferate as MNEs exercise a crucial role in international business (Ribau,

DOI: 10.4018/978-1-5225-3026-8.ch010

Moreira, & Raposo, 2015). However, there are still some controversies regarding FDI and its consequences in host counties, and the contribution of MNEs to local economies (e. g. Grimes & Du, 2013; Jiang, Branzei, & Xia, 2016). Those who contend that FDI affects negatively host countries defend that MNEs jeopardize the technological leadership of indigenous firms and drive them out of business (Günther, 2002). Those in favor of FDI argue that it is as a beneficial factor as it is a source of capital, technology and new knowledge (Wang and Yu, 2008), especially for developing countries (D'Amelio, Garrone, & Piscitello, 2016) as MNEs contribute to energy poverty alleviation. However, Gorg and Strobl (2001) and Irsova and Havranek (2013) found that the results are irrelevant.

Although the controversy remains, as MNEs are important players in the present global world, there has been a debate regarding, on one hand, how MNEs contribute to the development of indigenous firms generating endogenous conditions to promote a sustainable economic development in host countries, and, on the other hand, how indigenous suppliers are able to cope with their international technology demanding clients (Moreira, 2008; Perri & Peruffo, 2016; Reis, Heitor, Amaral, & Mendonça, 2016).

If it is clear that both a cooperative behavior is mandatory for suppliers to succeed in supplying their multinational clients, and that local suppliers and foreign MNEs need to interact with each other if local suppliers are to evolve strategically in this relationship (Moreira, 2008). Moreover, as Moreira (2009) claims, knowledge flows between both firms are mandatory for a symbiotic relationship to take place.

What is not known is what the patterns of technology acquisition among SMEs in their relationship with MNEs are. As such, this chapter seeks to analyze the accumulation process among suppliers as a result of the supplier (SME)-client (MNE) interface in the supply chain. It is assumed that the external network of relationships among suppliers is the result of their need to cope with technological change generated by their clients.

Two types of inter-firm relationships are going to be analyzed: informal and formal relationships. The following patterns of technology accumulation are going to be analyzed, based on Ribault, Martinet, and Lebidois (1995): catalogue purchase; specification purchase; capital equipment purchase; outsourcing; technological scanning; reverse engineering; patenting; licensing; spin offs; network of firms; joint venture; strategic alliances; cooperative R&D; and participation in European programs.

This chapter is divided in seven sections. After this introduction, the second section presents the literature review on the importance of FDI, MNEs, and the consequences of FDI for local economies. The third section lays down the research methodology. The main results are presented in section four. Section five presents the main conclusions. Section six presents future research directions and section seven presents solutions and recommendations.

BACKGROUND

FDI has become one of the key consequences of the erosion of barriers to international flows of goods and knowledge (Moreira, 2008). Gross domestic product (GDP) grew from 7% of world GDP in 1990 to 32% of world GDP in 2012 (Sun, Lee, & Hong, 2016), which gives a clear picture of the importance of FDI for the world economy.

As referred by Ribau et al. (2015), classical theories of international business addressed the articulation of international production with international trade and capital flows (Hymer, 1976). Hymer (1976) stressed that FDI was important as way of MNEs controlling foreign assets, and exercising market power benefiting from imperfect competition or from the possession of distinctive ownership advantages. The theories of the firm were also important to study the motivation for MNEs to operate, produce and market abroad in any industry and why MNEs have a special drive towards diversification (Buckley & Casson, 1976; Hymer, 1976; Ribau et al, 2015).

The eclectic paradigm, developed by Dunning (1977; 1981) was important to explain why, where, and how MNEs operate overseas. It was based on the premise that international investment requires the fulfilment of three main preconditions firms need to fulfil to invest abroad: called the *ownership*, *location*, and internalization (OLI) advantages. Ownership advantages are unique to a particular firm and enable it to take advantage of investment opportunities abroad. Locational advantages are those that are specific to a country. These types of advantages are especially attractive for foreign investors. Internalization advantages are the benefits that derive from internal markets and that allow firms to bypass external markets and the costs associated with them.

It is clear that, from the theories so far referred to, there is little reference to the endogenous conditions of the host country perspective. However, based on the eclectic paradigm, the investment development path (IDP) model contends that firms ownership advantages interact with countries location advantages, and as a result from those interactions both host and home countries' economies are shaped (Dunning & Narula, 1996; Narula & Dunning, 2010).

Although the presence of foreign firms has negative implications on local suppliers as they cannot comply with higher standards of supplied products (Weatherspoon & Reardon, 2003; Farina & Reardon, 2000), there are positive vertical impacts among domestic firms in supplier-client relationships (Moreira, 2008), in the adoption of new technologies (Gow & Swinnen, 1998), and in improved access to finance and product quality (Dries & Swinnen, 2004).

Jiang et al. (2016), based on a study of Chinese manufacturing firms, from 1998 to 2007, conclude that foreign equity dis-incentivizes endogenous knowledge while export orientation incentivizes investment on internal knowledge as there is a shift in the locus of innovation control from a firm-level dependence on imported technology to an indigenous-centered innovation perspective. This perspective is tuned with Grimes and Du's (2013) view that defend that dependence on external knowledge makes firms overly dependent on imported technology.

On the other hand, studies have shown negative economic and social impacts stemming from MNEs presence in developing countries (Günther, 2002). Some studies find that multinationals crowd out local firms and that technology, knowledge, and skills transfers do not occur over the long-term (Aitken & Harrison, 1999). In addition, MNEs pollute the environment, exploit child labor, adopt inadequate safety standards and are not effective in alleviating poverty with their social initiatives (Oetzel & Doh, 2009).

Perri and Perrufo (2016) address FDI knowledge spillovers from the international business perspective, and develop a framework that integrates macro- and micro-level antecedents spillovers and their consequences. They clearly differentiate between traditional models and new perspectives and propose that: first, consequences of FDI spillovers should be analyzed from both local (erosion of local firms' competitive knowledge and catch up process) and foreign firms perspective (subsidiaries' opportunity for knowledge sourcing, liability of foreignness, and embeddedness); second, antecedents of FDI spillovers should be analyzed from a macro level (emerging economy home context and informal institutions and coevolution); local firms level (degree of openness); MNE level (FDI motivation, effectiveness of central and lateral knowledge flows, leader vs laggard, and multiple-embeddedness); and subsidiary level (influence of social norms, knowledge strategies, and relationship with local business network). This is clearly a different view of the "dominated by economists" literature of the impact of FDI on host countries (Eden, 2009, p. 1065).

Based on the outcomes of the different studies, stablishing upstream and downstream linkages among foreign and domestic firms is one of the main concerns policy makers face (Altenburg & Mayer-Stamer, 1999; Schmitz & Nadvi, 1999; Belderbos, Capannelli, & Fukao, 2001; Costa & Queiroz, 2002; Dries & Swinnen, 2004; Andreoni & Chang, 2016; Hirsh, 2016).

Governments in many developing countries are using financial incentives (e.g. grants, subsidized credits), fiscal incentives (e.g. lower tax rates, tax holidays) and donations of land to aggressively attract FDI, which was influenced by the failure of important-substitution policies (Narula, 2014). The importance of the attraction of

FDI in Portugal has been addressed by Moreira and Carvalho (2012) and Reis et al. (2016), who claim that the benefits from attracting FDI is well beyond the obvious direct effect on job creation and income tax collection, and include the enhancement of absorptive capabilities among indigenous suppliers and of research & development (R&D) activities and fostering science and technology (C&T) partnerships between local C&T institutions and industrial players.

From a spillover point of view, Sun et al. (2016) analyzed 44,434 newly created firms in South Korea between 2000 and 2004. They found that the impact of FDI in low-tech industries is positive and significant in all four possible combinations of intra- / inter-regional and intra- / inter-sectoral channels. However, the impacts in high-tech industry are largely intra-sectoral within the host region. These differences are explained by the fact that agglomeration effects and location decisions favor regions of high quality of human quality with high wage rate. This clearly indicates that location advantages are sector specific, which has consequences for industrial policy. Moreover, if MNEs want to foster their relationships in upstream and downstream in the supply chain they need to be aware that knowledge spillovers are important but that there are spatial and sectorial differences (Sun et al., 2016).

RESEARCH METHOD

The methodology implemented was explorative in nature and was based in qualitative data, collected from semi-structured, in-depth interviews.

The research methodology involved three main steps. The first one consisted in the formulation of the patterns of technology acquisition among firms supplying Foreign MNEs in Portugal. These mechanisms are based on work done by Ribault et al. (1995) and Gomes and Kruglianskas (2009). These variables are assessed in SMEs.

The second step involved the selection of the sample. Firms were selected from four different industries – electronics, footwear, chemical, and automobile – in order to maximize the possible differences between the patterns of technology acquisition. The population of firms included two different sub-groups: the clients (MNEs) and the suppliers (SMEs). The clients were selected among the largest MNEs of the previously mentioned industries and the suppliers were selected among the set of firms supplying to those MNEs.

While the identification of the MNEs was carried out through secondary information, the identification of the suppliers was based on information released by MNEs during the interviews.

Eight MNEs were willing to co-operate in the field research. Data from the second subset of firms (suppliers) were obtained from released information from TNCs.

The objective was to select five suppliers from each multinational subsidiary and to reach a sample of forty firms. The final sample included 40 suppliers: 12 firms supplying automakers, 11 firms supplying electronics MNEs, 10 firms supplying footwear manufacturers and seven firms supplying chemical industry's MNEs. The gathering of data was carried out through in loco, semi-structured, tape-recorded interviews at both MNEs and suppliers' sites.

The interviews with local suppliers' executives addressed the following topics:

- General information about the firm;
- Evolution of production, operations and technological activities;
- Evolution of technological activities in downstream activities in the value chain with MNEs.

The third step consisted in the analysis of the patterns of technology acquisition of the suppliers of the MNEs of the four industries analyzed. The following patterns of technology accumulation were analyzed, based on Ribault et al. (1995) and Gomes and Kruglianskas (2009): catalogue purchase; specification purchase; capital equipment purchase; outsourcing; technological scanning; reverse engineering; patenting; licensing; spin offs; network of firms; joint venture; strategic alliances; cooperative R&D; and participation in European programs.

The process of know-how accumulation proposed by places the innovating firm as the center of an extended network of institutions and activities (Rothwell, 1994; Moreira, 2009). This perspective is used because it illustrates both the important interfaces between the suppliers and their clients and the various modes of external learning. While in the context under analysis the supplier-customer relationship implies learning from the direct relationship with the customer, other modes of external learning can be considered as a consequence of the supplier-customer interaction (Schiele, 2006; Moreira & Carvalho, 2015). While Figure 1 illustrates the supplier-customer interactions and their external networking relationships, Table 1 lays down the main findings.

The relationship between companies and the external environment plays a fundamental role in the technological development process. In the case of SMEs, and due to their diverse endogenous limitations, external relationships become an essential and indispensable instrument of technological accumulation.

RESULTS

There are two types of inter-firm relationship (Lowe, 1995; Veludo, Macbeth, & Purchase, 2006):

Figure 1. Client-supplier interactions and external relationships

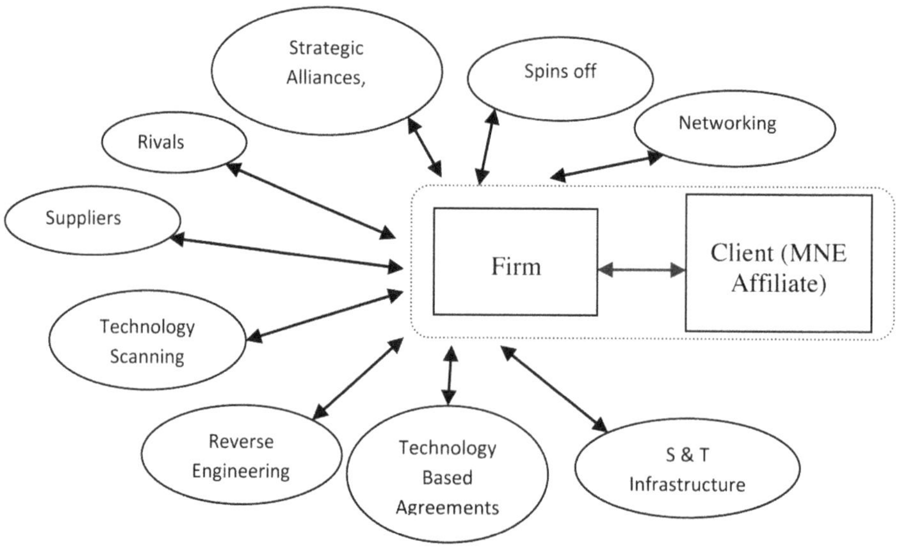

- **Informal Relationships:** Although they are not normally made public in written contracts they involve a continuous process of exchange of information among different organizations;
- **Formal Relationships:** That normally take the form of explicit - technology, productive, commercial or otherwise - co-operation agreements or strategic alliances that involve two or more companies.

Informal Relationships

Customers

The deepest relationship is established with the customers. All the suppliers mentioned the importance of listening to clients and analyzing clients' suggestions in the innovation process as well as in the new product development (NPD) process.

The characteristics of that relationship vary according to the industry type and the firms' technological strategy.

Although in all the four industries it was clear that the contact with clients is of fundamental importance, the footwear, electronics and automobile industries have more intense supplier-client relationships than the chemical industry. This is due to the vertical structure of supplier-client relationships. Generically, customers – normally larger than their suppliers – have a superior bargaining power than that

Table 1. Patterns of technology acquisition

	Suppliers to							
	Auto Industry		Chemical Industry		Electronics Industry		Footwear Industry	
	Number	%	Number	%	Number	%	Number	%
Catalogue Purchase	12	100.0	7	100.0	11	100.0	9	90.0
Specification Purchase	12	100.0	7	100.0	11	100.0	9	90.0
Capital Equipment Purchase	12	100.0	7	100.0	11	100.0	10	100.0
Outsourcing/ Subcontracting:								
1. Non-core products	3	25.0	-	-	5	45.5	2	20.0
2. Production	7	58.3	-		-		4	40.0
Technological Scanning:								
1. Broad Scope	8	66.7	5	71.4	6	54.5	2	20.0
2. Production	10	83.3	7	100.0	11	100.0	7	70.0
Reverse Engineering	5	52.1	-	-	2	18.2	4	40.0
Patenting	1	10.4	-	-	-	-	-	-
Licensing	-	-	-	-	-	-	2	20.0
Spin Outs	3	31.3	1	14.3	1	9.1	1	10.0
Network of Firms	2	20.8	-	-	-	-	-	-
Joint Venture	2	20.8	-	-	-	-	-	-
Strategic Alliances	2	20.8	-	-	-	-	-	-
Co-operative R&D:								
1. University	7	58.3	5	71.4	4	36.4	3	30.0
2. Governm. Sponsor. Res. Ins.	2	20.8	-	-	4	36.4	1	10.0
Participation European Progr.	3	25.0	2	28.6	2	18.2	2	20.0

of the suppliers and have a fundamental role in the introduction of innovation in the supply chain imposing new products, new designs or new features in upstream activities.

The supplier-client articulation grows deeper when clients successfully work with their suppliers the adaptation of existing products to new specific market conditions / applications or in the development of brand new products. Suppliers are then able not only to satisfy industrial production capabilities, but also to provide supporting activities in the NPD process, which enhances the long-term supplier-client relationship.

The suppliers' technological strategy has a very important role because it either underpins or hinders supplier-client relationships.

Innovative firms have very close relationships with their clients. These companies' scope goes beyond the mere development and production of a component/product; they have managed to accumulate enough technological capability to develop new products/new innovative solutions that satisfy the customers' needs behaving as credible, long-term partners with competencies of their own to create added value for the client.

In summary, despite the bargaining power differences between suppliers and clients and the industry's unique demands, the customers constitute the dynamic engine of the suppliers' external relationships.

Suppliers

The relationship with suppliers can be considered positive and quite widespread among the visited firms. Nevertheless, suppliers' influence seems to be lower than that of the clients. The main upstream relationships with the suppliers' suppliers were, as shown in Table1: catalogue purchase; specification purchase; capital equipment purchase; and outsourcing.

The relationship with capital equipment suppliers has been one of the primary ways used by Portuguese SMEs in their struggle for technological development. In the sample studied, capital equipment suppliers are important players because they transmit the technological novelties forward in the value chain, as well as supply an entire range of services that help to update firms. The dialogue with capital equipment vendors is important, above all, due to the introduction of improvements and adaptations to equipment and systems and to the introduction of new hardware technical solutions. Although the relationship with capital equipment suppliers is important, it was possible to notice that there were several sectoral differences. Its importance is felt above all, in the footwear industry and in companies that follow traditional and dependent strategies, *i.e.*, those that are likely to base their technology competence in production technology.

A factor that should not be ignored is the training provided by capital equipment vendors: it allows firms to overtake barriers without which the equipment would not be used in the best conditions; to access technical knowledge; and to diminish learning time, all of which are difficult to quantify due to their very intangible nature.

Raw materials and components suppliers also play an important role in technology accumulation among SMEs. All, except one firm, from the cork industry, expressed the importance of assessing input suppliers news and novelties as a means of being updated. Suppliers from the plastics and chemical industries showed a larger interest in their upstream relationship with input suppliers than the rest of the firms. The importance of this relationship lies in the importance that technical change has in the creation of new products.

The two chemical suppliers (one SME and one larger firm) supplying the shoemakers stated that input suppliers were crucial for keeping abreast of knowledge. Their suppliers of raw material were multinational firms with a wide accumulated technical knowledge that should not be disregarded as important technical source relevant to the creation of new products. Although this technical knowledge is passed on to the two chemical suppliers as new raw materials and new components both firms have different attitudes towards their suppliers. Whilst the SME has an internalization attitude towards novelties transmitted by vendors, the large firm has no development department. Although some technology flows from vendors of raw materials and components do occur, the large firm seems unable to make those technology flows endogenous due to lack of technical capability.

The rest of the chemical firms supplying the chemical industry, having large MNCs as suppliers of input materials as well, showed a lower dependence on their suppliers. This is not surprising taking into account that they are part of large conglomerates and consequently they acquire technology from various sources.

Outsourcing policies have been used differently across all sectors. Whilst suppliers to the automobile industry (seven firms) were the most active in subcontracting production capacity, suppliers to the electronics industry (five firms) were more oriented towards outsourcing non-core products. Not a single supplier to the chemical industry followed an outsourcing policy.

Outsourcing production capacity was more concerned with extending the firms' boundaries upstream in the supply chain than with accumulating technology. The eleven firms that outsourced part of the production claimed that had they had the possibility to produce it in-house they would have done it, i.e., they resorted to outsourcing due to their lack of capacity to serve the market.

For the suppliers, outsourcing non-core products and processes seem to be much more important than outsourcing production capacity: firms claimed they not only learned with subcontracted firms but that they also extended the firms' competencies.

Of the four upstream relationships studied the most important one was with capital equipment suppliers. Suppliers that belong to the metallic and plastics industry seem to have a deeper upstream relationship than other firms do. The suppliers to shoemakers showed a weaker upstream relationship with capital equipment vendors due to the lower complexity of production equipment and to the more labor-intense production systems.

Summing up, capital equipment suppliers influence a wide range of firms in a broad range of industries. The more complex the production equipment and the larger the variety of technologies incorporated the more intense seems to be the relationship with capital equipment suppliers. It can be argued that in those companies that base their technology competence on production equipment the influence is harder on hardware, while in companies that base their technology competence on product engineering the influence is more intangible in nature.

Formal Relationships

Technology Scanning

The firm's technological scanning reflects the degree of involvement the firm has in the assessment of certain technologies, as well as the company's awareness to assess the external environment.

Among the most mentioned mechanisms of technology scanning are: technical magazines and journals, national and international fairs, seminars, congresses, industrial associations and the firms' technical literature.

Although technological assessment activities were performed in all four industries, there are several important differences in their nature: in some firms the only technological activities assessed were the production-related ones, whereas in other firms the technological scope was broader. In order to help explain the situation two different perspectives were used: one taking into account only production activities and another with a broader scope.

In general, almost all suppliers were concerned with the assessment of production technology activities. Only two suppliers to the automotive industry and three suppliers to the footwear industry mentioned they were not assessing these activities. In four situations – two foreign suppliers to automakers and two foreign suppliers to footwear producers – the reason behind this lack of assessment was that these activities were normally performed at headquarters level. In the fifth situation, the firm has followed a retrenchment strategy.

Taking into account a broader technological scope, some differences arise. The suppliers to the chemical, automotive and electronics industries show a superior performance than those supplying to the footwear industry: whilst eight of the twelve suppliers to the automotive industry, five of the seven vendors to the chemical industry and six of the eleven suppliers to the electronics industry declared doing technological assessment beyond production activities only two of ten vendors to the footwear producers declared doing so.

Although this difference expresses the production orientation of most suppliers to the footwear producers, when compared to the rest of the suppliers the following should also be taken into account:

- Some foreign suppliers have reduced control over technological activities performed at headquarters' level; and
- The internal technology base of most small local suppliers is still production technology-based, which conditions most of their technology assessment activities.

Reverse Engineering

Only eleven suppliers claimed to practice reverse engineering activities. Taking into account sectoral activities some differences arise among suppliers:

- No suppliers to the chemical industry reverse engineer their products;
- Only two suppliers to the electronics industry have used reverse engineering activities;
- Four out of 10 suppliers to the footwear producers have reverse engineered products; and
- Five out of 12 suppliers to the automakers have frequently used reverse engineering activities.

In the chemical industry, all firms have a unanimous opinion: reverse engineering activities are hardly applicable because there is hardly any room to differentiate the commodities they produce.

Only two suppliers to the electronics cluster industry used reverse engineering activities. One is an automation engineering firm. One of the partners claimed that all developmental activities have competitors' activities and products as a starting point, and the firm's main objective is to improve upon them. The other firm produces high precision plastic components for the electronics industry. According to the firm's managing director, the firm has usually analyzed its competitors' products to try to come up with better solutions.

The suppliers to footwear producers are almost as active as automakers suppliers in reverse engineering activities. This is not surprising taking into account that the textile and the footwear industry are considered among the most active industries in reverse engineering products.

The automakers suppliers are those that most frequently reverse engineer. Nevertheless, some differences arise among them. Three of the seven metallic components suppliers extensively practice reverse engineering activities, while the other four suppliers claim there is hardly anything to reverse engineer in metallic products. This difference might be explained by the type of product and by the type of firm. Whilst metallic components producers that cater for assemblies or sub-assemblies normally depart from the client's assemblies or sub-assemblies those that cater for mere components do it at the client's request. While the former are used to depart from something that already exists (and sometimes have to compare the different designs/categories of the products) the latter normally depart from the clients' specification. Consequently, it is not surprising that the former are more used to reverse engineering activities than the latter.

Another feature that might be taken into account is that of the developmental activities. Firms that normally use developmental activities are those that have a more acute practice of reverse engineering activities, i.e., the pressure to assess what the clients and competitors are normally doing leads firms to reverse engineer in their search for new products/solutions.

Patenting

The fact that only one firm has been granted a patent reflects a low technological orientation among the suppliers analyzed. The firm is a supplier to the automotive industry which has a strong orientation towards technology-based activities.

Licensing

Within the sample studied, only two suppliers of the footwear industry have signed licensing agreements. While one produces glues and hot melts the other one produces a wide variety of synthetic foams.

The firm that produces synthetic foams produces a wide range of products, mattresses, car seats, pillows, cushions and insoles. The firm has used this license contract to have access to certain types of technologies and knowledge the firm lacks. Its concern has been concentrated on the development of new products. The firm does not have a development department. In a broad sense, despite this technology transfer contract the firm has not been able to take advantage from it: as the company lacks a development department the creation of new solutions has been quite static in nature.

Contrary to this first case, the second firm has taken advantage of its license agreements to accumulate technology. It has allowed the firm not only to accumulate on technological leaps generated by the technology transfer agreement, but also to make the knowledge transferred endogenous. Commercially, the firm has also yielded from this agreement. Part of the know-how generated has been used to enlarge the range of products offered in varied industries.

New Spinoffs

Spinoff as a result of an entrepreneurial process was not very popular among Portuguese suppliers. There are only seven cases of new spinoffs and in all of them the creation of the new firms was related to two different situations:

- The production of different types of products (product specialization); and
- The generation of new production capacity.

In any case, the creation of new spinoffs was associated with: the will of a young researcher to exploit the creation of new technologies/products developed within the firm, and the will to exploit the degree of exclusiveness of new products or new technologies. This situation reveals some of the fragilities associated with the R&D functions in SMEs.

The suppliers to the auto industry were the most active in the creation of spinoffs. Three among the 12 suppliers to the auto industry have created new spinoffs as a means of acquiring new technologies.

Among the 11 suppliers to the electronics industry, only two have spun off new firms. One to produce new plastic products based on new technologies. Another case is a firm of the package & label industry that has two different production sites, manufacturing different products.

Joint-Ventures

The participation in joint-ventures is low, though in the near future may grow due to the involvement of some suppliers to the automotive industry in broader, international markets.

Only two firms in the sample have signed joint-venture agreements. Both firms are suppliers to the auto industry.

Network of Firms

Although there are several types of relationships between suppliers and clients it is clear that there are some sectoral differences that must be taken into account. The work done by Lamming (1993) and Veludo et al. (2006) reveals how important the supplier-customer relationship is.

Only two firms, both from the auto industry, participated in a network of firms. Both firms exemplify how firms might evolve from learning-by-doing to learning-by-using to learning-by-interacting to finally learning-by-learning in a complex, competitive world, taking advantages of their accumulated experiences and of their relationship with other institutions to innovate and position themselves differently in the supply chain.

Co-Operative Agreements With Universities

Co-operative agreements with universities and other higher education institutions can be considered as moderate though there is some sectoral variation. In any situation the relationship with universities was considered as a priority. Suppliers to the chemical industry have better performance than the rest of the suppliers: five of the seven suppliers to the chemical cluster have co-operation agreements with universities.

In most situations contacts between universities and companies happen in a formal way, contrary to what Simões (1995) suggested. This may be the result of the industrial / innovation policy that has been taking place lately in the Portuguese industry.

36% of the suppliers to the electronics industry maintain contacts with universities. Of the four firms, three belong to the plastics industry and the other firm belongs to the metallic industry. Only one firm has an active involvement with the university. The firm has two projects with three universities. The first project involves the planning and control of production and logistics activities involving the U. of Minho. The other project involves the Technology Center of Marinha Grande and the Católica and Independente Universities.

Two companies have contacts with to U. of Minho involving the use of the laboratories for raw materials characterization. Finally, in the fourth case the contacts involve in-company university trainees mainly with the University of Lisbon.

The remaining suppliers to the electronics industry have kept a certain distance from universities.

Among suppliers to the automobile industry the panorama is slightly different. Although seven firms have had co-operative R&D projects with universities, only four of them have continued using the university as a means of acquiring technology. Three of the four companies that use universities do it systematically. The fourth one has had sporadic successful contacts with universities. One of the companies – a mold maker – has a protocol with the U. of Minho. It had a project with another university that was unsuccessful: it consisted of an image acquisition system installed within the mold. The firm knew that it was extremely difficult to carry it out. Another company has a contract with the University of Minho for the development and improvement of the production process. According to the firm, it has been a success. The firm also has projects with the Universities of Lisbon and Coimbra.

The third produces batteries and has contacts mainly with the universities of Lisbon and Évora. The fourth company with co-operative projects with universities is a metallic parts producer. Its contacts are with the University of Oporto. All these contacts have been sporadic in nature and have always had good results.

There are three cases of negative experiences. Three companies mentioned they had some projects with universities and that those contacts were complete fiascos. In all three situations it was mentioned that it had been the first contact with the university and that the firms did not intend to resort to universities again. They claimed that universities are very bureaucratic and have a time concept that is not adequate to the industry.

Five suppliers to the auto industry declared they have never had any contacts with universities. Four of them are foreign companies whose R&D strategy is centralized at corporate level. The fifth company is an SME whose technological competence is based on production technology.

Three of ten suppliers to footwear producers have contacts with universities and only one has regular contacts with the University of Minho. The other two firms have had projects with universities on a situational basis. One firm has developed several projects with the universities of Minho, Aveiro and Beira Interior for the development of laces and strings with different textile and plastic materials. The third firm has had several projects with the University of Oporto, namely the development of different types of leather.

Finally, the suppliers to the chemical industry seem to be the most active in exploiting university knowledge. Initially all the contacts were developed on a project basis. Successful results led firms to continue to resort to universities. This situation resulted in the creation of positive relationships among them. Chemical suppliers were normally working with the universities of Oporto, Coimbra, and Lisbon.

Co-Operative Agreements With Government-supported Research Institutions and Technology Centers

Relationships with this type of institutions have generally not been intense. Most of the firms resort to these institutions to test either product characteristics or product quality. Consequently, the research and/or developmental component is very reduced. Very few firms fall back upon the technological centers in a systematic way.

Only one supplier to the footwear industry uses the technological center of the footwear industry – CTC. Although the firm and the technology center have a common project – the recovery of rubber waste – the firm claims that the project has not had great progress.

The suppliers to the electronics industry have more active behavior than the suppliers to the footwear industry. Four suppliers have had projects with technology centers.

Only two suppliers to the auto industry claimed to have resorted to technology centers. In both projects, the major aim was to take advantage of the laboratory equipment of those institutions rather than of R&D activities.

No supplier to the chemical industry manifested any contact with technology centers or any other research institutions.

Participation in European Programs

The participation in European programs involving R&D projects has been embraced with moderate enthusiasm. Nine companies have been involved in European technology transfer projects. Three firms supply automakers. The other six firms are evenly distributed among the chemical, footwear and electronics industries.

The companies claimed they have an active involvement in this type of programs. Several companies have participated in more than one program and all firms claimed to have achieved the proposed objectives.

All companies manifested that they were involved in these projects to achieve long-term results, which demonstrates a certain technological maturity in the approach to possible solutions.

A company that participated in European programs for the first time showed a *sui generis* a point of view:

...at the beginning were we quite reluctant. It was the first time and we were not sure about the other partners' real objectives and their involvement. As time went by, we realized that not only were we not technologically behind them, but also they [project-partner firms] had the same doubts we had. .... the involvement has been quite positive: we have been improving. We realized they had different methodologies, and approaches and this helped us to question ourselves. If a new opportunity appears we intend to participate in a search for new, joint solutions.

All companies involved in European programs have played an active role in the search for new solutions as opposed to what Simões (1995) calls an "interested assessment role". The following interesting comment stresses the active role "... in this project everybody has to be involved actively, otherwise everybody loses. It is not advantageous to participate without having defined objectives. Curiosity plays no part here...".

Comparisons Between Foreign and Indigenous Suppliers

The patterns of technology acquisition among foreign suppliers are also very poor when compared with indigenous firms, as shown in Table 2. Cooperative agreements with universities and government sponsored research institutions were only present among foreign suppliers to the chemical industry.

In general, the orientation towards the low end of technology competence among most foreign suppliers is a clear indication of the low importance technological and innovative activities have among them.

Table 3 categorizes the type of factories among foreign suppliers, based on White et al (1984) typology. Table 3 characterizes the role of foreign suppliers and

Table 2. Comparison of patterns of technology acquisition between foreign and indigenous suppliers

	Foreign Suppliers		Indigenous Suppliers		Total	
	Number	**%**	**Number**	**%**	**Number**	**%**
Catalogue Purchase	11	100.0	28	96.6	39	97.5
Specification Purchase	11	100.0	28	96.6	39	97.5
Capital Equipment Purchase	11	100.0	29	100.0	40	100.0
Outsourcing/Subcontracting:						
1. Non-core products	2	18.2	8	27.6	10	25.0
2. Production	2	18.2	9	31.0	11	27.5
Technological Scanning:						
1. Broad Scope	4	36.4	17	58.6	21	52.5
2. Production	7	63.6	28	96.6	7	17.5
Reverse Engineering	3	27.3	8	27.6	4	10.0
Patenting	0	-	1	3.4	-	-
Licensing	0	-	2	6.9	-	-
Spin Outs	0	-	6	20.7	1	2.5
Network of Firms	0	-	2	6.9	-	-
Joint Venture	0	-	2	6.9	-	-
Strategic Alliances	0	-	2	6.9	-	-
Co-operative R&D:						
1. University	3	27.3	16	55.2	19	47.5
2. Governm. Sponsor. Res. Ins.	1	9.1	6	20.7	7	17.5
Participation European Progr.	1	9.1	8	27.6	9	22.5

Table 3. Type of factories among foreign suppliers

	Suppliers to Automakers	Suppliers Electronics Industry	Suppliers Chemical Industry	Suppliers to Shoemakers
Manufacturing Replica	2		4	2
Rationalized Manufacturer	1	1		
Production Specialist	1			

the scope of their activities, following Ferdows' (1997) typology. Clearly, most of the foreign suppliers play a secondary role in the creation of new products as well as in innovative activities, which is a consequence of the R&D policies of most of their mother firms. Following Ronstsdt's (1977) categorization, three suppliers to the chemical industry have mother firms with global technology units (GTU), one supplier to the auto industry has an indigenous technology unit (ITU) and all the rest use the mother firm transfer technology units (TTU) to access technology.

When comparing the types of factories of foreign suppliers and clients it is clear that they are closer to what Ferdows (1997) calls *offshore* factories than to *lead* factories, which is a clear indication that the *raison d'être* of those factories is the exploitation of operational/production investments rather than the creation of technology/knowledge investments. Nevertheless, at industry level, the clients play a more important role than the suppliers. A plausible explanation for the different technology management level is the type of product they produce: while the foreign clients analyzed – a clear exception is the chemical sector – are product-centered oriented, the foreign suppliers are component-centered oriented.

Table 4. Role and scope of foreign suppliers

	Suppliers to Automakers	Suppliers Electronics Industry	Suppliers Chemical Industry	Suppliers to Shoemakers
Offshore Factory	3	1	1	2
Source Factory	1			
Server Factory			3	
Contributor				

SUMMARY AND CONCLUSION

As described in the beginning of the chapter both formal and informal relationships between the companies and the external environment play a fundamental role in the process of technological development.

There are certain differences among suppliers as well as among industries they belong to. These differences, as it is obvious, are the result of a cumulative process through time, which reflect the different performances of the companies and their relationships with the environment. The analysis of the different components of the patterns of technology acquisition has led to the following conclusions:

1. The firms' capabilities to endogenize technology as a result of opportunities generated by either formal or informal relationships depends upon the internal technology base. Nevertheless, as was put forward throughout chapter it is plausible to say that the greater the technical context the greater the firms capabilities.
2. Informal relationships play an important role as technology acquisition mechanisms. The task environment – the clients and the suppliers, basically – is of fundamental importance for the suppliers to gain access to a continuous process of exchange of information.
3. The intensity of the relationships with the clients is of crucial importance. The interactions established with the clients are particularly important in the process of the creation and development of new products.
4. Although the intensity of the relationships with the suppliers is deep they are not as crucial as the relationships with the clients. The relationship with the capital equipment suppliers stands out among the relationships with the suppliers basically due to the tangible consequences in terms of modernization of equipment and productivity evaluations.
5. Formal relationships among firms are not as frequent as informal relationships. The lack of extensive use of formal technology transfer relationships stems from the low technological level of most Portuguese firms. Nevertheless, as some indigenous firms have managed to make use of formal relationships it is plausible to contend that those firms have not only seen added value on those relationships, but have also managed to accumulate technology from a wider variety of sources. The lack of interest of foreign firms in technology added value activities from the science and technology (S&T) institutions in Portugal stems not from the lack of offer from indigenous institutions, but from the easiness those firms have in using mother and sister firms in transferring technological assets.

6. Some firms have managed to accumulate technology from informal as well as from formal relationships. They have not only managed to complement their internal technology base with proper R&D departments, but have also extensively used other S&T institutions as well as joint-ventures and strategic alliances to reinforce their internal technology base. Then, it is plausible to argue that though the client is of fundamental importance, the firm's role in properly generating and internalizing technology from both informal and formal sources is crucial in endogenizing technology in the value chain.
7. Co-operative agreements with higher education institutions reached interesting figures when compared to other figures among formal relationships. Although it is generally acknowledged that universities and the industrial sector in Portugal are 'divorced' it is clear that while some successful relationships reinforce the virtuous cycle of the relationships, the negative experiences – especially the first one – create a barrier for future, continuous relationships.
8. Some of the formal relationships with universities and some government sponsored research institutions are underpinned by laboratory tests and not by research or development. The former, though positive, do not represent a great technological impact for companies as would be the case of either research or development.
9. For *technologically-oriented* companies, universities and government sponsored research institutions constitute one of the first priorities for future technological developments. The same cannot be said for *technologically-weak* firms. In a general way, it can be said that if the universities can offer some windows of opportunities to the companies the only form of surpassing the differences between the industrial and the academic world is the existence of an appropriate communication channel and a proper understanding of the logic of both partners' operation. This appropriate communication channel would involve: (a) more skilled human resources capable of internalizing knowledge and technology, on the part of the firms; and (b) a lower dependence on the state, *i.e.* a more acute tuning to the needs of the business world, on the part of the academic world.
10. Public policy needs to address not only the attraction of FDI of large MNEs of the auto, electronics, footwear, and chemical industries. However, when after comparing suppliers to those large MNEs, it is possible to conclude that certain foreign suppliers are less technologically endowed than indigenous suppliers. This calls for a public policy to support not only the attraction of FDI, but also the support of the relationship between suppliers and MNEs in upstream activities of the supply chain.

A point that also deserves to be addressed is the evolutionary conditions of foreign firms. If they are able to evolve technologically and organizationally it is because the production and the organization of knowledge-based assets among them have changed and thus, the boundaries of the firms as a consequence of the dissemination of those assets have changed as well. Addressing this point, Dunning (1997) claimed that the raison d´être for most initial conditions for FDI are tuned to resource-seeking and market-seeking investments, while the main motives for sequential investments are tuned to efficiency-seeking and strategic-seeking investments. Consequently, there is a considerable difference between initial and sequential conditions. While the former seeks an initial foreign entry the latter seeks to acquire resources and capabilities to augment core competencies in regional or global markets.

As a result, host governments have to properly address not only what investments are more likely to upgrade competitiveness of the indigenous economy, but also, and perhaps more importantly, how to foster upstream supply linkages to enhance the competitive advantage of the local suppliers in order to create the conditions for sequential foreign investments.

The challenges for host governments are increasing, rather than diminishing, because the demands for technology and the competitive pressure are becoming more pluralistic with the globalization process. Thus, the "buying" of foreign investment so popular until a decade ago is clearly insufficient. In order to generate a virtuous cycle of initial and subsequent investment, host governments must properly address the supply chain so that the indigenous conditions are more prevalent in the decision of MNC corporations.

SOLUTIONS AND RECOMMENDATIONS

The activities of MNEs are difficult to assess as markets are more volatile than over. However, it would be important if public policy could address FDI from a more holistic perspective taking into account not only initial conditions to attract FDI but also to consider sequential investments that are tuned to efficiency-seeking activities with local suppliers, which would allow local firms to augment and explore their core competencies creating endogenous condition for sustainable economic development.

FUTURE RESEARCH DIRECTIONS

Future research direction needs to seek new perspectives in which innovation- and knowledge-centered perspectives are addressed from the suppliers' point of view so that the supply chain might be aligned with the needs of MNEs in host countries, which is tuned with Perri and Perrufo's (2016) findings.

REFERENCES

Aitken, B. J., & Harrison, A. E. (1999). Do domestic firms benefit from foreign direct investment? Evidence from Venezuela. *The American Economic Review*, *89*(3), 605–618. doi:10.1257/aer.89.3.605

Altenburg, T., & Meyer-Stamer, J. (1999). How to promote clusters: Experiences from Latin America. *World Development*, *27*(9), 1693–1713. doi:10.1016/S0305-750X(99)00081-9

Andreoni, A., & Chang, H.-J. (2016). Industrial policy and the future of manufacturing. *Economia e Politica Industriale*, *43*(4), 491–502. doi:10.100740812-016-0057-2

Belderbos, R., Capannelli, G., & Fukao, K. (2001). Backward vertical linkages of foreign manufacturing affiliates: Evidence from Japanese multinationals. *World Development*, *29*(1), 189–208. doi:10.1016/S0305-750X(00)00086-3

Buckley, P. J., & Casson, M. (1976). *The future of the multinational enterprise*. London: Macmillan. doi:10.1007/978-1-349-02899-3

Costa, I., & Queiroz, S. (2002). Foreign direct investment and technological capabilities in Brazilian industry. *Research Policy*, *31*(8-9), 1431–1443. doi:10.1016/S0048-7333(02)00073-2

D'Amelio, M., Garrone, P., & Piscitello, L. (2016). Can multinational enterprises light up developing countries? Evidences from the access to electricity in sub-Saharan Africa. *World Development*, *88*, 12–32. doi:10.1016/j.worlddev.2016.06.018

Dries, L., & Swinnen, J. (2004). Foreign direct investment, vertical integration, and local suppliers: Evidences from the polish dairy sector. *World Development*, *32*(9), 1525–1544. doi:10.1016/j.worlddev.2004.05.004

Dunning, J. (1977). Trade, location of economic activity, and the multinational enterprise: a search for an eclectic approach. In B. Ohlin, P. Hesselborn, & P. Wijkman (Eds.), *The international allocation of economic activity*. London: Macmillan. doi:10.1007/978-1-349-03196-2_38

Dunning, J., & Narula, R. (1996). The investment development path revisited: some emerging issues. In J. Dunning & R. Narula (Eds.), *Foreign direct investment and governments: Catalysts for economic restructuring*. Basingstoke, UK: Edward Elgar.

Dunning, J. H. (1981). *International production and the multinational enterprise*. London: Allen and Unwin.

Dunning, J. H. (1997). *Alliance capitalism and global business*. London: Routledge.

Eden, L. (2009). Letter from the Editor-in-Chief: FDI spillovers and linkages. Journal of International Business Studies, 40, 1065-1069.

Ferdows, K. (1997, March). Making the most of foreign factories. *Harvard Business Review*, 73–88.

Gomes, C., & Kruglianskas, I. (2009). Indicadores e características de gestão de fontes externas de informação tecnológica e do desempenho inovador de empresas brasileiras. *RAC*, *13*(2), 172–188.

Gorg, H., & Strobl, E. (2001). Multinational companies and productivity spillovers: A meta-analysis. *Economic Journal (London)*, *111*(475), 723–739. doi:10.1111/1468-0297.00669

Gow, H., & Swinnen, J. (1998). Up- and downstream restructuring, foreign direct investment, and hold-up problems in agricultural transition. *European Review of Agriculture Economics*, *25*(4), 331–350. doi:10.1093/erae/25.3.331

Grimes, S., & Du, D. (2013). Foreign and indigenous innovation in China: Some evidence from Shanghai. *European Planning Studies*, *21*(9), 1357–1373. doi:10.1080/09654313.2012.755829

Günther, J. (2002). FDI as a multiplier of modern technology in Hungarian industry. *Inter Economics*, *37*(5), 263–269. doi:10.1007/BF02928885

Hirsch, S. (2016). Nation states and multinationals: Common interests, conflicting interests and public policies. *Transnational Corporations Review*, *8*(1), 17–27. doi:10.1080/19186444.2016.1162477

Hymer, S. H. (1976). *The international operations of national firms: A study of direct investment*. Cambridge, MA: MIT Press.

Irsova, Z., & Havranek, T. (2013). Determinants of horizontal spillovers from FDI: Evidence from a large meta-analysis. *World Development*, *42*, 1–15. doi:10.1016/j.worlddev.2012.07.001

Jiang, M., Branzei, O., & Xia, J. (2016). DIY: How internationalization shifts the locus of indigenous innovation for Chinese firms. *Journal of World Business*, *51*(5), 662–674. doi:10.1016/j.jwb.2016.07.005

Lamming, R. (1993). *Beyond partnership. Strategies for innovation and lean supply*. Cornwall, UK: Prentice-Hall.

Lowe, P. (1995). *The management of technology. Perceptions and opportunities*. London: Chapman.

Moreira, A. C. (2008). Upstream linkages between TNCs and local suppliers: Evidences from Portugal. *World Review of Science, Technology and Sustainable Development*, 5(1), 28–48. doi:10.1504/WRSTSD.2008.017811

Moreira, A. C. (2009). Knowledge capability flows in buyer-supplier relationships. Challenges for small domestic suppliers in international contexts. *Journal of Small Business and Enterprise Development*, *16*(1), 93–114. doi:10.1108/14626000910932908

Moreira, A. C., & Carvalho, A. C. (2012). Internationalization approaches of the automotive innovation system. A historical perspective. In A. Teixeira (Ed.), *Technological change*. Rijeka, Croatia: InTech.

Moreira, A. C., & Carvalho, A. C. (2015). Supply Chain Management: Identifying Innovative Suppliers. In L. C. Carvalho (Ed.), *Handbook of research on internationalization of entrepreneurial innovation in the global economy* (pp. 436–457). Hershey, PA: IGI Global. doi:10.4018/978-1-4666-8216-0.ch022

Narula, R. (2014). Foreign direct investment as a driver of industrial development: Why is there so little evidence? In R. Van Tulder, A. Verbeke, & R. Strange (Eds.), *International business and sustainable development* (pp. 45–678). Bingley, UK: Emerald. doi:10.1108/S1745-8862(2013)0000008008

Narula, R., & Dunning, J. (2010). Multinational enterprises, development and globalization: Some clarifications and a research agenda. *Oxford Development Studies*, *38*(3), 263–287. doi:10.1080/13600818.2010.505684

Oetzel, J., & Doh, J. P. (2009). MNEs and development: A review and reconceptualization. *Journal of World Business*, *44*(2), 108–120. doi:10.1016/j.jwb.2008.05.001

Perri, A., & Peruffo, E. (2016). Knowledge spillovers from FDI: A critical review from the international business perspective. *International Journal of Management Reviews*, *18*(1), 3–27. doi:10.1111/ijmr.12054

Reis, A., Heitor, M., Amaral, M., & Mendonça, J. (2016). Revisiting industrial policy: Lessons learned from the establishment of an automotive OEM in Portugal. *Technological Forecasting and Social Change*, *113*, 195–205. doi:10.1016/j.techfore.2016.04.006

Ribau, C. P., Moreira, A. C., & Raposo, M. (2015). Internationalisation of the firm theories: A schematic synthesis. *International Journal of Business and Globalisation*, *15*(4), 528–554. doi:10.1504/IJBG.2015.072535

Ribault, J. M., Martinet, B., & Lebidois, D. (1995). *A gestão das tecnologias*. Lisbon: Publicações Dom Quixote.

Ronstadt, R. C. (1977). *Research and development abroad by US multinationals*. New York: Preacher Publishers.

Rothwell, R. (1994). Issues in the User-Producer Relations in the Innovation Process: The Role of Government. *International Journal of Technology Management*, *9*(5/6/7), 629-649.

Schiele, H. (2006). How to distinguish innovative suppliers? Identifying innovative suppliers as new task for purchasing. *Industrial Marketing Management*, *35*(8), 925–935. doi:10.1016/j.indmarman.2006.05.003

Schmitz, H., & Nadvi, K. (1999). Clustering and industrialization: Introduction. *World Development*, *27*(9), 1503–1514. doi:10.1016/S0305-750X(99)00072-8

Simões, V. C. (1995). *Inovação e gestão em PME industriais portuguesas*. Lisbon: GEP – Gabinete de Estudos e Planeamento.

Sun, L., Lee, I. H., & Hong, H. (2016). Does foreign direct investment stimulate new firm creation? In search of spillovers through industrial and geographical linkages. *Small Business Economics*. doi:10.100711187-016-9803-0

Veludo, M., Macbeth, D., & Purchase, S. (2006). Framework for relationships and networks. *Journal of Business and Industrial Marketing*, *21*(4), 199–207. doi:10.1108/08858620610672560

Wang, C., & Yu, L. (2008). Do spillover benefits grow with rising foreign direct investment? An empirical examination of the case of China. *Applied Economics*, *39*(3), 397–405. doi:10.1080/00036840500428096

White, R. E., & Poynter, T. (1984). Strategies for Foreign-Owned Subsidiaries in Canada'. *Business Quarterly*, (Summer): 55–69.

KEY TERMS AND DEFINITIONS

Capital Equipment Purchase: It normally starts with a project justifying the investment. Once it is economically justified, the purchase happens. This technology-transfer mechanism has important repercussions for firms because it might change the production efficiency, the production flexibility, and the vertical integration across the supply chain.

Catalogue Purchase: The purchase of standard materials or components that can easily be acquired in the market.

Foreign Direct Investment: A foreign direct investment (FDI) is an investment made by a company or entity based in one country, into a company or entity based in another country. It normally includes mergers and acquisitions, building new facilities, reinvesting profits earned from overseas operations and intra company loans.

Joint Venture: A business arrangement in which two or more parties agree to pool their resources to accomplish a specific task that involves normally a new project or a business activity.

Licensing: A business arrangement in which one firm gives another firm permission to manufacture its product for a specified payment.

MNE: A multinational enterprise is a firm that has facilities and other assets in one country other than its home country. Such firms may have offices and/or factories in different countries but are usually centralized in the home country where they have the headquarters.

Outsourcing: A practice used by different companies to reduce costs by transferring portions of work to outside suppliers rather than completing it internally.

Reverse Engineering: The processes of extracting knowledge from anything competitors' products or reproducing anything based on the extracted information.

SMEs: Abbreviation of small and medium-sized enterprises. Although there are plenty of definitions across the world, the working definition used in this document is the one that was created by the European Commission to permit a coherent and effective access of SMEs to European community funds.

Specification Purchase: It is more complete than catalogue purchase as it involves information transfer as well as knowledge transfer. Although the know-how might not be accessible, it may be possible to know both what the key points and the limits of the technologies are and, consequently, be aware of the minimum limits that must be reached to be a potential competitor.

Technological Scanning: It is a technology transfer mechanism that allows the forecast of future technologies. It is normally done either by technology non-leaders that want to assess technology development without having to massively invest in research activities, and by technology leaders that want to keep abreast of technology.

Chapter 11
The Role of Governance on Foreign Direct Investment Inflows:
A New Theoretical Perspective and Cross-Country Analysis

Adem Gök
Kırklareli University, Turkey

ABSTRACT

The effect of governance on FDI inflows is firstly through the effect of institutions on investment environment of a country and secondly through the decreasing transaction costs, production costs, and uncertainty. The countries are divided into three clusters. A new theoretical perspective is developed considering governance as a base factor. System GMM methodology is used to deal with endogeneity problem. The empirical analysis covers 32 advanced, 70 developing, and 17 least developed countries for the period 1996-2010. Improving governance infrastructure as a base factor attracts more FDI in all country clusters. FDI made into advanced countries are efficiency seeking, FDI made into developing countries are market seeking, and FDI made into least developed countries are resource seeking. Finally, it is found that a motivation factor alone may not be sufficient for MNCs to take FDI decision since they also observe governance infrastructure in host countries and any deterioration in governance infrastructure leads to a decreasing amount of FDI inflows.

DOI: 10.4018/978-1-5225-3026-8.ch011

INTRODUCTION

Generally, the main reason for host countries to attract FDI is for the ultimate goal of sustaining long-run growth in the sphere of economics. But, there are conditions for host countries to reach this goal. FDI should contribute to knowledge spillovers from foreign affiliations to domestic companies in the host country. Entry of MNCs into host country market should not damage competitive market structure due to advantages gained by protection of knowledge. Governance should be established in a way that there should be no governance-impairment spillovers from domestic firms to foreign affiliations. Human capital in the host country should provide labor with necessary skill set to foreign affiliations in order the employment rate in the host country get increased. Host countries should prioritize FDI to short-term foreign capital inflows by considering above conditions at the same time, for the following reason. Because in time of economic crises, FDI inflows is less inclined to run away than short-term foreign capital inflows. Host countries should be on alert in time of economic crises for the expansion of MNCs by harming competitive market structure and to dictate their own practices, which may lead to impairment in governance structure of the host countries.

The study mainly concentrates on the effect of governance on FDI inflows by controlling other factors.

Instead of scholars who established the theories on the determinants of FDI, the most satisfying argument was established by North (1990) in his assessment of the role of institutions on economic performance of countries. North (1990) argued that formal institutions such as constitutions, prudential laws, regulations, government policies and informal institutions such as traditions, habits, customs affect the perception and willingness of investors in a country because they limit opportunism, build transactional trust in financial transactions, and ultimately influence international players to engage in cross border transactions. Together with the standard constraints of economics, institutions define the choice set and therefore determine transaction and production costs and hence the profitability and feasibility of engaging in economic activity whether it is domestic or foreign (North, 1990).

Based mainly on North (1990), Dunning and Lundan (2008) emphasize the significance of institutions for the ability of countries to attract FDI and to derive a sustained economic benefit from FDI.

All other theories of FDI referring to an aspect of governance as a determinant of FDI as follows;

According to Hymer (1976) first type of FDI requires prudent use of assets in a way that the investor seeks to control over the enterprise in order to ensure the safety of his investment. When the distrust of foreigners or when fear of expropriation are high, this type of direct investment will substitute for portfolio investment theory. Kindleberger (1969) considers the role of bribery, corruption, evasion, transgression, ethical standards, risks of confiscation, risks of governmental intervention in trade as institutional factors affecting FDI decision. According to Vernon (1966), producers setting up a new production facility in the importing country will have to balance a number of complex considerations at the maturing stage of production and political situation in the country of prospective investment is one of these considerations. According to Knickerbocker (1973), once a country has attained some threshold level of socio-political stability, or has re-established order after a period of turmoil, firms in oligopolistic industries simultaneously show an interest in making direct investments in the country. Magee (1977) argues that well-established property rights and efficient legal system are necessary conditions for the protection of knowledge created by the foreign investors. Buckley and Casson (1976) argue that political relations between nations affect FDI decision. Rugman (1980) argues that internalization allows MNE to establish property rights for information, which can be considered as an aspect of governance. Aliber (1970) argues that foreign firms operating in host countries incur political risk due to additional costs associated with management of an enterprise at some distance, which can be considered as a governance factor.

Looking at the empirical studies, Aysan et al. (2006) argues that low quality of governance negatively affects the investment climate of the host countries. In the literature, it is widely accepted that low quality of governance increases economic uncertainties and cost of doing business (Wei, 2000).

Low quality of governance affects investment climate of the host country in the following way. It leads to partial, inequitable and inconsistent legal system, which is unable to protect private property. It increases political uncertainties due to civil disobedience or internal and external conflicts. Finally it allows non-democratic practices of the governments in the form of unfair elections and electoral laws, absence of freedom of press, assembly and demonstration.

The study brings a new perspective to FDI theory based on extensive theoretical literature survey. It makes a distinction between base factors and motivation factors by considering governance structure as a base factor.

Countries are categorized according to UN classification of developed countries, developing countries except least developed countries and least developed countries. Thirty-two advanced countries, seventy developing countries and seventeen less developed countries for the period 1996-2010 is analyzed with System GMM methodology due to endogeneity problem. The countries are classified according to UN categorization of developed countries, developing countries except LDCs and LDCs.

The result of the previous empirical studies is going to be compared with the results found in the study, in the section of empirical analysis.

Next section presents a new perspective to FDI theory. Third section presents data, variables and methodology used in the study. Fourth section presents empirical analysis. Last section provides concluding remarks.

Any FDI decision taken by MNCs depends on two factors as base and motivation. Without the base that the host country offers to investors, especially the governance structure, any motivation behind the FDI decision may not put into practice. FDI theories in the literature has either totally excluded the base factor or partially included it as other determinants of FDI. Most of them concentrated on the motivation factor behind the FDI decision.

Base factor includes governance structure, physical infrastructure and human capital that the host countries offer to investors. Motivation factor refers to the advantages either imperfect markets offer to investors as locational attractions, the exploitation of firm-specific or ownership advantages (Dunning and Lundan, 2008), strategic behaviors behind the FDI decision as in the case of oligopolistic reaction theory by Knickerbocker (1973), internalizing operations of MNCs and finally investing abroad to diversify risks.

Figure 1. Theoretical perspective
Source: Author's own categorization based on extensive literature survey.

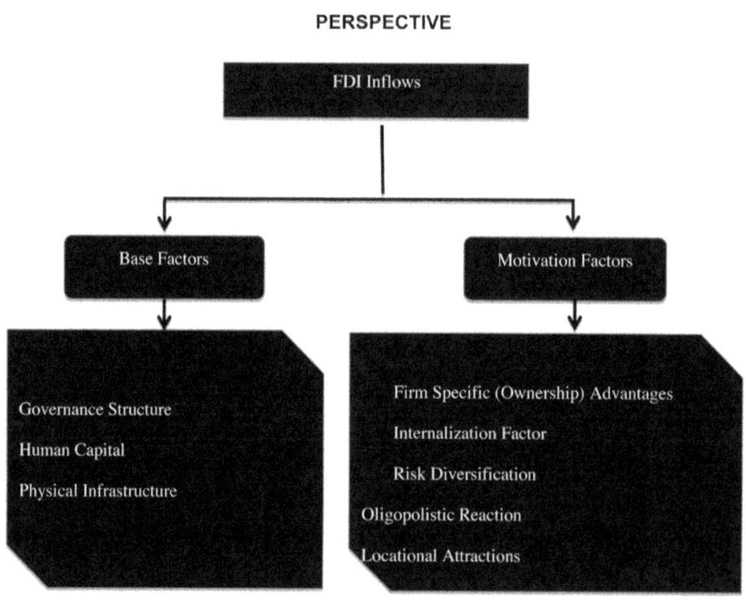

BASE FACTORS

Base factors are divided into three as governance structure, human capital and physical infrastructure.

Since foreign investors may invest in human capital or physical infrastructure in the host countries by ignoring the current development level of them altogether for future profits, governance structure bears more importance than human capital and physical infrastructure. Because, no foreign investor has rights or motivation to involve in investment for governance structure of the host countries.

Governance Structure

Governance structure of a country should be defined and measured by its politic, economic, administrative and democratic stand against internal and external events. However, this study only inquires stand of host country against FDI inflows.

Political dimension of governance affects the FDI decision of foreign affiliates in the following way. Politically unstable countries have higher amount of internal and external conflicts. Due to these conflicts governments are unstable and the probability of civil disobedience is high. Hence the protection of private property is hard to sustain. Without the protection of property rights, MNCs do not prefer to take FDI decision or foreign affiliates do not prefer to increase their FDI inflows. There is only one exception for this case. MNCs take action to suppress competitive market equilibrium for the sake of future profits in time of political turmoil.

Economic dimension of governance affects the FDI decision of foreign affiliates in the following way. MNCs consider the costs and returns on the FDI projects. If an economy is governed by inadequate and inconsistent economic policies and turns into unstable one, it constitutes the major cause of unpredictable high costs. Returns on FDI projects, which seems profitable at the beginning turn into losses mainly due to the exchange rate risks and inflation. Economic instability increases uncertainty and risks, which are detrimental to FDI inflows. Hence MNCs either prefer economically more stable host countries or just make FDI if they predicted that the time required to exploit full return on FDI comes before the time of the economy in the host country becomes unstable.

Administrative dimension of governance affects FDI decision of foreign affiliates in the following way. It includes bureaucratic quality of the host country, host country's stand against corruption and protection of investors against expropriation. MNCs taking FDI decision in a host country evaluates the performance of bureaucracy based on how responsive is the system to the need of investors, does it take too much time and effort even to initiate simple steps of investment plans. Whether investor have to deal with red tape. Hence the inefficiencies in bureaucracy are a detrimental factor for FDI, because it increases the time for implementation of investment plans; hence it increases the costs of investment due to time lags. Extensiveness of corruption for the initiation of FDI decision has two effects on the competitive market structure. The first one is the case where host country officials impose their corruption practices on foreign affiliates. In this case the price mechanism is harmed to the increase in cost due to corruption practices. The second one is that MNCs suborn host country officials in order to access better terms or privileges. The last constituent of administrative dimension of governance structure is the extent of protection of investor rights. MNCs also consider the protection against expropriation, contract viability by the risk of unilateral contract modification or cancellation, and payment delays by the extent that profits can be transferred out of the host country to home country bases.

Last dimension of governance is the stand of host country with respect to democracy. Democratic institutions "provide checks and balances on elected officials, which in turn reduces arbitrary government intervention and lowers the risk of policy reversal and strengthen private property protection" (Asiedu and Lien, 2011, p.1). The type of products and services supplied by MNCs to domestic markets are highly sensitive to the preferences of consumers if the consumer rights in the host country are well protected. Any reduction in the quality of goods and services offered to domestic consumers or any harm given to environment or public health is confronted with public reaction either by the legal system which provides those rights to consumers through lawsuits or by democratic actions through boycott, rallies, assembly against MNCs. Hence MNCs take this reality into account at the planning stage of their investment. Improvement in the protection of consumer rights either through legal system or democratic rights of the public do not constitute a detrimental factor for FDI inflows. On the contrary, they enlarge the preference set of consumers, which lead to increased amount of FDI inflows by MNCs.

The author is benefitted from Aysan et. al. (2006) and ICRG variable definitions of PRS while establishing his own stand. The three governance indicators; political stability, administrative quality and public voice are based on governance indicators developed by Aysan et.al. (2006). But, the reason to include these indicators, the motivation behind using them and the sub-indices of the indicators differ from Aysan et.al. (2006).

Human Capital

Lucas (1988), Barro, Mankiw and Sala-i-Martin (1995) argued that higher rates of human capital accumulation led to higher growth rates and thereby more investment including FDI. On the other hand, Benhabib and Spiegel (1994) argued that the countries having high level of human capital attract MNCs and assimilate new technologies with efficacy and thereby would be able to achieve higher growth rates. (Khan, 2007)

An enhanced level of human capital increases FDI inflows by making the investment climate more attractive to the foreign investors through a direct effect of upgraded skill level of the workforce as well as via indirect effects, such as improved socio-political stability and health (Humphreys, 2003) .

The level of human capital has been a crucial factor in determining the new location of operation by the MNCs as their production is becoming overly skill-conscious with an increasing number of high-technology manufacturing and services (Khan, 2007).

On the other hand, the FDI contributes to human capital because MNCs that are the providers of education and training. They bring new skills, information and technology to host countries (Khan, 2007). Because of this, insufficient human capital in the host countries may be a motivation factor for FDI.

Physical Infrastructure

Wheeler and Mody (1992), Asiedu (2002), Loree and Guisinger (1995), Richard et. al. (1999) all agree that investors search for markets where they can maximize the benefits and lower the cost of production. This can only be achieved if the infrastructure offered as a public good is in good conditions and supportive to investors (Abu Bakar et.al., 2012). The maximization of benefits and minimization of production costs are motivation factors that can only be achieved if the physical infrastructure as a base factor is well established. The argument of Bae (2008) that the infrastructure is not a motivator but an indicator to attract FDI in emerging economies is also parallel to author's argument. A good quality of physical infrastructure would improve the investment climate for FDI as the cost of total investment by foreign investors can be subsidized; therefore increase the rate of return.

Also, the quality of physical infrastructure affects the decision made by MNCs in relocating the export-platform production. (Abu Bakar et.al., 2012)

Khadaroo and Seetanah (2007) claimed that increase in the quality of physical infrastructure was associated with greater accessibility and reduction in transportation costs. Erenberg (1993) argued that if physical infrastructure were not extended to local and multinational enterprises publicly, then these enterprises would have been operating with less efficiency. Because, they had to build their own infrastructure resulting in duplication and wasting of resources.

MOTIVATION FACTORS

FDI decision of a typical foreign investor or a MNC is taken at least considering one of each or a combination of five motivation factors as;

1. Firm specific or ownership advantages
2. Internalization factor
3. Risk diversification
4. Oligopolistic Reaction
5. Locational attractions of the host country

The study only inquires locational attractions that the host country offers and oligopolistic reaction as motivation factors because other factors are mainly in the sphere of microeconomic theories of FDI.

Oligopolistic Reaction

According to Knickerbrocker (1973), FDI is an interactive kind of corporate behavior by which rival firms in an industry composed of a few large firms counter one another's moves by making similar moves themselves.

"Either the countering firms acquire about the same advantages as the firm that made the initial move, so that a new competitive balance is established in the industry, or the countering firms force the firm with the advantage to forego exploiting it by the threat of intensifying competition in the industry to the point where all rivals suffer. In this case the old competitive balance is restored" (Knickerbrocker, 1973, pp.6).

The concept of oligopolistic reaction does not try to explain the reason behind the initial move made by a specific MNC, it just tries to explain what rival(s) MNC(s) may react against it.

Although oligopolistic reaction is included in the microeconomic theories of FDI, it can be evaluated by considering all the aggregate responses of other MNCs against the initial move by a typical MNC.

Locational Attractions of the Host Country

Market Size and Its Growth

The main rationale is that the firms increase their investment in response to their sales and that domestic investment of a country rises with its rising GDP (Agarwal, 1980).

It is only natural that rapidly growing foreign markets should attract foreign investors interested in expanding their stakes overseas. After all, the gains in output needed to meet rapidly increasing demand offer opportunities for economies of scale. Although defensive investors may ignore scale considerations at the outset, they want assurance that scale advantages will be possible in the future; so rapid growth gives this assurance (Knickerbrocker, 1973).

Appropriability

By analyzing patent system, depreciation of the information investment, private rate of return on information, private and public R&D expenditure,

Magee (1977) argued that economic actors would invest resources in the generation of information until the expected private returns would be equated to the returns on other investments of equal risk. The extension of patent system in host countries, whether it provides full protection from imitation or not plays the crucial role on private returns of investment on information.

Natural Resources

The nature and composition of a country's comparative advantage based on its possession of a unique set of immobile natural resources and capabilities, offer a distinctive and non-imitable set of location bound created assets, including the presence of indigenous firms with which foreign MNCs might form alliances to complement their own core competencies (Dunning, 2000).

Costs

There are different types of costs when a MNC involved in FDI as;

1. Cost of acquiring information
2. Cost of making transaction

National firms have the general advantage of better information about their country and its economy. For the foreigner, acquiring the fixed cost of this information may be considerable; but once incurred no need to be incurred again (Hymer, 1976). According to (Hymer, 1976), in the case of high costs of acquiring information or of making transaction, equivalent securities in different countries sell at different rates, because the discrepancy is not known or because the cost of removing it, is too great.

3. Communication cost

There has been a great increase in communications between different countries in recent years, which may lead to the integration of the world economy or at least the economic integration of broader areas than in the past. The increased international operations of national firms may be a result of this fact, and they may also play their part in furthering integration of the world economy. (Hymer, 1976)

4. Transportation cost
5. Production cost

According to Vernon (1966), as long as the marginal production cost plus the transportation cost of the goods being exported from home country is less than the average cost of prospective production in the market of import (host countries), producers will avoid an investment.

6. Cost of capital
7. Unit labor costs

According to Vernon (1966), if economies of scale are being fully exploited, the principal differences between any two locations are likely to be labor costs.

All these type of costs are considered in FDI decision of MNCs whether to expand or cut back the production in host countries.

Market Imperfections

Kindleberger (1969) argues that in a world of perfect competition for goods and factors, direct investment cannot exist; domestic firms would have an advantage over foreign firms in the proximity of their operations to their decision-making centers, so that no firm could survive in foreign operation. For direct investment to thrive there must be some imperfection in markets for goods or factors including technology or some interference in competition by government or by firms, which separates markets.

Rugman (1980) argues that internalization theory serves to determine the reasons for the foreign production and sales of the MNE in response to imperfections in the goods and factor markets.

When MNE develops in response to imperfections in the goods or factor markets, the country specific advantage of a nation, which leads to trade, is replaced by a firm specific advantage internal to an MNE, which leads to FDI (Rugman, 1980).

Rugman (1980) concludes that imperfections in the factor markets, especially in the market for intermediate goods, always lead to the development of MNEs and if there were perfect goods or factor markets in the first place then there would be no reason for an MNE to develop and free trade would exist.

Barriers to Entry

In the area of foreign direct investment barriers to entry can take many forms as below;

1. **Government Limitations**: Government limitations include tariffs, non-tariff barriers, import duties, requirement of a share of the equity capital to be sold in the local market by MNC or a foreign investor, training of native labor, and finally stipulation of specified and generally rising proportions of inputs that must be procured locally (Kindleberger, 1969).
2. **Discrimination by Host Government:** The prohibition of foreigners or severe restrictions on the types of activity foreigners is permitted to engage in (Hymer, 1976).
3. **Discrimination by Consumers or Suppliers:** Although Hymer (1976) refers to this subject as a barrier to entry, he concludes that it is hard to tell whether consumers or suppliers really care about the nationality of the firm they deal with.
4. **Significant Economies of Large-Scale:** Hymer (1976) refers to Bain (1956) that typical circumstances discouraging entry by sustaining significant economies of large-scale firm as;
    a. Real or strictly pecuniary economies of large-scale production and distribution such that an optimal firm will supply a significant share of the market
    b. Real or strictly pecuniary economies of large-scale advertising or other sales promotion, having a similar effect

Where economies of scale exist, it is difficult to start small, hence international mergers and acquisitions may be a means of increasing competition rather than reducing it (Kindleberger, 1969).

Tax Policy

A government should tax those industries where private value is above social value and subsidize those where the opposite is true, such taxes and subsidies would apply to foreign and domestic entrepreneurs alike and to restrict only the foreigner is distortionary and uneconomic (Kindleberger, 1969).

Tax systems inevitably distort allocation. The underlining point is that one country will tax the income of a corporation on its foreign earnings to the extent that they are not already taxed abroad (Kindleberger, 1969).

Geographical Proximity to the Market

The entrepreneur's consciousness of and responsiveness to opportunity are a function of ease of communication and ease of communication is a function of geographical proximity to the market (Vernon, 1966).

Interest Rates

According to portfolio investment theory, capital will move from countries where the interest rate is low to countries where it is high until interest rates are equal everywhere in case of no risks, uncertainties, or barriers to movement (Hymer, 1976).

International Trade

International operations frequently were established to replace exports or to produce imports and in some cases, international operations occur only because there is actual or potential trade. Trade brings enterprises of one country into contact with enterprises of another country, which often causes conflict. International operations are one means of resolving this conflict. Not only advantages lead to trade but also trade leads to advantages. A firm may establish distribution channels or may establish differentiated product through its export activities, which improves its advantages leading to foreign operations (Hymer, 1976).

DATA, VARIABLES, AND METHODOLOGY

Data

Empirical analysis cover thirty-two advanced, seventy developing and seventeen less developed countries for the period 1996-2010 due to data availability. Interpolation and extrapolation techniques are used in the study. The countries are categorized according to UN classification of developed countries, developing countries except LDCs and LDCs. See Appendix for the list of countries.

Variables

FDI Inflows

The dependent variable is FDI inflows of the host countries as a percentage of GDP. "FDI includes equity capital, reinvested earnings and intra-company loans. Data on FDI flows are presented on net bases as credits less debits of capital transactions between direct investors and their foreign affiliates. Net decreases in assets or net increases in liabilities are recorded as credits with a positive sign, while net increases in assets or net decreases in liabilities are recorded as debits with a negative sign. FDI flows with a negative sign are called reverse investment or disinvestment that indicate that at least one of the three components of FDI is negative and not offset by positive amounts of the remaining components" (UNCTAD, 2014).

Lag of FDI Inflows

In case of oligopolistic reaction to exist, any FDI decision taken by a typical MNC involving increase (decrease) in the FDI for a specific host country i in year t-1 leads other MNCs to react to take similar FDI decision involving increase (decrease) in the FDI for that specific host country i in year t. But we must be careful that there are multiple MNCs not just one a typical MNC in period t-1 taking FDI decision in country i. Also we must assume that all the reaction of other MNCs taking FDI decision starting with time t. And time t starts no later than the beginning of the analysis; 1996.

Governance Variables

Political Stability Index (PSI)

This index is constructed to measure the safety of FDI due to political stability of the host countries. This index is the average of three indices from ICRG (2011); government stability, external conflict and internal conflict.

Economic Stability Index (ESI)

This index is constructed to measure the sustainability of FDI due to economic stability of the host countries. This index is the average of six indices from ICRG (2011); risk for budget balance, risk for current account, risk for exchange rate stability, risk for foreign debt, risk for inflation, risk for international liquidity. Another reason to use this index is to control the effect of economic and financial crises.

Administrative Quality Index (AQI)

This index is constructed to measure the quality of the relationship between investor and the administrative institutions of the host country, and the protection of investor rights. This index is the average of three indices from ICRG (2011); bureaucracy quality, investment profile and corruption.

Public Voice Index (PVI)

This index is constructed to measure the protection of consumer rights against investors. This index is the average of three indices; democratic accountability from ICRG (2011), political rights and civil liberties from FRH (2011).

Market Growth

Market growth is proxied by annual GDP growth rate of host countries.

Human Capital

This index is constructed by using Barro-Lee indicators (WDI, 2015). Since MNCs look for labor with graduation certificate, we used these indicators, which show the completion rather than attendance ratio. It is the weighted average of completed primary, completed secondary and completed tertiary.

Physical Infrastructure

In order to measure physical infrastructure of host countries, we created a physical infrastructure index, which is the average of three sub-indices, basic infrastructure, communication infrastructure and transportation infrastructure. Basic infrastructure is the average of two indices from WDI (2015), access to electricity and improved water source. Communication infrastructure is the average of two indices from WDI (2015); internet users and telephone lines. Transportation infrastructure is the average of three indices from WDI (2015); roads total network, rail lines total route-km and air transport passengers carried, all divided by population of the host countries.

Natural Resources

In order to measure the effect of available natural resources on FDI inflows, we used Total natural resources rents (% of GDP) from WDI (2015).

Financial Depth

In order to measure the effect of financial depth on FDI inflows, we used money and quasi money (M2) as % of GDP from WDI (2015).

Trade Openness

In order to measure the effect of trade openness on FDI inflows, we used trade (% of GDP) from WDI (2015).

Tariff Rate

In order to analyze the effect of barriers on FDI inflows, we used tariff rate, applied, simple mean, all products from WDI (2015).

Real Interest Rate

In order to test the portfolio investment theory, hence to measure the effect of interest rates on FDI inflows, we used real interest rate of the host countries from WDI (2015).

METHODOLOGY

The studies analyzing the role of governance on FDI inflows can be categorized first into categories as bilateral FDI studies analyzing institutional difference and unilateral FDI studies either analyzing the role of governance on FDI inflows or outflows. The analysis for unilateral FDI inflows can be categorized into five categories as; the single country studies, regional studies as Latin America or South Asia, multiple country studies based on one group of countries as transition economies or developing countries, multiple country studies without regarding the different structures of countries and multiple country studies regarding the different structures of countries.

The study aims to analyze the role of governance on FDI inflows in a broader sense by including as many countries as possible into the analysis by regarding their different structures for FDI, governance and human capital. Hence the aim of the study is completely different than first and second category of studies. The results of third category studies for developing countries will be compared with the results of the study. Fourth category studies do not regard the different structures of included countries in the regressions, hence their results are biased because it is known that the governance has different effects on FDI inflows for countries mainly based on their development level according to the literature review. For the studies under the fifth categories, actually there is only one study as Globerman and Shapiro (2002). It only categorizes countries into two as developed and developing without considering the difference between developing and less developed countries. The reason why the study categorizes countries into three clusters as developed, developing and less developed countries is as follows:

The reason to divide countries into three clusters is based on type of FDI inflows, governance structure developed in the historical content and the type of human capital required for FDI.

FDI inflows in advanced countries are generally technology intensive, high R&D based; hence they require high skilled human capital. The majority of FDI is technology driven FDI (TFDI) in advanced countries targeting local technology market and advancing their further technology (Amighini et.al, 2013). The volume of FDI inflows are highest compared to developing and less advanced countries, because the value-added created through FDI inflows are highest due to patents and protection of technical know-how. Advanced countries generally established their governance institutions long time ago during the colonization of world based on their experiences both on their mainland and colonies. They established their governance structures according to their own internal dynamics of historical and cultural background, customs, economic practices, belief and legal system. As Acemoglu et.al (2001) argued they sustained their governance structure with strong emphasis on private property and checks against government power. As a consequence, their governance structure is taken as a role model on a worldwide basis. That's why ex-colonizers of past and advanced countries of today have the highest governance quality in the world.

According to UN (2006), the bulk of FDI into LDCs is associated with natural-resource-related investments requiring lowest skilled level of human capital. Less developed countries are generally ex-colonies, did not find a chance to establish their own governance structures because they are ruled by the regimes of colonizers for many years. When they thought they won their independence, they were ruled by totalitarian regimes left behind and supported by advanced countries of today for sustaining political stability of the region or securing their economic interests (Beyer, 2008; Etzioni, 2008). The colonial state and extractive institutions persisted even after independence (Acemoglu et.al, 2001). That's why less developed countries have the lowest governance quality.

Between these two extremes; FDI inflows in developing countries are generally based on automated technology with capital-intensive production techniques that are developed in and imported from advanced countries. Either no or low R&D is made. As Amighini et.al (2013) argued even these countries started to invest in advanced countries to acquire technological assets and to create knowledge and innovation. The raw or semi materials are generally imported. Since know-how is brought by host country firms through patents from advanced countries and advanced countries do not generally build technology or R&D bases in these countries and the production process requires middle level of human capital, the value-added created through FDI inflows are not high, so the FDI inflows are not high as well. Although these countries generally were not colonized as in the case of less developed countries for many years, at least they were occupied. They could not adapt their historical and cultural inheritance, customs, economic practices, belief and legal system with modern practices and standards of advanced countries; instead they just merely imported governance structures of advanced countries to catch them up as soon as possible. That's why developing countries generally have middle performance of governance.

Hence, the reason why FDI inflows in these three country clusters are high, middle and low depend on the value-added created through FDI and the amount of resources that are accessible or exploitable through FDI. FDI inflows are highest in advanced countries because they are technology-intensive, R&D based. The cost of FDI and return on FDI is high because they also export the technology they created to developing and less developed countries. In developing countries, FDI inflows are at the middle level because MNCs do not establish technology centers and R&D bases to create know how. The main objective is to use the technology created in home country bases together with automated production process requiring middle level of human capital because wage rates are lower compared to advanced countries or near the growing markets. Since FDI inflows in less developed countries require lowest skilled human capital, their wage costs are lowest. But, keeping good relationship with the totalitarian regime requires financial support to the regime and increases cost with corruption. Also the natural resources exploitable in these countries are limited. That's why FDI inflows in these countries are at the lowest amount.

Hence, the results reached without taking these differences among countries lead to misleading conclusions because we are analyzing countries with different structures, regarding the type of FDI inflows, governance structure and human capital requirements. Three aggregate country clusters based on these three structural factors seems to be more appropriate way to classify countries, reaching results and advising policy implications.

EMPIRICAL ANALYSIS

Empirical Model

The general model to be estimated with System GMM (Roodman, 2006) is as below;
For Models 1.1-6.4;

$$FDI_{it} = \propto FDI_{i,t-1} + \beta_1 \; BASE_{it} + \beta_2 \; MOT_{it} + \varepsilon_{it} \qquad (1.1)$$

$$\varepsilon_{it} = \mu_i + \nu_{it} \qquad (1.2)$$

$$E\left(\mu_i\right) = E\left(\nu_{it}\right) = E(\mu_i \nu_{it}) = 0 \qquad (1.3)$$

$$\Delta FDI_{it} = \delta \; \Delta FDI_{i,t-1} + \phi \; \Delta BASE_{it} + \lambda \; \Delta MOT_{it} + \nu_{it} \qquad (1.4)$$

$$E\left(\Delta w_{it} \mu_i\right) = 0 \qquad (1.5)$$

FDI_{it} represents FDI inflows for country i in year t. $FDI_{i,t-1}$ represents FDI inflows for country i in year t-1 to measure the oligopolistic reaction. $BASE_{it}$ represents base factors including, human capital, physical infrastructure, our four governance variables and two governance indicators from WGI (2015). MOT_{it} represents motivation factors as GDP growth, availability of natural resources, financial depth, trade openness, tariff rates and real interest rates for country i in year t.

Except Model 1.5 and Model 1.6 all the regressions include governance indicators as base factor. Model 1.5 incorporates human capital and Model 1.6 incorporates physical infrastructure as base factors. Since there exists high correlation between governance infrastructure, human capital and physical infrastructure, all these base factors regressed separately. All the regressions include lag of FDI inflows. All regressions include GDP growth as motivation factor. All other motivation factors are included in the regressions separately.

Reduced form equations for Model 7;

$$FDI_{it} = \propto FDI_{i,t-1} + \beta_1 \, BASE_{it} + \beta_2 \, MOT_{it} + \beta_3 \, BASEMOT_{it} + \varepsilon_{it} \tag{2.1}$$

$$\varepsilon_{it} = \mu_i + \nu_{it} \tag{2.2}$$

$$E\left(\mu_i\right) = E\left(\nu_{it}\right) = E(\mu_i \nu_{it}) = 0 \tag{2.3}$$

$$\Delta FDI_{it} = \delta \Delta FDI_{i,t-1} + \phi \Delta BASE_{it} + \lambda \Delta MOT_{it} + \gamma \Delta BASEMOT_{it} + \nu_{it} \tag{2.4}$$

$$E\left(\Delta w_{it} \mu_i\right) = 0 \tag{2.5}$$

FDI_{it} represents FDI inflows for country i in year t. $FDI_{i,t-1}$ represents FDI inflows for country i in year t-1 to measure the oligopolistic reaction. $BASE_{it}$ represents one of our governance variables. MOT_{it} represents motivation factors, GDP growth or availability of natural resources for country i in year t. $BASEMOT_{it}$ represents interaction of a base and motivation factor for country i in year t.

System GMM Analysis

According to the estimation results in Table 1 to Table 6, lag of FDI inflows have positive significant effect on current FDI inflows in all country clusters, which confirms oligopolistic reaction theory. Hence it can be concluded that FDI is an interactive kind of corporate behavior by which rival firms in an industry composed of a few large firms counter one another's moves by making similar moves themselves. The results of the study supports Knickerbocker (1973), Flowers (1975) and Kinoshita (1998) even they use other proxies to measure oligopolistic reaction. Estimation results also support Cheng and Kwan (2000), Noorbaksh et. al. (2001), Biglaiser and DeRouen (2004), Biglaiser and Staats (2010), Cantah et.al. (2013) in the sense that there exists a clustering effect for FDI, the increase (decrease) in FDI made in previous year leads to increase (decrease) in FDI made in current year.

According to the estimation results in Table 1 to Table 6, all the governance variables have positive significant effect on FDI inflows in advanced and developing

Table 1. System GMM estimation results I for advanced countries (AC)

Dependent Variable: fdi						
	Model 1.1	**Model 1.2**	**Model 1.3**	**Model 1.4**	**Model 1.5**	**Model 1.6**
l.fdi	0.334***	0.338***	0.329**	0.330***	0.341***	0.334***
	-0.097	(0.101)	(0.126)	-0.105	(0.085)	(0.101)
psi	0.025***					
	0.009					
esi		0.032***				
		-0.011				
aqi			0.026**			
			(0.010)			
pvi				0.021**		
				(0.009)		
gdpgr	0.532***	0.503**	0.548***	0.518***	0.512***	0.531***
	-0.188	-0.211	-0.144	(0.189)	(0.179)	(0.175)
humcap					0.021**	
					(0.009)	
infra						0.028***
						(0.010)
Prob > F	0.000	0.000	0.000	0.000	0.000	0.000
Countries	32	32	32	32	32	32
Instruments	30	30	30	30	30	27
Hansen	0.431	0.257	0.421	0.398	0.437	0.343
AR(3)	0.212	0.227	0.226	0.215	0.217	0.218

Source: Author's Own Calculations

Notes: The values in parenthesis are robust standard errors. ***, ** and * denote significance levels at % 1, % 5 and % 10 respectively. AR(#) is test for #-order serial correlation in the #-differenced residuals, under the null of no serial correlation. Hansen test of over-identification is under the null that all instruments are valid. All the independent variables are treated endogenously. Appropriate lags of endogenous variables were instrumented according to AR(#) test of serial correlation.

countries. All the governance variables except political stability (psi) have positive significant effect on FDI inflows in less developed countries. Hence better governance attracts higher amount of FDI inflows in all country clusters. Since all governance variables except political stability in less developed countries have positive significant coefficients in each regression models with other control variables, it will not be a misleading conclusion that the governance structure is not a sufficient but a necessary base factor to attract FDI inflows in all country clusters. Our results regarding the

Table 2. System GMM estimation results II for advanced countries (AC)

Dependent Variable: fdi							
	Model 2.2	**Model 3.3**	**Model 4.1**	**Model 5.2**	**Model 6.4**	**Model 7.1**	**Model 7.2**
l.fdi	0.323***	0.327***	0.496*	0.374***	0.245*	0.332***	0.292***
	(0.092)	(0.118)	-0.28	-0.097	-0.131	(0.122)	(0.095)
psi			0.073**			0.030*	
			-0.034			(0.017)	
esi	0.037***			0.028*			0.034***
	(0.012)			-0.016			(0.011)
aqi		0.042**					
		(0.020)					
pvi					0.037*		
					-0.02		
gdpgr	0.505**	0.424***	0.608**	0.519***	0.353***	-1.503	-2.229
	(0.193)	(0.127)	-0.285	-0.172	-0.128	(1.002)	(1.401)
natural	-0.360**						
	(0.173)						
findep		-0.012					
		(0.015)					
trop			-0.049				
			-0.029				
tariff				-0.326			
				-0.329			
rint					0.022		
					-0.184		
psigdpgr						0.024*	
						(0.013)	
esigdpgr							0.034*
							(0.019)
Prob > F	0.000	0.000	0.000	0.000	0.000	0.000	0.000
Countries	32	32	32	32	30	32	32
Instruments	32	36	12	28	35	34	36
Hansen	0.353	0.564	0.455	0.299	0.61	0.675	0.530
AR(3)	0.232	0.226	0.196	0.225	0.199	0.205	0.280

Source: Author's Own Calculations

Notes: The values in parenthesis are robust standard errors. ***, ** and * denote significance levels at % 1, % 5 and % 10 respectively. AR(#) is test for #-order serial correlation in the #-differenced residuals, under the null of no serial correlation. Hansen test of over-identification is under the null that all instruments are valid. All the independent variables except tariff are treated endogenously. Appropriate lags of endogenous variables were instrumented according to AR(#) test of serial correlation.

Table 3. System GMM estimation results I for developing countries (DC)

Dependent Variable: fdi						
	Model 1.1	**Model 1.2**	**Model 1.3**	**Model 1.4**	**Model 1.5**	**Model 1.6**
l.fdi	0.604***	0.600***	0.416**	0.606***	0.758***	0.827***
	(0.120)	(0.103)	(0.189)	(0.121)	(0.072)	(0.111)
psi	0.023***					
	(0.008)					
esi		0.019**				
		(0.007)				
aqi			0.050**			
			(0.020)			
pvi				0.022**		
				(0.010)		
gdpgr	0.136**	0.136**	0.167*	0.190***	0.131**	0.174**
	(0.058)	(0.054)	(0.086)	(0.058)	(0.061)	(0.068)
humcap					0.010*	
					(0.006)	
infra						-0.008
						(0.011)
Prob > F	0.000	0.000	0.000	0.000	0.000	0.000
Countries	70	70	70	70	70	70
Instruments	24	23	24	24	24	27
Hansen	0.839	0.671	0.616	0.585	0.665	0.178
AR(4)	0.136	0.119	0.167	0.133	0.108	0.102

Source: Author's Own Calculations

Notes: The values in parenthesis are robust standard errors. ***, ** and * denote significance levels at % 1, % 5 and % 10 respectively. AR(#) is test for #-order serial correlation in the #-differenced residuals, under the null of no serial correlation. Hansen test of over-identification is under the null that all instruments are valid. All the independent variables are treated endogenously. Appropriate lags of endogenous variables were instrumented according to AR(#) test of serial correlation.

advanced countries support the findings of Globerman and Shapiro (2002) regarding the role of governance on FDI inflows in developed and richer countries. Our results regarding the developing countries support the findings of Globerman and Shapiro (2002), Buchanan et.al (2012) regarding governance structure, Ahmed (1975), Levis (1979), Busse and Hefeker (2007) regarding political stability, Asiedu and Lien (2011) for economic stability, Globerman and Shapiro (2002), Busse and Hefeker (2007) regarding administrative quality, Busse and Hefeker (2007) regarding public

Table 4. System GMM estimation results II for developing countries (DC)

Dependent Variable: fdi							
	Model 2.4	**Model 3.3**	**Model 4.1**	**Model 5.2**	**Model 6.2**	**Model 7.3**	**Model 7.4**
l.fdi	0.451**	0.542***	0.524**	0.501***	0.569***	0.602***	0.671***
	(0.173)	-0.13	(0.246)	(0.147)	(0.129)	-0.133	-0.102
psi			0.037**				
			(0.016)				
esi				0.020*	0.018*		
				(0.011)	(0.010)		
aqi		0.036*				0.054**	
		-0.02				-0.027	
pvi	0.034**						0.035**
	(0.017)						-0.017
gdpgr	0.202**	0.182***	0.118*	0.168***	0.191***	0.602***	-0.116
	(0.097)	-0.055	(0.066)	(0.059)	(0.072)	-0.133	-0.126
natural	-0.019						
	(0.033)						
findep		0.002					
		-0.022					
trop			-0.018				
			(0.015)				
tariff				-0.031			
				(0.031)			
rint					-0.016		
					(0.033)		
aqigdpgr						0.005**	
						-0.002	
pvigdpgr							0.005**
							-0.002
Prob > F	0.000	0.000	0.000	0.000	0.000	0	0
Countries	68	67	67	65	30	70	70
Instruments	36	44	24	33	35	40	48
Hansen	0.174	0.122	0.348	0.121	0.61	0.151	0.175
AR(3)	0.178	0.135	0.169	0.120	0.199	0.133	0.129

Source: Author's Own Calculations

Notes: The values in parenthesis are robust standard errors. ***, ** and * denote significance levels at % 1, % 5 and % 10 respectively. AR(#) is test for #-order serial correlation in the #-differenced residuals, under the null of no serial correlation. Hansen test of over-identification is under the null that all instruments are valid. All the independent variables except tariff are treated endogenously. Appropriate lags of endogenous variables were instrumented according to AR(#) test of serial correlation.

Table 5. System GMM estimation results I for less developed countries (LDC)

	Dependent Variable: fdi					
	Model 1.1	**Model 1.2**	**Model 1.3**	**Model 1.4**	**Model 1.7**	**Model 1.8**
l.fdi	0.604**	0.537**	0.533***	0.594***	0.618***	0.587***
	(0.237)	(0.244)	(0.174)	(0.205)	(0.202)	(0.172)
psi	0.009					
	(0.027)					
esi		0.050*				
		(0.026)				
aqi			0.115*			
			(0.061)			
pvi				0.084**		
				(0.037)		
gdpgr	0.284	0.038	0.062	0.039	-0.299	-0.088
	(0.287)	(0.369)	(0.141)	(0.261)	(0.207)	(0.157)
humcap					0.113*	
					(0.060)	
infra						0.118*
						(0.063)
Prob > F	0.001	0.000	0.007	0.000	0.000	0.000
Countries	17	17	17	17	17	17
Instruments	15	25	22	21	18	27
Hansen	0.608	0.962	0.756	0.465	0.410	0.885
AR()	0.455	0.374	0.382	0.474	0.582	0.466

Source: Author's Own Calculations

Notes: The values in parenthesis are robust standard errors. ***, ** and * denote significance levels at % 1, % 5 and % 10 respectively. AR(#) is test for #-order serial correlation in the #-differenced residuals, under the null of no serial correlation. Hansen test of over-identification is under the null that all instruments are valid. All the independent variables are treated endogenously. Appropriate lags of endogenous variables were instrumented according to AR(#) test of serial correlation.

voice. Our results regarding the less developed countries support the findings of Asiedu (2002) regarding political stability, Sekkat and Varoudakis (2004), Cantah et.al. (2013) for economic stability.

According to the estimation results, market gowth, proxied by GDP growth has a positive significant effect on FDI inflows in advanced and developing countries, according to Table 1 to Table 6. Hence we can conclude that rapidly growing foreign markets should attract foreign investors interested in expanding their stakes

Table 6. System GMM estimation results II for less developed countries (LDC)

Dependent Variable: fdi						
	Model 2.4	**Model 3.2**	**Model 4.4**	**Model 5.4**	**Model 6.2**	**Model 7.2**
l.fdi	0.567***	0.697*	0.552***	0.585***	0.552**	0.626***
	-0.142	(0.372)	(0.086)	(0.184)	(0.229)	-0.188
esi		0.050*			0.068*	0.052*
		(0.024)			(0.036)	-0.028
pvi	0.042*		0.029***	0.056*		
	-0.02		(0.007)	(0.026)		
gdpgr	0.093	0.055	-0.032	0.492	0.017	
	-0.057	(0.318)	(0.044)	(0.334)	(0.239)	
natural	0.085*					-0.359
	-0.041					-0.23
findep		-0.0144				
		(0.085)				
trop			0.027**			
			(0.010)			
tariff				-0.296**		
				(0.118)		
rint					-0.115**	
					(0.043)	
esinatural						0.007*
						-0.004
Prob > F	0.000	0.000	0.000	0.000	0.000	0
Countries	16	17	16	13	10	16
Instruments	36	32	28	19	17	21
Hansen	0.998	0.990	0.991	0.990	0.984	0.974
AR(3)	0.431	0.385	0.490	0.617	0.504	0.227

Source: Author's Own Calculations

Notes: The values in parenthesis are robust standard errors. ***, ** and * denote significance levels at % 1, % 5 and % 10 respectively. AR(#) is test for #-order serial correlation in the #-differenced residuals, under the null of no serial correlation. Hansen test of over-identification is under the null that all instruments are valid. All the independent variables except tariff are treated endogenously. Appropriate lags of endogenous variables were instrumented according to AR(#) test of serial correlation.

overseas. After all, the gains in output needed to meet rapidly increasing demand offer opportunities for economies of scale. Although MNCs may ignore scale considerations at current period, they want assurance that scale advantages will be possible in the future; so rapid growth gives this assurance. (Knickerbrocker, 1973) Although we found a significant positive effect for GDP growth, we cannot conclude FDI made into advanced countries is market seeking, because we know that GDP growth rate has a decreasing trend on average and even it takes negative values from Table 7. It can also be concluded that FDI made into developing countries is market seeking, because we know that GDP growth rate is highest for these countries. Our results support the findings of Noorbaksh et. al. (2001) regarding developing countries.

According to the estimation result of Model 1.5 in Table 1, human capital has a positive significant effect on FDI inflows in advanced countries. Hence it will not be a misleading conclusion that human capital is a base factor that attracts FDI in advanced countries. We can also conclude that FDI made into advanced countries is efficiency seeking, because we know that human capital has the highest values and has an increasing trend in these countries on average from Table 7. Our results support the findings of Globerman and Shapiro (2002) regarding the role of human capital on FDI inflows in developed and richer countries. According to the estimation result of Model 1.5 in Table 3, human capital has a positive significant effect on FDI inflows in developing countries. Hence it will not be a misleading conclusion that human capital is a base factor that attracts FDI in developing countries. But we cannot conclude that FDI made into developing countries is efficiency seeking, because we know that human capital is lower compared to advanced countries. Our results support the findings of Narula (1996), Noorbaksh et. al. (2001), Globerman and Shapiro (2002). According to the estimation result of Model 1.5 in Table 5, human capital has a positive significant effect on FDI inflows in less developed countries. Hence it will not be a misleading conclusion that human capital is a base factor that attracts FDI in less developed countries. But we cannot conclude that FDI made into less developed countries is efficiency seeking, because we know that human capital is lower compared to other two country clusters. Our results support the findings of Sekkat and Varoudakis (2004), Cantah et.al. (2013).

According to the estimation result of Model 1.6 in Table 1, physical infrastructure has a positive significant effect on FDI inflows in advanced countries. Hence it will not be a misleading conclusion that physical infrastructure is a base factor that attracts FDI in advanced countries. Our results support the findings of Loree and Guisinger (1995). According to the estimation result of Model 1.6 in Table 3, physical infrastructure has no significant effect on FDI inflows in developing countries. Hence we are not able to conclude whether physical infrastructure is a base or motivation factor in developing countries. Our results support the findings of Loree and Guisinger (1995). According to the estimation result of Model 1.6 in Table 5, physical infrastructure has a positive significant effect on FDI inflows in less developed countries. Hence it will not be a misleading conclusion that physical infrastructure is a base factor that attracts FDI in less developed countries. Our results support the findings of Sekkat and Varoudakis (2004), Kandiero and Chitiga (2006), Khadaroo and Seetanah (2007).

According to the estimation results of Model 2.2 in Table 2, availability of natural resources has a negative significant effect on FDI inflows in advanced countries. It will not be a misleading conclusion that the FDI made in natural resources is less efficient form of investment than FDI made to other sectors of the host countries, so that FDI channeled to sectors using natural resources reduce the total amount of FDI made into that advanced host country. Also, it can be concluded that FDI made into advanced countries are definitely not resource seeking. According to the estimation results of Model 2.4 in Table 4, availability of natural resources has no significant effect on FDI inflows in developing countries. Hence we can conclude that FDI made into developing countries is not resource seeking. According to the estimation results of Model 2.4 in Table 6, availability of natural resources has a positive significant effect on FDI inflows in less developed countries. Hence we can conclude that FDI made into less developed countries is resource seeking. Our results support the findings of Aseidu (2002), Biglaiser and Staats (2010), Cantah et.al. (2013) for less developed countries.

According to the estimation results of Model 3.3 in Table 2, Model 3.3 in Table 4 and Model 3.2 in Table 6, financial depth has no significant effect on FDI inflows in all country clusters. Our results support the findings of Aseidu (2002) for less developed countries.

According to the estimation results of Model 4.1 in Table 2 and Table 4, trade openness has no significant effect on FDI inflows in advanced and developing countries. Our results support the findings of Globerman and Shapiro (2002) regarding the role of trade openness on FDI inflows in developed and richer countries and Globerman and Shapiro (2002), Busse and Hefeker (2007) for developing countries. According to the estimation results of Model 4.4 in Table 6, trade openness has a positive significant effect on FDI inflows in less developed countries. Hence integration with global economy by increasing international trade and decreasing tariff rates may attract higher amount of FDI inflows in less developed countries. Decreasing real interest rates by central bank policies to allow foreign enterprises to borrow domestically seems to attract higher amount of FDI inflows in these countries. Our results support the findings of Aseidu (2002), Sekkat and Varoudakis (2004), Kandiero and Chitiga (2006), Cantah et.al. (2013) for the case of less developed countries.

According to the estimation results of Model 5.2 in Table 2 and Table 4, Model 6.4 in Table 2 and Model 6.2 in Table 4, tariff rates and real interest rate have no significant effect on FDI inflows in advanced and developing countries. According to the estimation results of Models 5.4 and 6.2 in Table 6, tariff rates and real interest rate have negative significant effect on FDI inflows in less developed countries.

According to the estimation results of Models 7.1 and 7.2 in Table 2 and Models 7.3 and 7.4 in Table 4, interaction term of governance indicators and GDP growth has a positive significant effect on FDI inflows in advanced and developing countries, even GDP growth has no significant effect in these models. It may be concluded that market growth as a motivation factor alone is not sufficient for MNCs to take FDI decision in advanced and developing countries if governance structure deteriorates in the host country. According to the estimation results of Model 7.2 in Table 6, interaction term of economic stability and natural resources has a positive significant effect on FDI inflows in less developed countries, even natural resources have no significant effect in the model. It may be concluded that natural resources, as a motivation factor alone, is not sufficient for MNCs to take FDI decision in less developed countries if economic instability as a governance deterioration occurs in the host country. These finding support the argument of the author that without the base that the host country offers to investors, especially the governance structure, any motivation behind the FDI decision may not put into practice.

CONCLUSION

According to the empirical findings, improvement in each aspect of governance structure attracts more FDI inflows in all country clusters except political stability in less developed countries. Following policies to increase GDP growth attract higher amount of FDI inflows in advanced and developing countries. It may not be a misleading conclusion that FDI made into developing countries are market seeking because developing countries have the highest growth rate compared with other country clusters on average. Improvement in human capital attracts more FDI inflows in all country clusters. It will not be a misleading to conclude that FDI made into advanced countries are efficiency seeking because we know that advanced countries on average have the highest human capital compared with other country clusters. Improvement in physical infrastructure attracts more FDI inflows in advanced and less developed countries. Hence it will not be a misleading conclusion that physical infrastructure is a base factor for FDI inflows in advanced and less developed countries. Channeling FDI into other sectors seems to be appropriate strategy for advanced countries because FDI made into these countries is not resource seeking. FDI inflows seem to be resource seeking for less developed countries. Although increase in available natural resources attracts more FDI inflows in these countries, relying solely on natural resources seems not an appropriate strategy to attract higher amount of FDI inflows. Because, natural resources are scarce and depletable. Integration with global economy by increasing international trade and decreasing tariff rates may attract higher amount of FDI inflows in less developed countries. Decreasing real interest rates by central bank policies to allow foreign enterprises to borrow domestically seems to attract higher amount of FDI inflows in these countries.

Finally, it is found that a motivation factor alone whether GDP growth or available natural resources may not be sufficient for MNCs to take FDI decision because they also observe governance in host countries and any deterioration in governance leads to decreasing amount of FDI inflows. It requires further research on the subject to determine whether governance is not a sufficient but a necessary base factor that attracts higher amount of FDI inflows, although our estimation results do not reject this possibility.

REFERENCES

Abu Bakar, N., & Mat, S. H. C. (2012). The impact of infrastructure on foreign direct investment: *The case of Malaysia. Procedia: Social and Behavioral Sciences*, *65*, 205–211. doi:10.1016/j.sbspro.2012.11.112

Acemoglu, D., Johnson, S., & Robinson, J. A. (2001). The colonial origins of comparative development: An empirical investigation. *The American Economic Review*, *91*(5), 1369–1401. doi:10.1257/aer.91.5.1369

Agarwal, J. P. (1980). Determinants of foreign direct investment: A survey. *Weltwirtschaftliches Archiv*, *116*(4), 739–773. doi:10.1007/BF02696547

Ahmed, A. A. (1975). *The determinants of direct investment, with special reference to developing countries* (Doctoral dissertation). Graduate School of Arts and Sciences, University of Pennsylvania.

Aliber, R. Z. (1970). A theory of direct foreign investment. The International Corporation.

Amighini, A., Cozza, C., Giuliani, E., Rabellotti, R., & Scalera, V. (2013). *Technology-Driven FDI: A Survey of the Literature* (No. 2013/17). Lund University, CIRCLE-Center for Innovation, Research and Competences in the Learning Economy.

Asiedu, E. (2002). On the determinants of foreign direct investment to developing countries: Is Africa different? *World Development*, *30*(1), 107–119. doi:10.1016/S0305-750X(01)00100-0

Asiedu, E., & Lien, D. (2011). Democracy, foreign direct investment and natural resources. *Journal of International Economics*, *84*(1), 99–111. doi:10.1016/j.jinteco.2010.12.001

Aysan, A. F., Nabli, M. K., & Véganzonès-Varoudakis, M. A. (2007). Governance institutions and private investment: an application to the Middle East and North Africa. *The Developing Economies, 45*(3), 339-377. doi: 10.1111/j.1746-1049.2007.00042.x

Beyer, C. (2008). *Violent globalisms: conflict in response to empire*. Ashgate Publishing, Ltd.

Biglaiser, G., & DeRouen, K. (2004). The expansion of neoliberal economic reforms in Latin America. *International Studies Quarterly*, *48*(3), 561–578. doi:10.1111/j.0020-8833.2004.00315.x

Biglaiser, G., & Staats, J. L. (2010). Do political institutions affect foreign direct investment? A survey of US corporations in Latin America. *Political Research Quarterly*, *63*(3), 508–522. doi:10.1177/1065912909331428

Buchanan, B. G., Le, Q. V., & Rishi, M. (2012). Foreign direct investment and institutional quality: Some empirical evidence. *International Review of Financial Analysis*, *21*, 81–89. doi:10.1016/j.irfa.2011.10.001

Buckley, P. J., & Casson, M. (1976). *The future of the multinational enterprise* (Vol. 1). London: Macmillan. doi:10.1007/978-1-349-02899-3

Busse, M., & Hefeker, C. (2007). Political risk, institutions and foreign direct investment. *European Journal of Political Economy*, *23*(2), 397–415. doi:10.1016/j.ejpoleco.2006.02.003

Cantah, W. G., Wiafe, E. A., & Adams, A. (2013). *Foreign direct investment and trade policy openness in Sub-Saharan Africa (No. 58074)*. University Library of Munich.

Cheng, L. K., & Kwan, Y. K. (2000). What are the determinants of the location of foreign direct investment? The Chinese experience. *Journal of International Economics*, *51*(2), 379–400. doi:10.1016/S0022-1996(99)00032-X

Dunning, J. H. (2000). The Eclectic Paradigm as an Envelope for Economic and Business Theories of MNE Activity. *International Business Review*, *9*(2), 163–190. doi:10.1016/S0969-5931(99)00035-9

Dunning, J. H., & Lundan, S. M. (2008). *Multinational enterprises and the global economy*. Edward Elgar Publishing.

Etzioni, A. (2008). *Security first: For a muscular, moral foreign policy*. Yale University Press.

Flowers, E. B. (1976). Oligopolistic reactions in European and Canadian direct investment in the United States. *Journal of International Business Studies*, *7*(2), 43–55. doi:10.1057/palgrave.jibs.8490700

FRH. (2011). *Freedom in the World Database*. Freedom House. Retrieved from https://freedomhouse.org/report/freedom-press/freedom-press-2016?gclid=CjwKEAjwsr-6BRCLvrj785rbhTsSJADjUxakfmi8db3cy-omU7DQ8jQkXcsQWjY13q9kx90R9_UPixoC_-Xw_wcB

Globerman, S., & Shapiro, D. (2002). Global foreign direct investment flows: The role of governance infrastructure. *World Development*, *30*(11), 1899–1919. doi:10.1016/S0305-750X(02)00110-9

Globerman, S., & Shapiro, D. (2003). Governance infrastructure and US foreign direct investment. *Journal of International Business Studies*, *34*(1), 19–39. doi:10.1057/palgrave.jibs.8400001

Humphreys, C. (2003). *Better governance for development in the Middle East and North Africa: enhancing inclusiveness and accountability*. World Bank Publications.

Hymer, S. H. (1976). *The international operations of national firms: A study of direct foreign investment* (Vol. 14). Cambridge, MA: MIT Press.

ICRG. (2011). *International country risk guide*. PRS Group. Retrieved from https://www.prsgroup.com/about-us/our-two-methodologies/icrg

Jadhav, P. (2012). Determinants of foreign direct investment in BRICS economies: Analysis of economic, institutional and political factor. *Procedia: Social and Behavioral Sciences*, *37*, 5–14. doi:10.1016/j.sbspro.2012.03.270

Kandiero, T., & Chitiga, M. (2014). Trade openness and foreign direct investment in Africa. *South African Journal of Economic and Management Sciences*, *9*(3), 355–370. doi:10.4102ajems.v9i3.1093

Khadaroo, A. J., & Seetanah, B. (2007, November). Transport Infrastructure and FDI: Lessons from Sub Saharan African Economies. In *African Economic Conference (AEC)* (pp. 15-17). Academic Press.

Khan, M. A. (2007). Role of human capital in attracting foreign direct investment: A South Asian perspective. *SAARC Journal HRD*, *3*(1), 5.

Kindelberger, C. P. (1969). *American business abroad: six lectures on direct investment*. New Haven, CT: Yale UP.

Kinoshita, Y. (1998). *Firm Size and Determinants of Foreign Direct Investment.* CERGE-EI Working Paper Series, 135.

Knickerbocker, F. T. (1973). *Oligopolistic reaction and the multinational enterprise.* Cambridge, MA: Harvard University Press.

Levis, M. (1979). Does political instability in developing countries affect foreign investment flow? An empirical examination. *Management International Review,* 59–68.

Loree, D. W., & Guisinger, S. E. (1995). Policy and non-policy determinants of US equity foreign direct investment. *Journal of International Business Studies, 26*(2), 281–299. doi:10.1057/palgrave.jibs.8490174

Magee, S. P. (1977). Information and the multinational corporation: An appropriability theory of direct foreign investment. University of Chicago, Department of Economics and Graduate School of Business.

Mengistu, A. A., & Adhikary, B. K. (2011). Does good governance matter for FDI inflows? Evidence from Asian economies. *Asia Pacific Business Review, 17*(3), 281–299. doi:10.1080/13602381003755765

Narula, R. (2002). *Multinational investment and economic structure: Globalisation and competitiveness.* Routledge.

North, D. C. (1990). *Institutions, institutional change and economic performance.* Cambridge university press. doi:10.1017/CBO9780511808678

Roodman, D. (2006). *How to do xtabond2: An introduction to difference and system GMM in Stata.* Center for Global Development working paper, 103.

Rugman, A. M. (1980). Internalization as a general theory of foreign direct investment: A re-appraisal of the literature. *Review of World Economics, 116*(2), 365–379. doi:10.1007/BF02696864

Sekkat, K., & Veganzones-Varoudakis, M. A. (2004). *Trade and Foreign Exchange Liberalization, Investment Climate, and FDI in the MENA Countries.* World Bank, Middle East and North Africa, the Office of the Chief Economist.

UN. (2006). FDI in least developed countries at a glance: 2005 / 2006. *United Nations Conference on Trade and Development.*

Vernon, R. (1966). International investment and international trade in the product cycle. *The Quarterly Journal of Economics, 80*(2), 190–207. doi:10.2307/1880689

WDI. (2015). *World development indicators*. World Bank Group. Retrieved from http://data.worldbank.org/data-catalog/world-development-indicators

Wei, S. J. (2000). How taxing is corruption on international investors? *The Review of Economics and Statistics*, *82*(1), 1–11. doi:10.1162/003465300558533

WGI. (2015). *Worldwide governance indicators*. World Bank Group. Retrieved from http://data.worldbank.org/data-catalog/worldwide-governance-indicators

Wheeler, D., & Mody, A. (1992). International investment location decisions: The case of US firms. *Journal of International Economics*, *33*(1), 57–76. doi:10.1016/0022-1996(92)90050-T

KEY TERMS AND DEFINITIONS

Administrative Quality Index: The index value of administrative quality in host country taking values between 0 and 100.

Economic Stability Index: The index value of economic stability in host country taking values between 0 and 100.

Financial Depth: The ratio of liquid assets as a percentage of host country GDP.

Governance Infrastructure: The quality of host country institutional capabilities.

Human Capital: Availability of educated human resources in host country.

Natural Resources: Availability of total natural resource rents as a percentage of host country GDP.

Physical Infrastructure: Availability of energy, water, communication, and transportation infrastructure in host country.

Political Stability Index: The index value of political stability in home country taking values between 0 and 100.

Public Voice Index: The index value of public voice in host country taking values between 0 and 100.

Real Interest Rate: The real interest rates of host countries.

Tariff Rate: The tariff rate of host countries.

Trade Openness: Total volume of exports and imports as a percentage of host country GDP.

APPENDIX: LIST OF COUNTRIES

Table 7. Advanced countries

Australia	Finland	Japan	Singapore
Austria	France	Korea, South	Slovakia
Belgium	Germany	Latvia	Slovenia
Canada	Greece	Malta	Spain
Cyprus	Iceland	Netherlands	Sweden
Czech Republic	Ireland	New Zealand	Switzerland
Denmark	Israel	Norway	United Kingdom
Estonia	Italy	Portugal	United States

Table 8. Developing countries

Albania	Dominican Republic	Kuwait	Romania
Algeria	Ecuador	Libya	Russia
Argentina	Egypt	Lithuania	Saudi Arabia
Armenia	El Salvador	Malaysia	South Africa
Bahrain	Gabon	Mexico	Sri Lanka
Bolivia	Ghana	Moldova	Syria
Botswana	Guatemala	Mongolia	Thailand
Brazil	Guyana	Morocco	Trinidad & Tobago
Brunei	Honduras	Namibia	Tunisia
Bulgaria	Hungary	Nicaragua	Turkey
Cameroon	India	Pakistan	United Arab Emirates
Chile	Indonesia	Panama	Ukraine
China	Iran	Papua New Guinea	Uruguay
Colombia	Iraq	Paraguay	Venezuela
Congo	Jamaica	Peru	Vietnam
Costa Rica	Jordan	Philippines	Zimbabwe
Côte d'Ivoire	Kazakhstan	Poland	
Croatia	Kenya	Qatar	

Table 9. Less developed countries

Bangladesh	Mozambique	Tanzania
Congo, DR	Myanmar	Togo
Gambia	Niger	Uganda
Haiti	Senegal	Yemen
Malawi	Sierra Leone	Zambia
Mali	Sudan	

Chapter 12
Econometric Analysis of India's Foreign Direct Investment Inflows

Debesh Bhowmik
International Institute for Development Studies, Kolkata, India

ABSTRACT

In this chapter, the author explains the trend lines, random walk, stationary, structural breaks, and volatility of FDI inflows in India during 1971-2015. Both log linear and exponential trends are significant. FDI inflows are stationary and showed four structural breaks in 1985, 1994, 2000, and 2006. The author found the relation among FDI inflows, growth rate, interest rate, inflation rate, exchange rate, fiscal deficit, external debt, and trade openness with the help of Granger causality, Johansen cointegration test, and vector error correction models. Trace statistic has four cointegrating equations, and Max Eigen statistic has three cointegrating equations. The speed of the vector error correction process is more or less slow except for change in interest rate and change in inflation rate, which are significant where VECM is stable and diverging. Limitations and future scope of research is added. Policy recommendations are also included.

INTRODUCTION

Foreign direct investment (FDI) is an investment in a business by an investor from another country for which the foreign investor has control over the company purchased. The Organization of Economic Cooperation and Development (OECD) defines control as owning 10% or more of the business. Businesses that make foreign direct investments are often called multinational corporations (MNCs) or multinational enterprises (MNEs). FDI provides a win – win situation to the host and the home

DOI: 10.4018/978-1-5225-3026-8.ch012

countries. FDI as a strategic component of investment is needed by India for its sustained economic growth and development. FDI is necessary for creation of jobs, expansion of existing manufacturing industries and development of the new one. Indeed, it is also needed in the healthcare, education, R&D, infrastructure, retailing and in long term financial projects. Need of FDI depends on saving and investment rate in any country. Foreign Direct investment acts as a bridge to fulfill the gap between investment and saving. In the process of economic development foreign capital helps to cover the domestic saving constraint and provide access to the superior technology that promotes efficiency and productivity of the existing production capacity and generate new production opportunity. Foreign investments mean both foreign portfolio investments and foreign direct investments (FDI). FDI brings better technology and management, marketing networks and offers competition, the latter helping Indian companies improve, quite apart from being good for consumers. The effectiveness of FDI in bringing about the desired growth may be constrained by the level of infrastructural developments and other macroeconomic variables . Infrastructural development, openness and domestic market size are major determinants of FDI. Even, exchange rate and interest rate may influence FDI inflows. Besides, balance of payments adjustment is a good correlation with FDI flows. Political instability and financial crises influence FDI flows negatively. Alongside opening up of the FDI regime, steps were taken to allow foreign portfolio investments into the Indian stock market through the mechanism of foreign institutional investors. The objective was not only to facilitate non-debt creating foreign capital inflows but also to develop the stock market in India, lower the cost of capital for Indian enterprises and indirectly improve corporate governance structures. FDI have helped India to attain a financial stability and economic growth with the help of investments in different sectors. FDI has boosted the economic life of India.

By allowing MNC in Indian economy, the government of India with the help of World Bank and IMF introduced the macro-economic stabilization and structural adjustment program. As a result of these reforms India open its door to FDI inflows and adopted a more liberal foreign policy in order to restore the confidence of foreign investors. Further, under the new foreign investment policy Government of India constituted FIPB (Foreign Investment Promotion Board) whose main function was to invite and facilitate foreign investment.

OBJECTIVE OF THE STUDY

In this paper, the author endeavors to explain the patterns of behavior of India's foreign direct investment inflows during 1971-2015. Besides, the author tries to relate FDI inflows with macro variables like growth rate, interest rate, inflation rate, exchange rate, fiscal deficit, external trade and trade openness of India during the specified period with the help of causality, cointegration and vector error correction models.

REVIEW OF LITERATURE

There are innumerable economic literature on FDI and other related variables in general and in country specific. The author showed some important literatures which are related with Indian economy. Basu, Chakraborty and Reagle (2003), for 23 developing countries from (1978-1996), found a cointegration relationship between FDI and GDP. Moreover, Hansen and Rand (2006), for 31 developing countries from 1970-2000, found that there is a cointegration relationship between FDI and GDP. Their findings indicated that FDI inflows are positively correlated with GDP, whereas GDP has no long-run effect on FDI. Chakraborty and Mukherjee (2012) argued that foreign direct investment (FDI) inflow positively influences economic growth through technology diffusion, human capital formation, etc., and found that there is a unidirectional causality from India's economic growth to FDI and from FDI to domestic investment raises important policy implications. Higher FDI inflow in India in recent period can be argued to be facilitated by the relatively stable GDP growth rate, which in turn acted as a major boost towards a sustainable high domestic investment. The growth effects of the FDI on GDP in the short run are, however, less pronounced since the post reform period in India. Chakraborty and Basu (2010) linked between foreign direct investment and growth for India using a structural cointegration model with vector error correction mechanism. The existence of two cointegrating vectors between GDP, FDI, the unit labor cost and the share of import duty in tax revenue is found, which captures the long run relationship between FDI and GDP. Their VECM model reveals three important features: (a) GDP in India is not Granger caused by FDI; the causality runs more from GDP to FDI; (b) trade liberalization policy of the Indian government had some positive short run impact on the FDI inflow; and (c) FDI tends to lower the unit labor cost suggesting that FDI in India is labor displacing. Sarbapriya Ray (2012) analyzed the causal relationship between Foreign Direct Investment (FDI) and economic growth in India during 1990-91 to2010-11. The cointegration test confirmed an existence of long run equilibrium relationship between the two as confirmed by the Johansen cointegration test results. The Granger causality test finally confirmed the presence of uni-directional causality which runs from economic growth to foreign direct investment. The error correction estimates gave evidence that the Error-Correction Term is statistically significant and has a negative sign, which confirms that there isn't any problem in the long-run equilibrium relation between the independent and dependent variables. For FDI to be a noteworthy provider to economic growth, India would do better by focusing on improving infrastructure, human resources, developing local entrepreneurship, creating a stable macroeconomic framework and conditions favorable for productive investments to augment the process of development. Wang (1990), as part of an empirical verification of the FDI-growth relationship in china, found that there are two potential routes by which FDI affects economic growth namely: rate of physical capital accumulation and productivity growth. Thus, according to Wang (1990), FDI is not only an additional source of financing growth, but also helps increase productivity. Dash, R.K. & Parida, P.C. (2013) examined the linkages between inward FDI, services trade (export and import) and economic output using co-integration and VECM causality test. Their study confirmed the long-run relationship among these variables. Causality results indicate the presence of bi-directional causal relationship between FDI and economic output as well as between services exports and economic output. The results also bring out feedback relationship between services export and FDI, reconfirming the presence of complementary relationship between the two. At the sectoral level, they found at least a unidirectional causality from FDI and services exports to both manufacturing and services output and also cross-sectoral spillover effects from manufacturing output to services output and vice versa. Bhattacharjee and Bhattacharjee (2011) investigated whether the volume of merchandise trade and FDI inflows influences economic growth during in India 1996-97:Q1 to 2008-09:Q3. After investigating the stationarity of the variables, cointegration analysis has been conducted followed by VECM analysis and Granger Causality Test. The variables are I(1) processes. While unidirectional causality is observed from merchandise trade to economic growth, feedback causality has been observed between FDI inflows and economic growth. T.G. Saii (2013) investigates the causal relations between foreign direct investment and economic growth in a developing country like India. The analysis has been made under Johansen's cointegration framework based on 21 years of data covering the post reform era of the country. The cointegration analysis finds strong positive relation between FDI and economic growth in India. The study concludes with a suggestion that the policy makers in India should develop investor friendly environment conducive for attracting more amount of capital from the developed world. Osinubi and Amaghionyeodiwe (2009) studied that the empirical evidence on the effect of exchange rate volatility on foreign direct investment (FDI) in Nigeria, using secondary time series data from1970 to 2004 which revealed a significant positive relationship between real inward FDI and exchange rate. This implies that, depreciation of the Naira increases real inward FDI. So, major challenge before the Central Bank of Nigeria therefore, is to attain a stable and realistic exchange rate that will boost domestic production, increase real inward FDI and maintain internal and external balance. Froot and Stein (1991) claimed that the level of exchange rate may influence FDI. This is because depreciation of the host country currency against the home currency increases the relative wealth of foreigners thereby increasing the attractiveness of the host country for FDI as firms are able to acquire assets in the host country relatively cheaply. Thus a depreciation of the host currency should increase FDI into the host country, and conversely an appreciation of the host currency should decrease FDI. Numerous empirical studies have supported this view. Cushman (1988) and Stokman and Vlar (1996) find a significantly positive relationship between exchange rate volatility and FDI flows into and out of the US and the Netherlands. Siddiqui, Hira Aijaz Ahmed & Aumeboonsuke, Vesarach (2014) relate foreign direct investment (FDI) inflow and its determinant in ASEAN 5. The analysis is based on the data over the years, 1986 to 2012 using Vector Auto regression (VAR) Technique. Singapore and Malaysia does not support the ideas that low interest rates attract the FDI inflow. There is one directional relationship between FDI inflow and INF in Thailand, Singapore and Indonesia. According to this finding we can say that due to increase in FDI inflow inflation decreases and interest rate decreases this implies the price stability target. Vanita Tripathi, Seth, Ritika and Bhandari, Varun (2015) showed that a significant correlation between FDI and all macroeconomic variables (except for Exchange rate). Causality results show that IIP/GDP, WPI and S&P CNX 500 Equity Index are Granger causing FDI inflows in India while Trade Openness is Granger caused by the same. All the macroeconomic variables taken in the article (except exchange rate) are significantly affecting FDI inflows and the overall explanatory power of the regression model (i.e., Adjusted R square) is 75.7 per cent. The results of Johansen's cointegration test disclose that there is long-run causal relation between FDI and IIP; FDI and S&P CNX 500 Equity, FDI and Trade Openness and FDI and WPI. VAR and impulse response function analysis show that FDI is caused more by its own lagged values rather those of other macroeconomic factors. Shanta Parajuli (2012) indicates a unidirectional Granger causality between GDP and exports, which suggests that there is a significant and positive Granger causal relationship running from exports to GDP in Mexico during the period from 1970 to 2008. There is a positive impact of FDI on economic growth of Mexico. Under the causality test, a unidirectional Granger causality between FDI and GDP running from GDP to FDI was observed, and Surprisingly, no Granger causality was found from FDI to GDP, However, the causality relationship from GDP to FDI has disappeared in the presence of imports; just then export-led FDI hypothesis is supported suggesting that imports are the channel through which the growth in exports spurs growth in FDI. That is, there is a positive long-run relationship between a pair of variables from GFCF to imports and labor force to imports. This suggests that Granger causality between GDP and exports, FDI and GDP, exports to FDI derived from bivariate (model 1 and 3) and multivariate (model 4) frameworks are through a channel of imports, GFCF, and the labor force. Khan and Mitra(2014) showed that there prevails long run equilibrium among the concerned variables. The Granger-causality test results conclude that exchange rate and GDP statistically significantly influence FDI, whereas, inflation rate is insignificant variable to predict FDI inflows. Further, the growth analysis result claims that the total FDI inflows grow exponentially at a rate of 23% per annum. However, as stated by the results of Chow test, 1991-92 (the year of initiation of New Economic Policy in India) is a statistically significant structural break year in the context of FDI inflows in India. Uwubanmwen, Ahmed E. & Ajao, Mayowa G. (2012) showed that macroeconomic variables (exchange rate, interest rate, inflation) and openness of the economy are among the major and important factors that determine the inflow of FDI into Nigeria during 1972-2009. The GDP and government size exhibited positive but insignificant influence on FDI. The analysis revealed the presence of a long-run equilibrium relationship between FDI and GDP, but FDI does not have any significant effect on the growth as well as the development of Nigeria economy during this period. The study therefore recommends that government should ensure stable macroeconomic policies (as motivating factor for the attraction of FDI into Nigeria) and also increase its expenditure in the area of infrastructural development as ways to accelerate the growth of Nigerian economy which will reduce the excessive dependence of Nigeria on FDI.

METHODOLOGY AND DATA

Semi-log linear model and exponential model are taken for computing trend of FDI. Random walk with drift model was used to find randomness. ARIMA (1,1,1) and ARIMA (2,1,2) model were used to find stationary of the series. Bai-Perron (2003) model was applied to show structural breaks. Hodrick-Prescott-Filter (1997) model was taken for minimizing cyclical behavior to get smooth trend path. Johansen (1988,1991) models were used to find cointegration and VECM of the determinants of FDI during 1971-2015.Granger model (1969) was used to find causality of the determinants of FDI. Even the residual tests were shown for finding autocorrelation, serial correlation and normality. Assume, x_1=GDP growth rate per cent per year,x_2=interest rate per cent per year(discount rate),x_3=exchange rate of rupee per US dollar,x_4=inflation rate(per cent change of CPI),x_5=fiscal deficit per cent of GDP,x_6=external debt per cent of GDP,x_7= trade openness per cent, y= FDI inflows in India in million US dollar. Data have been collected from the World Bank, and International Financial Statistics of IMF from 1971 to 2015.

ECONOMETRIC MODELS: SOME OBSERVATIONS

Nature of FDI Inflows in India

India's FDI inflows have been increasing at the 21.56% per year during 1971-2015 which is significant at 5% level.

Log(y)=1.4485+0.215672t

(4.11)* (16.16)*

R^2=0.858, F=261.37*, DW=1.53, *=significant at 5% level, y=FDI inflows in million dollars., t=year(time).

In Figure 1, the actual and fitted trend line have been plotted. The fitted line is steeply rising upward.

The exponential fitted trend line of Indian FDI inflows during 1971-2015 is also significant and exponentially rising at the rate 0.6044% per year.

$$y = e^{0.6651+t^{0.604473+ut}}$$

Figure 1. Trend line of FDI inflows
Source: Computed by author

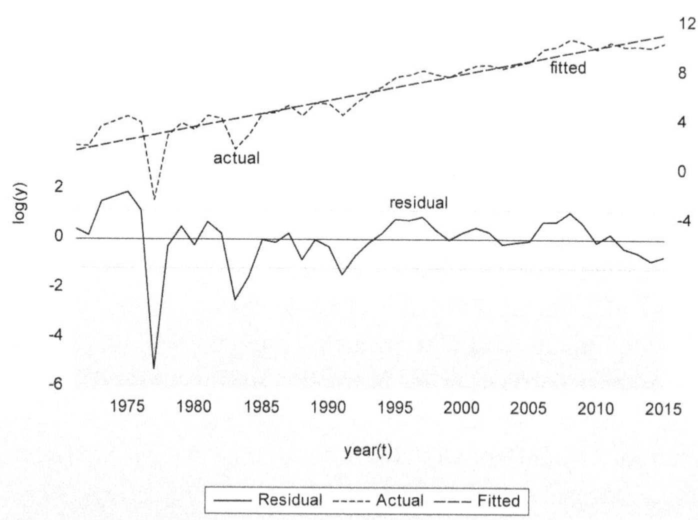

where U_t=-0.117016U_{t-1}

(-0.7077)

R^2=0.828, DW=2.13, Inverted AR root=0.50±0.30i, -0.34, the t values of 0.6651 and 0.604473 are 5.064583 and 112.5020 respectively. The estimated exponential trend line as well as actual line is shown in Figure 2.

The FDI inflows do not follow random walk with a drift during 1972-2015 which is estimated below.

$d\log(y_t)=1.134923-0.772167\log(y_{t-1})+0.16737t$

(2.768)* (-5.063)* (4.65)*

R^2=0.38, F=12.82* DW=1.93

In Figure 3, the random walk with drift are seen clearly.

The FDI inflows in India from 1971 to 2015 is stationary, convergent and stable which is proved by the ARIMA(1,1,1) model.

Figure 2. Exponential trend of FDI
Source: Computed by author

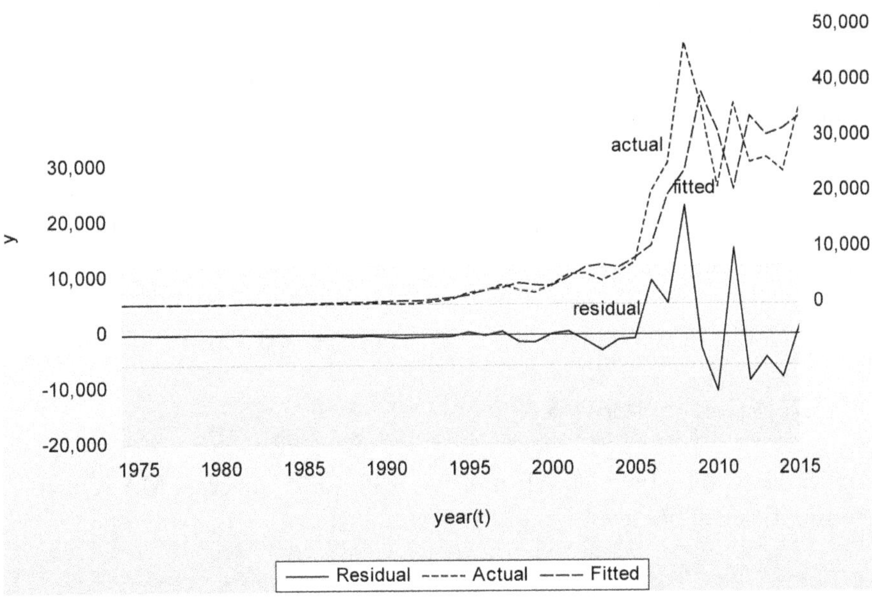

Figure 3. Random walk
Source: Computed by author

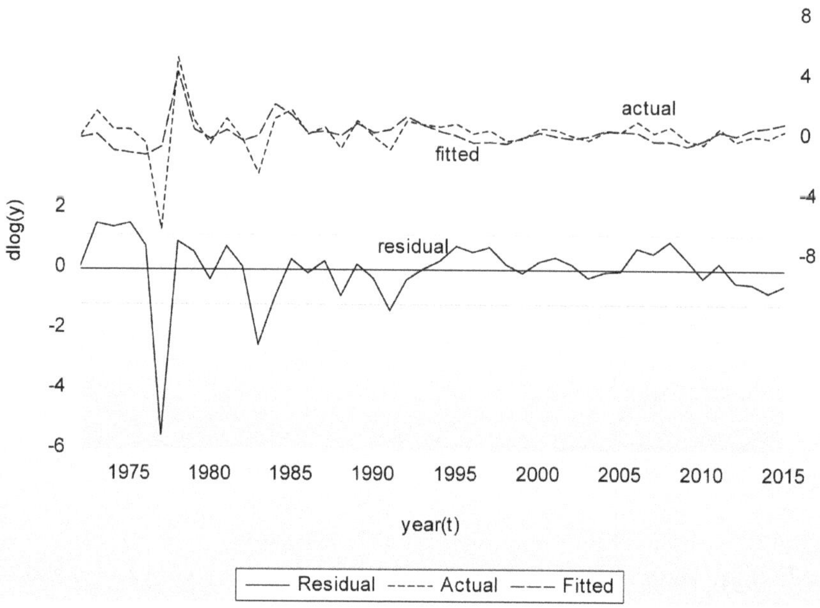

$Log(y_t)=282.1647+0.999log(y_{t-1})+\varepsilon_t-0.970609\varepsilon_{t-1}$

(0.08) (100.96)* (-35.92)*

R^2=0.84, DW=1.53, F=114*, Inverted AR root=1.0, Inverted MA root=0.97, *=significant at 5% level.

But in AR(2) the FDI inflows is convergent and significant but MA(1) process is convergent while MA(2) process is divergent, thus why ARIMA(2,1,2) is non stationary but stable.

$Log(y_t)=17.91567+0.3378log(y_{t-1})+0.6367log(y_{t-2})+\varepsilon_t+0.2061\varepsilon_{t-1}-0.7938\varepsilon_{t-2}$

(0.88) (2.76)* (5.45)* (1.36) (-5.28)*

R^2=0.858, F=57.63*, Inverted AR roots =, 0.98, -0.65, Inverted MA root=0.79,-1.0,*=significant at 5% level.

Table 1. Structural breaks

Variable	Coefficient	Std. Error	t-Statistic	Prob.
		1971 - 1984 -- 14 obs		
C	2.968555	0.483099	6.144817	0.0000
		1985 - 1993 -- 9 obs		
C	5.184334	0.198430	26.12671	0.0000
		1994 - 1999 -- 6 obs		
C	7.690081	0.173512	44.32012	0.0000
		2000 - 2005 -- 6 obs		
C	8.566927	0.102723	83.39861	0.0000
		2006 - 2015 -- 10 obs		
C	10.26461	0.087104	117.8438	0.0000
		R^2=0.889,F=80.4*,DW=1.99		
Break test: Sequential F-statistic determined breaks:4				
Break Test	F-statistic	Scaled F-statistic	Critical Value**	
0 vs. 1 *	136.9461	136.9461	8.58	
1 vs. 2 *	133.9357	133.9357	10.13	
2 vs. 3 *	19.38291	19.38291	11.14	
3 vs. 4 *	18.00003	18.00003	11.83	
4 vs. 5	0.999666	0.999666	12.25	

Source: Computed by author, *=significant at 5% level

Assuming Bai-Perron test (2003) of L+1 vs.L sequential determined breaks selecting Trimming 0.15,maximum breaks 5 with 5% significant level, we found 4 upward breaks in 1985, 1994, 2000,2006 following HAC standard errors and covariance and Newey-West fixed bandwidth=4.0.In Table 1,the significant values are given.

In Figure 4, the successive four upward breaks have been plotted in the fitted line showing actual line of FDI inflows in terms of log.

The cyclical path is minimized by the trend line by Hodrick Prescott Filter model and we got the smooth nonlinear trend line shown in Figure 5.

For Stationary I(0),the H.P.Filter is made to asymmetric noncyclical rather than cyclical model shown in Figure 6.

For Random walk I(1) process the HP Filter model is changed to asymmetric noncyclical trend line which is more than the previous asymmetric model (Figure 7).

FDI inflows in India during 1971-2015 showed high volatility as measured by GARCH (1,1) model which is estimated below.

Figure 4. Structural breaks in FDI inflows
Source: Computed by author.

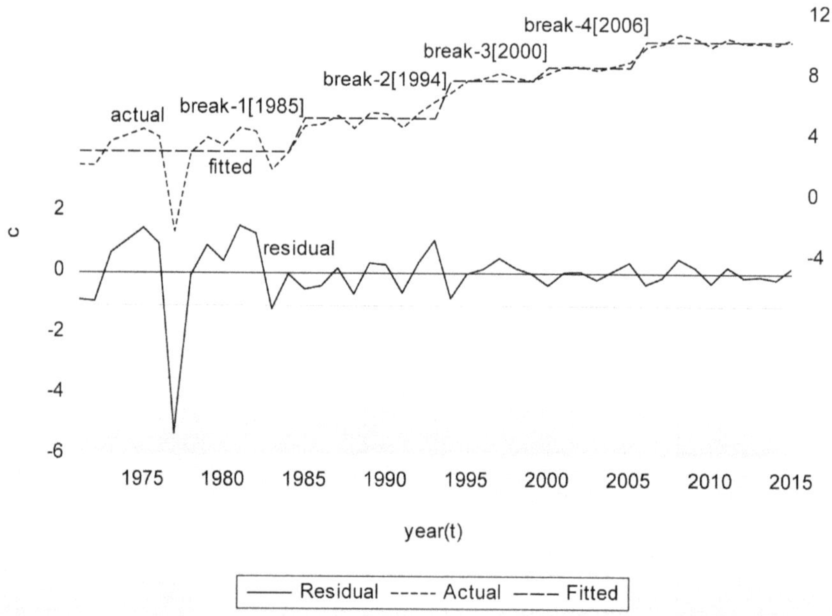

Figure 5. H.P. filter model
Source: Computed by author

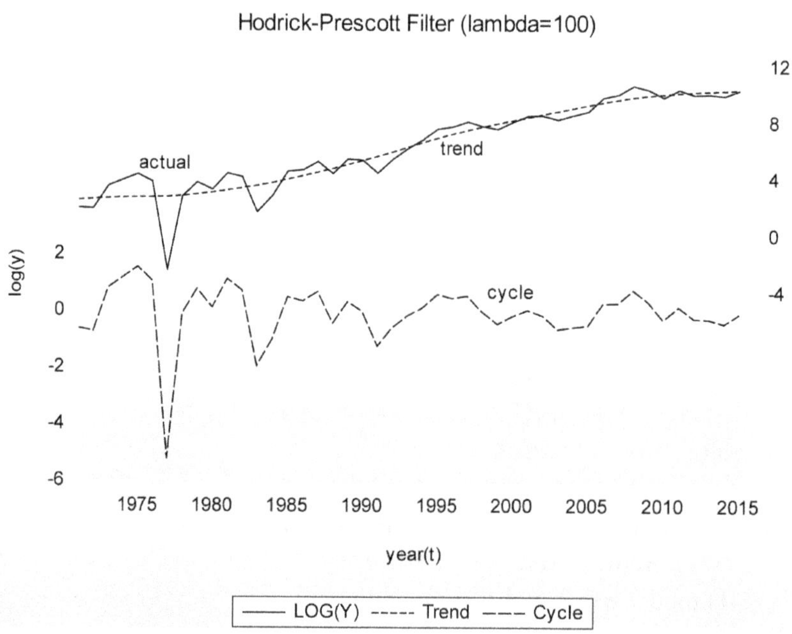

Figure 6. Asymmetric filter
Source: Computed by author

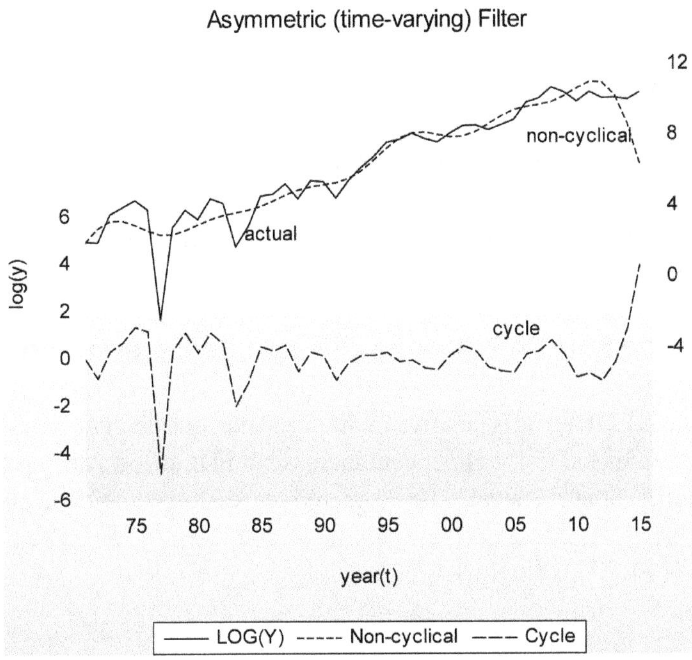

Figure 7. Random walk asymmetric filter
Source: Computed by author

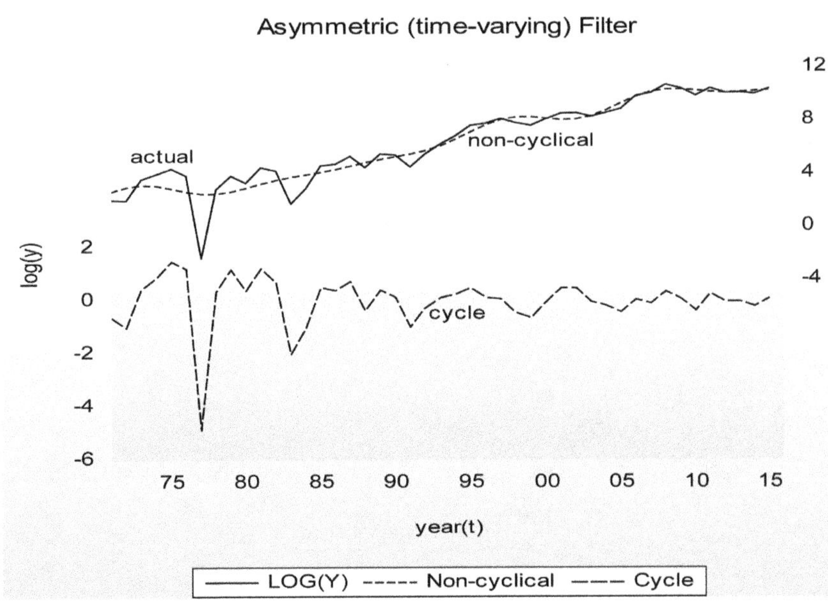

$h_t=3.932117+0.894068\sigma^2_t+0.045933h_{t-1}$

(0.137) (0.242) (0.0127)

R^2=-4.49, loglikelihood=-144.71,

Since the z statistic of the coefficients are insignificant, therefore, the model shows volatilc.

In Figure 8, the conditional variance showed the nature of volatility of FDI inflows during 1971-2015.

Cointegration and VAR Among FDI and Its Determinants

In India, growth-FDI nexus is positive in the sense that one percent increase in GDP growth rate in India led to 1.204 per cent increase in FDI inflows during 1971-2015 which is significant at 5% level. The estimated regression equation is given below.

$Log(y)=4.574+1.204228log(x_1)$

Figure 8. Conditional variance
Source: Computed by author

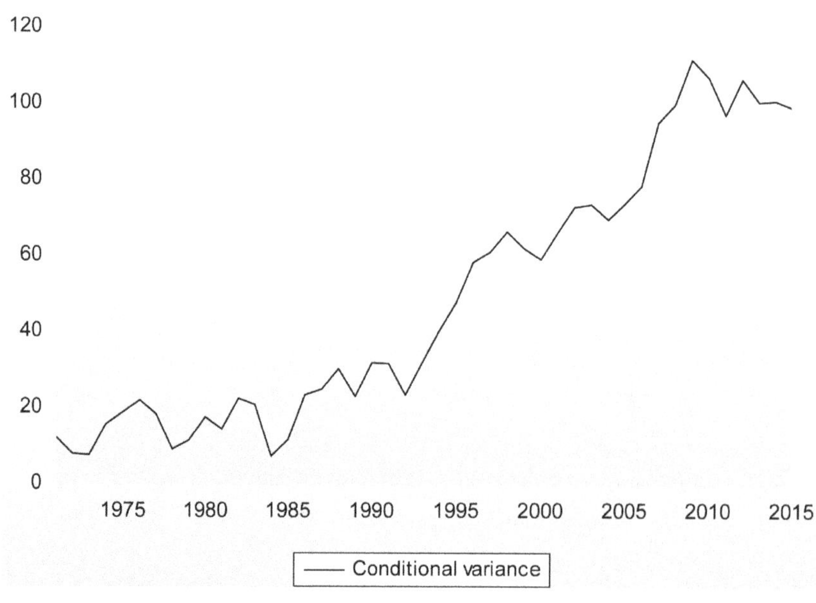

(5.72)* (2.71)*

R^2=0.14, F=7.34*, DW=0.63,

where x_1= GDP growth rate, y=FDI inflows in India, *=significant at 5% level.

In Figure 9, the growth-FDI nexus is plotted.

Granger causality test assured that there are no causality between growth rate and interest rate, growth rate and openness, FDI inflows and openness respectively but there exists uni-directional causality between growth and exchange rate, growth and inflation, interest rate and openness, exchange rate and external debt, exchange rate and FDI inflows, fiscal deficit and FDI inflows, fiscal deficit and external debt respectively during 1971-2015 and rest of variables showed bi-directional causality. In Table 2, the results of Granger causality test are given.

Johansen unrestricted cointegration rank test showed that Trace statistic has four cointegrating equations and Max Eigen Statistic has three cointegrating equations which are shown in Table 3. Therefore the variables are cointegrated in order of CI(1).

Since the variables are cointegrated, thus the estimated vector error correction model is given below.

$$\Delta x_{1t}=-0.024378-0.46107\Delta x_{1t-1}-0.0624\Delta x_{2t-1}+0.2556\Delta x_{3t-1}+0.1718\Delta x_{4t-1}+0.3480\Delta x_{5t-1} \quad (1)$$

Figure 9. Growth FDI nexus
Source: Computed by author

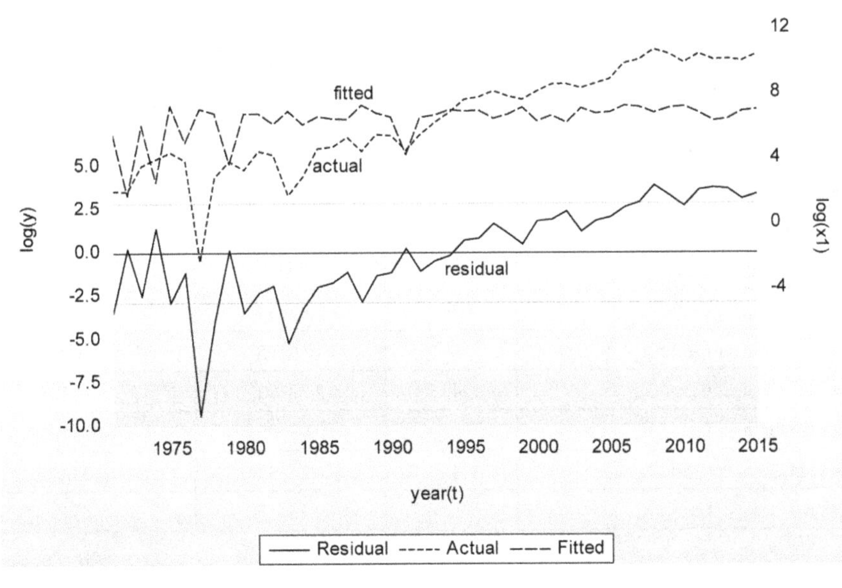

Table 2. Granger causality test

Null Hypothesis:	Obs	F-Statistic	Prob.
X_2 does not Granger Cause X_1	44	1.73801	0.1947
X_1 does not Granger Cause X_2		0.74632	0.3927
X_3 does not Granger Cause X_1	44	7.62229	0.0086
X_1 does not Granger Cause X_3		0.14968	0.7008
X_4 does not Granger Cause X_1	44	0.97870	0.3283
X_1 does not Granger Cause X_4		4.78031	0.0346
X_5 does not Granger Cause X_1	44	0.42533	0.5179
X_1 does not Granger Cause X_5		0.01272	0.9107
X_6 does not Granger Cause X_1	44	1.16506	0.2867
X_1 does not Granger Cause X_6		0.59396	0.4453
X_7 does not Granger Cause X_1	44	7.10295	0.0110
X_1 does not Granger Cause X_7		4.14904	0.0481
Y does not Granger Cause X_1	44	3.76020	0.0594
X_1 does not Granger Cause Y		2.65379	0.1110
X_3 does not Granger Cause X_2	44	6.02424	0.0184
X_2 does not Granger Cause X_3		4.80786	0.0341
X_4 does not Granger Cause X_2	44	0.40073	0.5302
X_2 does not Granger Cause X_4		0.25303	0.6176
X_5 does not Granger Cause X_2	44	0.33362	0.5667
X_2 does not Granger Cause X_5		0.55810	0.4593
X_6 does not Granger Cause X_2	44	0.17375	0.6790
X_2 does not Granger Cause X_6		0.06494	0.8001
X_7 does not Granger Cause X_2	44	0.70864	0.4048
X_2 does not Granger Cause X_7		8.90190	0.0048
X_7 does not Granger Cause X_3	44	0.60191	0.4423
X_3 does not Granger Cause X_7		1.21653	0.2765
Y does not Granger Cause X_2	44	0.06276	0.8034
X_2 does not Granger Cause Y		3.24339	0.0791
X_4 does not Granger Cause X_3	44	1.91647	0.1737
X_3 does not Granger Cause X_4		1.69565	0.2001
X_5 does not Granger Cause X_3	44	2.33792	0.1339
X_3 does not Granger Cause X_5		0.09696	0.7571
X_6 does not Granger Cause X_3	44	4.87837	0.0328
X_3 does not Granger Cause X_6		0.35427	0.5550

continued on following page

Table 2. Continued

Null Hypothesis:	Obs	F-Statistic	Prob.
X_7 does not Granger Cause X_3	44	0.60191	0.4423
X_3 does not Granger Cause X_7		1.21653	0.2765
Y does not Granger Cause X_3	44	0.27972	0.5997
X_3 does not Granger Cause Y		3.35859	0.0741
X_5 does not Granger Cause X_4	44	0.07100	0.7912
X_4 does not Granger Cause X_5		0.97114	0.3302
X_6 does not Granger Cause X_4	44	0.08489	0.7723
X_4 does not Granger Cause X_6		1.06878	0.3073
X_7 does not Granger Cause X_4	44	0.35750	0.5532
X_4 does not Granger Cause X_7		0.21981	0.6417
Y does not Granger Cause X_4	44	0.10544	0.7470
X_4 does not Granger Cause Y		1.27829	0.2648
X_6 does not Granger Cause X_5	44	0.38607	0.5378
X_5 does not Granger Cause X_6		7.22076	0.0104
X_7 does not Granger Cause X_5	44	1.87525	0.1783
X_5 does not Granger Cause X_7		0.68293	0.4134
Y does not Granger Cause X_5	44	9.75678	0.0033
X_5 does not Granger Cause Y		0.00764	0.9308
X_7 does not Granger Cause X_6	44	0.18516	0.6692
X_6 does not Granger Cause X_7		0.02489	0.8754
Y does not Granger Cause X_6	44	0.53797	0.4674
X_6 does not Granger Cause Y		0.07397	0.7870
Y does not Granger Cause X_7	44	6.74823	0.0130
X_7 does not Granger Cause Y		14.6940	0.0004

Source: Computed by author

(-0.043) (-2.75)* (-0.089) (1.048) (1.94) (0.78)

$$-0.28909\Delta x_{6t-1}-0.0729\Delta x_{7t-1}+2.28E\text{-}05\Delta y_{t-1}-0.2381EC$$

(-0.714) (-0.29) (-1.02) (-1.02)

R^2=0.48, F=3.4, AIC=5.14 , SC=5.55

Table 3. Johansen Cointegration test

Hypothesized No. of CE(s)	Eigen value	Trace Statistic	0.05 Critical Value	Prob.**
None *	0.732982	219.9294	159.5297	0.0000
At most 1 *	0.659855	163.1505	125.6154	0.0000
At most 2 *	0.612689	116.7800	95.75366	0.0008
At most 3 *	0.495951	75.99326	69.81889	0.0148
At most 4	0.348309	46.53476	47.85613	0.0662
At most 5	0.309576	28.12279	29.79707	0.0770
At most 6	0.240770	12.19346	15.49471	0.1479
At most 7	0.008086	0.349106	3.841466	0.5546
Hypothesized No. of CE(s)	**Eigen value**	**Max Eigen Statistic**	**0.05 Critical Value**	**Prob.****
None *	0.732982	56.77893	52.36261	0.0166
At most 1 *	0.659855	46.37050	46.23142	0.0483
At most 2 *	0.612689	40.78672	40.07757	0.0415
At most 3	0.495951	29.45849	33.87687	0.1540
At most 4	0.348309	18.41197	27.58434	0.4612
At most 5	0.309576	15.92934	21.13162	0.2290
At most 6	0.240770	11.84435	14.26460	0.1166
At most 7	0.008086	0.349106	3.841466	0.5546

* denotes rejection of the hypothesis at the 0.05 level, **MacKinnon-Haug-Michelis (1999) p-values, H0=No cointegration, Source: Computed by author

$$\Delta x_{2t}=-0.0924+0.1129\Delta x_{1t-1}-0.2025\Delta x_{2t-1}+0.0076\Delta x_{3t-1}+0.0068\Delta x_{4t-1}+ 0.0207\Delta x_{5t-1} \quad (2)$$

(-0.72) (2.88)* (-1.27) (0.137) (0.337) (0.203)

$$-0.0855\Delta x_{6t-1}+0.0303\Delta x_{7t-1}+ 3.02E\text{-}05\Delta y_{t-1}-0.23196EC$$

(-0.92) (0.529) (1.129) (-4.33)*

R^2= 0.49, F=3.6, AIC=2.19, SC=2.6

$$\Delta x_{3t}==1.3603+-0.00155\Delta x_{1t-1}+0.711074\Delta x_{2t-1}+ 0.2534\Delta x_{3t-1}-0.05331\Delta x_{4t-1}- 0.762132\Delta x_{5t-1} \quad (3)$$

(2.92)* (-0.011) (1.23) (1.25) (-0.72) (2.06)*

$-0.39126\Delta x_{6t-1}-0.157501\Delta x_{7t-1}-0.157501\Delta y_{t-1}-0.179943EC$

(-1.16) (-0.76) (-0.51) (-0.92)

$R^2= 0.19$, F=0.87, AIC=4.7, SC=5.1

$$\Delta x_{4t}=0.388400-0.007038\Delta x_{1t-1}-0.907988\Delta x_{2t-1}+ 0.079949\Delta x_{3t-1}-0.246616\Delta x_{4t-1}- \quad (4)$$

(2.92)* (-0.082) (0.68) (0.17) (-1.47)

$0.097889\Delta x_{5t-1}-0.952970\Delta x_{6t-1}-0.442524\Delta x_{7t-1}+0.000244\Delta y_{t-1}-1.025525EC$

(-0.115) (-1.24) (-0.93) (1.10) (-2.31)*

$R^2= 0.26$, F=1.33, AIC=6.42, SC=6.83

$$\Delta x_{5t}=-0.106383+0.007038\Delta x_{1t-1}+-0.071309\Delta x_{2t-1}+ 0.109699\Delta x_{3t-1}+0.013372\Delta x_{4t-1} \quad (5)$$

(-0.49) (0.109) (-0.26) (1.17) (0.17)

$+ 0.158234\Delta x_{5t-1} -0.053390\Delta x_{6t-1}-0.016278\Delta x_{7t-1}+ 0.000125\Delta y_{t-1}-0.004321EC$

(0.92) (-0.34) (-0.17) (2.8)* (-0.04)

$R^2= 0.33$, F=1.86, AIC=3.22, SC=3.68

$$\Delta x_{6t}= 0.325363+0.204180\Delta x_{1t-1}-0.386254\Delta x_{2t-1}-0.073751\Delta x_{3t-1}+0.010424\Delta x_{4t-1}- \quad (6)$$

(0.87) (1.83) (-0.83) (-0.073) (0.17)

$0.134339\Delta x_{5t-1}+0.175616\Delta x_{6t-1}-0.059622\Delta x_{7t-1}+2.09E\text{-}05\Delta y_{t-1}-0.277907EC$

(-0.45) (0.65) (-0.36) (0.27) (-1.79)

R^2= 0.2 F=1.04, AIC=4.31, SC=4.72

$$\Delta x_{7t}=1.557461+0.064348\Delta x_{1t-1}-0.445270\Delta x_{2t-1}-0.675446\Delta x_{3t-1}+0.033164\Delta x_{4t-1} \quad (7)$$

(4.24)* (0.58) (-0.97) (-4.22)* (0.57)

$$-0.264192\Delta x_{5t-1}+0.345774\Delta x_{6t-1}+0.345774\Delta x_{7t-1}-0.000255\Delta y_{t-1}+0.051273EC$$

(-0.90) (0.49) (2.11)* (-3.33)* (0.33)

R^2= 0.59, F=5.32*, AIC=4.29, SC=4.7

$$\Delta y_t=2834.112-89.85084\Delta x_{1t-1}+842.2183\Delta x_{2t-1}-1391.315\Delta x_{3t-1}-174.3453\Delta x_{4t-1}-1692.335\Delta x_{5t-1} \quad (8)$$

(2.86)* (-0.3) (0.68) (-3.22)* (-1.11) (-2.14)*

$$+155.3180\Delta x_{6t-1}+147.5783\Delta x_{7t-1}-0.348757\Delta y_{t-1}+202.9272EC$$

(0.21) (0.33) (-1.69) (0.49)

R^2= 0.42 F=2.71, AIC=20.09, SC=20.50

The speed of the vector error correction process is more or less slow except for Δx_{2t} and Δx_{4t} which are significant but most of the estimated equations are poor fit except Δx_{1t},Δx_{2t} and Δx_{7t} in this vector error correction model.

Yet this VECM is stable since it has one unit root, six roots are imaginary(0.518961 ± 0.209573i, -0.308760 ± 0.428752i, -0.165298 ± 0.346439i)and other three (-0.543200, 0.328063, 0.138599) are less than one, all of which lie in the unit circle. It is shown in the Figure 10.

The impulse response functions of VECM have been diverging away from equilibrium which means that exogenous shocks do not turn the model into equilibrium. It is shown in Figure 11.

Residual tests of this VECM assure that the residuals have the problem of autocorrelations which is shown in Figure 12.

Vector Residual Serial correlation LM test suggested that the variables are serially correlated which is seen in the Table 4.

The VEC residual normality test as done by Doornik-Hansen (2008) has shown that the joint components of skewness, kurtosis and Jarque-Bera (1987) are significant

Figure 10. Unit circle
Source: Computed by author

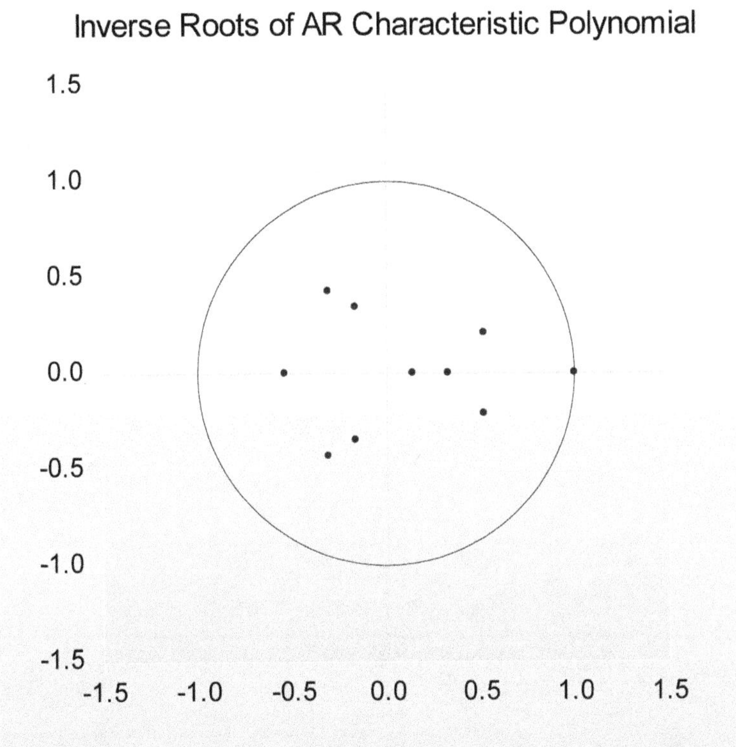

but other components of them are not significant according to the values of Chi-square distribution, therefore, the residuals are not multivariate normal. In Table 5, their values are given.

LIMITATIONS AND FUTURE SCOPE OF RESEARCH

In India, FDI inflows has much impact on balance of payments and on three sectors of the economy which were not explained in this model. Results will be different if whole sale price index is taken for inflation rate. The paper could be divided into pre reform and post reform parts so that comparison would be available for two periods. Multiple determinants of FDI in this econometric model is rather different from the economic reality of the utilization of inflows in India. External debt and FDI inflows nexus is a great research field which is to be explored along with growth-FDI inflows nexus.

Figure 11. Impulse response functions
Source: Computed by author.

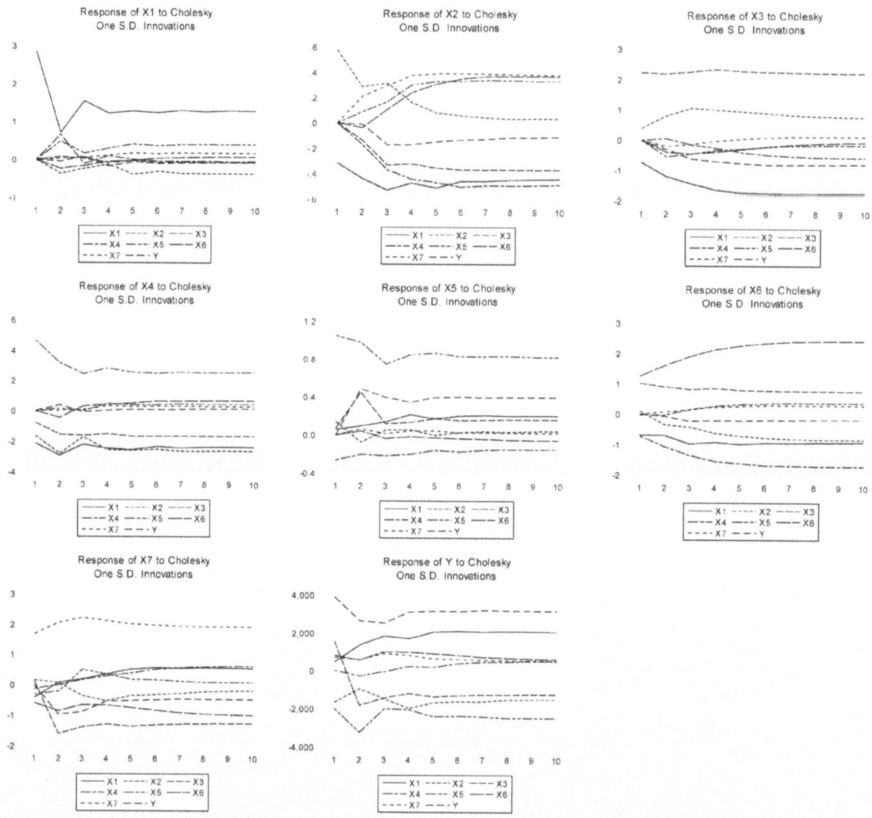

SOME RECOMMENDED POLICIES

Some general economic policies are urgent like [i] to reduce current account deficit,[ii] to reduce external debt,[iii] to cut down fiscal deficit,[iv] to fix target rate of inflation,[v] to follow monetary policy to reduce interest rate when needed,[vi] to increase trade openness respectively to get fruitful outcome of FDI inflows.

Utilization of FDI inflows is considered as to what extent welfare might increase or productivity might rise, even FDI inflows and employment nexus should be positive so that FDI in manufacturing or agri-ouput must accelerate as a result of inflows. Policy makers should put increased weight on infrastructure improvements, training productive workers, and encouraging domestic firms to invest in technology in order to achieve sustained benefits from FDI. Stimulating knowledge transfers both in terms of labor training and skill acquisition and by introducing alternative management practices and better organizational arrangements are required.

Figure 12. Autocorrelation problem
Source: Computed by author

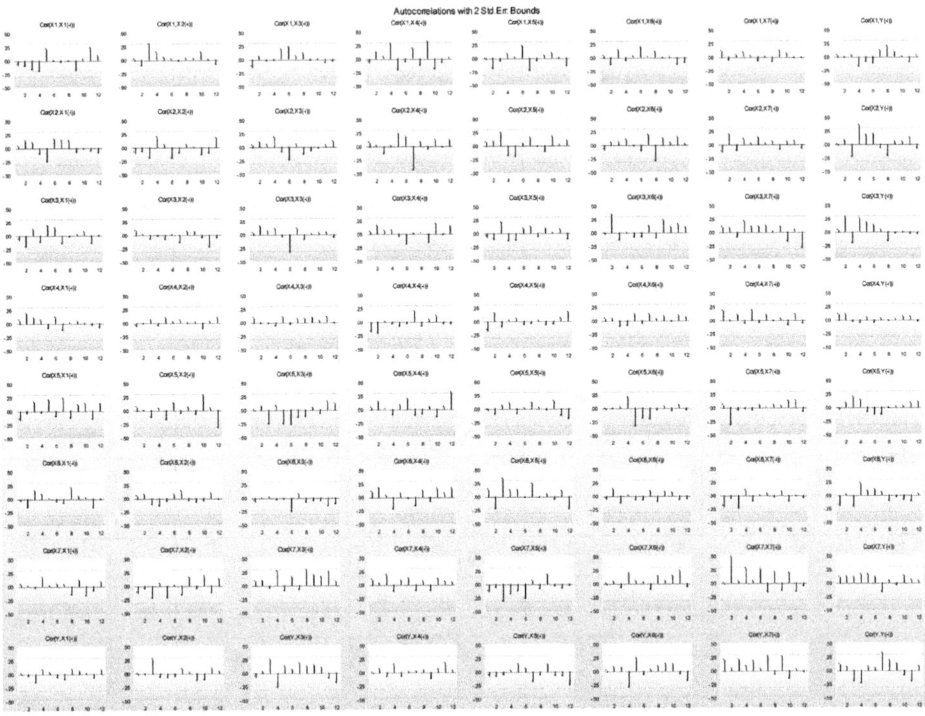

Table 4. VEC residual serial correlation LM test

Lags	LM-Stat	Prob
1	69.08543	0.3097
2	76.00517	0.1447
3	60.44998	0.6028
4	67.75267	0.3504
5	51.45797	0.8709
6	82.35328	0.0610
7	63.05198	0.5100
8	61.63928	0.5605
9	56.77821	0.7272
10	42.09907	0.9844
11	65.69198	0.4180
12	75.12452	0.1612

Source: Computed by author

Table 5. Doornik-Hansen normality test

Component	**Skewness**	**Chi-sq**	**df**	**Prob.**
1	-0.084242	0.064756	1	0.7991
2	-0.194496	0.341888	1	0.5587
3	0.158327	0.227451	1	0.6334
4	-0.642132	3.360874	1	0.0668
5	-0.460680	1.822804	1	0.1770
6	0.710372	4.022242	1	0.0449
7	0.395926	1.367554	1	0.2422
8	0.672477	3.650127	1	0.0561
Joint		14.85770	8	0.0620
Component	**Kurtosis**	**Chi-sq**	**df**	**Prob.**
1	2.806869	0.180811	1	0.6707
2	3.673029	3.119953	1	0.0773
3	2.743956	0.054829	1	0.8149
4	8.172222	31.27463	1	0.0000
5	3.160990	0.104753	1	0.7462
6	5.533883	7.996608	1	0.0047
7	2.384901	1.219767	1	0.2694
8	3.384075	0.017875	1	0.8936
Joint		43.96922	8	0.0000
Component	**Jarque-Bera**	**df**	**Prob.**	
1	0.245568	2	0.8845	
2	3.461841	2	0.1771	
3	0.282280	2	0.8684	
4	34.63550	2	0.0000	
5	1.927557	2	0.3814	
6	12.01885	2	0.0025	
7	2.587321	2	0.2743	
8	3.668003	2	0.1598	
Joint	58.82692	16	0.0000	

Source: Computed by author

CONCLUSION

The paper concludes that India's FDI inflows from 1971 to 2015 has been increasing at the rate of 21.56% per year and exponentially increasing at the rate of 0.604% per year. It has no random walk with drift. It is stationary as suggested by ARIMA (1,1,1) model. It has four upward structural breaks in 1985,1994,2000 and 2006 respectively. It is highly volatile as shown by GARCH (1,1) model. Granger causality test assured that there are no causality between growth rate and interest rate, growth rate and openness, FDI inflows and openness respectively but there exists uni-directional causality between growth and exchange rate, growth and inflation, interest rate and openness, exchange rate and external debt, exchange rate and FDI inflows, fiscal deficit and FDI inflows, fiscal deficit and external debt respectively during 1971-2015 and rest of variables showed bi-directional causality. Johansen unrestricted cointegration rank test showed that Trace statistic has four cointegrating equations and Max Eigen Statistic has three cointegrating equations. The speed of the vector error correction process is more or less slow except for Δx_{2t} and Δx_{4t} which are significant but most of the estimated equations are poor fit except Δx_{1t}, Δx_{2t} and Δx_{7t} in this vector error correction model. Yet this VECM is stable and diverging. VEC residuals are not multivariate normal having problems of autocorrelations and serial correlations.

REFERENCES

Agrawal, P. (2005). Foreign direct investment in South Asia: Impact on economic growth and local investment. In E. M. Graham (Ed.), *Multinationals and foreign investment in economic development* (pp. 94–118). Basingstoke, UK: Palgrave Macmillan. doi:10.1057/9780230522954_5

Agrawal, R., & Shahani, R. (2005). Foreign investment in India: issues and implications for globalisation. In C. Tisdell (Ed.), *Globalisation and world economic policies: effects and policy responses of nations and their groupings* (pp. 644–658). New Delhi: Serials Publication.

Asiedu, E. (2002). On the Determinants of Foreign Direct Investment to Developing Countries: Is Africa Different? *World Development, 30*(1), 107-119.

Asiedu, E. (2003). Capital Control and Foreign Direct Investment. *World Development, 32*(3), 479-490.

Bai, J., & Perron, P. (2003). Critical values for multiple structural change tests. *The Econometrics Journal, 6*, 72–78.

Basu, P., Chakraborty, C., & Reagle, D. (2003). Liberalization, FDI, and growth in developing countries: a panel cointegration approach. *Economic Inquiry, 41*(3), 510–516.

Bhattacharjee, M., & Bhattacharjee, S. (2011). The interrelationship between merchandise trade, economic growth and FDI inflows in India. *South Eastern Europe Journal of Economics*, *2*, 229–244.

Bhowmik, D. (1999). Foreign Investment in India: Theories, evidences, policies. *ArthaBeekshan, 8*(2), 20-32.

Bhowmik, D. (2003). *Essays on International Money*. New Delhi: Deep and Deep Publications Pvt.Ltd.

Bhowmik, D. (2011). US financial crisis, recovery packages and dollar hegemony. In R.K.Sen (Ed.). *Modern Indian economy: Essays in honour of Prof. Alok Ghosh* (pp 26-378), New Delhi: Deep and Deep Publications Pvt.Ltd.

Bhowmik, D. (2014a). *An analysis of financial integration: Now and then*. Paper selected for presentation at World conference on Finance and Banking, December, Singapore.

Bhowmik, D. (2014b). *FDI, financial crises and BW-II*. Paper selected for presentation at 2014 Asia Conference on Economics and Business Research, November, Singapore.

Bhowmik, D. (2014c, December). FDI, financial crises and BW-II. *The Indian Economic Journal*, 1–18.

Bhowmik, D. (2014d). *The Euro crisis and international Liquidity Problems*. New Delhi: Synergy Books India.

Bhowmik, D. (2015a). Foreign Direct investment, Economic growth and financial crises. *DMIETR International Journal on Financial Management*, *1*, 32-53.

Bhowmik, D. (2015b, July). The determinants of foreign direct investment: An econometric study with special reference to India. *Political Economy Journal of India*.

Bhowmik, D., & Dey, T. (2014). *Financial crises, US shut down and FDI*. Paper presented in Kalyani University on 27-28 March at UGC seminar.

Chakraborty, C., & Basu, P. (2010). Foreign Direct Investment and growth in India: A Cointegration Approach. *Applied Economics, 34*(9), 1061-1073.

Chakraborty, C., & Nunnenkamp, P. (2008). Economic Reforms, FDI, and Economic Growth in India: A Sector Level Analysis. *World Development, 36*(7), 1192–1212. doi:10.1016/j.worlddev.2007.06.014

Chakraborty, D., & Mukherjee, J. (2012). Is there any relationship between foreign direct investment and economic growth in India? A time series analysis. *Review of Market Integration*, *4*, 309–337.

Cushman, D. O. (1988). Exchange-Rate Uncertainty and Foreign Direct Investment in the United States. *Weltwirtschaftliches Archiv*, *124*(2), 322–336. doi:10.1007/BF02706782

Dash, R. K., & Parida, P. C. (2011). Services trade and economic growth in India: an analysis in the post-reform period. *International Journal Economics Business Research, 4*(3), 326–345.

Dhawan, U., & Biswal, B. (1999). Re-examining export led growth hypothesis: A multivariate cointegration analysis for India. *Applied Economics*, *31*(4), 525–530. doi:10.1080/000368499324246

Doornik, J. A., & Hansen, H. (2008). An Omnibus test for Univariate and Multivariate normality. *Oxford Bulletin of Economics and Statistics*, *70*, 927–939.

Enders, W. (2011). *Applied Econometric Time Series*. Wiley Student Edition.

Engle, R. F., & Granger, C. W. J. (1987). Cointegration and error correction: Representation, estimation and testing. *Econometrica, 55*(2), 251–276. doi:10.2307/1913236

Froot, K., & Stein, J. (1991). Exchange Rates and Foreign Direct Investment: An Imperfect Capital Markets Approach. *Quarterly Journal of Economics, Vol*, *196*(4), 1191–1218. doi:10.2307/2937961

Goldberg, S., & Klein, W. (1998). Foreign Direct Investment and Real Exchange Rate Linkages in Developing Countries. In R. Glick (Ed.), *Managing Capital Flows and Exchange Rates:Lessons from the Pacific Basin*. Cambridge University Press.

Goswami, G., & Saikia, K. K. (2012). FDI and its Relation with Exports in India,Status and Prospect in North East Region. *Procedia: Social and Behavioral Sciences*, *37*, 123–132. doi:10.1016/j.sbspro.2012.03.280

Granger, C. W. J. (1969). Investigating Causal Relations by Econometric Models and Cross-spectral Methods. *Econometrica*, *37*(3), 424–438.

Grosse, R., & Trevino, L. (1996). Foreign direct investment in the United States: An analysis by country of origin. *Journal of International Business Studies*, *27*(1), 139–155. doi:10.1057/palgrave.jibs.8490129

Hansen, H., & Rand, J. (2006). On the causal links between FDI and Growth in developing countries. *World Economy*, *29*, 21–43.

Hodrick, R., & Prescott, E. C. (1997). Post-War U.S. Business Cycles: An Empirical Investigation. *Journal of Money, Credit and Banking*, *29*(1), 1–16.

Hooda, M. S. (2011). A study of FDI and Indian Economy. Department of Humanities and Social Sciences National Institute of Technology (Deemed University), Durgapur.

Jarque, C. M., & Bera, A. K. (1987). A Test for normality of observations and regression residuals. *International Statistical Review*, *55*(2), 163–172.

Johansen, S. (1988). Statistical Analysis of Cointegrating Vectors. *Journal of Economic Dynamics & Control*, *12*(2-3), 231–254. doi:10.1016/0165-1889(88)90041-3

Johansen, S. (1991, November). Estimation of Hypothesis Testing of Cointegration Vectors in Gaussian Vector Autoregressive Models. *Econometrica*, *59*(6), 1551–1580. doi:10.2307/2938278

Johansen, S. (1994, January). The role of the constant and linear terms in cointegration analysis of nonstationary variables. *Econometric Reviews*, *13*(2), 205–229. doi:10.1080/07474939408800284

Johansen, S. (1995). *Likelihood-Based Inference in Cointegrated Vector Autoregressive Models*. Oxford University Press. doi:10.1093/0198774508.001.0001

Johansen, S. (1996). Likelihood-Based Inference in Cointegrated Vector Autoregressive Models (2nd ed.). Oxford University Press.

Johnson, A. (2006). *The effects of FDI inflows on Host Country Economic growth*. CESIS Electronic working paper series No-58.

Juselius, K. (1990). Maximum likelihood estimation and cointegration with application to the demand of money. *Oxford Bulletin of Economics and Statistics*, *52*(2), 169–210.

Kalecki. (1937). Economic and Political Determinants of Foreign Direct Investment. *World Development*, *13*(2), 161-175.

Khan, G. S., & Mitra, P. (2014). Semtember-October). A Causal Linkage between FDI Inflows with Select Macroeconomic Variables in India – An Econometric Analysis. *Journal of Economics and Finance*, *5*(5), 124–133.

Kumar, A. (2007). What are the Determinants of the Location of Foreign Direct Investment? *Journal of International Economics*, *51*, 379-400.

Lipsey, R. E. (1999). The Role of FDI in International Capital Flows. In M. Feldstein (Ed.), *International Capital Flows*. Chicago: Chicago University Press.

Mattoo, A., & Stern, R. M. (2003). *India and the WTO*. World Bank and Oxford University Press.

Moosa, I. A. (2002). *Foreign Direct Investment: Theory, Evidence and Practice*. London: Palgrave. doi:10.1057/9781403907493

Moosa, I. A., & Cardak, B. A. (2006). The Determinants of Foreign Direct Investment: An Extreme Bound Analysis. *Journal of Multinational Financial Management*, *16*(2), 199–211. doi:10.1016/j.mulfin.2005.07.002

Odozi, V. A. (1995). *An Overview of Foreign Investment in Nigeria 1960-1995*. Occasional Paper No. 11, Research Department, Central Bank of Nigeria.

Osinubi, T. S., & Amaghionyeodiwe, L. A. (2009). Foreign Direct Investment and exchange rate volatility in Nigeria. *International Journal of Applied Econometrics and Quantitative Studies*, *6*(2), 83-116.

Parajuli, S. (2012). *Examining the relationship between the exchange rate, foreign direct investment and trade* (PhD Thesis). Louisiana State University.

Ray, S. (2012). Impact of FDI on economic growth in India: A Cointegration Analysis. *Advances in Information Technology and Management*, 2(1), 187-201.

Saji, T G. (2013). Does Foreign Direct Investment Lead Economic Growth in India? *International Journal of Financial Management, 3*(2), 38-45.

Siddiqui, H. A. A., & Aumeboonsuke, V. (2014). Role of interest rate in attracting FDI: Study on ASEAN5 Economy. *International Journal of Technical Research and Applications*, 2(S3), 59-70.

Stokman, A. C. J., & Vlar, P. J. G. (1996). *Volatility*. Amsterdam: International Trade and Capital Flows.

Tripathi, V., Seth, R., & Bhandari, V. (2015). Foreign Direct Investment and MacroEconomic Factors: Evidence from the Indian Economy. *Asia-Pacific Journal of Management Research and Innovation, 11*, 46-56.

Uwubanmwen, A. E., & Ajao, M. G. (2012). The determinants and impact of Foreign Direct Investment in Nigeria. *International Journal of Business and Management*, *7*(24), 67–77.

Wang, J. Y. (1990). Growth, technology transfer and long run theory of International Capital Movement. *Journal of International Economics*, *29*, 255–271.

Compilation of References

Abdou, D. S., & Zaazou, Z. (2013). The Egyptian revolution and post socio-economic impact *Topics in Middle Eastern and African Economies, 15*(1), 91-115.

Abraham, F., Konings, J., & Slootmaekers, V. (2006). *FDI spillovers, firm heterogeneity and degree of ownership: evidence from Chinese manufacturing* (Unpublished Paper). Department of Economics, Catholic University of Leuven.

Abu Bakar, N., & Mat, S. H. C. (2012). The impact of infrastructure on foreign direct investment: *The case of Malaysia. Procedia: Social and Behavioral Sciences, 65*, 205–211. doi:10.1016/j.sbspro.2012.11.112

Accolley, D. (2003). *The Determinants and Impact of Foreign Direct Investment* (Master's Dissertation). Retrieved from: http://mpra.ub.uni-muenchen.de/3084/

Acemoglu, D., Johnson, S., & Robinson, J. A. (2001). The colonial origins of comparative development: An empirical investigation. *The American Economic Review, 91*(5), 1369–1401. doi:10.1257/aer.91.5.1369

Adam, A., & Kammas, P. (2007). Tax policies in a globalized world: Is it politics after all? *Public Choice, 133*(3-4), 321–341. doi:10.100711127-007-9190-9

Adams, S. (2009). Foreign direct investment, domestic investment, and economic growth in Sub-Saharan Africa. *Journal of Policy Modeling, 31*(6), 939–949. doi:10.1016/j.jpolmod.2009.03.003

ADB. (2004). *Asian Development Outlook 2004*. Retrieved from http://www.adb.org/Documents/Books/ ADO/2004/default.asp

Adewumi, S. (2006). *The impact of foreign direct investment on growth in developing countries: An African Experience*. Jönköping International Business School Jönköping University Jonkoping University.

Agarwal, J.P. (1980). Determinants of Foreign Direct Investment: A Survey. *Weltwirtschaftliches Archive, 116*, 739-773.

Agarwal, J. P. (1980). Determinants of foreign direct investment: A survey. *Weltwirtschaftliches Archiv, 116*(4), 739–773. doi:10.1007/BF02696547

Aghion, P., Bloom, N., Blundell, R., Griffith, R., & Howitt, P. (2005). Competition and innovation: An inverted-U relationship. *The Quarterly Journal of Economics, 120*(2), 701–728.

Aghion, P., & Tirole, J. (1994). The management of innovation. *The Quarterly Journal of Economics, 109*(4), 1185–1209. doi:10.2307/2118360

Agosin, M., & Mayer, R. (2000). *Foreign investment in developing countries: Does it crowd in Domestic investment.* UNCTAD Discussion Paper No. 146.

Agosin, M., & Machado, D. (2005). Foreign Investment in Developing Countries: Does it Crowd in Domestic Investment? *Oxford Development Studies, 33*(2), 149–162. doi:10.1080/13600810500137749

Agrawal, P. (2005). Foreign direct investment in South Asia: Impact on economic growth and local investment. In E. M. Graham (Ed.), *Multinationals and foreign investment in economic development* (pp. 94–118). Basingstoke, UK: Palgrave Macmillan. doi:10.1057/9780230522954_5

Agrawal, R., & Shahani, R. (2005). Foreign investment in India: issues and implications for globalisation. In C. Tisdell (Ed.), *Globalisation and world economic policies: effects and policy responses of nations and their groupings* (pp. 644–658). New Delhi: Serials Publication.

Ahmed, A. A. (1975). *The determinants of direct investment, with special reference to developing countries* (Doctoral dissertation). Graduate School of Arts and Sciences, University of Pennsylvania.

Ahmed, A. D., Cheng, E., & Messinis, G. (2011). The role of exports, FDI and imports in development: Evidence from Sub-Saharan African countries. *Applied Economics, 43*(26), 3719–3731. doi:10.1080/00036841003705303

Ahya, C., & Xie, A. (2004). India and China: A Special Economic Analysis. Morgan Stanley Equity Research.

Aitken, B. J., & Harrison, A. E. (1999). Do domestic firms benefit from direct foreign investment? Evidence from Venezuela. *The American Economic Review, 89*(3), 605–618. doi:10.1257/aer.89.3.605

Akbas, Y. E., Senturk, M., & Sancar, C. (2013). Testing for causality between the Foreign Direct Investment, Current Account Deficit, GDP and Total Credit: Evidence from G7. *Panoeconomicus, 6*(6), 791–812. doi:10.2298/PAN1306791A

Akcaci, T., & Akkaya, O. (2012). How have FDI flows effected to Current Account Balance: In Turkey Case. China-USA Business Review, 11(12), 1565-1571.

AlAzzawi, S. (2012). Innovation, productivity and foreign direct investment-induced R&D spillovers. *The Journal of International Trade & Economic Development, 21*(5), 615–653. doi: 10.1080/09638199.2010.513056

Alfaro, Chanda, Kalemli-Ozcan, & Sayek. (2002). *FDI and Economic Growth: The Role of Local Finance Markets.* Harvard Business School.

Alfaro, L., Chanda, A., Kalemli-Ozcan, S., & Sayek, S. (2004). FDI and economic growth: The role of local financial markets. *Journal of International Economics, 64*(1), 89–112. doi:10.1016/S0022-1996(03)00081-3

Alguacil, M., Cuadros, O. A., & Orts, V. (2011). Inward FDI and growth: The role of macroeconomic and institutional environment. *Journal of Policy Modeling, 33*(3), 481–496. doi:10.1016/j.jpolmod.2010.12.004

Aliber, R. Z. (1970). A theory of direct foreign investment. The International Corporation.

Aliber, R. Z. (1970). A theory of direct foreign investment. In C. P. Kindleberger (Ed.), *The International Corporation*. Cambridge, MA: MIT Press.

Alper & Teoman. (2011). *Foreign Direct Investment and Technology Spillovers in the Turkish Manufacturing*. Industry, Science and Techonology Policies Research Center TEKPOL Working Paper series, 11/3.

Altenburg, T., & Meyer-Stamer, J. (1999). How to promote clusters: Experiences from Latin America. *World Development, 27*(9), 1693–1713. doi:10.1016/S0305-750X(99)00081-9

Amighini, A., Cozza, C., Giuliani, E., Rabellotti, R., & Scalera, V. (2013). *Technology-Driven FDI: A Survey of the Literature* (No. 2013/17). Lund University, CIRCLE-Center for Innovation, Research and Competences in the Learning Economy.

Anderson, M. (1999). *Access to justice & legal process: making legal institutions responsive to poor people in LDCs*. Discussion Paper at WDR 2000 Conference.

Andreoni, A., & Chang, H.-J. (2016). Industrial policy and the future of manufacturing. *Economia e Politica Industriale, 43*(4), 491–502. doi:10.100740812-016-0057-2

Anfofum, A. A., Gambo, J. S., & Suleiman, T. (2013). Estimating the impact of foreign direct investment in Nigeria. *International Journal of Humanities and Social Science, 3*(17), 138–145.

Anken, F., & Beasley, E. J. (2012). Corporate structure optimization for multinational companies. *Omega, 40*(2), 230–243. doi:10.1016/j.omega.2011.06.003

Appleton, A. E., & Plummer, M. G. (2007). *The world trade organization: Legal, economic and political analysis*. Berlin, Germany: Springer Science & Business Media.

Arellano, M., & Bond, S. (1991). Some tests of specification for panel data: Monte Carlo Evidence & an application to employment equations. *The Review of Economic Studies, 58*(2), 277–297. doi:10.2307/2297968

Artige, L., & Nicolini, R. (2006). *Evidence on the determinants of foreign direct investment. The case of three European regions*. CREPP working paper.

Asano, T. (2010). Optimal tax policy and foreign direct investment under ambiguity. *Journal of Macroeconomics, 32*(1), 185–200. doi:10.1016/j.jmacro.2009.12.006

Asiedu, E. (2002). On the Determinants of Foreign Direct Investment to Developing Countries: Is Africa Different? *World Development, 30*(1), 107-119.

Asiedu, E. (2003). Capital Control and Foreign Direct Investment. *World Development, 32*(3), 479-490.

Asiedu, E. (2002). On the Determinants of Foreign Direct Investment to Developing Countries: Is Africa Different? *World Development*, *30*(1), 107–119.

Asiedu, E. (2002). On the determinants of foreign direct investment to developing countries: Is Africa different? *World Development*, *30*(1), 107–119. doi:10.1016/S0305-750X(01)00100-0

Asiedu, E., & Lien, D. (2011). Democracy, foreign direct investment and natural resources. *Journal of International Economics*, *84*(1), 99–111. doi:10.1016/j.jinteco.2010.12.001

Asteriou, D., & Stephen, G. (2011). *Applied Econometrics* (2nd ed.). London, UK: Palgrave MacMillan.

Atique, Z., Ahmad, M., Azhar, U., & Khan, A. (2004). The Impact of FDI on economic growth under foreign trade regimes: A case study of Pakistan. *Pakistan Development Review*, *43*(4), 707–718.

Aysan, A. F., Nabli, M. K., & Véganzonès-Varoudakis, M. A. (2007). Governance institutions and private investment: an application to the Middle East and North Africa. *The Developing Economies, 45*(3), 339-377. doi: 10.1111/j.1746-1049.2007.00042.x

Azman-Saini, W., Baharumshah, A. Z., & Law, S. H. (2010b). Foreign direct investment, economic freedom and economic growth: International evidence. *Economic Modelling*, *27*(5), 1079–1089. doi:10.1016/j.econmod.2010.04.001

Azman-Saini, W., Law, S. H., & Ahmad, A. H. (2010a). FDI and economic growth: New evidence on the role of financial markets. *Economics Letters*, *107*(2), 211–213. doi:10.1016/j.econlet.2010.01.027

Bacchetta, P., & Wincoop, E. V. (2000). Does Exchange Rate Stability increase Trade and Capital Flows? *The American Economic Review*, *90*(5), 1093–1109. doi:10.1257/aer.90.5.1093

Bai, J., & Perron, P. (2003). Critical values for multiple structural change tests. *The Econometrics Journal*, *6*, 72–78.

Bajal, Tuli, &Srivastava. (2009). *Retail management*. Oxford University Press.

Balasubramanyam, V. N., Salisu, M., & Sapsford, D. (1996). Foreign direct investment and growth in EP and IS countries. *Economic Journal (London)*, *106*(434), 92–105. doi:10.2307/2234933

Baltagi, H. (2005). *Econometric Analysis of Panel data*. New York: John Wiley and Sons.

Barrell, R., & Pain, N. (1997). Foreign Direct Investment, Technological Change, and Economic Growth Within Europe. *Economic Journal (London)*, *107*(445), 1770–1786. doi:10.1111/j.1468-0297.1997.tb00081.x

Barrios, S., Görg, H., & Strobl, E. (2005). Foreign direct investment, competition and industrial development in the host country. *European Economic Review*, *49*(7), 1761–1784. doi:10.1016/j.euroecorev.2004.05.005

Barro, R. J., & Lee, J. W. (1993). International comparisons of educational attainment. *Journal of Monetary Economics*, *32*(3), 363–394. doi:10.1016/0304-3932(93)90023-9

Barro, R. J., & Lee, J. W. (2013). A net data set of educational attainment in the world, 1950-2010. *Journal of Development Economics*, *104*, 184–198. doi:10.1016/j.jdeveco.2012.10.001

Basu, P., Chakraborty, C., & Reagle, D. (2003). Liberalization, FDI, and growth in developing countries: a panel cointegration approach. *Economic Inquiry*, *41*(3), 510–516.

Bayraktar, N. (2013). Foreign Direct Investment and Investment Climate. *Procedia Economics and Finance*, *14*, 83–92. doi:10.1016/S2212-5671(13)00013-0

Becker, J., & Fuest, C. (2010). Taxing Foreign Profits with International Mergers and Acquisitions. *International Economic Review*, *51*(1), 171–186. doi:10.1111/j.1468-2354.2009.00575.x

Becker, J., & Riedel, N. (2012). Cross-border tax effects on affiliate investment-Evidence from European Multinationals. *European Economic Review*, *56*, 1495–1511. doi:10.1016/j.euroecorev.2012.07.001

Belderbos, R., Capannelli, G., & Fukao, K. (2001). Backward vertical linkages of foreign manufacturing affiliates: Evidence from Japanese multinationals. *World Development*, *29*(1), 189–208. doi:10.1016/S0305-750X(00)00086-3

Benassy-Quere, A., Coupet, M., & Mayer, T. (2007). Institutional Determinants of Foreign Direct Investment. *World Economy*, *30*(5), 764–782. doi:10.1111/j.1467-9701.2007.01022.x

Berman & Evans. (2010). *Retail management a strategic approach* (8th ed.). Prentice Hall of India Publication.

Beyer, C. (2008). *Violent globalisms: conflict in response to empire*. Ashgate Publishing, Ltd.

Bhasin, N. (2012). *Foreign Direct Investment (FDI) in India: Policies, Conditions and Procedures*. New Delhi: New Century Publications.

Bhattacharjee, M., & Bhattacharjee, S. (2011). The interrelationship between merchandise trade, economic growth and FDI inflows in India. *South Eastern Europe Journal of Economics*, *2*, 229–244.

Bhowmik, D. (1999). Foreign Investment in India: Theories, evidences, policies. *ArthaBeekshan*, *8*(2), 20-32.

Bhowmik, D. (2011). US financial crisis, recovery packages and dollar hegemony. In R.K.Sen (Ed.). *Modern Indian economy: Essays in honour of Prof. Alok Ghosh* (pp 26-378), New Delhi: Deep and Deep Publications Pvt.Ltd.

Bhowmik, D. (2014a). *An analysis of financial integration: Now and then*. Paper selected for presentation at World conference on Finance and Banking, December, Singapore.

Bhowmik, D. (2014b). *FDI, financial crises and BW-II*. Paper selected for presentation at 2014 Asia Conference on Economics and Business Research, November, Singapore.

Bhowmik, D. (2015a). Foreign Direct investment, Economic growth and financial crises. *DMIETR International Journal on Financial Management*, *1*, 32-53.

Bhowmik, D. (2015b, July). The determinants of foreign direct investment: An econometric study with special reference to India. *Political Economy Journal of India*.

Bhowmik, D., & Dey, T. (2014). *Financial crises, US shut down and FDI*. Paper presented in Kalyani University on 27-28 March at UGC seminar.

Bhowmik, D. (2003). *Essays on International Money*. New Delhi: Deep and Deep Publications Pvt.Ltd.

Bhowmik, D. (2014c, December). FDI, financial crises and BW-II. *The Indian Economic Journal*, 1–18.

Bhowmik, D. (2014d). *The Euro crisis and international Liquidity Problems*. New Delhi: Synergy Books India.

Biglaiser, G., & DeRouen, K. (2004). The expansion of neoliberal economic reforms in Latin America. *International Studies Quarterly*, *48*(3), 561–578. doi:10.1111/j.0020-8833.2004.00315.x

Biglaiser, G., & Staats, J. L. (2010). Do political institutions affect foreign direct investment? A survey of US corporations in Latin America. *Political Research Quarterly*, *63*(3), 508–522. doi:10.1177/1065912909331428

Blalock, G., & Gertler, P. (2004). *Firm capabilities and technology adoption: Evidence from foreign direct investment in Indonesia* (Working Paper). Department of Applied Economics and Management, Cornell University.

Blanton, R. G., & Apodaca, C. (2007). Economic globalization and violent civil conflict: Is openness a pathway to peace?'. *The Social Science Journal*, *44*(4), 599–619. doi:10.1016/j.soscij.2007.10.001

Blomstrom, M., & Kokko, A. (2003). *The economic of foreign direct investment incentives*. Retrieved November 20, 2016, from http://www.nber.org/papers/w9489

Blundell, R., & Bond, S. (1988). Initial conditions & moment restrictions in dynamic panel data models. *Journal of Econometrics*, *87*(1), 115–143. doi:10.1016/S0304-4076(98)00009-8

Borensztein, E., De Gregorio, J., & Lee, J. (1998). How does foreign direct investment affect economic growth? *Journal of International Economics*, *45*(1), 115–135. doi:10.1016/S0022-1996(97)00033-0

Bowles, S., Durlauf, S. N., & Hoff, K. (2006). *Poverty traps*. Princeton, NJ: Princeton University Press.

Braczyk, H. J., Cooke, P. N., & Heidenreich, M. (1998). *Regional innovation systems: the role of governances in a globalized world.* Psychology Press.

Breusch, T. S., & Pagan, A. R. (1980). The Lagrange multiplier test and its applications to model specification in econometrics. *The Review of Economic Studies, 47*(1), 239–253. doi:10.2307/2297111

Broner, F. A., & Rigobon, R. (2006). Why are Capital Flows so Much More Volatile in Emerging than in Developed Countries? In R. J. Caballero, C. Calderon, & L. F. Cespedes (Eds.), *External Vulnerability and Preventive Policies*. Santiago: Central Bank of Chile.

Brouthers, K., & Dikova, D. (2010). Acquisitions and Real Options: The Greenfield Alternative. *Journal of Management Studies, 47*(6), 1048–1071. doi:10.1111/j.1467-6486.2009.00875.x

Buchanan, B., Lee, V. Q., & Rishi, M. (2012). Foreign direct investment and institutional quality: Some empirical evidence. *International Review of Financial Analysis, 4*, 81–89. doi:10.1016/j.irfa.2011.10.001

Buckley, P. J., & Casson, M. (1976). *The Future of Multinational Enterprise*. London: MacMillan. doi:10.1007/978-1-349-02899-3

Buckley, P., Clegg, J., & Wang, C. (1995). The impact of inward FDI on the performance of Chinese manufacturing firms. *Journal of International Business Studies, 33*(4), 637–655. doi:10.1057/palgrave.jibs.8491037

Busse, M., & Hefeker, C. (2007). Political risk, institutions and foreign direct investment. *European Journal of Political Economy, 23*(2), 397–415. doi:10.1016/j.ejpoleco.2006.02.003

Bussmann, M. (2010). Foreign direct investment and militarized international conflict. *Journal of Peace Research, 47*(2), 143–153. doi:10.1177/0022343309354143

Bussmann, M., & Schneider, G. (2007). When globalization discontent turns violent: Foreign economic liberalization and internal war. *International Studies Quarterly, 51*(1), 79–97. doi:10.1111/j.1468-2478.2007.00440.x

Calvet, A. L. (1981). A synthesis of foreign direct investment theories and theories of the multinational firm. *Journal of International Business Studies, 12*(1), 43–59. doi:10.1057/palgrave.jibs.8490570

Calvo, G. A., Leiderman, L., & Reinhart, C. M. (1996). Inflows of Capital to Developing Countries in the 1990s. *The Journal of Economic Perspectives, 10*(2), 123–139. doi:10.1257/jep.10.2.123

Campbell, T. (2001). Foreign Direct Investment Inflows and their Impact on Barbados' Current Account: Implications for Policy. In *Canadian Economic Association (2001) annual meeting*. McGill University.

Cantah, W. G., Wiafe, E. A., & Adams, A. (2013). *Foreign direct investment and trade policy openness in Sub-Saharan Africa (No. 58074)*. University Library of Munich.

Caporale, G. M., & Pittis, N. (1999). Efficient estimation of cointegration vectors and testing for causality in vector autoregressions. *Journal of Economic Surveys*, *13*(1), 1–35. doi:10.1111/1467-6419.00073

Carlos Pinho, J. (2007). The impact of ownership: Location-specific advantages and managerial characteristics on SME foreign entry mode choices. *International Marketing Review*, *24*(6), 715–734. doi:10.1108/02651330710832676

Caves, R. E. (1971). International Corporations: The Industrial Economics of Foreign Investment. *Economica*, *38*(149), 1–27. doi:10.2307/2551748

Caves, R. E. (1974). 'Causes of Direct Investment: Foreign Firms' Share in Canadian and UK Manufacturing Industries'. *The Review of Economics and Statistics*, *56*(3), 272–293. doi:10.2307/1923965

Cazzavillan, G., & Olszewski, K. (2012). Interaction between foreign financial services and foreign direct investment in Transition Economies: An empirical analysis with focus on the manufacturing sector. *Research in Economics*, *66*(4), 305–319. doi:10.1016/j.rie.2012.08.001

Chakraborty, C., & Basu, P. (2010). Foreign Direct Investment and growth in India: A Cointegration Approach. *Applied Economics*, *34*(9), 1061-1073.

Chakraborty, C., & Nunnenkamp, P. (2008). Economic Reforms, FDI, and Economic Growth in India: A Sector Level Analysis. *World Development*, *36*(7), 1192–1212. doi:10.1016/j.worlddev.2007.06.014

Chakraborty, D., & Mukherjee, J. (2012). Is there any relationship between foreign direct investment and economic growth in India? A time series analysis. *Review of Market Integration*, *4*, 309–337.

Chakravati, A. (2001). The Determinants of Foreign Direct Investments: Sensitvity Analysis of Cross- Country Regressions. *International Review for Social Sciences*, *54*(1), 89–114.

Cheng, L. K., & Kwan, Y. K. (2000). What are the determinants of the location of foreign direct investment? The Chinese experience. *Journal of International Economics*, *51*(2), 379–400. doi:10.1016/S0022-1996(99)00032-X

Chesnais, F., Ietto-Gillies, G., & Simonetti, R. (Eds.). (2003). *European integration and global corporate strategies*. London, UK: Routledge.

Cheung, K. Y., & Ping, L. (2004). Spillover effects of FDI on innovation in China: Evidence from the provincial data. *China Economic Review*, *15*(1), 25–44. doi:10.1016/S1043-951X(03)00027-0

Chopra, S., & Kaur, S. (2014). Analysis of FDI Inflows and Outflows in India. *Journal of Advanced Management Science*, 2(4), 326–332. doi:10.12720/joams.2.4.326-332

Chowdhury, A., & Mavrotas, G. (2006). FDI and growth: What causes what? *World Economy*, *29*(1), 9–19. doi:10.1111/j.1467-9701.2006.00755.x

Chun, B. G. (2012). Host country's strategic policies and multinational firm's choice of entry mode. *Economic Modelling*, *29*(2), 435–443. doi:10.1016/j.econmod.2011.11.014

Ciruelos, A., & Wang, M. (2005). International technology diffusion: Effects of trade and FDI. *Atlantic Economic Journal*, *33*(4), 437–449. doi:10.100711293-005-2871-1

Conyon, M., Girma, S., Thompson, S., & Wright, P. (2002). The Productivity and Wage Effect of Foreign Acquisition in the United Kingdom. *The Journal of Industrial Economics*, *50*(1), 85–102. doi:10.1111/1467-6451.00169

Ćorić, B., & Pugh, G. (2013). Foreign direct investment and output growth volatility: A worldwide analysis. *International Review of Economics & Finance*, *25*, 260–271. doi:10.1016/j.iref.2012.07.011

Cosh, A., Fu, X., & Hughes, A. (2005). *Management characteristics, collaboration and innovative efficiency: Evidence from UK survey data*. Cambridge, UK: Centre for Business Research, University of Cambridge.

Costa, I., & Queiroz, S. (2002). Foreign direct investment and technological capabilities in Brazilian industry. *Research Policy*, *31*(8-9), 1431–1443. doi:10.1016/S0048-7333(02)00073-2

Crespo, N., & Fontoura, M. P. (2007). Determinants factors of FDI spillovers – what we really know? *World Development*, *35*(3), 410–425. doi:10.1016/j.worlddev.2006.04.001

Cushman, D. O. (1988). Exchange-Rate Uncertainty and Foreign Direct Investment in the United States. *Weltwirtschaftliches Archiv*, *124*(2), 322–336. doi:10.1007/BF02706782

D'Amelio, M., Garrone, P., & Piscitello, L. (2016). Can multinational enterprises light up developing countries? Evidences from the access to electricity in sub-Saharan Africa. *World Development*, *88*, 12–32. doi:10.1016/j.worlddev.2016.06.018

Dabla-Norris, E., Ho, G., Kochhar, K., Kyobe, A., & Tchaidze, R. (2014). Anchoring Growth: The Importance of Productivity-Enhancing Reforms in Emerging Market and Developing Economies. *Journal of International Commerce Economic Policy*, *5*(02), 1–29.

Dabour, N Md. (2000). The Role of Foreign Direct Investment in Development and Growth in OIC Member Countries. *Journal of Economic Cooperation*, *21*(3), 27–55.

Damijan, J., Rojec, M., Majcen, B., & Knell, M. (2013). Impact of firm heterogenity on direct and spillover effects of FDI: Micro-evidence from the transition countries. *Journal of Comparative Economics*, *41*(3), 895–922. doi:10.1016/j.jce.2012.12.001

Dangi. (2013). fdi in retail sector opportunities and challenges. *Innovative Journal of Business and Management, 2*, 103 - 108.

Dash, R. K., & Parida, P. C. (2011). Services trade and economic growth in India: an analysis in the post-reform period. *International Journal Economics Business Research, 4*(3), 326–345.

Das, S. (1987). Externalities, and technology transfer through multinational corporations A theoretical analysis. *Journal of International Economics, 22*(1-2), 171–182. doi:10.1016/0022-1996(87)90028-6

Davies, R., & Voget, J. (2008). *Tax Competition in an Expanding European Union.* Retrieved December 5, 2016, from http://sbs.ox.ac.uk/sites/default/files/Business_Taxation/Docs/Publications/Working_Papers/Series_08/WP0830.pdf

Davies, R. B., & Desbordes, R. (forthcoming). Greenfield FDI and Skill Upgrading: A Polarised Issue. *The Canadian Journal of Economics. Revue Canadienne d'Economique.*

De Mello, L. R. (1999). Foreign direct investment-led growth: Evidence from time series and panel data. *Oxford Economic Papers, 51*(1), 133–151. doi:10.1093/oep/51.1.133

De Simone, G., & Manchin, M. (2012). Outward Migration and Inward FDI: Factor Mobility between Eastern and Western Europe. *Review of International Economics, 20*(3), 600–615. doi:10.1111/j.1467-9396.2012.01041.x

De Sousa, B. S. (2002). Procesi globalizacije. *Časopis za književnost i kulturu, i društvena pitanja, 68*(14), 5–65.

Demirhan, E., & Masca, M. (2008). Determinants of Foreign Direct Investments to Developing Countries: A Cross – Section Analysis. *Prague Economic Papers, 4*(4), 356–369. doi:10.18267/j.pep.337

Dhawan, U., & Biswal, B. (1999). Re-examining export led growth hypothesis: A multivariate cointegration analysis for India. *Applied Economics, 31*(4), 525–530. doi:10.1080/000368499324246

Dhrifi, A. (2015). Foreign direct investment, technological innovation and economic growth: Empirical evidence using simultaneous equations model. *International Review of Economics, 62*(4), 381–400. doi:10.100712232-015-0230-3

Dickey, D. A., & Fuller, W. A. (1981). Likelihood ratio statistics for autoregressive time series with a unit root. *Econometrica, 49*(4), 1057–1072. doi:10.2307/1912517

Din, M. U. (1994). Export processing zones and backward linkages. *Journal of Development Economics, 43*(2), 369–385. doi:10.1016/0304-3878(94)90014-0

Domazet, I., & Marjanović, D. (2016). *Improving the business environment in Serbia through tax incentives for foreign investors. Institute of Economics Sciences.*

Doornik, J. A., & Hansen, H. (2008). An Omnibus test for Univariate and Multivariate normality. *Oxford Bulletin of Economics and Statistics, 70*, 927–939.

Dries, L., & Swinnen, J. (2004). Foreign direct investment, vertical integration, and local suppliers: Evidences from the polish dairy sector. *World Development*, *32*(9), 1525–1544. doi:10.1016/j.worlddev.2004.05.004

Drogendijk, R., & Slangen, A. (2006). Hofstede, Schwartz, or Managerial Perceptions? The Effects of Different Cultural Distance Measures on Establishment Mode Choices by Multinational Enterprises. *International Business Review*, *15*(4), 361–380. doi:10.1016/j.ibusrev.2006.05.003

Du, J., Lu, Y., & Tao, Z. (2012). Institutions and FDI location choice: The role of cultural distances. *Journal of Asian Economics*, *23*(3), 210–223. doi:10.1016/j.asieco.2010.11.008

Dumludag, D., Saridogan, E., & Kurt, S. (2007). *Determinants of Foreign Direct Investment: An Institutionalis Approach.* Retrieved November 27, 2016, from http://www.researchgate.net/publication/237732834

Dunning John, H. (1988). The Eclectic Paradigm of International Production: A Restatement and Some Possible Extensions. *Journal of International Business Studies*, *19*(1), 1–31. doi:10.1057/palgrave.jibs.8490372

Dunning, J., & Zhang, F. (2007). *Foreign Direct Investment and the Locational Competitiveness of Countries.* Retrieved December 6, 2016, from http://www.researchgate.net/publication/255605733

Dunning, J. (1977). Trade, location of economic activity, and the multinational enterprise: a search for an eclectic approach. In B. Ohlin, P. Hesselborn, & P. Wijkman (Eds.), *The international allocation of economic activity*. London: Macmillan. doi:10.1007/978-1-349-03196-2_38

Dunning, J. H. (1980). Toward an Eclectic Theory of International Production. *Journal of International Business Studies*, *11*(1), 9–31. doi:10.1057/palgrave.jibs.8490593

Dunning, J. H. (1981). *International Production and the Multinational Enterprise*. London: Allen & Unwin.

Dunning, J. H. (1981). *International production and the multinational enterprise*. London: Allen and Unwin.

Dunning, J. H. (1993). *Multinational Enterprises and the Global Economy*. Addison-Wesley Publishing Company.

Dunning, J. H. (1997). *Alliance capitalism and global business*. London: Routledge.

Dunning, J. H. (1998). Location and the multinational enterprise: A neglected factor? *Journal of International Business Studies*, *29*(1), 45–66. doi:10.1057/palgrave.jibs.8490024

Dunning, J. H. (2000). The Eclectic Paradigm as an Envelope for Economic and Business Theories of MNE Activity. *International Business Review*, *9*(2), 163–190. doi:10.1016/S0969-5931(99)00035-9

Dunning, J. H., & Lundan, S. M. (2008). *Multinational enterprises and the global economy*. Edward Elgar Publishing.

Dunning, J., & Narula, R. (1996). The investment development path revisited: some emerging issues. In J. Dunning & R. Narula (Eds.), *Foreign direct investment and governments: Catalysts for economic restructuring*. Basingstoke, UK: Edward Elgar.

Eapen. (2006). *Economic Growth in India and china-a comparative study* (vols. 1-2). ICFAI University Press.

Eden, L. (2009). Letter from the Editor-in-Chief: FDI spillovers and linkages. Journal of International Business Studies, 40, 1065-1069.

Edwards, S. (1993). Openness, trade liberalisation and growth in developing countries. *Journal of Economic Literature, 31*(3), 1358–1393.

Eicher & Kang. (2005). Trade, foreign direct investment or acquisition: Optimal entry modes for multinationals. *Journal of Development Economics, 77*, 207–228.

Ekholm, K., Forslid, R., & Markusen, J. R. (2003). *Export-Platform Foreign Direct Investment.* NBER Working Paper, No 9517.

Enders, W. (2011). *Applied Econometric Time Series.* Wiley Student Edition.

Engle, R. F., & Granger, C. W. J. (1987). Cointegration and error correction: Representation, estimation and testing. *Econometrica, 55*(2), 251–276. doi:10.2307/1913236

Erdal, L., & Göçer, I. (2015). The Effects of Foreign Direct Investment on R&D and Innovations: Panel Data Analysis for Developing Asian Countries. *Procedia: Social and Behavioral Sciences, 195*, 749–758. doi:10.1016/j.sbspro.2015.06.469

Erramilli, M. K., Agarwal, S., & Kim, S. S. (1997). Are firm-specific advantages location-specific too? *Journal of International Business Studies, 28*(4), 735–757. doi:10.1057/palgrave.jibs.8490117

Ersoy, I. (2011). The Causal Relationship between the Financial Account and the Current Account: The Case of Turkey. *International Research Journal of Finance and Economics, 75*, 187–193.

Esqueda, O., Assefa, A. T., & Mollick, V. A. (2012). Financial globalization and stock market risk, *International Financial Markets. Institutions and Money, 22*(1), 87–102. doi:10.1016/j.intfin.2011.07.006

Etzioni, A. (2008). *Security first: For a muscular, moral foreign policy.* Yale University Press.

Falvey, R., Foster, N., & Greenaway, D. (2004). Imports, exports, knowledge spillovers and growth. *Economics Letters, 85*(2), 209–213. doi:10.1016/j.econlet.2004.04.007

Fan, E. X. (2002). *Technological spillovers from foreign direct investment: A survey (No. 33).* Manila, Philippines: Asian Development Bank.

Ferdows, K. (1997, March). Making the most of foreign factories. *Harvard Business Review*, 73–88.

Fergusson, L. (2006). Institutions for financial development: What are they and where do they come from? *Journal of Economic Surveys, 20*(1), 27–70. doi:10.1111/j.0950-0804.2006.00275.x

Flowers, E. B. (1976). Oligopolistic reactions in European and Canadian direct investment in the United States. *Journal of International Business Studies*, *7*(2), 43–55. doi:10.1057/palgrave.jibs.8490700

Forogue, A., & Veloce, W. (1990). Causality and Structure of Canada's Balance of Payments. *Empirical Economics*, *15*(3), 267–283. doi:10.1007/BF02426969

Forssbaeck, J., & Oxelhelm, L. (2011). Corporate financial determinants of foreign direct investment. *The Quarterly Review of Economics and Finance*, *51*(3), 269–282. doi:10.1016/j.qref.2011.05.002

Fowowe, B. (2013). Financial liberalization in Sub-Saharan Africa: What do we know? *Journal of Economic Surveys*, *27*(1), 1–37. doi:10.1111/j.1467-6419.2011.00689.x

Frankel, J., & Romer, D. (1999). Does trade cause growth? *The American Economic Review*, *89*(3), 379–399. doi:10.1257/aer.89.3.379

FRH. (2011). *Freedom in the World Database*. Freedom House. Retrieved from https://freedomhouse.org/report/freedom-press/freedom-press-2016?gclid=CjwKEAjwsr-6BRCLvrj785rbhTsSJADjUxakfmi8db3cy-omU7DQ8jQkXcsQWjY13q9kx90R9_UPixoC_-Xw_wcB

Froot, K. A., & Stein, J. C. (1991). Exchange Rates and Foreign Direct Investment: An Imperfect Capital Markets Approach. *The Quarterly Journal of Economics*, *106*(4), 1191–1217. doi:10.2307/2937961

Fry, M. J. (1996). How Foreign Direct Investment in Pacific Asia improves the Current Account. *Birmingham Journal of Asian Economics*, *7*(3), 459–486. doi:10.1016/S1049-0078(96)90021-4

Fu, X. (2007). Trade-cum-FDI, Human Capital Inequality and the Dual Economy in China: The Signer Perspective. *Journal of Economic Change and Restructuring*, *2*(1), 55–71.

Fu, X. (2008). Foreign direct investment, absorptive capacity and regional innovation capabilities: Evidence from China. *Oxford Development Studies*, *36*(1), 89–110. doi:10.1080/13600810701848193

Gassebner, M., & Méon, P.-G. (2010). *Where do Creditor Rights Matter? Creditor Rights, Political Constraints and Cross-border M&A Activity*. CEB Working Paper No. 10-019.

Girma, S., Kneller, R., & Pisu, M. (2007). Do exporters have anything to learn from foreign multinationals? *European Economic Review*, *51*(4), 993–1010. doi:10.1016/j.euroecorev.2006.07.003

Globerman, S., Shapiro, D., & Tang, Y. (2004). *Foreign direct investment in emerging and transition European countries*. Retrieved December 10, 2016, from http://www.emeraldinsight.com/doi/abs/10.1016/S1569-3767%2805%2906017-6

Globerman, S., & Shapiro, D. (2002). Global foreign direct investment flows: The role of governance infrastructure. *World Development*, *30*(11), 1899–1919. doi:10.1016/S0305-750X(02)00110-9

Globerman, S., & Shapiro, D. (2003). Governance infrastructure and US foreign direct investment. *Journal of International Business Studies*, *34*(1), 19–39. doi:10.1057/palgrave.jibs.8400001

Globerman, S., & Shapiro, D. (2004). Assessing International Mergers And Acquisitions As A Mode Of Foreign Direct Investment. [EconWPA.]. *International Finance*, 0404009.

Goldberg, S., & Klein, W. (1998). Foreign Direct Investment and Real Exchange Rate Linkages in Developing Countries. In R. Glick (Ed.), *Managing Capital Flows and Exchange Rates:Lessons from the Pacific Basin*. Cambridge University Press.

Gomes, C., & Kruglianskas, I. (2009). Indicadores e características de gestão de fontes externas de informação tecnológica e do desempenho inovador de empresas brasileiras. *RAC*, *13*(2), 172–188.

Gondor, M., & Nistar, P. (2012). Fiscal Policy and Foreign Direct Investment: Evidence from some Emerging EU Countries. *Procedia: Social and Behavioral Sciences*, *58*, 1256–1266. doi:10.1016/j.sbspro.2012.09.1108

Görg, H., & Greenaway, D. (2004). Much ado about nothing? Do domestic firms really benefit from foreign direct investment? *The World Bank Research Observer*, *19*(2), 171–197. doi:10.1093/wbro/lkh019

Gorg, H., & Strobl, E. (2001). Multinational companies and productivity spillovers: A meta-analysis. *Economic Journal (London)*, *111*(475), 723–739. doi:10.1111/1468-0297.00669

Gorodnichenko, Y., Svejnar, J., & Terrell, K. (2007). *When Does FDI Have Positive Spillovers? Evidence from 17 Emerging Market Economies*. IZA Discussion Paper No. 3079.

Goswami, C., & Saikia, K. K. (2012). FDI and its relation with exports in India, status and prospect in north east region. *Procedia: Social and Behavioral Sciences*, *37*, 123–132. doi:10.1016/j.sbspro.2012.03.280

Gow, H., & Swinnen, J. (1998). Up- and downstream restructuring, foreign direct investment, and hold-up problems in agricultural transition. *European Review of Agriculture Economics*, *25*(4), 331–350. doi:10.1093/erae/25.3.331

Goyal & Bansal. (2016). Trends of FDI inflows in retail sector. International Journal of Innovative Research and Development, 5(2).

Goyal, S., Kumar, K.P., & Rao, K.S. (2012). Retail Sector in India – Is it Necessary for Inviting FDI? *Indian Journals.com, 12*(4), 286-295.

Granger, C. W. J. (1969). Investigating Causal Relations by Econometric Models and Cross-spectral Methods. *Econometrica*, *37*(3), 424–438.

Granger, C. W. J. (1988). Some recent developments in the concept of causality. *Journal of Econometrics*, *39*(1-2), 199–211. doi:10.1016/0304-4076(88)90045-0

Greenhill, B., Mosley, L., & Prakash, A. (2009). Trade-based diffusion of labor rights: A panel study, 1986–2002. *The American Political Science Review*, *103*(04), 669–690. doi:10.1017/S0003055409990116

Grimes, S., & Du, D. (2013). Foreign and indigenous innovation in China: Some evidence from Shanghai. *European Planning Studies*, *21*(9), 1357–1373. doi:10.1080/09654313.2012.755829

Grosse, R., & Trevino, L. (1996). Foreign direct investment in the United States: An analysis by country of origin. *Journal of International Business Studies*, *27*(1), 139–155. doi:10.1057/palgrave.jibs.8490129

Grossman, G. M., & Helpman, E. (1991). Trade, knowledge spillovers, and growth. *European Economic Review*, *35*(2-3), 517–526. doi:10.1016/0014-2921(91)90153-A

Grossman, J., & Helpman, E. (1991). *Innovation and Growth in the Global Economy*. Cambridge, MA: MIT Press.

Günther, J. (2002). FDI as a multiplier of modern technology in Hungarian industry. *Inter Economics*, *37*(5), 263–269. doi:10.1007/BF02928885

Gurgul, H., & Lach, L. (2014). Globalization and economic growth: Evidence from two decades of transition in CEE. *Economic Modelling*, *36*, 99–107. doi:10.1016/j.econmod.2013.09.022

Haddad, M., & Harrison, A. (1993). Are there positive spillovers from direct foreign investment?: Evidence from panel data for Morocco. *Journal of Development Economics*, *42*(1), 51–74. doi:10.1016/0304-3878(93)90072-U

Hall, S. G., & Wickens, M. R. (1993). *Causality in integrated systems.* Centre for Economic Forecasting Discussion Paper No. 7-93, London Business School.

Hall, S. G., & Milne, A. (1994). The relevance of P-star analysis to UK monetary policy. *Economic Journal (London)*, *104*(424), 597–604. doi:10.2307/2234634

Hanousek, J., Kočenda, E., & Maurel, M. (2011). Direct and indirect effects of FDI in emerging European markets: A survey and meta-analysis. *Economic Systems*, *35*(3), 301–322. doi:10.1016/j.ecosys.2010.11.006

Hansen, H., & Rand, J. (2006). On the causal links between FDI and Growth in developing countries. *World Economy*, *29*, 21–43.

Heady, C., Johansso, A., Arnold, J., Brys, B., & Vartia, L. (2009). *Tax Policy for Economic Recovery and Growth.* Retrieved December 21, 2016, from https://kent.ac.uk/economics/documents/research/papers/2009/0925.pdf

Hebous, S., Ruf, M., & Weichenrieder, A. J. (2011). The Effects Of Taxation On The Location Decision Of Multinational Firms: M&A Versus Greenfield Investments. *National Tax Journal*, *64*(3), 817–838. doi:10.17310/ntj.2011.3.03

Helpman, E., Melitz, M. J., & Stephen, R. Y. (2004). Exports Versus FDI with Heterogenous Firms. *The American Economic Review*, *94*(1), 300–316. doi:10.1257/000282804322970814

Hermes, N., & Lensink, R. (2003). Foreign direct investment, financial development and economic growth. *The Journal of Development Studies*, *40*(1), 142–163. doi:10.1080/00220380412331293707

Herzer, D. (2012). How does foreign direct investment really affect developing countries' growth? *Review of International Economics*, *20*(2), 396–414. doi:10.1111/j.1467-9396.2012.01029.x

Herzer, D., Klasen, S., & Nowak-Lehmann, D. F. (2008). In search of FDI-led growth in developing countries: The way forward. *Economic Modelling*, *25*(5), 793–810. doi:10.1016/j.econmod.2007.11.005

Hirsch, S. (2016). Nation states and multinationals: Common interests, conflicting interests and public policies. *Transnational Corporations Review*, *8*(1), 17–27. doi:10.1080/19186444.2016.1162477

Hodrick, R., & Prescott, E. C. (1997). Post-War U.S. Business Cycles: An Empirical Investigation. *Journal of Money, Credit and Banking*, *29*(1), 1–16.

Hong, Q., & Smart, M. (2010). In praise of tax havens: International tax planning and foreign direct investment. *European Economic Review*, *54*(1), 82–95. doi:10.1016/j.euroecorev.2009.06.006

Hooda, M. S. (2011). A study of FDI and Indian Economy. Department of Humanities and Social Sciences National Institute of Technology (Deemed University), Durgapur.

Hood, N., & Young, S. (1979). *The economics of multinational enterprise*. London, UK: Longman.

Hossain, M. A. (2008). *Impact of Foreign Direct Investment on Bangladesh's Balance of Payments: Some Policy Implication. Policy Note No. 08005*. Dhaka: Bangladesh Bank.

Hsiao, F. T., & Hsiao, M. W. (2006). FDI, exports, and GDP in East and Southeast Asia: Panel data versus time-series causality analyses. *Journal of Asian Economics*, *17*(6), 1082–1106. doi:10.1016/j.asieco.2006.09.011

Hu, A. G., & Jefferson, G. H. (2002). FDI impact and spillover: Evidence from China's electronic and textile industries. *World Economy*, *25*(8), 1063–1076. doi:10.1111/1467-9701.00481

Humphreys, C. (2003). *Better governance for development in the Middle East and North Africa: enhancing inclusiveness and accountability*. World Bank Publications.

Hunady, J., & Orviska, M. (2014). Determinants of Foreign Direct Investment in EU Countries-Do Corporate Taxes Really Matter? *Procedia Economics and Finance*, *12*, 243–250. doi:10.1016/S2212-5671(14)00341-4

Hundt, R. (2006). *In China's Shadow: The Crisis of American Entrepreneurship*. Yale University Press.

Hymer, S. H. (1960). *The International Operations of National Firms: A Study of Direct Investment* (Ph.D. Thesis). MIT.

Hymer, S. H. (1976). *The international operations of national firms: A study of direct foreign investment* (Vol. 14). Cambridge, MA: MIT Press.

Hymer, S. H. (1976). *The international operations of national firms: A study of direct investment.* Cambridge, MA: MIT Press.

Hyndman, R., Koehler, B. A., Snyder, D. R., & Grose, S. (2002). A state space framework for automatic forecasting using exponential smoothing methods. *International Journal of Forecasting, 18*(3), 439–454. doi:10.1016/S0169-2070(01)00110-8

ICRG. (2011). *International country risk guide.* PRS Group. Retrieved from https://www.prsgroup.com/about-us/our-two-methodologies/icrg

IMF (International Monetary Fund). (n.d.). *DOTS (Direction of Trade Statistics), IFS (International Financial Statistics).* Retrieved from https://www.imf.org/external/pubs/cat/longres.aspx?sk=19305.0

IMF. (2014). *Macroeconomic developments in low-income developing countries.* Washington, DC: International Monetary Fund.

Iqbal, S. M., Shaikh, F. M., & Shar, A. H. (2010). Causality Relationship between Foreign Direct Investment, Trade and Economic Growth in Pakistan. *Asian Social Science, 6*(9). doi:10.5539/ass.v6n9p82

Irsova, Z., & Havranek, T. (2013). Determinants of horizontal spillovers from FDI: Evidence from a large meta-analysis. *World Development, 42*, 1–15. doi:10.1016/j.worlddev.2012.07.001

Jadhav, P. (2012). Determinants of foreign direct investment in BRICS economies: Analysis of economic, institutional and political factor. *Procedia: Social and Behavioral Sciences, 37*, 5–14. doi:10.1016/j.sbspro.2012.03.270

Jansen, K. (1995). The macroeconomic effects of Foreign Direct Investment: The Case of Thailand. *World Development, 23*(2), 193–210. doi:10.1016/0305-750X(94)00125-I

Jarque, C. M., & Bera, A. K. (1987). A Test for normality of observations and regression residuals. *International Statistical Review, 55*(2), 163–172.

Javed, K., Sher, F., Awan, R. U., & Ashfaq, M. (2012). Foreign Direct Investment, Trade and Economic Growth: A Comparison of selected South Asian Countries. *International Journal of Humanities and Social Science, 2*(5).

Javorcik Smarzynska, B., & Saggi, K. (2004). *Technological asymmetry and the mode of foreign investment.* World Bank Policy Research Working Paper, 3196.

Jensen, N. M. (2003). Democratic governance and multinational corporations: Political regimes and inflows of foreign direct investment. *International Organization*, *57*(3), 587–616. doi:10.1017/S0020818303573040

Jensen, N. M., & Rosas, G. (2007). Foreign direct investment and income inequality in Mexico, 1990–2000. *International Organization*, *61*(03), 467–487. doi:10.1017/S0020818307070178

Jhamb, S., & Bhardwaj, A. (2006). The Case of FDI in Retail Sector in India. *Asia Pacific Business Review*, *2*(2), 55–60. doi:10.1177/097324700600200207

Jiang, M., Branzei, O., & Xia, J. (2016). DIY: How internationalization shifts the locus of indigenous innovation for Chinese firms. *Journal of World Business*, *51*(5), 662–674. doi:10.1016/j.jwb.2016.07.005

Johansen, S. (1996). Likelihood-Based Inference in Cointegrated Vector Autoregressive Models (2nd ed.). Oxford University Press.

Johansen, S. (1988). Statistical Analysis of Cointegrating Vectors. *Journal of Economic Dynamics & Control*, *12*(2-3), 231–254. doi:10.1016/0165-1889(88)90041-3

Johansen, S. (1991). Estimation and hypothesis testing of cointegration vectors in Gaussian vector autoregressive model. *Econometrica*, *59*(6), 1551–1580. doi:10.2307/2938278

Johansen, S. (1994, January). The role of the constant and linear terms in cointegration analysis of nonstationary variables. *Econometric Reviews*, *13*(2), 205–229. doi:10.1080/07474939408800284

Johansen, S. (1995). *Likelihood-Based Inference in Cointegrated Vector Autoregressive Models*. Oxford University Press. doi:10.1093/0198774508.001.0001

Johnson & Tellis. (2008). Drivers of success for market entry into India and china. *Journal of Marketing*, *72*.

Johnson, A. (2005). *Host country effects of foreign direct investment: The case of developing and transition economies.* Retrieved December 02, 2016, from http://hj.diva-portal.org/smash/get/diva2:4009/FULLTEXT01.pdf

Johnson, A. (2006). *FDI inflows to the Transition Economies in Eastern Europe: Magnitude and Determinants.* Retrieved December 15, 2016, from https://ideas.repec.org/p/hhs/cesisp/0059.html

Johnson, A. (2006). *The effects of FDI inflows on Host Country Economic growth.* CESIS Electronic working paper series No-58.

Jones, G. (1996). The Evolution of International Business: An Introduction. Routledge.

Joseph, M., & Soundarajan. (2009). *Retail in India: A critical assessment.* New Delhi: Academic Foundation, in association with Indian Council for Research on International Economic Relations.

Joseph, M., Soundararajan, N., Gupta, M., & Sahu, S. (2008). *Impact of Organized Retail on Unorganized Retail.* Indian Council for Research on International Economic Relations.

Jurcic, L., Bilas, V., & Franc, S. (2011). *The effects of FDI on the Recipient Country*. Academic Press.

Juselius, K. (1990). Maximum likelihood estimation and cointegration with application to the demand of money. *Oxford Bulletin of Economics and Statistics*, *52*(2), 169–210.

Kalamov, Z. Y. (2013). Risk sharing and the efficiency of public good provision under tax competition. *Regional Science and Urban Economics*, *43*(4), 676–683. doi:10.1016/j.regsciurbeco.2013.03.002

Kalecki. (1937). Economic and Political Determinants of Foreign Direct Investment. *World Development*, *13*(2), 161-175.

Kandiero, T., & Chitiga, M. (2014). Trade openness and foreign direct investment in Africa. *South African Journal of Economic and Management Sciences*, *9*(3), 355–370. doi:10.4102ajems.v9i3.1093

Kaplinsky, R., & Morris, M. (2009). Chinese FDI in Sub-Saharan Africa: Engaging with large dragons. *European Journal of Development Research*, *21*(4), 551–569. doi:10.1057/ejdr.2009.24

Kaur, M., Yadav, S. S., & Gautam, V. (2012). Foreign Direct Investment and Current Account Deficit- A Causality Analysis in context of India. *Journal of International Business and Economy*, *13*(2), 85–106.

Kawai, M. (2005). East Asian Economic Regionalism: Progress and Challenges. *Journal of Asian Economics*, *16*(1), 29–55. doi:10.1016/j.asieco.2005.01.001

Keen, M., & Konrad, A. K. (2011). *International Tax Competition*. Retrieved December 11, 2016, from http://eml.berkeley.edu/~burch/Keen-Konrad-handbook-11.pdf

Kerner, A. (2014). What we talk about when we talk about foreign direct investment. *International Studies Quarterly*, *58*(4), 804–815. doi:10.1111/isqu.12147

Khadaroo, A. J., & Seetanah, B. (2007, November). Transport Infrastructure and FDI: Lessons from Sub Saharan African Economies. In *African Economic Conference (AEC)* (pp. 15-17). Academic Press.

Khan, G. S., & Mitra, P. (2014). Semtember-October). A Causal Linkage between FDI Inflows with Select Macroeconomic Variables in India – An Econometric Analysis. *Journal of Economics and Finance*, *5*(5), 124–133.

Khan, M. A. (2007). Role of human capital in attracting foreign direct investment: A South Asian perspective. *SAARC Journal HRD*, *3*(1), 5.

Khondoker, A. M., & Kalirajanb, K. (2010). *Determinants of Foreign Direct Investment in Developing Countries: A Comparative Analysis*. ASARC working paper 2010/13.

Kim, C. H., & Kim, D. (2010). Do Capital Inflows Cause Current Account Deficits? *Applied Economics Letters*, *18*(5), 497–499. doi:10.1080/13504851003724267

Kim, Y. (2007). Impacts of regional economic integration on industrial relocation through FDI in East Asia. *Journal of Policy Modeling*, *29*(1), 165–180. doi:10.1016/j.jpolmod.2006.04.008

Kim, Y. H. (2009). Cross-border M&A vs. greenfield FDI: Economic integration and its welfare impact. *Journal of Policy Modeling*, *31*(1), 87–101. doi:10.1016/j.jpolmod.2008.08.005

Kindelberger, C. P. (1969). *American business abroad: six lectures on direct investment*. New Haven, CT: Yale UP.

Kindleberger, C. P. (1969). American Business Abroad. *The International Executive*, *11*(2), 11–12. doi:10.1002/tie.5060110207

Kinoshita, Y. (1998). *Firm Size and Determinants of Foreign Direct Investment*. CERGE-EI Working Paper Series, 135.

Kishor, N., & Singh, R. P. (2015). Determinants of FDI and its Impact on BRICS Countries: A Panel Data Approach. *Transnational Corporations Review*, *7*(3), 269–278. doi:10.5148/tncr.2015.7302

Klein, M. W., & Rosengren, E. S. (1994). The Real Exchange Rate and Foreign Direct Investment in the United States: Relative Wealth vs. Relative Wage Effects. *Journal of International Economics*, *36*(3-4), 373–389. doi:10.1016/0022-1996(94)90009-4

Knickerbocker, F. T. (1973). Oligopolistic reaction and multinational enterprise. *Thunderbird International Business Review*, *15*(2), 7–9.

Knickerbocker, F. T. (1973). *Oligopolistic reaction and the multinational enterprise*. Cambridge, MA: Harvard University Press.

Kokko, A., Tansini, R., & Zejan, M. C. (1996). Local technological capability and productivity spillovers from FDI in the Uruguayan manufacturing sector. *The Journal of Development Studies*, *32*(4), 602–611. doi:10.1080/00220389608422430

Konana & Doggnet. (2004). *Comparing India and China Growth Strategies: Chaotic Or Planned?* Retrieved from faculty.mccombs.utexas.edu/prabudeva.konana/indiachina.pdf

Kophaiboon, A. (2003). Foreign trade regimes and the FDI-Growth nexus: A case study of Thailand. *The Journal of Development Studies*, *40*(2), 55–69. doi:10.1080/00220380412331293767

Kophaiboon, A. (2006). Foreign direct investment and technology spillover: A cross-industry analysis of Thai manufacturing. *World Development*, *34*(3), 541–556. doi:10.1016/j.worlddev.2005.08.006

Kose, M., Prasad, E., Rogoff, K., & Wei, J. S. (2009). Finansijska globalizacija: Ponovna procena. *Panoeconomicus*, *2*, 143–197. doi:10.2298/PAN0902143K

Kumar, A. (2007). What are the Determinants of the Location of Foreign Direct Investment? *Journal of International Economics*, *51*, 379-400.

Kutan, A. M., & Vukšić, G. (2007). Foreign direct investment and export performance: Empirical evidence. *Comparative Economic Studies*, *49*(3), 430–445. doi:10.1057/palgrave.ces.8100216

Lall, S. (2002). *FDI and development: research issues in the emerging context* (B. Bora, Ed.). Routledge. doi:10.4324/9780203469699.ch19

Lall, S., & Narula, R. (2004). Foreign direct investment and its role in economic development: Do we need a new agenda? *European Journal of Development Research*, *16*(3), 447–464. doi:10.1080/0957881042000266589

Lall, S., & Streeten, P. (1980). *Foreign Investment Transnational's and Developing countries.* London: Macmillan Press Ltd.

Lamming, R. (1993). *Beyond partnership. Strategies for innovation and lean supply*. Cornwall, UK: Prentice-Hall.

Lessmann, C. (2013). Foreign direct investment and regional inequality: A panel data analysis. *China Economic Review*, *24*, 129–149. doi:10.1016/j.chieco.2012.12.001

Levin, A., Lin, F., & Chu, C. (2002). Unit root tests in panel data: Asymptotic and finite sample properties. *Journal of Econometrics*, *108*(1), 1–24. doi:10.1016/S0304-4076(01)00098-7

Levis, M. (1979). Does political instability in developing countries affect foreign investment flow? An empirical examination. *Management International Review*, 59–68.

Li, C., Murshed, S. M., & Tanna, S. (2017). The impact of civil war on foreign direct investment flows to developing countries. *The Journal of International Trade & Economic Development*, *26*(4), 488–507. doi:10.1080/09638199.2016.1270347

Lipsey, R. E. (1999). The Role of FDI in International Capital Flows. In M. Feldstein (Ed.), *International Capital Flows*. Chicago: Chicago University Press.

Lipsey, R. E. (2004). Home-and host-country effects of foreign direct investment. In *Challenges to globalization: Analyzing the economics* (pp. 333–382). University of Chicago Press. doi:10.7208/chicago/9780226036557.003.0010

Lipsey, R. E., & Sjöholm, F. (2004). FDI and wage spillovers in Indonesian manufacturing. *Review of World Economics*, *140*(2), 321–332. doi:10.1007/BF02663651

Li, Q., & Resnick, A. (2003). Reversal of fortunes: Democratic institutions and foreign direct investment inflows to developing countries. *International Organization*, *57*(01), 175–211. doi:10.1017/S0020818303571077

Li, X., Wang, J., & Liu, X. (2013). Can locally-recruited R&D personnel significantly contribute to multinational subsidiary innovation in an emerging economy? *International Business Review*, *22*(4), 639–651. doi:10.1016/j.ibusrev.2012.12.002

Loree, D. W., & Guisinger, S. E. (1995). Policy and non-policy determinants of US equity foreign direct investment. *Journal of International Business Studies*, *26*(2), 281–299. doi:10.1057/palgrave.jibs.8490174

Loukil, K. (2016). Foreign Direct Investment And Technological Innovation In Developing Countries. *Oradea Journal of Business and Economics*, *1*(2), 31–40.

Lowe, P. (1995). *The management of technology. Perceptions and opportunities*. London: Chapman.

Lucas, R. (1990). Why doesn't capital flow from Rich to Poor countries? *The American Economic Review*, *80*(2), 92–96.

Lucas, R. E. Jr. (1988). On the mechanics of economic development. *Journal of Monetary Economics*, *22*(1), 3–42. doi:10.1016/0304-3932(88)90168-7

Madaan. (2009). *Fundamentals of Retailing*. Tata McGraw Hill Education Private Ltd.

Magee, S. P. (1977). Information and the multinational corporation: An appropriability theory of direct foreign investment. University of Chicago, Department of Economics and Graduate School of Business.

Manda, S. (2014). Capital flows and Current Account Dynamics in Zimbabwe. *Journal of Economics and International Business Management*, *2*(4), 82–99.

Marjanović, D., & Ahmetagić, D. (2013). Multinational Companies as Carriers of Foreign Direct Investment. In Tudomanyos Mozaik, 10 Kotet (pp. 265-274). Kalocsa, HU: Tomori Pal Foiskola.

Marjanović, D., & Radojević, P. (2013). Foreign Direct Investments As An Engine Of Economic Growth And Development of Serbia. In Post Crisis Recovery (pp.349-364). Belgrade: Belgrade Banking Academy.

Markusen, J. R. (1995). The boundaries of multinational enterprises and the theory of international trade. *The Journal of Economic Perspectives*, *9*(2), 169–189. doi:10.1257/jep.9.2.169

Markusen, J. R. (2002). *Multinational Firms and the Theory of International Trade*. Cambridge, MA: MIT Press.

Markusen, J. R., & Venables, A. J. (1998). Multinational firms and the new trade theory. *Journal of International Economics*, *46*(2), 183–203. doi:10.1016/S0022-1996(97)00052-4

Markusen, J. R., & Venables, A. J. (1999). Foreign direct investment as a catalyst for industrial development. *European Economic Review*, *43*(2), 335–356. doi:10.1016/S0014-2921(98)00048-8

Martínez-Martín, J. (2010). *On the dynamics of exports and FDI: the Spanish internationalization process*. IREA–Working Papers, 2010, IR10/010.

Mastroyiannis, A. (2012). Causality Relationships in the Structure of Portugal's Balance of International Payments. *International Journal of Business and Social Science*, *3*(15), 54–61.

Mattoo, A., & Stern, R. M. (2003). *India and the WTO*. World Bank and Oxford University Press.

McKinney, L. A. (2014). Foreign direct investment, development, and overshoot. *Social Science Research*, *47*, 121–133. doi:10.1016/j.ssresearch.2014.04.003 PMID:24913949

Mencinger, J. (2008). *Direct and Indirect effects of Foreign Direct Investment on Current Account*. Academic Press.

Mengistu, A. A., & Adhikary, B. K. (2011). Does good governance matter for FDI inflows? Evidence from Asian economies. *Asia Pacific Business Review*, *17*(3), 281–299. doi:10.1080/13602381003755765

Mercado, R. Jr, & Park, C.-Y. (2011). What Drives Different Types of Capital Flow and their Volatilities in Developing Asia? *International Economic Journal*, *25*(4), 655–680. doi:10.1080/10168737.2011.636628

Mishkin, F. S. (2009). Globalization and financial development. *Journal of Development Economics*, *89*(2), 164–169. doi:10.1016/j.jdeveco.2007.11.004

Moosa, I. A. (2002). *Foreign Direct Investment: Theory, Evidence and Practice*. London: Palgrave. doi:10.1057/9781403907493

Moosa, I. A., & Cardak, B. A. (2006). The Determinants of Foreign Direct Investment: An Extreme Bound Analysis. *Journal of Multinational Financial Management*, *16*(2), 199–211. doi:10.1016/j.mulfin.2005.07.002

Moran, T. H., Graham, E. M., & Blomström, M. (2005). *Does Foreign Direct Investment Promote Development?* Washington, DC: Institute for International Economics, Center for Global Development.

Moreira, A. C. (2008). Upstream linkages between TNCs and local suppliers: Evidences from Portugal. *World Review of Science, Technology and Sustainable Development*, *5*(1), 28–48. doi:10.1504/WRSTSD.2008.017811

Moreira, A. C. (2009). Knowledge capability flows in buyer-supplier relationships. Challenges for small domestic suppliers in international contexts. *Journal of Small Business and Enterprise Development*, *16*(1), 93–114. doi:10.1108/14626000910932908

Moreira, A. C., & Carvalho, A. C. (2012). Internationalization approaches of the automotive innovation system. A historical perspective. In A. Teixeira (Ed.), *Technological change*. Rijeka, Croatia: InTech.

Moreira, A. C., & Carvalho, A. C. (2015). Supply Chain Management: Identifying Innovative Suppliers. In L. C. Carvalho (Ed.), *Handbook of research on internationalization of entrepreneurial innovation in the global economy* (pp. 436–457). Hershey, PA: IGI Global. doi:10.4018/978-1-4666-8216-0.ch022

Morrissey, O. (2012). FDI in Sub-Saharan Africa: Few linkages, fewer spillovers. *European Journal of Development Research*, *24*(1), 26–31. doi:10.1057/ejdr.2011.49

Mosconi, R., & Giannini, C. (1992). Noncausality in cointegrated systems: Representation, estimation and testing. *Oxford Bulletin of Economics and Statistics*, *54*(3), 399–417. doi:10.1111/j.1468-0084.1992.tb00009.x

Mukherjee & Patel. (2005). *FDI in Retail sector India*. Academic Foundation in Association with ICRIER and Ministry of Consumer Affairs, Food and Public Distribution (Govt. of India).

Mukhrjee, P., & Patel, N. (2005). *FDI in Retail Sector in India*. Academic Foundation.

Muller, T. (2007). Analyzing Modes of Foreign Entry: Greenfield Investment versus Acquisition. *Review of International Economics*, *15*(1), 93–111. doi:10.1111/j.1467-9396.2006.00634.x

Nafziger, W. (2012). *Economic development* (5th ed.). New York, NY: Cambridge University Press. doi:10.1017/CBO9781139028295

Nandal, S. (2013). Impact Analysis of FDI on Retail Industry in India. *International Journal of Marketing, Financial Services & Management Research*, *2*(1), 12–20.

Narula, R. (2002). *Multinational investment and economic structure: Globalisation and competitiveness*. Routledge.

Narula, R. (2014). Foreign direct investment as a driver of industrial development: Why is there so little evidence? In R. Van Tulder, A. Verbeke, & R. Strange (Eds.), *International business and sustainable development* (pp. 45–678). Bingley, UK: Emerald. doi:10.1108/S1745-8862(2013)0000008008

Narula, R., & Dunning, J. (2010). Multinational enterprises, development and globalization: Some clarifications and a research agenda. *Oxford Development Studies*, *38*(3), 263–287. doi:10.1080/13600818.2010.505684

Ndikumana, L., & Verick, S. (2008). The linkages between FDI and domestic investment: Unravelling the developmental impact of foreign investment in Sub-Saharan Africa. *Development Policy Review*, *26*(6), 713–726. doi:10.1111/j.1467-7679.2008.00430.x

Nelson, R., & Phelps, E. (1966). Investment in humans, technological diffusion and economic growth. *The American Economic Review*, *51*, 69–75.

Neto, D., & Veiga, J. F. (2013). Financial globalization, convergence and growth: The role of foreign direct investment. *Journal of International Money and Finance*, *37*, 161–186. doi:10.1016/j.jimonfin.2013.04.005

Neto, P., Brando, A., & Cerqueira, A. (2009). *The Macroeconomic Determinants of Cross Border Mergers and Acquisitions and Greenfield Investments. GEE Papers 0017*. Gabinete de Estratgia e Estudos, Ministrio da Economia e da Inovao.

Nguku, E. K. (2013). *Relationship between Foreign Direct Investment and Balance of Payments in Kenya*. Academic Press.

Nishiyama, H., & Yamaguchi, M. (2010). Foreign direct investment, international trade, and firm heterogeneity. *Economic Modelling*, *27*(1), 184–195. doi:10.1016/j.econmod.2009.08.005

Nocke, V., & Yeaple, S. (2008). An Assignment Theory of Foreign Direct Investment. *The Review of Economic Studies*, *75*(2), 529–557. doi:10.1111/j.1467-937X.2008.00480.x

North, D. C. (1990). *Institutions, institutional change and economic performance*. Cambridge university press. doi:10.1017/CBO9780511808678

Nunnenkamp, P. (2004). To what extent can foreign direct investment help achieve international development goals? *World Economy*, *27*(5), 657–677. doi:10.1111/j.0378-5920.2004.00620.x

Nunnenkamp, P., & Julius, S. (2002). *Determinants of FDI in Developing Countries: Has Globalization Changed the Rules of the Game?* (Vol. 11). Transactional Corporations.

Odozi, V. A. (1995). *An Overview of Foreign Investment in Nigeria 1960-1995*. Occasional Paper No. 11, Research Department, Central Bank of Nigeria.

OECD. (2002). *Global Forum on International Investment: Attracting Foreign Direct Investment for Development*. Retrieved December 12, 2016, from https://oecd.org/investment/investmentfordevelopment/2764407.pdf

Oetzel, J., & Doh, J. P. (2009). MNEs and development: A review and reconceptualization. *Journal of World Business*, *44*(2), 108–120. doi:10.1016/j.jwb.2008.05.001

Okada, K., & Samreth, S. (2014). How does corruption influence the effect of foreign direct investment on economic growth? *Global Economic Review*, *43*(3), 207–220. doi:10.1080/1226508X.2014.930671

Omisakin, O., Adeniyi, O., & Omojolaibi, A. (2009). Foreign direct investment, trade openness and growth in Nigeria. *Journal of Economic Theory*, *3*(2), 13–18.

Organisation for Economic Cooperation and Development. (2008). *OECD Benchmark Definition of Foreign Direct Investment* (4th ed.). OECD.

Osinubi, T. S., & Amaghionyeodiwe, L. A. (2009). Foreign Direct Investment and exchange rate volatility in Nigeria. *International Journal of Applied Econometrics and Quantitative Studies*, *6*(2), 83-116.

Outreville, J. F. (2008). Foreign affiliates of the largest insurance groups: Location-specific advantages. *The Journal of Risk and Insurance*, *75*(2), 463–491. doi:10.1111/j.1539-6975.2008.00268.x

Pal. (2013). FDI in multi-brand retailing: opportunities and threats for rural India. *Innovative Journal of Business and Management, 2*(6), 131 - 136.

Pandit, Levy, & Weitz. (2009). *Retailing management*. Tata McGraw Hill Companies.

Parajuli, S. (2012). *Examining the relationship between the exchange rate, foreign direct investment and trade* (PhD Thesis). Louisiana State University.

Park, C.-Y., Byun, H.-S., & Lee, H.-H. (2012). *Assessing Factors Affecting M&As versus Greenfield FDI in Emerging Countries*. Papers and Briefs, Economics Working Papers 18414, National Bureau of Economic Research, Inc.

Penelope & Kulkarni. (2007). *Economic Development in India and China*. Serial Publication.

Perović, J. (2005). Međunarodno kretanje kapitala kao generator i akcelerator globalizacije. *Ekonomija, 12*(2), 369–383.

Perri, A., & Peruffo, E. (2016). Knowledge spillovers from FDI: A critical review from the international business perspective. *International Journal of Management Reviews, 18*(1), 3–27. doi:10.1111/ijmr.12054

Pesaran, M. H. (2004). *General diagnostic tests for cross section dependence in panels.* University of Cambridge Working Papers in Economics, No 0435.

Pesaran, M. H. (2007). A simple panel unit root test in the presence of cross-section dependence. *Journal of Applied Econometrics, 22*(2), 265–312. doi:10.1002/jae.951

Pesaran, M. H., Ullah, A., & Yamagata, T. (2008). A bias-adjusted LM test of error cross-section independence. *The Econometrics Journal, 11*(1), 105–127. doi:10.1111/j.1368-423X.2007.00227.x

Pesaran, M. H., & Yamagata, T. (2008). Testing slope homogeneity in large panels. *Journal of Econometrics, 142*(1), 50–93. doi:10.1016/j.jeconom.2007.05.010

Piggott, J., & Cook, M. (2006). *International business economics: A European perspective.* Basingstoke, UK: Palgrave Macmillan. doi:10.1007/978-0-230-62776-5

Polachek, S., Seiglie, C., & Xiang, J. (2005). *Globalization and international conflict: can fdi increase peace? (*Department of Economics Working Paper). Rutgers University.

Polachek, S. W., Seiglie, C., & Xiang, J. (2011). Globalization and international conflict: Can FDI increase cooperation among nations? In M. R. Garfinkel & S. Skaperdas (Eds.), *The Oxford Handbook of the Economics of Peace and Conflict* (pp. 733–762). New York, NY: Oxford University Press.

Polachek, S., Seiglie, C., & Xiang, J. (2007). The impact of foreign direct investment on international conflict. *Defence and Peace Economics, 18*(5), 415–429. doi:10.1080/10242690701455474

Prasanna, N. (2010). Impact of foreign direct investment on export performance in India. *Journal of Social Science, 24*(1), 65–71.

Psacharopoulos, G. (1994). Returns to investment in education: A global update. *World Development, Elsevier, 22*(9), 1325–1343. doi:10.1016/0305-750X(94)90007-8

Raff, H. (2004). Preferential Trade Agreements and Tax Competition for Foreign Direct Investment. *Journal of Public Economics, 88*(12), 2745–2763. doi:10.1016/j.jpubeco.2004.03.002

Raff, H., Ryan, M., & Sthler, F. (2009). The Choice of Market Entry Mode: Greenfield investment, M&A and Joint Venture. *International Review of Economics & Finance, 18*(1), 3–10. doi:10.1016/j.iref.2008.02.006

Rahman, M. N. (2016). Impact of Foreign Direct Investment Inflows on Capital Account of India's Balance of Payments. *Business and Economic Review, 6*(1), 111–128. doi:10.5296/ber.v6i1.8965

Rahman, N. (2015). Trends in FDI Inflows and Current Account of India's BOP Since 1991. *International Journal of Economics. Commerce and Research*, *5*(5), 1–12.

Rahman, S. M. Z., & Bristy, J. F. (2015). Macroeconomic Impact of Foreign Direct Investment: A Study on SAARC Countries. *European Journal of Business and Management*, *7*(34), 2222–2839.

Ramkishen, Rongala, & Ghost. (2008). *Attracting Foreign Direct Investment (FDI) to India.* International Professional Services Organization.

Rao. (2004). *Chinese economy- Issues and perspectives.* ICFAI Publishing House.

Ravindra, P. S., Murthy, O. N., & Rao, C. T. (2013). Will FDI in Retail Sector is Viable for Indian economy. *Asian Journal of Research in Economics and Business Management*, *3*(2), 110–123.

Ray, S. (2012). Impact of FDI on economic growth in India: A Cointegration Analysis. *Advances in Information Technology and Management*, *2*(1), 187-201.

Reis, A., Heitor, M., Amaral, M., & Mendonça, J. (2016). Revisiting industrial policy: Lessons learned from the establishment of an automotive OEM in Portugal. *Technological Forecasting and Social Change*, *113*, 195–205. doi:10.1016/j.techfore.2016.04.006

Reiter, S., & Steensma, K. H. (2010). Human Development and Foreign Direct Investment in Developing Countries: The influence of FDI Policy and Corruption. *World Development*, *38*(12), 1678–1691. doi:10.1016/j.worlddev.2010.04.005

Renuka, R., Ganesan, M., & Durgamani, M. K., (2013). Impact of FDI in Indian Economy with special reference to Retail sector in India. *Global Research Analysis, 2*(1), 22-24.

Ribau, C. P., Moreira, A. C., & Raposo, M. (2015). Internationalisation of the firm theories: A schematic synthesis. *International Journal of Business and Globalisation*, *15*(4), 528–554. doi:10.1504/IJBG.2015.072535

Ribault, J. M., Martinet, B., & Lebidois, D. (1995). *A gestão das tecnologias*. Lisbon: Publicações Dom Quixote.

Rodriguez-Clare, A. (1996). Multinationals, linkages and economic development. *The American Economic Review*, *86*(4), 852–873.

Rodriguez, F., & Rodrik, D. (2000). Trade policy and economic growth: A sceptic's guide to the cross-country evidence. In B. Bernanke & K. Rogoff (Eds.), *NBER Macroeconomics Annual 2000, 15*. Cambridge, MA: MIT Press.

Rodrik, D. (2006). Goodbye Washington Consensus, Hello Washington Confusion? A Review of the World Bank's Economic Growth in the 1990s: Learning from a Decade of Reform. *Journal of Economic Literature*, *44*(4), 973–987. doi:10.1257/jel.44.4.973

Romer, P. M. (1990). Endogenous technological change. *Journal of Political Economy*, *98*(5, Part 2), S71–S102. doi:10.1086/261725

Ronstadt, R. C. (1977). *Research and development abroad by US multinationals.* New York: Preacher Publishers.

Roodman, D. (2006). *How to do xtabond2: An introduction to difference and system GMM in Stata.* Center for Global Development working paper, 103.

Rothwell, R. (1994). Issues in the User-Producer Relations in the Innovation Process: The Role of Government. *International Journal of Technology Management, 9*(5/6/7), 629-649.

Roy, S. K., & Pandit, S. K., (2012). FDI in Multi Brand Retailing: What are they fighting about in India. *The Management Accountant, 47*(6), 652–658.

Rugman, A. M. (1980). Internalization as a general theory of foreign direct investment: A re-appraisal of the literature. *Review of World Economics, 116*(2), 365–379. doi:10.1007/BF02696864

Sabirianova Peter, K., Svejnar, J., & Terell, K. (2004). *Distance to the Efficiency Frontier and FDI Spillovers.* William Davidson Institute Working Paper Number, No 721.

Saggi, K. (2002). Trade, foreign direct investment, and international technology transfer: A survey. *The World Bank Research Observer, 17*(2), 191–235. doi:10.1093/wbro/17.2.191

Saglam, B. B., & Yalta, A. Y. (2015). Current Account Imbalances and Capital flows: Further Evidence from Emerging Markets. *Global Journal of Emerging Market Economies, 7*(2), 201–213. doi:10.1177/0974910115574170

Sahoo, P. (2006). *Foreign Direct Investment in South Asia: Policy, Trends, Impact and Determinants.* ADB Institute Discussion Paper No. 56.

Saji, T G. (2013). Does Foreign Direct Investment Lead Economic Growth in India? *International Journal of Financial Management, 3*(2), 38-45.

Saluja, M. S., Bhatia, N. K., & Patel, N. (2013). A Cointegration and VECM approach in explaining relationship of FDI with Current and Capital Account of India. *International Journal of Advanced Research in Computer Science and Management Studies, 1*(6).

Sanjo, Y. (2012). Country risk, country size, and tax competition for foreign direct investment. *International Review of Economics & Finance, 21*(1), 292–301. doi:10.1016/j.iref.2011.08.002

Sarode, S. (2012). Effects of FDI on Capital Account and GDP: Empirical Evidence from India. *International Journal of Business and Management, 7*(8), 102–107. doi:10.5539/ijbm.v7n8p102

Satguru, Y. S., & Satsangi, P. (2013). FDI & Developing Countries, Role of World Bank. *Global Journal of Management and Business Studies, 3*(8), 929–934.

Schiele, H. (2006). How to distinguish innovative suppliers? Identifying innovative suppliers as new task for purchasing. *Industrial Marketing Management, 35*(8), 925–935. doi:10.1016/j.indmarman.2006.05.003

Schmitz, H., & Nadvi, K. (1999). Clustering and industrialization: Introduction. *World Development, 27*(9), 1503–1514. doi:10.1016/S0305-750X(99)00072-8

Schwab, K., & Porter, M. (2008). *The Global Competitiveness Report 2008-2009*. Geneva, Switzerland: World Economic Forum.

Sekkat, K., & Veganzones-Varoudakis, M. A. (2004). *Trade and Foreign Exchange Liberalization, Investment Climate, and FDI in the MENA Countries*. World Bank, Middle East and North Africa, the Office of the Chief Economist.

Sen, P. (1995). Foreign Direct Investment: A Solution to Balance Of Payments Problems? *Economic and Political Weekly*, *30*(30), 1921–1927.

Siddiqui, D. A., & Ahmad, M. H. (2012). The Causal Relationship between Foreign Direct Investment and Current Account: An Empirical investigation for Pakistan Economy. *European Journal of Economics, Finance and Administrative Sciences, 44*.

Siddiqui, H. A. A., & Aumeboonsuke, V. (2014). Role of interest rate in attracting FDI: Study on ASEAN5 Economy. *International Journal of Technical Research and Applications*, *2*(S3), 59-70.

Simões, V. C. (1995). *Inovação e gestão em PME industriais portuguesas*. Lisbon: GEP – Gabinete de Estudos e Planeamento.

Singh. (2009). *Retail management- A global perspective text and cases*. S. Chand & Company Ltd Edition.

Sivalogathasan, V., & Wu, X. (2014). The effect of foreign direct investment on innovation in south asian emerging markets. *Global Business and Organizational Excellence*, *33*(3), 63–76. doi:10.1002/joe.21544

Slangen, A., & Hennart, J.-F. (2007). Greenfield or Acquisition Entry: A review of the Empirical Foreign Establishment Mode Literature. *Journal of International Management*, *13*(4), 403–429. doi:10.1016/j.intman.2007.08.001

Slesman, L., Baharumshah, A. Z., & Wohar, M. E. (2015). Capital inflows and economic growth: Does the role of institutions matter? *International Journal of Finance & Economics*, *20*(3), 253–275. doi:10.1002/ijfe.1514

Solow, R. M. (1956). A contribution to the theory of economic growth. *The Quarterly Journal of Economics*, *70*(1), 65–94. doi:10.2307/1884513

Solow, R. M. (1957). Technical Change and the Aggregate Production Function. *The Review of Economics and Statistics*, *39*(3), 312–320. doi:10.2307/1926047

Srinivasan & Tendulkar. (2003). *Reintegrating India with the World Economy*. Washington, DC: Institute for International Economics.

Srivastava. (2007, September). India retail new face of India. *Marketing Mastermind*, 59-61.

Stamatiou, P., & Dritsakis, N. (2014). Exports, Foreign Direct Investment and Economic Growth for Five European Countries: Granger Causality Tests in Panel Data. *Applied Economics*. doi:10.3790/aeq.60.4.253

Stock, J., & Watson, W. M. (2001). Vector auto regressions. *The Journal of Economic Perspectives*, *15*(4), 101–115. doi:10.1257/jep.15.4.101

Stokman, A. C. J., & Vlar, P. J. G. (1996). *Volatility*. Amsterdam: International Trade and Capital Flows.

Sultan, Z. A. (2013). A causal relationship between FDI inflows and export: The case of India. *Journal of Economics and Sustainable Development*, *4*(2), 1–9.

Sun, L., Lee, I. H., & Hong, H. (2016). Does foreign direct investment stimulate new firm creation? In search of spillovers through industrial and geographical linkages. *Small Business Economics*. doi:10.100711187-016-9803-0

Swenson, D. L. (2001). Transaction Type and the Effect of Taxes on the Distribution of Foreign Direct Investment in the United States. In J. J. Hines (Ed.), *International Taxation and Multinational Activity* (pp. 89–112). University of Chicago Press. doi:10.7208/chicago/9780226341750.003.0005

Tanna, S., & Li, C. (2018). *FDI and economic growth: An external debt threshold effect*. Paper presented at the Annual Conference of the American Economic Association (AEA) in conjunction with the Allied Social Sciences Associations (ASSA), January 2018, Philadelphia, PA.

Temiz, D., & Gökmen, A. (2011). Foreign direct investment (FDI) and export relation in Turkey: 1991–2010. *Journal of Transnational Management*, *16*(3), 157–180. doi:10.1080/15475778.2011.596779

The Economist. (2001, February 24). The Cutting Edge. *The Economist*, 90.

Themnér, L., & Wallensteen, P. (2013). Armed conflicts, 1946–2012. *Journal of Peace Research*, *50*(4), 509–521. doi:10.1177/0022343313494396

Tian, X. (2007). *Managing International Business in China*. Cambridge University Press. doi:10.1017/CBO9780511810558

Toda, H. Y., & Phillips, P. C. B. (1993). Vector autoregressions and causality. *Econometrica*, *61*(6), 1367–1393. doi:10.2307/2951647

Toda, H. Y., & Yamamoto, T. (1995). Statistical inference in vector autoregressions with possibly integrated processes. *Journal of Econometrics*, *66*(1-2), 225–250. doi:10.1016/0304-4076(94)01616-8

Topalli, N. (2015). A Causal Relationship between Foreign Direct Investment, Economic Growth and High Technology Exports. *International Journal of Social Sciences and Education Research*, *1*(1).

Townsend, I. (2003). *Does Foreign Direct Investment Accelerate Economic Growth in Less Developed Countries?* (Working Paper). St. Olaf College.

Trakman, L. (2010). *Foreign direct investment: An Australian perspective*. UNSW Law Research Paper No. 2010-4. Retrieved from https://papers.ssrn.com/sol3/papers.cfm?abstract_id=1540289

Tripathi, V., Seth, R., & Bhandari, V. (2015). Foreign Direct Investment and MacroEconomic Factors: Evidence from the Indian Economy. *Asia-Pacific Journal of Management Research and Innovation, 11*, 46-56.

UN. (2006). FDI in least developed countries at a glance: 2005 / 2006. *United Nations Conference on Trade and Development.*

UNCTAD. (1998). World Investment Report (WIR) 1998: Trends and Determinants. New York: UNCTAD.

UNCTAD. (1999). *World Investment Report 1999: foreign direct investment and the challenge of development.* UNCTAD.

UNCTAD. (2001). *Host country operational measures.* New York: United Nations.

UNCTAD. (2007). *World Investment Report 2007: Cross-border Mergers and Acquisitions and Development.* Geneva: United Nations.

UNCTAD. (2009). *World investment report.* Retrieved from www.unctad.org/wir

UNCTAD. (2011). *Foreign direct investment in LDCs: Lessons learned from the decade 2001-2010 and the way forward.* New York: United Nations.

UNCTAD. (2011). *Foreign Direct Investment in LDCs: Lessons Learned from the Decade 2001-2010 and the Way Forward.* New York: United Nations.

UNCTAD. (2013). *The least developed countries report 2013: Growth with employment for inclusive and sustainable development.* New York: United Nations.

UNCTAD. (2014). *World Investment Report 2014.* New York: United Nations.

UNCTAD. (2014). *World investment report.* Retrieved from www.unctad.org/wir

UNCTAD. (2016). *World Investment Report (Chapter II Regional Investment Trends).* Retrieved from http://unctad.org/en/pages/PublicationWebflyer.aspx?publicationid=1555

Uppal, R., And, K., & Juneja, A. (2013). Emerging Trends of FDI inflows in India: Responses and Challenges. *Asian Journal of Research in Business Economics and Management, 3*(9), 218–222.

Uwubanmwen, A. E., & Ajao, M. G. (2012). The determinants and impact of Foreign Direct Investment in Nigeria. *International Journal of Business and Management, 7*(24), 67–77.

Veludo, M., Macbeth, D., & Purchase, S. (2006). Framework for relationships and networks. *Journal of Business and Industrial Marketing, 21*(4), 199–207. doi:10.1108/08858620610672560

Vernon, R. (1966). International investment and international trade in the product cycle. *The Quarterly Journal of Economics*, 190–207.

Vernon, R. (1966). International investment and international trade in the product cycle. *The Quarterly Journal of Economics, 80*(2), 190–207. doi:10.2307/1880689

Vijayakumar, N., Sridhran, P., & Rao, K.C.S. (2010). Determinants of FDI in BRICS Countries: A Panel Analysis. *International Journal of Business Sciences and Applied Management, 5.*

Vongpraseuth, T., & Choi, C. G. (2015). Globalization, foreign direct investment, and urban growth management: Policies and conflicts in Vientiane, Laos. *Land Use Policy*, *42*, 790–799. doi:10.1016/j.landusepol.2014.10.003

Wamser, G. (2011). Foreign (in)direct investment and corporate taxation. *The Canadian Journal of Economics. Revue Canadienne d'Economique*, *44*(4), 1498–1524. doi:10.1111/j.1540-5982.2011.01682.x

Wang & Li. (2005). The Development of the Retailing Industry in China: 1981-2005. School of Economics and Management Tsinghua University (China).

Wang, C., & Yu, L. (2008). Do spillover benefits grow with rising foreign direct investment? An empirical examination of the case of China. *Applied Economics*, *39*(3), 397–405. doi:10.1080/00036840500428096

Wang, J. Y. (1990). Growth, technology transfer and long run theory of International Capital Movement. *Journal of International Economics*, *29*, 255–271.

Wang, J. Y., & Blomström, M. (1992). Foreign investment and technology transfer: A simple model. *European Economic Review*, *36*(1), 137–155. doi:10.1016/0014-2921(92)90021-N

Wang, M. (2010). Foreign Direct Investment and Domestic Investment in the host country: Evidence from Panel Study. *Applied Economics*, *42*(29), 3711–3721. doi:10.1080/00036840802314580

Wang, M., & Wong, M. C. S. (2009). What Drives Economic Growth? The Case of Crossborder M&A and Greenfield FDI Activities. *Kyklos*, *62*(2), 316–330. doi:10.1111/j.1467-6435.2009.00438.x

Wasaki, I., & Suganuma, K. (2015). Foreign direct investment and regional economic development in Russia: An econometric assessment. *Economic Change and Restructuring: Empirical and Policy Research on the Transitional and Emerging Economies*, *48*(3-4), 209–255. doi:10.100710644-015-9161-y

WDI. (2015). *World development indicators.* World Bank Group. Retrieved from http://data.worldbank.org/data-catalog/world-development-indicators

Wei, S. J. (2000). How taxing is corruption on international investors? *The Review of Economics and Statistics*, *82*(1), 1–11. doi:10.1162/003465300558533

Welch, G., & Nuru, Z. (2005). *Governance for the future: Democracy and development in the least developed countries.* New York, NY: UN-OHRLLS.

Westerlund, J. (2008). Panel cointegration tests of the Fisher effect. *Journal of Applied Econometrics*, *23*(2), 193–233. doi:10.1002/jae.967

WGI. (2015). *Worldwide governance indicators.* World Bank Group. Retrieved from http://data.worldbank.org/data-catalog/worldwide-governance-indicators

Wheeler, D., & Mody, A. (1992). International Investment Location Decisions: The Case of US Firms. *Journal of International Economics*, *33*(1-2), 57–76. doi:10.1016/0022-1996(92)90050-T

White, R. E., & Poynter, T. (1984). Strategies for Foreign-Owned Subsidiaries in Canada'. *Business Quarterly*, (Summer): 55–69.

World Bank. (2016). *Indicators*. Retrieved January 26, 2017, from http://data.worldbank.org/indicator

World Bank. (2016). *World development indicators. Data for various years*. Retrieved from www.worldbank.org

World Bank. (n.d.). *World Development Indicators*. Retrieved from http://data.worldbank.org/data-catalog/world-development-indicators

World investment report. (1998). *Trends and Determinants*. Retrieved December 05, 2016, from http://unctad.org/en/Docs/wir1998_en.pdf

Xiaoying, L., & Xiaming, L. (2005). Foreign direct investment and economic growth: An increasingly endogenous relationship. *World Development*, *33*(3), 393–407. doi:10.1016/j.worlddev.2004.11.001

Yan, H. (2007). Does capital mobility finance or cause a Current Account imbalance? *The Quarterly Review of Economics and Finance*, *47*(1), 1–25. doi:10.1016/j.qref.2005.08.001

Zafir, C. Z., & Funda, H. S. (2012). Analysis of the effects of Foreign Direct Investment on the financing of Current Account Deficits in Turkey. *International Journal of Business and Social Science*, *3*(10), 68–78.

Zhang, K. H. (2005). How does FDI affect a host country's export performance? The case of China. *International Conference of WTO, China and the Asian Economies*.

Zhang, K. H. (2001). China's inward FDI boom and the greater Chinese economy. *Chinese Economy*, *34*(1), 74–88. doi:10.2753/CES1097-1475340174

Zhang, K. H., & Song, S. (2002). Promoting exports: The role of inward FDI in China. *China Economic Review*, *11*(4), 385–396. doi:10.1016/S1043-951X(01)00033-5

Zhang, K., & Markusen, J. (1999). Vertical multinationals and host-country characteristics. *Journal of Development Economics*, *59*(2), 233–252. doi:10.1016/S0304-3878(99)00011-5

Zhang, X. (1999). Foreign investment polic, contribution and performance. In *Foreign direct investment and economic growth in China*. University of Michigan Press.

Zhao, H., & Zhu, G. (2000). Location factors and country-of-origin differences: An empirical analysis of FDI in China. *Multinational Business Review*, *8*(1), 60.

Zheng, P., Siler, P., & Giorgioni, G. (2004). FDI and the export performance of Chinese indigenous firms: A regional approach. *Journal of Chinese Economic and Business Studies*, *2*(1), 55–71. doi:10.1080/1476528031000163138l

About the Contributors

Venkataramanaiah Malepati received his Ph.D (Finance) from Department of Commerce and Management, Sri Venkateswara University. He is presently working as Associate Professor in the Department of Accounting and Finance, Faculty of Business and Economics, University of Gondar, Ethiopia. He has written two text books (Study material), namely,*Organisational Behaviour* and *Business Law for School of Distance Education*, Sri Venkateswara University, Tirupati. He has written two textbooks, namely *Performance Evaluation of the Bombay Stock Exchange Limited* and *Non-Performing Assets in Private and Public Sector Banks* by Research India Publication Limited. He has published 31 research articles in different national and international journals so far. And, he has organised a National Level Management Symposium entitled Panacea-2012 at KMM Group of Institutions, Tirupati and attended around 20 national and international conferences and 4 workshops so far.

* * *

Tezcan Abasiz is an Assistant Professor of Economics at Bulent Ecevit University, Zonguldak-Turkey. Dr. Abasiz has a BS in Economics from Karadeniz Technical University (2003), a Master in Economics from Zonguldak Karaelmas University (2004) and a Ph.D. in Economics from Kocaeli University (2013). He worked as a research assistant at Kocaeli University from 2008-2012. His research interests lie in empirical economics. He teaches Econometrics, Macroeconomics, and Microeconomics, at both graduate and undergraduate levels.

Christopher Boachie is a lecturer of Central Business School, Central University in Ghana, an academic and a practising Chartered Accountant (ACCA-UK) with specialisation in corporate finance, international trade, auditing, financial statement fraud and financial risk management. He was educated in Kwame Nkrumah University of Science and Technology in Kumasi Ghana, Technical University of Freiberg in Germany and the London School of Accountancy (UK). He is currently reading his PhD at Open University of Malaysia. He has considerable, teaching, consulting and practise experience in the application of accountancy and finance theory and risk management.

Kumar Choudhury is presently working as an Assistant Professor, Department of Economics, Sri Sathya Sai Institute of Higher Learning, Andhra Pradesh, India. Previously he was with Sri Venkateshwara College, University of Delhi as an Assistant Professor in Economics. He also worked at Indian Institute of Management, Ahmedabad (IIMA) as an Academic Associate. He did his B.A (Hons) in Economics from Sri Sathya Sai Institute of Higher Learning (SSSIHL), Prashanti Nilayam, Andhra Pradesh and M.Sc. in Economics from Madras School of Economics (MSE), Chennai. His current research interests in the areas of Economics of Investment, Trade and Development. His other areas of interest are Industrial Economics and Applied Econometrics.

Ivana Domazet is a Senior Researcher at the Institute of Economic Sciences and Associate Professor at the Faculty for Banking, Insurance and Finance, Union University. She teaches courses on Marketing Management, Market Research and Competitiveness Enhancement (postgraduate studies). Her scientific interest refers to: Improving Competitiveness, Marketing Research and Strategy, CRM and Strategic Management. She published a numerous papers related to foregoing topics. She is President of Scientific Council at the Institute of Economic Sciences, Vice-president of Board member of the Institute of Economics Sciences, Board member of the Institute of Social Science, member of Serbian Scientific Association of Economists and Serbian Marketing Association.

Rita Khatri is an Assistant Professor with academic experience of 12 years at H.R College of Commerce and Economics, affiliated to University of Mumbai, India.she has received PhD in Trade and transport covering retail trade focusing on consumer behavior toward modern retail formats in India. she has undertaken research project on Digital marketing in India and published various research papers across national and international Journal. She has also being recognized as the PhD guide in Commerce at University of Mumbai.

Chengchun Li is presently Assistant Professor at Changzhou University, China, having recently qualified with a PhD from Coventry University.

Darko Marjanovic has completed undergraduate studies and master's degree at the Faculty of Economics in Subotica, University of Novi Sad. PhD thesis entitled "Tax competition and foreign direct investment in the countries of Southeastern Europe" defended in February 2015 at the Faculty of Economics in Subotica, University of Novi Sad. He is currently employed in the company "BB TRADE" AD in the workplace financial director. He is author or co-authored more than 40 papers, and participated in several international conferences. He was hired as a researcher on the project funded by the Provincial Secretariat for Science and Technological Development of the Autonomous Province of Vojvodina in the project cycle 2011-2015.

António C. Moreira obtained a Bachelor's degree in Electrical Engineering and a Master's degree in Management, both from the University of Porto, Portugal. He received his PhD in Management from UMIST-University of Manchester Institute of Science and Technology, England. He has a solid international background in industry leveraged working for a multinational company in Germany as well as in Portugal. He has also been involved in consultancy projects and in research activities. He is Assistant Professor at the Department of Economics, Management, Industrial Engineering, and Tourism, University of Aveiro, Portugal, where he headed the Bachelor and Master Degrees in Management for five years. He is member of GOVCOPP research unit.

Nida Rahman is presently doctoral fellow in the department of economics, Aligarh Muslim University. She holds M.Phil degree in Economics and her area of research includes international trade and applied econometrics. She is presently working on FDI.

Prabhakara Rao presently Professor and Head of Economics at Sri Sathya Sai Institute of Higher Learning (SSSIHL) Andhra Pradesh, India. He worked as a Lecturer in the department of Mathematics and Computer Science, University of Hyderabad. He was a Research Associate, Council for Scientific and Industrial Research (CSIR), New Delhi. He was a Visiting Scientist, Department of Mathematics and Statistics, Memorial University of Newfoundland, Canada. He obtained his Master's as well as PhD degrees in statistics from Andhra University, Visakhapatnam, Andhra Pradesh, India. He is a recipient of 'Sai Krishna' award for excellence in research for the year 2012-13 for his contributions towards research at SSSIHL. He is a member of several professional and academic bodies. He is a Reviewer of American Mathematical Society (AMS), Journal of the Indian Society for Probability and Statistics (JISP) and other academic journals. He published more than 40 research articles in referred national and international journal such as Journal of Multivariate Analysis, Canadian Journal of Statistics, Sankhya: The Indian Journal of Statistics, The Journal of Statistical Computations and Simulations, The Brazilian Journal of Probability and Statistics, WEAS Journal of Systems, The Journal of Quantitative Economics. He attended several national and international conferences and presented his research papers. His current research interests are Statistical Modeling, Theoretical and Applied Econometrics.

Shehroz Alam Rizvi is a full-time professor at the Department of Economics, Aligarh Muslim University. His area of expertise includes International Economics, Quantitative Economics and Micro Economics.

Sailesh Tanna is Principal Lecturer (Associate Professor) in the Business School at Coventry University, having previously held research positions at South Bank University, Imperial College, University of Warwick, and as Lecturer in Economics at the University of Leicester. At Coventry University, he has taught various undergraduate and postgraduate courses in the economics, business and finance disciplines and has been instrumental in the development of postgraduate degrees in Finance and Banking. He has previously researched in the area of macroeconomic modelling and policy analysis and international economics, but his main research interests are now in banking, international finance and economic development.

Arzu Tay is an Assistant Professor of Economics at Bulent Ecevit University, Zonguldak, Turkey. Dr. Tay has a BS in Economics from Marmara University (2004), a Master in Economics from Zonguldak Karaelmas University (2007) and a Ph.D. in Economics from Istanbul University (2012). She worked as a research assistant at Istanbul University from 2008 to 2012. Her research interests lie in Macroeconomics. She has Macroeconomics classes at both graduate and undergraduate levels. Dr. Tay has her post-doctoral research at Lamar University Department of Economics and Finance, Beaumont, TX, USA.

Index

F

G

H

I

J

L

M

N

www.ingramcontent.com/pod-product-compliance
Lightning Source LLC
LaVergne TN
LVHW081338300926
849161LV00008B/2002

* 9 7 8 1 5 2 2 5 3 0 2 6 8 *